MW01133932

LIEBLING
AT *THE*
NEW YORKER

LIEBLING AT *THE NEW YORKER*

UNCOLLECTED ESSAYS

Edited by James Barbour and Fred Warner

University of New Mexico Press
Albuquerque

University of New Mexico Press edition 1994
published by arrangement with
the estate of A. J. Liebling.

First edition

**Library of Congress
Cataloging-in-Publication Data**

Liebling, A. J. (Abbott Joseph), 1904–1963.
Liebling at the New Yorker: uncollected essays/
edited by James Barbour and Fred Warner.—1st ed.
p. cm.
ISBN 0–8263–1535–6
I. Barbour, James, 1933– .
II. Warner, Fred.
III. Title.
PN4874.L44A5 1994
070.92—dc20
94–18988
CIP

Liebling at *The New Yorker*

UNCOLLECTED ESSAYS

Introduction

FRED WARNER

HE HAD A GRAND LIFE, but it wasn't nearly long enough. He left more than a dozen books, but no one who reads and admires those books can refrain from wanting more. I have had, with James Barbour, the privilege of putting together this volume and *A Neutral Corner*, an earlier book of uncollected boxing pieces, and the feeling is always the same about Liebling: there is so much good stuff; why couldn't there have been more? One wishes for his rendering of the great Ali fights, the Parisian eruptions of 1968, the grand meals. One thinks of the surging New York life that he could have chronicled. Perhaps his thoughts and his enormous talents might have turned to the wars he had seen and the fresh wars that have gone on since his death. One watches on television the raucous antics of a southern politician and wishes that Liebling were around to transform the fellow into a successor to Earl Long, the outlandish hero of Liebling's *The Earl of Louisiana*.

Once a person makes Liebling's acquaintance, there is the inevitable wonderment about what he would have said about the parade of burlesque characters that has gone on since his death: prize fighters, soldiers, reporters, con men, hucksters, writers, politicians, chefs, New Yorkers, and Parisians. Of course, he liked and even admired some of these people; if ever Liebling were venomous, writing about American newspapers, for instance, there always was the Liebling touch of bemused irony. Then one thinks of the many things he *did* write and the good life that he led, and one is grateful.

Abbott Joseph Liebling was born in New York in 1904 and died there in 1963. He attended Dartmouth College, which expelled him for cutting chapel, and he received a degree from the Columbia University School of Journalism. After the *New York Times* fired him for taking certain journalistic liberties with the accounts of basketball games, a sport, like baseball, that he found profoundly uninteresting, he got a newspaper job in Providence. In 1926 he convinced his father that he needed further study in Paris, and there he went, ostensibly to be a student of medieval history but in fact to devote himself to French food, French wine, and French culture, passions that remained happily with him for a lifetime. He returned to the United States a year later and took up his old job in Rhode Island. From 1930 to 1935 he worked for the *New York World-Telegram,* and then the great thing in his professional life happened—Harold Ross hired him to write for *The New Yorker,* and save for a brief interlude in Chicago, at *The New Yorker* he remained until his death.

In the fall of 1939, Ross decided that Europe had become too dangerous for Janet Flanner, who, as Genêt, had for many years covered Paris and France for *The New Yorker.* Liebling flew to Lisbon on the Pan American Clipper, went on to Paris, and checked into the Hotel Louvois, about which he would write so fondly for the rest of his life. It was the twelfth of October, 1939, and until the Germans came, his was the best American voice in France. He followed the retreating French government to Tours and then to Bordeaux. France fell to the invading Nazis on June 16, 1940, and on June 25 he took the Clipper from Lisbon back to New York. He is eloquent about his beloved France in many books, but perhaps *The Road Back to Paris* best expresses how he felt about a nation whose people, history, and cuisine he loved. He went to England in July 1941, returned to New York on a Norwegian ship, and then returned to England and on to North Africa with the invading American army.

Always he wrote. The inestimable *New Yorker* pieces, long and short, were much more than reportage, and I like to believe that Liebling knew this. Conrad's maritime writings are, of course, irreplaceable, but is there anything better in our literature than "Westbound Tanker," Liebling's account of his return to America at the end of 1941? That piece and the rest of *The Road Back to Paris* (1944) announced to those people who hadn't been reading *The New Yorker* and to those who had read the earlier books and pieces that here was the country's best reportorial voice.

After Africa, he returned to England and waited for D-Day. The account of his return to France is in *Mollie and Other War Pieces* (1964) and *Normandy Revisited* (1958). Here we have filled in some small gaps in that story. This writing may make you want to read his books about the Second World War, for in them he is at the top of his game, showing us what writing about war ought to be—compassionate, fierce, amusing, kind, and always just right. Bill Mauldin has seen more war than any man I know, and has put his observations into splendid drawings and words. I once asked him to rate the writers of the Second World War, and he said kind and generous things about a number of people, and then he paused and said, "Of course, Joe Liebling was the best."

It is more than amazing to consider the kinds of writing at which Liebling *was* the best. I doubt that any American has written better about soldiers, about the ecstasy and horror of combat, about food, about men who maintain high standards of decency while following difficult and unforgiving professions: boxers and their handlers, mustang wranglers, hustlers of ever sort, handicappers, and those who believe with Colonel Stingo, Liebling's friend and the subject of a biography, that taking an honest dollar was beneath contempt.

There are few places in the literary pantheon for the writer who does not chiefly write poems, plays, stories, and novels. One reads that W. H. Auden admired M. F. K. Fisher, but one hears also that most of her work is just about food and travel, and that her lean, supple prose ought to have embraced *real* writing. (There was with Fisher, as with Liebling, some fiction.) So where does one put Liebling and his compatriots at *The New Yorker*—Joseph Mitchell, S. N. Behrman, Philip Hamburger, Wolcott Gibbs, Janet Flanner, and many more? Dorothy Parker and Robert Benchley receive, from time to time, a bit of notoriety, but one wonders if anyone actually reads their wonderful work.

There is in *The Road Back to Paris* a summation of the feelings Liebling brought to his writing: "Millions of men meriting more than I have lived and died in humiliating periods of history. Free men and free thinking always gets a return match with the forces of sadism and anti-reason sometimes. But I had wanted to see a win, I had wanted my era to be one of those that read well in the books. Some people like to live in a good neighborhood; I like to live in a good age. I am a sucker for a happy ending—the villain kicked in the teeth, the stepchildren released from the dark basement, the hero in bed with the heroine. Maybe the curtain will go up on the same first act tomorrow night, but I won't be in the audience." He was always sad when the world and its best traditions let him down, when Pétain, France's great hero of the Great War, became a Nazi puppet in the Occupied France of the Second World War, when America gave in to the nut-case maunderings of Joe McCarthy and the House Un-

American Activities Committee, when, in their first fight, the hedonistic Ingemar Johansson trained on ice cream sodas and then knocked out the ascetic Floyd Patterson, the American champion who was a model of Spartan rigor. (Patterson's victories in the subsequent rematches confirmed Liebling's cherished belief that, in the words of Jack McAuliffe, an old bare-knuckle lightweight champion, "once down is no battle," words that Liebling applied to war and to life as well as to prize fights.) Like most people of mind and talent, Liebling professed strong opinions that at times may have seemed contradictory; he preferred not only Patterson to Johanssen but also General Omar Bradley to the gaudier General George S. Patton, and he wrote lovingly about such full-blown eccentrics as Earl Long and Colonel John R. Stingo.

To the reader encountering Liebling for the first time, I haven't any advice, only a nostalgic good wish as I remember my own luck of forty-odd years ago when my father, who had remarkable prescience about boxers and solid taste in literature, handed me a *New Yorker* and said, "Read the Liebling piece about the Robinson-Turpin fight. It's good," It was. And it is, thank God, securely collected in Liebling's first book of fight pieces, *The Sweet Science.* When I was living in London, I frequently walked past the arena where Turpin had defeated Robinson in their long-ago first match, and I always thought not of the ill-conditioned Robinson who had been training in Paris on women and good food but of Liebling's magisterial rendering of Robinson's eventual triumph.

This book is, I suppose, just a *soupçon* of Liebling's work. There is plenty more out there, much of it, alas, out of print—*The Republic of Silence* his splendid edition (to which he contributed) of writing from and about the French Resistance; there are his unpublished letters, and there are the scattered, ungathered pieces that appeared not only in *The New Yorker* but also in the *New York World-Telegram* and other newspapers and magazines. There are short stories to be gathered, and when one totes it up, the unpublished things and the many books that slip in and out print, the troublesome question arises again: how can a writer this good not be better known and not more available? It is small grace to know that few people other than academic specialists read Ring Lardner and H. L. Mencken and Heywood Broun, and it is meagre succor to be told by polls that most living Americans have not read a book since, let's say, the Rome Olympics in 1960 (which Liebling wonderfully covered for *The New*

Yorker). Perhaps the simple and admirable truth is that his writing is for those whom Stendhal, one of Liebling's literary heroes, called "the happy few." Liebling's own literary tastes were extremely catholic and had nothing to do with fashion and trend. He admired, respected, and read Frank Sullivan, Stephen Crane, Milt Gross, George Borrow, Defoe, Cobbett, Sterne, Stendhal, Fielding, Colonel Stingo (John A. Macdonald), Camus, Sartre, Mauriac, Robert Benchley; there were his special favorites, Pierce Egan, the "Sire de Joinville of the London prize ring," a sporting journalist of the late eighteenth and early nineteenth centuries, and Ibn Khaldûn, the fourteenth-century Tunisian historian. It is probably accurate and would be pleasing to Liebling if one compared him to Khaldûn, whom Liebling described as "not really a scholar. He was, by turns, or concurrently, a judge, a soldier, an educator, a political adventurer, a savant, and a talented but untrustworthy diplomat who worked all sides of the streets in the same time, in a North Africa torn among minor dynasties, as Machiavelli's Italy was to be." What joins Liebling to Egan and Khaldûn is that the three of them, like so many of the writers he admired, were wide and knowledgeable likers, writers who easily could range over a number of unlikely and unrelated subjects and write keenly and intelligently about them all. When Liebling died, there was in his office at *The New Yorker* a jumble of books, newspapers, and unfinished pieces. There were Pierce Egan's three-volume *Boxiana,* Harold Nicolson's *The Congress of Vienna,* the collected works of Camus, the Annual Budget of the New York Historical Society, the volumes of Stendhal's *Journals,* and, *inter alia,* Von Bernhardi's *Cavalry in War and Peace.*

With *A Neutral Corner* and this book, James Barbour and I have added a bit to what, as Liebling would have said, the boys in the academy call the Liebling canon. One soon realizes that behind his many accounts of war, New York, sport, and the untidy affairs of humankind, there is another story, the story of his life, the story of a good, talented man who went down too soon. One thinks of his late, happy marriage to the eminent American writer Jean Stafford. She lived on without him until 1979, and one likes to think that had he lived her later years would have been more pleasant and more productive. But Liebling was right when he said in his Introduction to *The Sweet Science* that "A boxer, like a writer, must stand alone."

If you want to understand the troubled relation between making money and making literature, then read what Liebling says about Stephen Crane. Liebling quotes what Melville wrote to Hawthorne:

"Dollars damn me!" (Melville was trying to finish *Moby Dick* and at the same time get in a crop of potatoes.) You don't have to go to graduate school to see the troubling, macabre analogies that Liebling found in Melville and Crane, who strove in lives long and short with the tough battle of making money out of writing. Liebling, of course, lived fully and well, but he lived with the curse of knowing how good he was, and, in the later years, how good Jean Stafford was. He possessed a lovely cynicism about American universities, and he wasn't at all surprised that they had jolly well taken their time in discovering Melville and Crane. Jean Stafford's novels and stories have, in recent years, made their way into the undergraduate classroom and the chambered seminar. As I write, it is nearly thirty years since A. J. Liebling died, and it is high time that his works become known at last, to readers in and out of colleges who know a truly good writer when they see one. Liebling and Jean Stafford are buried side by side, and on the grave stone is carved for her a snowflake and for him a *fleur-de-lys.*

1
The Line

PRECISELY at one-thirty o'clock on every afternoon of the racing season in New York, six or eight bookmakers' clerks gather under the grandstand, near the stationer's booth. They have come to get the day's prices from Augustine J. Grenet. Mr. Grenet, an elderly man with a soft hat pulled down over his eyes and a pair of binoculars joggling against his lower abdomen, hands to each of the clerks an ordinary ten-cent racing program. In the margin to the left of each entry, he has written, in pencil, odds against the horse to win, place, and show.

Just as the last clerk receives his program, the group is joined by a stocky colored man with straight brown features and a grizzled mustache. The colored man, whose name is Ollie Thomas, clocks horses for Grenet. Ollie spent his young manhood as a Pullman porter, and he is as punctual as a well-conducted railroad. He has just obtained the list of horses scratched from the day's racing, and he reads the names off to his employer.

Grenet notes the scratches on his own program, and then, without any perceptible pause for calculation, reels off the changes in the odds on each race. When a horse with an appreciable chance is withdrawn, the odds against the remaining entries must be lowered proportionately. The clerks record the changes on their program margins. Grenet adds a few words of advice about certain entries, and the clerks go to their respective employers.

Half an hour later, when the clerks' bosses write up the opening odds on their slates, the figures agree substantially with those on the Grenet programs. Some bookmakers employ a younger expert named Gene Austin, who is Grenet's sole competitor in pricemaking. A few even take both lines of prices and average them. Bookmakers who operate on a small budget wait until the Grenet and Austin subscribers chalk up the prices and then adapt them for their own slates.

Before post time some of the odds are forced down by heavy betting on certain horses and some odds are increased. But aside from these fluctuations, the New York racing public bets against the considered opinions of the two pricemakers.

Grenet, who invented the profession of making prices, has been evaluating thoroughbreds for fifty years. During all but two of them, pricemaking has furnished him with a comfortable living. There was no racing in New York State during 1911 and 1912, and in those years he worked as a statistician in Wall Street. On any track where there are bookmakers, they need guidance, Grenet explains, because bookmakers, as a class, are not horsemen but tradesmen.

"The average bookmaker has as much idea of horses as a hog has of heaven," he says sometimes.

ON the race course, Grenet is known as Tex. He was born in San Antonio in 1861, and it pleases him to tell new acquaintances that his father owned the Alamo, the disused mission where Santa Ana massacred a hundred and eighty-one Texan heroes during Texas's own revolution. His father bought the Alamo in 1877, to use as an annex to a dry-goods store. His estate sold it in 1886.

Tex today is a middling tall man who walks slowly but covers a couple of miles in an afternoon, between the head of the stretch, where he observes the races, and the betting ring. This round trip he completes a half-dozen times during a card of races. Usually he is dressed in a suit of brown gabardine, and he wears eyeglasses with thick lenses and a scarfpin with a painting of a horse's head on glass. Tex has a wide, pleasant mouth, screened by a straggling, clipped mustache, and a somewhat flattened nose. The nose was broken by a pitched ball when he caught for the Manhattan College nine in 1879. Catchers wore no masks or gloves at that time. The pricemaker's only surviving Manhattan classmate is the Right Reverend Monsignor Thomas J. McMahon, of Our Lady of Lourdes Church on West 143rd Street. Nine of the eighteen members of his college class went into the priesthood.

The Grenet's mode of living when Tex was a boy in San Antonio did not accord with any trite conception of frontier life. His father, Honoré Grenet, was a son of the proprietor of the Maison Dorée, one of the most celebrated Parisian restaurants of the Second Empire. Honoré had learned to cook in the kitchens of that glorious gastronomic institution. But he had not liked the commercial side of the restaurant business, so had gone to Mexico in the fifties to plant cotton. In 1861, when the French fleet bombarded Vera Cruz, Mexico became a nation of Francophobes, and Honoré Grenet, with his wife, three daughters, and one son, removed to Texas, where Augustine was almost immediately born. Grenet received new capital from France, and became the largest jobber and retailer of general merchandise in southern Texas. The railroad ran only as far as Austin then; goods travelled in wagons between that place and San Antonio. Yet Grenet père carried a vast stock, including a line of champagnes, brandies, and cordials unparalleled even in Chicago. He returned to his cooking, *en amateur*, as a social duty. The board at the hotels was notoriously bad. No traveller of any standing came to San Antonio without a letter of introduction to Honoré Grenet.

Tex says his father was the best cook in the United States, and could have been the richest man in Texas if he had been more avaricious. He just didn't have it in his heart to jack up prices. On Sundays, Tex remembers, the ladies would leave the table after dessert (dinner was served in the middle of the day) and the males would sit around the table all afternoon drinking champagne and talking. There were ranchers, salesmen, railroad builders, and Army officers on their way to border forts. The name all mentioned most often was that of Lexington, who, Tex says, was "the most revered being in America." Lexington was the ante-bellum Man o' War. He was foaled in 1850, and lived on, at stud, until 1875. Never a guest came to the Grenet board without some tale of the super-horse's deeds. At sundown, Honoré Grenet would serve a rum omelet, and Augustine, gratified with a small portion, would be sent off to bed to dream of a gigantic racehorse that ran one hundred and twenty miles an hour.

Although his conception of life was not austere, Honoré Grenet was of a family traditionally Catholic. So Augustine went to New York to study at a Catholic college. It took five days to get from San Antonio to Chicago, even though the railroad from Austin had been completed by that time. Manhattan College, which is up in Riverdale now, then stood at the corner of 131st Street and the Boulevard, which was the old name for upper Broadway. Augustine Grenet was the first undergraduate from Texas in the history of the college. Automatically, he became Tex. During Tex's senior year, his father died, leaving an involved estate. Tex went home for the funeral, then returned to New York to await the settlement. His older brother, Edouard, by that time was living in France, painting, and his three sisters had all married Army officers, so Tex felt more at home here. To increase his limited allowance from the estate, he began to attend the races at Jerome Park, on the present site of the Hillview Reservoir in Westchester. Naturally, he lost money. But he got a job as a sheet-writer with a bookmaker named Atkinson at fifteen dollars a day. Every bookmaker has a sheet-writer, a race-track bookkeeper who records his bets and adds up wins and losses on each race. The sheet-writer usually achieves a balance, to a dollar, a couple of minutes after the finish of the race.

Jerome Park was the only metropolitan track in 1880. There were five races a day four days a week. If the weather threatened in the morning, a flag would be raised over the downtown office of the American Jockey Club to warn the public that there would be no racing that day. This would spare the coaching element an all-morning drive to the course.

Tex was so efficient that after a couple of seasons Dave Johnson, one of the leading bookmakers of his time, hired him at twenty-five dollars a day, a figure unexcelled among sheet-writers even now. The settlement of the estate dragged, and young Grenet definitely became a racing man. In the mid-eighties he began to make the prices for Johnson and for Sol Lichtenstein, another leader of the betting ring. Both books were backed by a gambler named Lucius Appleby. Tex's services gave the Appleby books a certain advantage over their competitors, since none of the other bookmakers had any systematic method of working out their prices.

During the first hundred years of American racing, which began almost contemporaneously with the Republic, the heavy wagering had been done in auction pools. The pools usually were held on the night before the race meeting, in the salon of the leading local hotel. Horsemen bid on the entries' chances, just as passengers now bid for numbers in a ship's pool. The high bidder for a horse's chances took the whole pot, if his horse won. When the favorite had been "sold," the auctioneer asked for bids on other horses. Finally, when he reached the horses on which he could get no individual bid, he would lump them all as "the field" and ask for bids on their collective chances. If, for example, the favorite sold for $4,000 in the pool, second choice for $3,000, third choice for $1,000, and the field for $2,000, and the favorite won, the lucky bidder had a profit of $6,000, odds of 3 to 2 for his $4,000 stake. The bidders were almost all professional horsemen, with excellent grounds for their opinions. So the bookmakers waited for the result of the auction, and then based their odds upon it. These odds they, in turn, offered to the plebeian punters who turned out for the actual race. But racing, in the eighties, had begun to outgrow the pool system. There were too many tracks, too many races, and too many new horses, shifted rapidly from one region to another by railroad. The experts could not bid accurately on these strange horses, and preferred to wait until they had horses of their own entered. Then they bet with the bookies, taking advantage of the odds-layers' ignorance.

Betting coups were the order of the day. Marcus Daly, the Montana copper magnate, put over a horse named Senator Grady, at 100 to 1. A man named McCafferty came up from Texas with a string which he rode himself. He won on a mare named Helen Nichols, at 80 to 1. McCafferty, in his first Eastern races, appeared in danger of falling off his mounts. But he rode Helen Nichols quite competently—at 80 to 1. The bookmakers needed some form of protective information service. This Tex had supplied for Johnson, and other bookmakers were eager to buy his guidance.

Quitting Johnson in 1890, Tex set up as an independent bookmaker for a while. He had accumulated a modest capital by betting. Tex also campaigned a string of ten horses on New Jersey tracks, and continued to sell his opinions of horses as a side line. But as the number of horses in training increased, the task of observing them took up more of his time. In 1892 he adopted pricemaking as his sole profession.

Tex has owned and ridden horses from his seventh birthday; he has an eye for their idiosyncrasies and a prodigiously exact memory. For example, it is not enough for him to remember that he saw a horse named Tremont beat another known in history as Kingston at Jerome Park in 1886. He recalls also that Kingston at that time had no name, but was called "the Kapanga colt" (Kapanga was his dam). And further that Tremont, a very nervous horse, was distracted at the start by the passage of wagons on a road which ran by the course, so that he wheeled and was left ten lengths at the post. Despite which Tremont won. Nor is he content with a casual mention of a horse named King Thomas, once owned by Senator Hearst of California, father of William R. Tex feels impelled to specify that Hearst bought King Thomas for $38,000, and the horse was "one of the most notorious clucks that ever lived and died a maiden."

He has a passion for estimating mathematical probabilities, and for arithmetical short cuts. His conversation bristles with sentences like "the percentage on Bradley's roulette wheel, with 0 and the double 0, is 5 and 5/19ths against you." He likes people to ask him, without warning, for figures like the square of 495 (245,025) or the product of 6448 multiplied by 8749 (56,413,552). He jots the answers down on his race program, tears out the page, and invites you to check up on them.

Tex believes that horse racing, like history, moves in cycles, and that everything that happens on a race course is bound to recur. Since he forgets nothing, each year adds to his estimative equipment. Standing on a bench at the head of the Belmont or Aqueduct stretch during a race, peering through his binoculars, he notices dozens of minutiae that do not appear in past-performance charts. He may note that a certain horse, started from an outside position, shows a tendency to bear over to the rail. If this proves impossible, the horse sulks. Started from an inside post position next time, the "rail runner" may win the race. That mental note may be worth more for future reference than a bale of statistics about weight carried and the number of lengths back of the winner that the horse finishes. Or Tex may note a jockey sedulously flogging a horse that won very easily last time out without being whipped. Some horses sulk under the whip. On the former occasion the horse may have been priced at 6 to 1, while this time it is favorite, and loses. Tex will advise an increased price against the horse the next time it runs, but he will warn his clients that if any stable money appears for it, the odds must be slashed drastically. If the stable money does appear, he will not be astonished to see the rider without a whip.

"You must know your horses," he says, "and you must know your tracks. But the most important thing is to know your muggs." In support of this theorem, he sometimes cites the defeat of Man o' War by Upset at Saratoga in 1919, describing the highly involuted course steered by Man o' War's jockey. Under the general heading of muggs he includes ninety-eight per cent of the human race.

The indispensable qualification of a pricemaker is integrity. All racing people credit Tex with this form of eccentricity. A dishonest pricemaker, by withholding information from his clients, might leave the field clear for a gamblers' cleanup. A clocker, by withholding the time of a fast workout, might in the same way throw off the pricemaker who employs him. But Tex has complete faith in the probity of his clocker, Ollie Thomas, the ex-Pullman porter. Clocking, or timing horses in their trials, came into racing at an even later date than pricemaking because accurate split-second stopwatches appeared only toward the turn of the century. Clockers work on the theory that in timing a horse, one-fifth of a second is equivalent to one length. Human athletes are timed in fifth-seconds because the watchmakers produce an instrument to satisfy the horse-racing people. But more important than the time of a trial is the manner of its accomplishment, and since Tex doesn't get to the track in the early morning, he must depend upon Ollie to report on the workouts.

Ollie is draped in the suave decorum of his Pullman *métier.* He measures his words as if awed by his own sapience, and serves them out in a rich, deep, portentous voice. Every morning at daybreak, from April through July, Ollie may be found in the grandstand at Belmont Park. In August he is at Saratoga; then until November he is back at Belmont, where he usually sits by the glass windbreak at one end of the Turf and Field Club section. This place he chooses not from snobbishness but because it provides an unobstructed view of the whole course.

Most trainers work their horses at seven o'clock, but sometimes a "sharpshooter" tries to sneak in a time trial early. Ollie takes no chances. In his morning vigil he has the company of five or six colleagues—Austin's man, a couple from racing newspapers, and one or two who work for bettors. He carries a $450 Tiffany stopwatch in his right vest pocket. In his left hand he holds a $45 steel watch with which he does his work. He doesn't want to "wear out the works" of his expensive watch.

Each of his co-workers, like Ollie, carries a good watch, which he rests, and a comparatively cheap one with which he earns his living. The good watch is for prestige, occasional collateral, and insurance. The first professional clocker was a colored man named Hoggie Shields. "His was the common end of clockers," Tex says. "They auctioned his watch to bury him." Lou Salyers, a white clocker, carries Shields' watch now. He bought it at the sale.

The first item in a clocker's stock is the knack of identifying horses. Trainers cannot bar observers from the course, but they do what they can to confuse them. There are no colors or numbers to distinguish one thoroughbred from another. They break from any furlong or sixteenth marker on the track, and sometimes three or four time trials are going on simultaneously. At Belmont, especially in the spring, a large proportion of the horses working are two-year-olds that have never raced. The clockers may have had no opportunity of seeing them.

To Ollie, however, each horse has an unmistakable identity. To begin with, thoroughbreds have a surprising variety of markings. Many have black or white socks. A great number have a star or a blaze on the face. The clocker does not merely speak of a star; he distinguishes between heart stars, diamond stars, crescent stars, comet stars "with the tail coming toward you," and other varieties. He is sensitive to shades of horse color, and never forgets a peculiarity of conformation. This is the most important of all, for trainers may work a horse in bandages, which hide the leg markings, or blinkers, which hide the face. Ollie attends the yearling sales at Saratoga every summer, studying each offering. A colleague in Kentucky attends the Blue Grass sales, and Ollie and the Kentuckian exchange completely annotated catalogues. Often, when a two-year-old steps out on the Belmont track for his first spin of the season, Ollie is able to enter its correct lineage and identity in his big loose-leaf notebook. As for horses that have raced, they are like old friends. The clockers comment that they have lost or gained weight, look brisk or sluggish, move sorely or have recovered from a lameness, as if they were discussing human acquaintances.

When several spins are on at once, the clockers divide the work and exchange results. In the same way, Ollie trades information with clockers at Jamaica and Aqueduct, the other Long Island tracks. He prefers to work at Belmont because most of the young horses are quartered there. "Learn a horse when he's young and you know him when he's old," Ollie says. Being of a sanguine, energetic temper, he consistently catches workouts two-fifths of a second faster than they really are. He stops his watch too soon. Some of his confreres, pessimists with low blood pressure, catch all their work slow. "Those moody types are the only ones you can't count on," Ollie's employer says. "They're fast one day and slow the next. But if you know you have a fast clocker, you can allow for it."

If a horse runs a fast trial, it shows he has speed, but not that he will show it next time out. It means only that the trainer has tested him. A month may pass and several poor races and slow trials intervene before the animal truly goes for the money. But few workouts in any case are actually fast by competitive standards, because the horses are ridden under heavy saddles, by exercise boys considerably heavier than jockeys. Trainers, moreover, have a quaint fashion of placing thirty pounds of lead in a horse's saddle blanket or fitting him with thick, heavy shoes to befuddle the morning observers.

It happened, a few years ago, that a trainer substituted one horse for another in a race in Maryland, without bothering to notify officials of the change. This is known as "ringing," and doesn't often happen. It is almost impossible to paint one horse to look like another. "When the sun shine on one of them painted horses, it look streaky, like one of them women that dye her hair," Ollie says. "What the good ringer look for is a horse that don't amount to nothing, yet he look exactly like another horse that do amount to something. Then the ringer buy both them horses, and enter the one that don't amount to nothing in a race, and he run the one that do amount to something." That's what happened in Maryland when a horse named Akhnaton was substituted for an inferior one called Shem. Ollie wasn't at that meeting. He is sure he could have detected the sham Shem.

When the last workout is over, toward nine, Ollie mounts to the deserted press box and types out his work sheets for Tex. He is enormously proud of his typing. On the sheets, he records each workout, with the time by furlongs. Then, when Tex has finished his conference with the bookmakers' clerks in the afternoon, he and Ollie discuss the imponderables of the morning's trials.

Their consultation ends before the start of the first race, and Tex strolls down to his bench at the head of the stretch to sun himself. Sometimes, when the meeting is at Belmont, he sits under a shade tree in the paddock, ignoring the first race if it involves cheap horses. He has a constitutional hatred of $1,500 selling-platers. He reserves for them his bitterest epithet: "trotting horses." Cheap horses, like cheap people, are unpredictable, he says. They reduce his equine science to something like the match game or bingo.

During the two annual meetings at the Empire City track in Yonkers, Tex lives in his own house, a good-sized place in Hartsdale which cost $50,000 to build. During the rest of the year he and his wife live in hotels. They have been married for forty-nine years. Mrs. Grenet is a Dresden-shepherdess type of woman, with miraculously small feet and ankles. She was a New York girl, and met Tex through one of his Manhattan College classmates. They have three mature daughters.

While the races are on Long Island, the Grenets live in an apartment hotel called the Homestead, at Kew Gardens. One of the daughters lives there, too. She is married to a man named Teddy Steimer, a betting commissioner. Steimer places large sums of money for customers at the best possible odds, exactly as a broker executes orders on the Stock Exchange. The Grenets and Steimers travel to Saratoga in August, and in the winter attend the race meetings in Florida.

There was a time, between 1913 and 1934, when New York bookmakers were forbidden by law to operate with fixed stands or slates. Since it was then impossible to crib prices from a competitor's slate, every bookmaker had to buy a line from somebody. In those boom years, Tex had thirty-eight subscribers and employed three men to distribute bulletins to his customers, whom they had to track through the swirling crowds. Now he has about eight clients. Bookmakers in the clubhouse pay fifty dollars a week for the line; operators in the grandstand betting ring pay thirty dollars. The bookmaker's volume of business, per capita, is larger in the clubhouse. But Tex's most important single patron is a racing news agency which distributes his line, by telegraph, for the guidance of five thousand poolrooms in the United States which accept bets on New York racing. His income during the New York season of approximately six months runs to about five hundred dollars a week.

There are no books on Florida tracks, but Tex sends out a line on Florida races for the news service all through the winter. He just about makes his Southern expenses.

Tex is an early riser. At half past seven every morning he is at work compiling his prices. Besides the entries, he has his file of work sheets, past-performance charts, and his memory. There are "speed handicappers," who base their predictions entirely on the times of past races. Others pay attention only to consistency: "A has beaten B and B has beaten C, therefore A *must* beat C." Tex blends both schools of thought, and adds a generous dash of personal observation. By ten-thirty he has finished his computations. At eleven the news service calls up for his poolroom line. Then for an hour or so he is free to work on a history of the American turf, which he is writing. It is filled with such episodes as the authenticated steeplechase in Virginia wherein all eight entries fell at the second fence, seriously injuring all eight riders; and the race in which the rider of the winning horse died before the finish but remained in the saddle. In the first of these races one jockey, although dazed, recalled that he had bet $300 on his mount. He remounted, with a broken collarbone, finished the course, and won the race. In the other the stewards ruled that the result was official. There is to be a chapter on plungers and big bettors, whom Tex deems two entirely different breeds, and another on equine nomenclature, which he thinks is terrible. He cites the case of a horse named Xerxes, which bettors unanimously pronounced "Exercise."

At noon Tex's son-in-law drives him out to the track, and at about one o'clock he is sunning himself in front of the stationer's booth, waiting for Ollie and his clients.

The estate of Honoré Grenet, after the creditors and the Texas lawyers finished with it, pretty well evaporated. The trustees sold the Alamo to a pair of Germans who had succeeded Honoré Grenet as the leading wholesale grocers of San Antonio, for $28,000. They used it as a whiskey storehouse for thirty years. Finally the state appropriated enough money to buy the shrine of Texas liberty. Because it had held whiskey, the Daughters of the Texas Revolution wanted to tear it down and turn the site into a memorial park, but they were dissuaded. When Tex visited San Antonio last, in 1931, the roof needed repair, and the Daughters were soliciting contributions to buy shingles. Ten dollars for three shingles was the price. Tex bought six.

Tex has never been brash enough to plunge on the results of his own calculations. He doesn't think he can predict the winner of every race, and none of his clients expects him to. It is enough if he points out where the dangers lie and arranges prices so that, if the book fills, it will be sure of a decent profit. He likes to walk around the outside of the betting ring, though, and see if any bookmaker is widely out of line. If, for example, a book has quoted 20 to 1 against a horse Tex rates an 8 to 1 shot, or 3 to 5 against a 2-to-5 favorite, he likes to hop on with a bet of perhaps thirty dollars. He wins pretty often, and it gives him satisfaction.

2
The Navy's Only Mutiny

MIDSHIPMAN PHILIP SPENCER had two distinctions among the officers of the United States Navy in 1842. He was the son of John Canfield Spencer, Secretary of War in President Tyler's cabinet, and, according to Commander Alexander Slidell Mackenzie of the United States brig-of-war Somers, he had "the faculty of throwing his lower jaw out of joint and of thus playing with it a variety of musical airs." Midshipman Spencer achieved a third distinction by the manner of his death, unique in the history of the service, when he was hanged for "intended mutiny" without the formality of a court-martial. That event occurred on the first of December, 1842, aboard the Somers, about two hundred and fifty miles from the West Indian island of Antigua. Two other "intending mutineers" were hanged with Spencer: Samuel A. Cromwell, a tall boatswain, and a short seaman named Elisha Small.

Only one circumstance in Spencer's early youth might be interpreted as a portent. While a freshman at Hobart, then known as Geneva College, Spencer loved to read pirate stories. His favorite volume in the college library was an anthology called "The Pirate's Own Book," and he frightened the children of a professor by telling them tales from it. He stayed at Geneva long enough to learn a little Latin and the Greek alphabet, and then left to join the Navy. That was in 1841, before the founding of the Naval Academy at Annapolis. Spencer was put aboard the schoolship North Carolina, which was tied up all year round at the Navy Yard in Brooklyn as a training base for officers and enlisted men. Classmates on the vessel later recalled him as a moody fellow—tall, delicate, and taciturn. Accustomed to being bullied by his father, a tyrannical lawyer-politician, the young man had developed a protective habit of daydreaming, and he occasionally intensified his reveries with alcohol. After a few months on the North Carolina, Spencer served aboard the frigates Potomac and John Adams. He was eighteen when he was appointed to the Somers in the fall of 1842.

Like Spencer, many of the crew of the Somers were recent graduates of the North Carolina. Only twenty-four of the brig's hundred and twenty officers and men were old enough to vote, and most of the sailors, rated as apprentice seamen, were from thirteen to nineteen years old. The Somers was a smart new sailing vessel of two hundred and sixty-six tons, measuring one hundred and five feet over all. She mounted ten guns. The Navy had a few steam vessels, but the heroes of the War of 1812, who still guided naval thought, regarded steam craft as a fad and saw to it that the Brooklyn yard kept building sailing ships.

Alexander Slidell Mackenzie, commanding the Somers on her maiden voyage, was an unusual naval officer. He had been in the service for twenty-five years, but he was best known as the author of a number of travel books, written in a style that archly reflected Washington Irving's. Three of them were "A Year in Spain," "Two Years in Spain," and "Spain Re-visited." Commander Mackenzie had also composed flattering biographies of the naval heroes Stephen Decatur and Oliver Hazard Perry. A member of a wealthy New York merchant family named Slidell, he had added the Mackenzie in honor of a generous uncle on his mother's side. Mackenzie was thirty-nine when he took the Somers to sea. Contemporaries have described him as a man "of amiable and pleasing rather than stern and commanding presence." Despite this apparent amiability, Mackenzie had a bad name with the enlisted men. A pamphlet published a couple of years before his voyage on the Somers described him as a particularly revolting specimen of naval martinet. The seaman author of the tract said Mackenzie "was noted for his cruelty to the men for small offences and trifling accidents, and for his hypocrisy in public worship aboard the ship." Mackenzie's reputation as a stern disciplinarian and a religious man was considered excellent reason for assigning him to a vessel with a crew of boys.

Besides Spencer, there were six midshipmen on the Somers, more than usual for a brig of her size. Two were related to Commander Mackenzie by blood, two by marriage, and the remaining two had been placed in his care by family friends. The other midshipmen considered Spencer an interloper because of his father's position in the War Department. They made their feelings plain, and soon Spencer began talking to enlisted men more often than to his messmates.

Sometimes, to amuse the sailors, he would throw his lower jaw out of joint and produce what his commander regarded as music.

THE destination of the Somers was the west coast of Africa, then a favorite cruising and training ground for the American Navy. The United States was obliged by treaty to cooperate with Great Britain in a patrol to suppress the slave trade and, while the warships seldom made captures, their green crews were kept on the alert. They practiced handling the sails during chases after strange vessels sighted. The apprentices aboard the Somers exercised with broadswords and shot at floating barrels with thirty-two-pounders. They also listened to many rousing sermons by Commander Mackenzie and absorbed a tremendous amount of flogging—in all, during this cruise, 2,313 lashes were distributed upon the bare backs of less than a hundred homesick, seasick boys. Sermons and flogging came under the head of character-building. Mackenzie meticulously entered all floggings in the ship's log. The causes most frequently noted were "fighting," "skulking," and "being dirty." A fourteen-year-old named Bellinger Scott received, altogether, sixty-nine lashes at different times. Another recidivist, Dennis Manning, had his character fortified with a hundred and one. He was fifteen.

Cromwell, the boatswain, had to lay on the lashes. This naturally detracted from his popularity with his shipmates. He was a scarred, powerful fellow of thirty-five, almost a patriarch on that ship. There was a story among the boys that Cromwell had once sailed on a slaver.

Commander Mackenzie later testified before a naval board of inquiry in Brooklyn that the crew was an extremely depraved one. He said the boys, though lacking mature judgment, had the strength of men. Commodore Jacob Jones, one of the judges, remarked that "the Somers must have been in an extraordinary state to have required ten times the amount of flogging ordinarily necessary."

The African cruise was not eventful. On November 11th, Mackenzie thought they had been gone long enough, and decided to sail for the United States by way of St. Thomas, in the Virgin Islands, where he intended to take on provisions and fresh water. The exercises, the sermons, and the floggings continued on the westward passage. Mackenzie, despite what he was to say afterward about the morale of the crew, recorded nothing suspicious in its conduct and apparently considered his ship to be in a state of good discipline.

THEN an odd thing happened. On November 25th, Lieutenant Guert Gansevoort, the second in command, came to Mackenzie's cabin to report that in a roundabout manner he had heard of a mutinous conspiracy aboard the Somers. The Commander, aware that he was noted for what he called his "just severity," listened apprehensively. Perhaps, without considering the extreme youthfulness of his crew, he feared he had aroused his cowed apprentices to the active resentment he might have expected among older men. Whatever his thoughts, Mackenzie was ready instantly to believe that Lieutenant Gansevoort's rumor was true.

The Lieutenant had learned of the plot from the purser and the purser had heard it from his mate, a man named Wales, whose duties were to preside over the slop chest and dole out soap and tobacco to the crew. Wales (all this is according to testimony later brought out ashore) told the purser that the purpose of the conspiracy was "to murder the captain, bring over as many of the crew as possible, murder the rest, and convert the vessel into a pirate." The chief conspirator, Wales said, was Midshipman Spencer. The middle of the nineteenth century was not precisely an age of piracy, and an ordinary commander, if he believed Wales, might have considered young Spencer a lunatic. That he might be, however, did not occur to Commander Mackenzie.

Wales said that Spencer had called him from his berth on the previous evening and asked him to swear an oath of secrecy. Wales, with nice regard for the Commander's religious fervor, said he had sworn, but not upon a Bible. Spencer then had asked Wales to go up on the booms with him and there had "divulged all the details of his plan, which were admirably suited for his purpose." The mutineers were to murder Mackenzie first, of course, and then take the ship to the Isle of Pines. There, Wales said he had been told, they would meet a confederate of someone on the Somers who was not only Spencer's ally but a former pirate.

The description of the ally aboard ship, Lieutenant Gansevoort thought and Commander Mackenzie agreed, clearly pointed to the boatswain Cromwell, who, if he had not acknowledged himself an ex-pirate, was at least suspected of having been a slaver. It also indicated that Seaman Small, as Cromwell's closest friend, must be a leading conspirator.

With a good mind for details, Wales said that Spencer had told him they "would attack no vessels that they could not capture, and destroy all they captured," and that "they would select from the captured vessels such females as were proper, use them, and then dispose of them." Spencer had it all worked out in writing, Wales said, and he kept the paper in the back folds of his cravat. He had let Wales feel the paper.

Whether Spencer really told Wales all these things must remain doubtful, since he never had a chance to answer the charge. If he did, he may have popped his preposterous plan to frighten the slop clerk. Or he may have been slightly mad. But the terrified Mackenzie now remembered the business of Spencer's musical jawbone, and recalled that he had noticed him playing on it in the presence of members of the crew. This he saw as clearly part of a scheme to wean his men from allegiance to their lawful commander. Mackenzie testified later that "Mr. Spencer was often in the habit of joking with them and smiling at them whenever he met them . . . and I had frequently noticed in him a strange flashing of the eye."

THE COMMANDER sent Lieutenant Gansevoort to look for Spencer. He found him in the foretop with a sailor named Green, who was tattooing some love devices on his arm. The tattooing, Gansevoort thought, was obviously a pretext for mutinous conversation, and he ordered Spencer to come aft. At this, the Lieutenant said afterward, "Spencer looked at me with the most infernal expression I have ever seen upon a human face—it satisfied me at once of the man's guilt." When Spencer reached the quarterdeck, Commander Mackenzie ordered him placed under arrest.

"Did you not," Mackenzie asked, "tell Mr. Wales that you had a mutinous project on foot, that you intended to kill the commander and officers of the Somers and such of the crew as you could not seduce to your plans, and to enter upon a course of piracy?"

"I may have told him something like that," the midshipman replied, "but it was only in joke."

"This joke, sir," the Commander said, "may cost you your life." The dialogue, so reported by Mackenzie, shows that he could be gallant and restrained in a crisis. Spencer was ordered into double irons.

No paper was found in the prisoner's cravat, but a search of his sea chest turned up a razor case containing a memorandum in cryptic characters, which Henry Rodgers, another midshipman, recognized as Greek letters. The names of several members of the crew were thus spelled out on the paper. Four names—Spencer, Andrews, McKinley, and Wales—were marked "certain." Ten others were listed as "doubtful." There was nobody named Andrews on the Somers, so Mackenzie and Gansevoort decided the name must stand for Cromwell. McKinley was thrown into irons, but no charges were ever pressed against him and he was released after the Somers got back to New York. Small was among the men marked only "doubtful," but Mackenzie appears to have been unwaveringly certain of his guilt. Mackenzie ordered Cromwell and Small arrested.

The Commander explained afterward that Small sealed his fate by "shifting his weight from side to side—his eye was never for a moment fixed, but always turned from me." Cromwell sealed *his* fate by looking very cocky and self-assured—a hardened character, the Commander reasoned. Both men denied knowledge of a plot. "They had perhaps sworn a pirate's oath of secrecy upon a dirk," Commander Mackenzie said. He was not deceived for an instant.

ST. THOMAS was within easy reach and if the Commander thought an emergency existed, he could have put in at Antigua, even closer by. Mackenzie had the putative mutineers safely in irons, his apprentices were unarmed, and he had distributed carbines, cutlasses, and pistols among his officers and petty officers. Under the circumstances, another man might have felt secure. But the Commander of the Somers by that time was in a funk. His apprehension doubled when Wales reported he had seen the chained prisoners nodding significantly at members of the crew. That reminded Mackenzie that he had noticed seamen gathered in groups, "talking and giving sidelong glances."

Nor was that all. Early in the afternoon of the next day, the Commander ordered skysails and studding sails, the topmost and slightest of a ship's outfit, to be set to increase the ship's speed. Presently they were carried away by a gust of wind. Nothing happened except the loss of canvas, but Mackenzie was certain that some member of the crew had deliberately jerked too suddenly on a stay, hoping that in the confusion caused by the disappearing sails other potential mutineers would be able to free the prisoners. Still worse, on the following morning, as Mackenzie subsequently described it, a "crime of considerable magnitude came to light." A man named Waltham had stolen three bottles of wine and had hidden them in a boat. The appalled Commander decided to hang the three imprisoned conspirators immediately as a means of overawing the rest.

He had no right to hold a court-martial on his little ship, but he wrote a note to his officers asking if they thought it possible to bring the brig into port with the prisoners alive. Gansevoort was the only adult line officer aboard. He conferred with the surgeon and the purser, both young, and with the four oldest of the six midshipmen, leaving two youngsters, who were fifteen and sixteen, out of it. Gansevoort, after the conference, wrote, "We think that the safety of our lives, and honor to the flag entrusted to our charge, requires that the prisoners be put to death, as the course best calculated to make a salutary impression on the rest of the crew." Mackenzie concurred and the decision was put into effect on the morning of December 1st. "Whips," or hanging ropes, were passed over the yardarm. The Commander put on his full-dress uniform and came on deck to preside over the executions.

"If there be in your breast one feeling true to nature," he told Spencer, or so he recalled his words a month later, "you will be grateful for the premature disclosure of your horrible designs." Spencer "asked if the Commander had not exaggerated the danger, and if he was not going too far and too fast—if the law justified him."

"I told him 'No,' " Mackenzie subsequently reported. "I reminded him that his opinion was not unprejudiced."

Cromwell continued to insist that he was innocent, and Spencer said he had never talked to the boatswain about any sort of plot. "This, I confess, staggered me," Mackenzie admitted. "But the evidence of Cromwell's guilt was conclusive. Lieutenant Gansevoort said there was not a shadow of doubt of it."

Small did not seem to know why he was being hanged, but he was sporting about it. "Nobody cares for me but my poor old mother," he said, "and I would rather she should not know what has become of me. This is what I get for shipping in a Guineaman. Take example from me, mates, and never ship in a Guineaman."

Mackenzie gave the men ten minutes for prayer and then black handkerchiefs were adjusted over their eyes. A cannon shot was to be the signal. Spencer asked that he be allowed to give the word of command for his own execution. Mackenzie granted the request, but at the end of the ten minutes the boy's nerve failed him, so the Commander barked the order. As the cannon went off, Lieutenant

Gansevoort shouted "Whip!" and the seamen on the ends of the hanging ropes hauled the three conspirators into the air.

Commander Mackenzie delivered one of his mawkish sermons and then called for all hands to cheer ship. "Three *heartier* cheers never went up from the deck of an American ship," he wrote. "Dinner was piped."

The bodies were slid over the side after the meal. On the following Sunday, Commander Mackenzie preached a bang-up sermon. Even the frequently flogged apprentice Manning wept with emotion. In conclusion, Mackenzie called on his crew, "as they had given three cheers for their country, now to give three cheers for God by singing His praise." The colors were then hoisted and above the American ensign flew the Banner of the Cross.

The crew performed no mutinous act during the remainder of the voyage. By December 14th, when the Somers dropped anchor off Brooklyn, Mackenzie must have begun to suspect he had made a mistake, for he never pressed charges against another member of the crew. Instead, he made this modest recommendation: "Let every officer and seaman of the Somers who remained true to his flag receive the thanks of Congress accompanied with promotion or a sword to the officers and an appropriate medal to each of the petty officers and seamen." This meant either that he proposed to decorate a band of frustrated mutineers or that there had been no great risk of a general mutiny. Only the very imminent danger of such a mutiny, however, could have justified him in executing his prisoners instead of bringing them into port for trial. This fact was commented upon by friends of the hanged.

SINCE the Somers had touched at no port on her way up from the place of the hangings—Commander Mackenzie had changed his mind about stopping at St. Thomas—the public knew nothing of the executions until a day or two after her arrival. Mackenzie kept all his crew aboard while he sent dispatches to the Secretary of the Navy in Washington and a letter to J. Watson Webb, editor of the *Morning Courier & New York Enquirer*. This was a conservative newspaper largely supported by shipowners. The public first learned in the *Courier* of the supposed mutinous plot, and the account was decidedly favorable to Commander Mackenzie. He had spent most of a fortnight at sea composing it.

But when Mackenzie began to testify before a naval court of inquiry, summoned on board the North Carolina at the Brooklyn yard, public opinion turned against what James Gordon Bennett called "the despotism of the quarterdeck." James Fenimore Cooper, the nation's leading writer on naval affairs, pounced on the flaws in Mackenzie's story and daily wrote stinging critiques of the court's sessions. Friends of the executed men tried to have Mackenzie indicted for murder by a federal grand jury in New York, but the circuit court ruled that the hangings had occurred outside its jurisdiction. It appeared unfair to landsmen that Mackenzie, while his acts were subject to inquiry, should retain command of his ship and hold all the witnesses in the case incommunicado, having them flogged at the gangway whenever the notion seized him. Even before the hearings of the court of inquiry ended, President Tyler ordered a formal court-martial for the Commander. This court, consisting of twelve officers of high rank, also met on board the North Carolina. It followed so soon after the conclusion of the court of inquiry that the whole business seemed one continuous trial; it dragged on for three months. Commander Mackenzie was charged with murder at the court-martial, but his brother officers voted nine to three for acquittal and he went free. He died six years later, after retiring briefly and returning to the service. Lieutenant Gansevoort had a long career in the Navy and died a retired commodore in 1868. Henry Rodgers, the erudite midshipman who could read Greek letters, was drowned while attached to the frigate Albany, in 1850. The Somers, known from the date of the executions as a hard-luck ship, justified her reputation when she capsized off Vera Cruz in 1847 during the Mexican War. Twenty-one men lost their lives with her.

Philip Spencer is still recalled by Navy officers as the young fellow from the War Department who tried to start a mutiny. Few of them remember his name correctly or know the details of his case, but they say that there never has been a mutiny in the Navy since.

OCTOBER 29 (BY CABLE)

3
Letter from Paris

THE author of the current best-seller in Paris is Michel Nostradamus, the astrologer who died in 1566. Nostradamus left about 5,000 lines of prophecy in a crabbed mixture of French and what New Yorkers would call "double talk"—each quatrain lends itself to dozens of conflicting interpretations. He has been the object of a tiny cult for a long time, but became an important publishers' item only when war began. You can buy small condensed versions of his prophecies on the bookstalls for two francs or a large annotated definitive edition by a Dr. de Fontbrune for thirty at the big bookstores; the Boulevard des Italiens branch of Flammarion alone has sold 3,000 copies of the expensive edition in the last month.

In one prophecy, Nostradamus speaks of the destruction of Paris by "birds from the East." Some Nostradamists hold that his forecast is for 2040, while others believe it was intended for 1937, in which case Nostradamus, like the German General Staff, has missed the boat. All adepts agree that the astrologer predicted an eventual overwhelming French victory. Nostradamus's "little epidemic," as the booksellers call it, represents one element in the Parisian mood of the moment. Few readers admit taking him seriously, and yet *c'est une guerre tellement bizarre.*

NOW the bad weather has set in, heavily handicapping the German mechanized units. The French, eminently reasonable, cannot understand why the Germans have withheld their attack. There is the same astonishment in the high-ceilinged salons of retired generals as in the lodges of their concierges. Even the *chansonniers,* those knowing fellows who sing to intimate café audiences about love and politics, confess themselves stumped; they give exceedingly funny imitations of Hitler's radio voice—bawling, spitting, and sneezing—in what sounds at the same time like a dog fight and the Führer's

German, but as to future developments the refrain of a new song says only *"On n'en sait plus."*

This uncertainty, however, is no indication of a lack of confidence. *"On les aura"* has been revived from the other war. All last Sunday afternoon, a crowd of thousands stood around a little song-plugger in the Place Blanch in Montmartre, shouting the chorus of a new kind of war song, with nothing about smashing the Siegfried Line or taking Berlin but with merry references to Hitler's deficiencies in supplies, in munitions, in courage, and, since this is still Paris, in virility. The plugger, a youth of fifteen who wore four hats, one on top of another, howled with indelicate gaiety, and the changing crowd of soldiers and Montmartrois joined him in a long, happy yell.

DESPITE such surface exuberance, this, for the French, is a war of cold exasperation. They are self-conscious about expressions like "heroic poilu" and "sacred soil" and "accursed Boche," which had a vogue in War '14–'18. People just say that life with the Germans is impossible—that they mess up business, disarrange your private life, cause you to send your wife and children to the country, which is expensive, and are *tout simplement* a race of liars, cutthroats, and persons without shame, who, if you deprive them of their present Führer as one did in the case of the Kaiser, will push you a third one presently in the face. *Alors, faut en finir.* It is not a pretty state of mind, but it is an understandable one, and most of the Paris newspapers this week have given it intellectual expression in editorials advocating the partition of Germany after the war so that France, at least, will be sure of "peace for a hundred years."

AMONG Frenchmen, the most famous radio speaker in Europe is one Georges Ferdonnet, who is known to a public that would dearly love to tear him apart as "the traitor of Stuttgart." He is a Frenchman who broadcasts from Stuttgart in unmistakably authentic French, and he has done more than almost any other man to consolidate French hatred for Germany. Nothing seems so comical to a Frenchman as a foreign language, even in time of peace; on the other hand, there is something sacred for the French in the sound of their own tongue, and what Ferdonnet does is like the profanation of the Host. "Ah, that," the Parisians say, "that is too much. One expects filthy tricks of the Germans, but that *salaud,* he speaks French with a good accent."

Only the women now cling to the hope of a continuing miracle—a war without hard fighting. "Hitler will surely blow out his brains," they say, or "Just think how much money the English must be spending for the revolution in Germany." They circulate with grave optimism the story that a gipsy woman got into an autobus and sat down next to a Parisienne who moved her handbag out of the gipsy's reach. The gipsy said, "Why do you do that when you have only eighteen francs in your bag?" The woman had exactly that sum. Then the gipsy told each of the other passengers how much he or she had, down to the last sou. "Since you know so much," one passenger asked, "tell us when Hitler will die." "On December second," the gipsy said, and got out at the next stop. A story like this gains currency here not because Frenchwomen are silly but because they refuse to believe that their sons and husbands will be killed—those sons and husbands who until now have been so unexpectedly preserved.

It is hard for one to believe in the imperialism of a country where the army and the people are physically identical, where the bourgeoisie, which, by Marxist theory, is supposed to fatten on the profits of war, is the same bourgeoisie which has to shut up shop and move into the advanced zone.

By the way, cooties have reappeared at the front and have been rechristened. The French call them "breadcrumbs on springs."

NOVEMBER 12 (BY CABLE)

4
Letter from Paris

ANYBODY who thinks there are no Americans left here should attend a Thursday luncheon of the American Club in the white-and-gold banquet hall of the Cercle Interallié, a scene which always suggests the Rotary Club in Babylon. At least five hundred male Americans appeared at the last one, bravely enduring the rigors of wartime Paris while their families put up with expensive and bad accommodations in far-away Brittany or the Massif Central. These families have been the sufferers from the arrangement, while the beneficiaries have been the owners of houses in places like Tours and Nevers. The luncheon attendance was particularly large because the speaker was Paul Reynaud, Minister of Finance, an eager man who talked English with the restrained impatience of a fox terrier on a strange and heavy leash. Before M. Reynaud made his address there was an introduction of guests of honor with applause for each one, exactly as at the Dutch Treat Club, and after he had finished, a simultaneous rush for the cloakroom in the best American tradition. Some members have fought off nostalgia in this fashion for years.

PARIS is a city which comprises a little of everything. The distance between the American Club and the tiny Cirque Médrano on the Boulevard Rochechouart cannot be measured by the changing figures on a taxi clock; the club and the circus belong in different worlds. Even the Médrano reopening has made a concession to the American mode, however; the row of extra-comfortable *fauteuils* around the rim of the ring has been christened *le rang des Pullmans,* a designation completely unintelligible to habitués. Jérôme Médrano, the proprietor of this family circus, has been mobilized, but a couple of employees are carrying on for him.

This will be the forty-second season for the enterprise. As in the nineteenth century, the clowns and the *haute-école* riders are the stars;

the talking clowns hold the centre of the ring longer than any other act. The riders show their skill by galloping around the periphery without trampling *les mesdames et messieurs des Pullmans.* During the entracte the audience fraternizes with both clowns and horses, the bar being situated in cozy proximity to the horse stalls.

The artists are introduced from the ring as citizens of allied or friendly nations—a couple of American acrobatic dancers, the Arlette Sisters, are allowed to lead the *Défilé des Nations;* a troupe of Yugoslav riders is presented as Czech because this has a more sentimental appeal; and a program note assures the public that even the Arab tumblers are citizens of the French Empire and that several of the clowns were severely wounded in the other war. Having complied with the *convenances* of wartime presentation, the Médrano leaves the events of the day outside its orbit; it is a genre completely without malice, without even that element of danger inherent in the performance of acts like Clyde Beatty's or the Wallendas'. The soldiers on leave, nuzzling luxuriously against their wives in the *fauteuils de premier,* roar happily as the clowns act out the immemorial French jest of the deceived husband; the children (this is a brilliant year for the children left in Paris, because the elementary schools haven't opened) wriggle ecstatically when Boulicot, the clown grotesque, says "*des chevals*" instead of "*des chevaux.*" Nevertheless, everybody gets a slip with his ticket telling where to go in case of an air raid.

THE Sorbonne has begun another year in the four major faculties: law, medicine, letters, and sciences. Ninety per cent of the students are women. There are still enough males either under age or of foreign nationality to give the Latin Quarter some animation at night, but the sight of two or three girls sitting around a café table after dark no longer means what it used to. The co-eds even drink tomato juice and milk shakes in the big Dupont Restaurant on the Boulevard St. Michel, formerly the Restaurant Soufflet. They go hatless and wear windbreakers and socks in a belated rush to repeat the errors of the flapper period. Many of the foreign students stay on because they do not want to lose the benefit of university careers on which they have already spent years; besides, they are probably safer in Paris than they would be in Denmark, say, or Rumania. Virtually all the French students fit for military service have been mobilized; twelve hundred from the Sorbonne are in an officers' training camp.

Montparnasse has reverted to its pristine state of being a quiet residential section. On the sunniest afternoon of the last fortnight there were only two persons on the *terrasse* of the Dôme, three at Le Select, and none at La Rotonde or La Coupole. The *patron* of La Closerie des Lilas, which marks the boundary between the Latin Quarter and Montparnasse, says he might as well close his door on the Boulevard Montparnasse since what little trade there is comes through the St. Michel side.

THERE is, naturally, endless talk here about what they call *l'affaire de la brasserie* at Munich. In America, you probably have much fuller news of it. Practically everyone in Paris believes the explosion was staged by the Gestapo as a pretext, but people wonder for what—a purge in the Nazi Party, perhaps, or another massacre of Jews, or that absolutely definite attack on England which Hitler has so often promised? The most encouraging event of the week was the reported victory of French pursuit planes over a superior number of German fliers behind the French lines.

The aviators have become the first popular heroes of the war; even their unfortunate fashion of wearing a beard along the line of the jawbone, but no mustache (which gives them the aspect of early Mormon elders), cannot detract from the esteem in which they are held. The Royal Air Force uniform, rather like a Madison Avenue bus-driver's, is becoming common in Paris for the first time since the war began and one hears girls again speaking of *mon Tommy.* Yesterday, as you may have heard, was an anniversary.

NOVEMBER 17 (BY CABLE)

5
Letter from Paris

DURING EACH FORTNIGHT, the city lives through two or three periods of intense preoccupation with the war and as many of groping toward an approximation of peacetime life. Once the Netherlands crisis had subsided, the supposed decapitation of the German Crown Prince became the principal item of foreign news (most editors recapitated him yesterday morning). The war has had to cede much of the first page during the last few days to the murder of three detectives by bicycle thieves on the Ile St.-Germain. Because of the requisitioning of automobiles and the difficulty of obtaining gasoline, more civilians are awheel than ever and bicycles have become almost as negotiable as legal tender.

An interest in the ordinary amenities of life does not indicate that Frenchmen are tired of the war but rather that they are trying to make themselves comfortable, just as they did in the trenches of War '14. The object of civilization, the French say, is well-being; a disdain for well-being implies a contempt for civilization. Hitler, they like to remind you, drinks tap water and eats unsavory vegetables. In La Sologne, horse-racing men have been importuning the government to permit meetings. There has been racing in England this fall and French horses have done well there. The breeders complain piteously that unless they are allowed to race in France they will have to sell their brood mares and young stock to the horse butchers, who flourish here, to turn into *entrecôtes* and sausages. So there will probably be racing on Saturdays and Sundays in 1940.

Frenchmen are the most enthusiastic hunters in the world. The government gave out 1,500,000 shooting licences last year as against about 200,000 issued in England, which is usually thought of as more of a shooting country than France. When War '39 began, the French government forbade all shooting for sport. Its reasons were obscure, since shotgun ammunition is not particularly useful against tanks, and sportsmen have been lobbying about the restriction ever since. Last week, while editorials were denouncing Hitler for inventing pretexts to attack weaker nations, the hunters of France found a *casus belli* against wild rabbits, which, they said, offering the testimony of farmers who like to shoot on Sundays, were destroying the nation's crops. Apprised of this provocation, the Ministry proclaimed an open season on wild rabbits, and it is now beginning to receive complaints about the aggressive attitude of pheasants.

THE first *alerte* in a month began at half past four one morning last week with a madrigal of air-raid-warning sirens. The normal reflex action of a modern human upon being awakened by a vast noise is to switch on the light. Thousands of people did that instantly, and it developed that many of them had failed to draw their curtains as tightly as in the first frightened days after the war began. Every time a light showed, a police whistle shrilled, and the night was resonant with shouts of "Hey you, up there, the light!" Since it was difficult for Parisians behind their curtains to know whose lights were visible outdoors, most of them switched their lights off and searched for their clothes in the dark. In the end it seemed simplest to decide that the whole thing was just not worth the bother and to go back to bed, trying to think of something extraneous until the sirens stopped.

Most people here thought the recent *alerte* was a dress rehearsal called by General Hering, the military governor of Paris, to remind the population that danger still existed. (As a matter of fact, so far as Paris was concerned, it did turn out to be a false alarm.) Nevertheless, some thousands of less skeptical Parisians went down into the *abris,* renewing the informal camaraderie of the early days of the war, and many women had their first opportunity to wear their pajamas *d'alerte,* the costume designed by the big dressmaking houses to be worn in air-raid shelters. Skepticism, however, received a rebuke two mornings later, when there was another *alerte* at about the same hour. This time, almost as the sirens began, one could hear the cannon of the D.A.T. (Défense Antiaérienne du Territoire) in the suburbs. There was no doubt that they were shooting "*pour de bon,*" and people in town, judging from the shouts in the street, were rather proud about it. "Say, is it really here?" a boy on his way to a shelter shouted to a policeman in the little Square Louvois by the Bibliothèque Nationale, and the policeman shouted back, "It's really here!"

Both seemed to feel a sense of importance. In hotels, the guests who didn't go down to the shelters congregated in the lobbies for a cup of coffee. Some male French guests said they thought it would be bad for business "just when people were beginning to go out a bit in the evening." "It" turned out not to be really here after all, for the firing died down and everybody went back to bed. Afternoon newspapers reported that German planes had been seen over the suburbs, but these were only reconnaissance machines which had flown in across Belgium trying to spot nocturnal troop movements on the railways.

There was more firing at reconnaissance planes during the next afternoon, but although the shots were plainly audible, few paid much attention to them, acting on the principle that if the danger didn't justify an *alerte,* it certainly should not be allowed to interfere with traffic. The city was not entirely unmoved by the *alertes,* however. Neighborhood druggists, who for weeks now have found few purchasers for the gas masks they have been displaying in their windows, reported a lively demand for their goods after the first cannonade.

NOVEMBER 24 (BY CABLE)

6
Letter from Paris

THE French government is determined to convince its citizens that children are a handy thing to have. Not only have fathers of five or more been demobilized but the phrasing of a new decree imposing a 15-per-cent tax on incomes and affecting most male civilians indicates clearly the desire for a higher birth rate. The tax applies to incomes of more than 7,000 francs (roughly $160), but allowances for children are progressive—1,000 francs for the first child, 2,000 for the second, 3,000 for the third, and so on without any limit except the propagative impulse of the parents.

Frenchmen remain individualists. The Gallic resistance to intellectual pressure is manifested every day, to the annoyance of those who insist that what France needs is more discipline. The censorship is personalized as an old spinster called Anastasie, who is depicted in cartoons with a pince-nez, a chignon, and, of course, a pair of shears. This concept dates from War '14 and was standard here as Rollin Kirby's bluenose used to be in prohibition days in America. Anastasie is equally severe toward Charles Maurras of *L'Action Française* on the extreme Right and Léon Blum and Geneviève Tabouis on the Left, and is consequently under a continual cross fire of intelligent criticism. Blum says he will make an issue of the censorship of ideas when Parliament opens, and he probably will.

The French radio, which is now ruled by M. Georges Duhamel of the Académie-Française, is an even more inviting target for gibes, and is referred to by the press as "the worst in the world," which must annoy M. Duhamel, who once wrote an unkind book about things American, including the National and Columbia broadcasting systems. Every time M. Duhamel tries to raise the intellectual level of the radio public, he receives hundreds of letters from soldiers asking for more tunes like "J'Ai Deux Amours" and "Sérénade sans

Espoir," which is known in New York as "Penny Serenade." This refusal to agree with everything the government proposes indicates that morale is good. When Frenchmen do not grumble, they are sick. They are fighting in their minds to defend themselves against a German conformity that repels them more than massacres.

Even General Pierre Hering, the austere military governor of Paris, has had to make a small concession to popular demands. There has been no public dancing here since the war began, but tomorrow, which is St. Catherine's Day, consecrated to unmarried women over twenty-five, dancing will be permitted from two until eleven. The Governor, who was born in Alsace, the son of an Alsatian officer in the French Army, is a Calvinist and a disciplinarian. He came back from retirement to assume this command, and Parisians, while they are sometimes annoyed by his restrictions, feel a deep confidence in him precisely because he is so unlike them. They feel that anything he permits them to do must be extremely safe.

MONTMARTRE is opening up. Liberty's and the Savoy, the first two *boîtes* to resume, are doing such an excellent business that others are bound to follow. It is a repetition in the café world of the series of theatrical reopenings of a month ago. People go to Montmartre for dinner now and stay until eleven. At the Savoy, an entertainer comes to your table at 10:45 with an alarm clock, which he sets off to remind you to buy the last round. Exactly at eleven, most of Paris is on the sidewalks. All the cafés and theatres in town close at the same minute. By two minutes past eleven it is impossible to get a taxi anywhere, and whether it is raining or merely drizzling (at this season it is never dry), the wretched revellers walk home.

The Opéra has returned to its own building. There was a gala opening, all complete with the President of the Republic and "Faust"—a sombre combination. The Opéra-Comique remains as pleasant and shabby as ever, with a placid public of reserve officers and their wives and daughters listening sympathetically while Manon sings "Adieu, Notre Petite Table." Each officer, despite his uniform, remains palpably the lawyer, the doctor, or the university professor that he was last August; taking no pleasure in his metamorphosis, he is still an intelligent bourgeois. In his intelligence lies Germany's danger.

THE cinema, too, had a gala première this week at the old Olympia—the first of the season. The theatre had been donated for the occasion to an Army charity, under the patronage of M. Lebrun, M. Daladier, and General Gamelin. The film was "L'Homme du Niger," a modest evocation of the white man's burden in French Africa. In one scene, several hundred naked black children sing "La Madelon" in what I took to be Senegalese. There are some really wonderful African shots and the film pleased a patriotic audience immensely. Walking home in the dark, you could recognize other people who had been at the première, because they carried white souvenir programs and hummed the "Marseillaise."

A NEW type of British uniform has appeared in the Ritz and Crillon bars—the one worn by war correspondents. The journalists are only slightly less resplendent than generals, and the French, who are assiduous readers of Kipling and the Colonel Bramble sketches, admire them profoundly. A barman in a small café even refused to serve a reporter in the afternoon because it is forbidden to sell liquor to soldiers from 2:30 to 5:30. Torn between pride and thirst, the miserable Briton decided to forego his drink and walked out into the street, while the barman explained to his customers, "I feel a great regret not to be permitted to serve the English colonel, but what would you?"

DECEMBER 22 (BY CABLE)

7
Letter from Paris

UNLESS something unexpected happens within the next ten days, 1939 will be remembered in France as the year that began in uncertainty and ended in mild boredom. Many of the same people who three months ago were ready to pop into their cellars like prairie dogs at the first purring of an airplane motor, expecting Paris to be expunged between dark and dawn, are complaining now because the restaurants do not serve beefsteak on Mondays, Tuesdays, and Fridays, and because the season has produced no new plays worth seeing. Persons who in October, 1938, predicted that the least opposition to Hitler would mean the end of Western civilization should logically feel an enormous admiration for General Gamelin, who has protected France completely with a loss of human life slightly less than the annual mortality from tuberculosis in New York City. Curiously enough, however, there is a certain disappointment among the less reflective elements of the population; the appetite for disaster in some human beings is so strong that they feel let down when nothing terrible happens. Cartoonists here have developed a number of wartime civilian characters on the order of Caspar Milquetoast. One of them, a *petit bourgeois* called Bajus, was shown in a recent comic strip listening to a radio address by Hitler. At each howl from the radio set ("I will destroy England before breakfast," "I will show the French what total war means"), little Bajus's hair stood on end, and at the close of the speech he turned to his radio, saying, "Oh, please, Adolf, don't stop; frighten me again."

Thousands of Bajuses feel deprived of the terror which had become the most interesting component of their daily lives. If the people who warned that a Hitler provoked might tear the world apart feel silly, the equally numerous Frenchmen who said that the West couldn't be saved without the aid of Russia feel even sillier, for the floundering of the Russian army in Finland and the ineffectiveness of the Soviet's vintage-1911 battleships have convinced everybody here that the Russians would have been of no use against Germany. Silliest of all appear the Frenchmen who, like Colonel de La Rocque, insisted that what France needed was a totalitarian government, on the ground that dictatorships are more efficient than democracies because they make up their minds quicker. It is obvious that Hitler hasn't made up his mind for months.

IN the absence of major disasters, small annoyances have reassumed peacetime proportions. A few weeks ago, for example, a shortage of lemons happened to coincide with the oyster season, a fact which Parisians found hard to bear, and thus the rigors of war were brought home to the metropolis. Now there is a scarcity of coffee in the grocery shops, although you can still get all you want in hotels and restaurants. Fauchon's great food shop by the Madeleine has a sign over one of its counters reading, "Fresh caviar, no coffee."

The recent speech by M. Reynaud, Minister of Finance, in which he hinted that the war might involve a long period of military inactivity and that it would be won by economy at home, pointed up his rôle as one of the strong members of the government. It is a sensible policy, but the strain upon French patience will increase as the Germans and Russians gobble neutrals. There will then be the danger that a miracle man will emerge, like General Nivelle in 1916, who will promise to break the Siegfried Line, capture Hitler, and send the boys home in six weeks—the classic etiology of catastrophe.

NINETEEN THIRTY-NINE will also be remembered as a bad year for crime and the French novel. There was a definite cause for the first phenomenon: on the first day of war the police here rounded up every criminal fit for military service and got him a good place in the army, not too far from the front. Criminals unfit for military service and aliens with police records were clapped into concentration camps. Then a decree made looting during *alertes* punishable by death. Finally, since people do not stay out late nights, the opportunities for housebreakers have been decreased. The result of all this, according to the police, has been a reduction in the number of crimes committed since the war to only three per cent of what it was during the corresponding months last year.

The reason 1939 has been a bad year for novels is not so clear. All the novels which were entered for the Prix Goncourt were written before the war began and the winner, Phillippe Hériat's "Les Enfants Gâtés," is said by reviewers to have deserved the award, but a comparison with, say, 1933, when André Malraux's "La Condition Humaine" won the prize, shows a lamentable falling off. In literature, as in champagnes, there are non-vintage years. "Les Enfants Gâtés" is in part the story of a French girl's exotic romance in America; when she wants to do something typically American, she breakfasts at the Rainbow Room on grapefruit and malted milk, which should give you the idea.

THE Military Governor of Paris plans to let people stay in bars and restaurants until two o'clock Christmas morning—the latest closing hour since August. The Governor could not well insist on his usual eleven-o'clock shutdown of subways and bus lines because the churches want to hold midnight Mass and the restaurant men said that if Catholics could stay out until all hours of the night without provoking an air raid, there was no reason non-believers shouldn't stay out for a little fun. The Catholics then said they would like an hour for refreshment and possible song after Mass, and the Governor finally set the two-o'clock closing hour.

For the rest, it has so far been a nearly normal Paris Christmas season, with carillons and life-size mechanical figures in the windows of the Galeries Lafayette, postcard hucksters' stalls along the Boulevards, and a special Christmas circus at the Médrano, with the three Fratellinis appearing as guest stars. The great clowns are not as limber as they used to be, and they take fewer falls, but they have some good mechanical gags and their marvellous faces. The oldest brother got one of the big laughs of the evening when he made his entrance carrying an ordinary gas mask—which shows how the atmosphere of the city has changed since September. The French like old favorites. They go to see them over and over again to observe how time is treating them, and if a performer appears to be in good health, they are delighted. "*Tiens,*" a Parisian will say, "I went to see Mistinguett last night and she is as good as she was in 1936"—when, of course, she was already the oldest soubrette in the world. Mistinguett, as a matter of fact, has just opened in a revue and Cécile Sorel may be expected back from Belgium any minute now.

ANGERS, FEB. 11 (BY WIRELESS)

8
Letter from France

UNTIL last November, when the French government decided upon Angers as the place where the Poles could set up a new capital, most Frenchmen thought of this quiet old city in the valley of the Loire only as the home of Cointreau and of a certain sweet white wine. The people of Angers, in their way, were equally provincial, for although the Cointreau factory is the largest local industry, before the arrival of the diplomatic corps practically none of the 90,000 inhabitants of the community had ever heard of a cocktail called the Side Car. Now all that has changed; the Angevins have a broader point of view and the rest of France knows the city as the headquarters, until further notice, of a nation's President and Premier as well as of a group of diplomats which includes United States Ambassador Biddle, a Papal Nuncio, and, most remarkable of all, a French Ambassador.

When the Angevins, a friendly and unadventurous people, learned that their city was to become the capital of a distant nation, they were flattered but not altogether happy, for it occurred to many of them that the new distinction might attract bombers when and if the bombing started. However, once the Poles began to arrive and the bombers did not, civic pride overcame apprehension, and now the natives seem pleased that things turned out as they did. The townsfolk have rented any number of furnished rooms to white-collar workers employed in the offices of the various dignitaries, and the owners of several large, drafty buildings have been able to lease their properties as chancelleries. Every local notable, from the Prefect to the president of the Angers Rotary Club, has had a chance to welcome at least one batch of newly arrived diplomats.

THE winter climate of Angers is wet and fairly chilly, but palm trees grow here and people go about their business in the rain just as they do in Dublin. When the Poles arrived in this atmosphere of humid calm, many of them succumbed to a kind of inverted shell shock; Angers was so quiet that it frightened them, and they ran up to Paris, a hundred and seventy miles away, every chance they could get. These days, however, bureau chiefs have difficulty finding men to go on out-of-town missions, because the Poles have come to love a calm they had forgotten existed. They are by no means happy, though, even in this retreat. Among the young Polish diplomats in Angers are some who once contributed largely to the gaiety of several world capitals, including Washington; they have become a grim bunch, living in cheap hotel rooms and, when they are not at work, discussing the unbelievable brutality of the Nazis in Poland. The older men, who once worked for a free Poland, achieved it, and have seen it sink beneath the surface again, are an even sadder crowd. They try to cheer themselves by reminding one another that the Belgian government carried on at Le Havre for four years during the last war.

Like the Belgians then, the Poles now have their own army in France. When fully organized, it probably won't amount to more than one army corps, but it already includes Polish volunteers from nearly every country in the world. The Poles have their own hoard of gold in France, too, and their government borrows against it for running expenses, which are cut to the bone. The gold amounts to about $30,000,000—Poland's national reserve, which was taken out of the country in trucks, some of it through the Baltic countries and some of it through the Balkans, just before the converging German and Russian armies closed in.

THE Biddles occupy a small château (small, that is, as châteaux go hereabouts) at Seiches, a village a few kilometres from Angers. It is owned by a retired cavalry officer and has a moat around it which creates a mist even when the sun is shining, however weakly, on the rest of the countryside. The American Chancellery is a small house on the Rue de la Préfecture; it looks just about like any other house in Angers and would be hard to find if it were not directly across the street from the office of the city's most prosperous midwife, whose large swinging sign is something of a landmark. Most of the attachés and secretaries who formerly served under Mr. Biddle have been transferred to busier diplomatic posts on the Continent, and the personnel here at present consists only of the Ambassador; a third secretary, Mr. C. B. Elbrick; an interpreter; and a stenographer named Miss McWhorter.

If titles meant what they used to in Warsaw, one of the busiest men in the United States Foreign Service at the moment would be Mr. Elbrick, who, since the staff has been thinned out, has become acting first and second secretary as well as military and naval attaché at the Embassy. Mr. Elbrick, however, does not find his duties in Angers too burdensome; in fact, he considers his life here restful after what he has recently been through in Central Europe. He and his wife dodged bombs from Warsaw to the Rumanian border and got to Bucharest on the day King Carol had nine Iron Guards shot and left in the street to show the others how he felt about them. Continuing on their way, the Elbricks reached Munich on the evening of the beer-hall explosion. The rest of their journey was comparatively uneventful.

THE diplomats visit to some extent among themselves. Besides Mr. Biddle and the French Ambassador, there are the British and Turkish Ambassadors, and Brazil, Chile, Egypt, and a couple of other countries have legations here. The receptions are invariably informal, however, because almost all members of the corps lost their dress clothes and decorations when they fled from Poland.

MARCH 9 (BY WIRELESS)

9
Letter from Paris

SUMNER WELLES arrived in Paris on the fourth anniversary of the German reoccupation of the Rhineland. If the French in 1936 had squelched the Nazis without worrying about possible repercussions on public opinion abroad, the visit of an American Assistant Secretary of State now would be important news only for the Paris edition of the *Herald Tribune.* As it is, the French expect little good and no harm from his visit; Paris newspapers bade him welcome in their editorials, M. Daladier invited him to dinner, and everybody went right on thinking about a long war.

There are already at least fourteen versions in Paris of what Hitler said to Mr. Welles in Berlin; everyone agrees that the German Chancellor talked a tremendous fight, and most say that it was all a bluff. Next week people will be trying to reconstruct what M. Daladier and Mr. Chamberlain said to Mr. Welles; then the American will take an Italian boat and be forgotten—or so Paris thinks.

Mr. Welles' presence in Europe has had one mildly reassuring effect: people are confident the Germans won't start their great offensive while he is here. Not many of them think that there will be an offensive after he leaves, either; a couple of military critics and several dozen astrologers are the only really confident prophets of Armageddon. The astrologers say that Hitler has always made decisive moves in March, a month he considers lucky. The generals argue, more soundly, that great offensives usually start in the spring or not at all. The constant discussion of a German offensive completely muffles any general talk about an Allied attack, although the French and British are certainly in as good a position for an aggressive move as the army on the other side of the line. For one thing, a drawn battle probably would be a disaster for the Germans but of advantage to the Allies, because it would exhaust the German supply of gasoline. This sort of talk has largely displaced other kinds of table conversation in Paris; it has been going on so long that it seems as impersonal as what people used to say about the Davis Cup prospects or women's hats. It is only in the army zone that you recover a feeling of the war's relevance to the flesh and blood of your friends.

PARIS had its first *alerte* of 1940 a few nights ago. The excitement, but not the sirens, started at about eight-thirty in the evening, when an anti-aircraft battery began banging away at a German reconnaissance plane, wounding half a dozen Frenchmen with its spent shells. Later that night, a druggist returning home from his shop found a shell standing on his slippers by the foot of his bed. It was a dud which had fallen through the roof and the garret floor. There was no *alerte,* because of a sensible rule that the traffic in the streets is not to be interrupted just for one or two stray airplanes. At about four o'clock that morning, however, the sirens began, but this time there was no anti-aircraft activity. When Parisians could hear no gunfire, they decided the danger was not serious and went back to sleep. As it turned out, they were right.

That same night, when the British flew over Berlin dropping tracts, the German batteries didn't fire, either. This is a war in which the refined instruments of destruction are restrained by even more refined instruments of detection; there are whole regiments of artillery at the front which have never fired a shot in earnest, because when a battery opens up nowadays, even for a few rounds, it has to move elsewhere immediately. Both sides have a virtually foolproof system of detecting a gun's position by sound measurements and simple mathematics. Occasionally a regiment is withdrawn from the front for practice.

AMERICANS who came to Paris to escape prohibition in the good old days would be shocked by the most recent sumptuary decree here. Bars and restaurants can't sell hard liquor on Tuesdays, Thursdays, or Saturdays; after July 1st, retail stores will not be permitted to sell less than two litres of it at a time—a strange bit of legislation, since, as Paul Reynaud, the law's sponsor, will soon find out, it is almost certain to increase the consumption of alcohol in homes. M. Reynaud has never lived in a package-law state. Small bistros are less hard hit on the taboo days than the flashier places with a foreign patronage, for they have always done a good business in wine by the glass, and scarcely any of their customers mind switching to wine. Elsewhere, things are different; for example, the Crillon Bar was a stricken place at cocktail time on the Tuesday the new law went into effect. The diplomats and the newspapermen were home mixing their own drinks, and the only customers were several British aviators who were on furlough and had no flats to go to. The government maintains that the decree will help build a reserve of industrial alcohol, although it is hard to imagine the French mixing cognac with their aviation gasoline. Meanwhile the winegrowers, who have the most powerful legislative lobby in France, are not complaining.

THERE has been racing at Auteuil on the last two Sundays. All the events, which are over jumps, drew fields of from twenty to twenty-five horses; small stables and public trainers have won most of the purses. Steeple-chasing here has the same picaresque attraction that flat racing has in America—an identical atmosphere of engaging skulduggery motivated by avarice which nobody is ashamed to display on a race course. The most striking feature of the Auteuil reopening, aside from the spring costumes, was the way the big shots of racing were outshone by many of the common spectators. The owners who appeared in uniform were almost all sergeants or second lieutenants, while scores of less affluent chaps, who in other years were inconspicuous fifty-franc bettors, showed up as majors or colonels of cavalry, wearing long red spahi capes and so many spurs and buckles that they sounded like Swiss bell-ringers.

APRIL 6 (BY CABLE)

10
Letter from Paris

ANYONE who may have doubts about French tenacity of purpose should consider the Gallic method of capturing a carp. The fisherman walking along the bank of a sluggish stream sees a carp idling in a spot it likes; he knows that if it did not like the spot, it would have moved on, for such is the nature of carp. The fisherman goes home and cuts up three or four pounds of old Gruyère cheese into small cubes. Early the next morning he returns to the basking spot and throws some of the cheese into the river, and repeats the offering regularly for several days. The carp, at first suspicious, begins on the second or third morning to eat the Gruyère and soon is joined by other carp, which compete for the cubes. Each fish tries to get as much of the cheese as it can, and before long all are grabbing without their customary caution. After about ten days of this, the fisherman baits a large hook with a cube of Gruyère, drops it into the water, and one of the carp seizes it. The fisherman then has some anxious moments, for the carp is not only strong but intelligent for a fish, and instead of wasting energy on fancy leaps, it rushes for a rock or some tree roots likely to foul the line.

Sometimes the fisherman comes upon a carp that will not eat cheese, in which case he tries boiled potatoes or bread rubbed with garlic. It may take weeks to please the palate of a carp, but the Frenchman doesn't mind; he finds an inner satisfaction in the conquest. He respects the carp for its conservatism, its common sense, its discriminating tastes in food, and its ability to survive in large numbers without the aid of fish hatcheries and fish-and-game associations.

RIGHT NOW, every Frenchman not in uniform seems to be buying a reel, a bait pail, a landing net, or a bamboo pole at one of the fishermen's-supply stores on the right bank of the Seine between the Louvre and the Samaritaine. If a Frenchman has no chance for carp, he tries for perch, and if there are no perch near him, he fishes for minnows. The fishermen along the *quais* of the Seine, who are already out in considerable numbers, are of the same stamp as Americans who try for swordfish on a light line—they seldom catch anything, but they are looked upon as sportsmen and get their pictures in the papers. War or no war, Paris editors find space to print these pictures with such captions as "Spring brings the fishermen and the book merchants back to the Seine."

Gardeners are just as optimistic as the fishermen at this season. The seedsmen's shops in the same district near the Seine are filled with stubby men and pleasant, unfashionable matrons deciding together whether to plant Spring New or Rose of May lettuce. The compilers of French seed catalogues are just as handy as their colleagues in New York at thinking up enticing names for new varieties. The White Snowflake, the Year Round Marvel, and the Perfection of Massy (all three cauliflowers), the Long Violet Early Improved Eggplant, and the Stringless King of the Summer (which is, of course, a bean) all help Paris suburbanites forget the war, at least while they are looking at the beautiful pictures on the packages of seeds and making up their minds what to plant. "The presence of garden flowers will aid us to traverse this difficult period," one seedsman's sign proclaims. Mixtures of fertilizers are sold in trifling amounts, like bonbons, because most French gardeners think that every plant has its own peculiar tastes, and they regard their dahlias and petunias and so on as individuals, as they do carp.

Children, when their parents bring them shopping in this neighborhood, stand fascinated in front of the pet stores, where ferrets, Brahma roosters, Australian finches, and frogs that climb little flights of stairs are displayed in crates piled haphazardly on the sidewalk. The customers the animal men really like are the soldiers on leave, who are continually buying mascots for their platoons and companies—white mice, box tortoises, parakeets, and mongrel puppies. The mortality among such mascots is high, but the soldiers are hard to discourage; when one pet dies, the next man leaving the unit *en permission* is commissioned to buy another. The soldiers don't care much about pedigree; one will say, "I'll take that kitten. He's got an agreeable mug," and let it go at that. All this would be profoundly discouraging to people like Hitler if they had sense enough to understand it. A nation that continues to cultivate its gardens and to fish for gudgeons does not give the impression of having taken much stock in Teutonic big talk.

ANOTHER indication that nothing important has changed in France is the revival of "Les Cloches de Corneville" at the Théâtre de Mogador. Audiences continue to howl when the bailiff loses his peruke and at his monstrously bad puns; when the heavy villain, Gaspard, makes his melodramatic speech about the hallucination of the bells, everybody applauds, just as Italians do at the end of a favorite aria; the ingénue is very arch without being very pretty, and the soubrette very pert without being very carnal—all is in tradition.

The French are both innovators and traditionalists; they produce new things and hold on like grim death to the old. Moving through the ages under a constantly accumulating burden of plays, customs, books, and indestructible architecture of uneven value, they have sometimes seemed momentarily grotesque, but the very load they carry has served them well as ballast. They don't have to dig up a past, like the Italians, or invent one, like the Germans. They have had their past with them always.

POLITICALLY, the past fortnight has been quiet, but there is, of course, no guarantee that the calm will last. During the recent change in Ministries, Daladier descended a step in the hierarchy here and Chamberlain apparently had a fairly narrow squeak on the other side of the Channel. All the people one meets are talking about a war in the Levant, but nobody is sure who is going to fight. Finland is already being forgotten except by stubbornly reasonable people like a general named Duval, who wrote in the last *Revue des Deux Mondes* that the Allies, even if Sweden had refused to let them pass, could have gone to the ice-free ports of Petsamo and Murmansk to help the Finns. Sir Francis Drake, when he raided Cadiz, did not march across Europe to get there. He went in a boat. But then, Sir Francis never wore a school tie.

APRIL 21 (BY CABLE)

11
Letter from Paris

THE LOW POINT of French morale in this war was reached in the middle of March, after what many people thought of as the abandonment of Finland; the high point came about a month later, with the news of the defeat of the German squadron at Narvik. The change is graphically expressed in the two votes of the Chamber of Deputies on the Reynaud government. In March, the government survived by one vote on the question of confidence; last week, on the same question, no votes were cast against the government and 515 were recorded in its favor. The news from Norway that has given most satisfaction here was yesterday's report: "French troops have landed." Frenchmen's admiration for the British Navy is unlimited, but they regard the British on land in something of the spirit of a husband watching his wife drive an automobile.

People who have advocated an "energetic war" are pleased with the impression which the Allied stand in Norway has made upon the constantly less numerous neutrals. After the defeat of Finland, Rumania and the Scandinavian countries became extremely conciliatory toward the Nazis, but since Narvik, all the neutrals have been clapping German agents into jail and announcing their determination to fight if invaded. Even Italy, while its official press continues to deny Allied successes, is giving a pretty good impersonation of a man who has taken a mouthful of unexpectedly hot *minestrone* and would like to get rid of it without prejudice to his dignity.

The great question here is Führer Hitler: after his Norwegian adventure is settled, one way or another, will he turn toward the Balkans or France? If Hitler becomes engaged in the Balkans, the French say, the war may last longer than it would otherwise, but the shock of an eventual attack on France will be less violent, since, like a hooked fish, he will lose strength with every lunge. Most Parisians, however, would prefer the "big knock" as soon as possible, in order, as they are likely to put it, "to finish with a *sale type* who has ceased to interest us."

Le Français moyen—that average Frenchman who is the national hero—has always had a low opinion of the average German; it was only in the upper economic and social groups, here as in England, that Germanism made in-roads during the late thirties. Now that the attempt to take Europe by surprise has failed, the common man's cockiness is an inestimable asset. The French will not be shaken by initial defeats, if such there are to be, because they remember the early years of the 1914 war, and are convinced that the Germans always quit, if one holds on long enough. The Nazis, for all their bluster, can have no such confidence; even a Göring must remember sometimes that in 1917 the Central Powers held Bucharest and Brussels and Lille—advanced posts considerably more impressive than Copenhagen.

THE lightheartedness with which people here face things to come was illustrated beautifully at a gala held at the Opéra for the benefit of soldiers' recreation centres. The striking thing about it was not the enormous turnout or the presence of MM. Lebrun and Reynaud, but the joyous inconsequentiality of the entertainment. Two clowns from the Cirque Médrano played a serenade on a bicycle pump which was much appreciated by the President of the Republic, and an Englishman, introduced as "Stinker" Murdoch, performed on something that sounded like a peanut whistle. The official stars of the occasion were Maurice Chevalier, who has become a truly national figure, and Gracie Fields, who, like Yorkshire pudding, arouses enthusiasm among the British and to other people seems merely inoffensive. The setting represented an improvised theatre behind the lines, and Paul Goube, one of the Opéra's best dancers, who is now in the Army, came back from the front to lead a ballet. The audience was almost as much British as French and those who weren't bilingual caught only half of the show, but French and British alike enthusiastically applauded the parts they didn't understand in a touching demonstration of mutual faith.

PARIS is having its first major Salon since the war began—a joint showing of the Salon d'Automne, the Salon des Tuileries, and the Artistes Décorateurs, all at the Palais Chaillot on the Place du Trocadéro. There are seven hundred paintings. None of them, perhaps, will ever be listed in guidebooks, but neither are any of them representative of those slicked-up, colored-photograph sort of thing which used to get into the Salon shows of twenty years ago, and which has been restored to the position of high art on the other side of the Westwall.

Soldiers on leave are as numerous, in proportion to the other visitors, at the Salon as in the music halls. They study every landscape gravely to see whether the painter has done justice to the French stones and the French grass and the French waves, in all of which, as Frenchmen, they take a highly personal interest. What use is there in defending three chestnut trees or an old church in Poitou if some dauber is permitted to malign them behind one's back?

THE great joke of the past fortnight has been the publication in a newspaper here of a speech by Herr Goebbels, in which he is supposed to have said that Hitler would be in Paris by June 15th. "What pretension!" exclaimed a girl in a crowd surrounding a news kiosk. She sounded as indignant as if Herr Goebbels *in propria persona* had pinched her where no gentleman would. Most of the readers, though, seemed merely amused. That night at the Petit Casino, the great proletarian music hall on the Boulevards, a comic stepped down to the footlights and asked the orchestra leader, "Have you been to the Ecole Berlitz?" The leader asked why. "To learn German," the comic said, "so you can talk to Adolf when he gets here." The answering howl of laughter was a more impressive vote of confidence than M. Reynaud got from the Chamber of Deputies.

MAY 24 (BY WIRELESS)

12
Letter from Paris

It is slightly disconcerting, when one enters Burberry's tailoring establishment for a fitting these days, to find all the salesmen busily engaged in taking an inventory of goods on hand, but a minute or two of eavesdropping in front of the desk where a venerable Frenchman keeps the appointment book for fittings restores one's confidence. The French customers on their way out complain of sleeve lengths or bad backs as if they had never heard of the "events" in the north, and confidently make deposits on garments to be ready ten days from now.

Parisians are still calm, as confident as the English are supposed to be in novels. The government declared yesterday that it was staying in Paris because of what it called the amelioration of the situation; it had not previously mentioned that it was considering departure. People who live by newspapers and by rumors are having a hard time. Those whose only business is to stay here and observe acquire a sort of meteorological sensibility which cannot be described as barometric, because barometers work on known principles. Such observers fluctuate between cheer and melancholy fifty times a day, while the supposedly volatile French set their teeth and go quietly about their business.

It was difficult to sleep last Tuesday night after M. Reynaud's "Fatherland is in danger" speech in the Senate, in which he announced that the Germans had taken Arras. Wednesday, when it was learned that the Germans in Arras had been only a handful of motorcyclists dashing about in the fashion of a Dillinger gang and had been driven out by the first serious Allied detachment to reach them, the world seemed beautiful. The Germans appear to have made virtually no advance toward Paris in the last five days, and since, during that interim, General Weygand has taken over, great masses of troops have been brought up from the south and east, and the French soldiers have acquired a familiarity with the German offensive technique, the chances for a successful defence appear to be enormously improved.

THE morning's citations include the names not only of aviators and soldiers who have died but of postmen killed delivering letters under fire in the invaded provinces and of conductors of Parisian autobuses who were sent up into the north to help evacuate refugees and were killed on vehicles that had carried them for many peaceful years between the Madeleine and the Porte Maillot. Almost as remarkable as the courage such men have shown under fire is the simple, friendly way ordinary folk keep attending to their jobs—girl operators in beauty parlors, bookkeepers in offices, boys delivering fancy cakes for first-Communion parties, and waiters solicitous of the diminished appetites of favorite clients. They refuse to believe that their day-to-day way of life, which has endured from century to century, can be submerged; noncombatant Parisians simply live their faith.

The Army puts faith into action and the Army is not discouraged. One of the rumors current here on that pessimistic night of last Tuesday was that General Weygand had gone to the front to look things over and see if further resistance was worth while. It was a rumor which had a bracing after-effect, at any rate, because the seventy-three-year-old Weygand, setting a historic example of *panache*, came back to Paris, after flying over the entire war area in a military plane, to tell the government he was confident of victory. Like a pitcher going in with the bases full, Weygand will have to start out carefully, but everything in his past indicates that if he once nurses his army past the emergency, he may change the whole complexion of the war in a few days. Weygand, mystic, devout, and a great specialist in the campaigns of Marshal de Turenne, whose biographer he is, has always believed that war against Germans should be fought in Germany, moving through the river valleys that de Turenne knew. Such a notion seems fantastically optimistic at the moment, but the Germans have penetrated only a few miles into France by American standards of distance—from Sedan to Paris is about as far as from Albany to New York, and the invaders have come only about a third of the way.

THE first divisions rushed north into Belgium had a terrible experience with an air force that overwhelmed them, but the troops now fighting belong either to units that have stood the test or to good divisions which didn't suffer at all from the first impact because they were still on the supposedly vital eastern frontier when the blow fell from the north. The French artillery has been decidedly better than the German. The possibility of victory almost surely depends on the quantity of airplanes the Allies still have or can get immediately. It is not a canard that they are outflying the Germans; the question is whether this point in their favor will be enough to offset Germany's apparently inexhaustible supply of slightly inferior machines and pilots.

If French and British factories had been working since September as they have now decided to work, the Allies might have been successful in the struggle to accumulate the greater equipment, but the effort to whip a wildcat with one hand appears to have been a mistake. Hitler has proved that democracies can be forced to turn into dictatorships in self-defence. He has also proved, perhaps fortunately for the world, that good-natured French boys can be turned into cruel and effective combatants in a very few days if they are lucky enough to survive an initial setback.

German parachutists and spies are now killed casually and right on the spot. One driver of a large French tank succeeded in running over and crushing six small German tanks, one after another. The German assault troops' fanatical devotion to a cause appears less impressive as the French get to know them. Parachutists are herded into planes and dropped through trapdoors. If they land among troops or hostile civilians and see that they are to be killed, they will fight, but if there's a chance for them to surrender, they often do.

French boys you've known for years—since they had their first tennis racquets, since they collected autographs of Joan Crawford—boys who last summer used to ask you gravely if Margaret Mitchell was really a significant American author, tell you about these things now when they come back from the front to get spare parts for their motors. The French, one of them said a while ago, are an unbelievable mixture of pettiness and grandeur. At this moment, they are purely grand.

JUNE 1 (BY WIRELESS)

13
Letter from Paris

THESE have been three strained weeks in Paris. Each Tuesday has brought a shock, and after each disappointment the French have rebounded and gone on more grimly than ever about the business of winning a war which, they say, has just begun. The Dutch surrendered Holland on Tuesday, May 14th, freeing a part of the invading German army for use in Belgium; on Tuesday, May 21st, M. Reynaud made his famous "danger" speech, announcing the enemy's advance and the change in the High Command; on Tuesday, May 28th, all France learned of the surrender of King Leopold.

The press is already preparing for what may be next Tuesday's blow by predicting that the speech Mussolini is scheduled to make then will announce Italy's entry into the war on Germany's side. It would seem that the editors are purposely appearing more pessimistic than they feel, for at the moment there is still no certainty that Il Duce has made up his mind. If his speech turns out to be anything less than a declaration of war, everybody will feel encouraged. Meanwhile, the army is strengthening itself.

THE first reaction to Leopold's desertion was one of indignation; at last, it was clear, the war had developed a traitor of major stature capable, unlike such small fry as Quisling, of absorbing the quantity of ill will which the public had to bestow. Then, as the heroic fight by the betrayed French and British troops in Flanders continued, Paris, for the first time since the outbreak of the war, began to identify itself with an army in battle. The withdrawal of the Anglo-Franco-Belgian Army of the North toward the Channel ports, at first a purely strategic retreat, had been viewed, as was only natural, in a rather discouraged fashion. When the Belgians, constituting about half of the army, stepped aside, leaving their comrades almost surrounded by Germans, and that remnant of an army, instead of quitting, lashed out harder than ever, the public was galvanized.

Five days have passed since Leopold's surrender. The army of Flanders is still fighting, thousands of soldiers have been evacuated to England (despite the boast of the German radio that the Reich's aviators would sink every ship that tried to take men off), and each day of battle eliminates German troops and material from the next offensive.

From a military standpoint, the Belgian defection was a blow, for a large army solidly established on the coast between Zeebrugge and Calais would have been a lasting threat to German maneuvers, and a great counter-offensive could have been prepared while the men there held the attention of many German divisions. The battle in its present form, however, may have a greater influence on the result of the war: it is the battle of the breaking of the spell. The quick German invasion, after the long, indolent winter, had a hypnotic effect. People wondered at first whether the armies of the democracies had lost their fighting qualities and whether the enemy might not be just a trifle superhuman after all, but five days of battle by French and British troops against four times their number of Germans, days in which the trapped divisions have pierced enemy lines repeatedly, have restored national pride.

There has even been a minor break in "Hitler luck." For the past two days the Allied troops embarking at Dunkerque have been favored by cloudy skies, which have made accurate bombing of boats more difficult. Parisians who had relatives in the French Army of the North, and who for a few hours Tuesday had resigned themselves to the thought that those men would soon be dead or prisoners, are now in some cases smiling, for a great many "landed safe" messages are coming through from England.

PUBLIC OPINION in the Allied countries, as a matter of fact, reacts miraculously to disaster. The regime of complacency in the first seven inactive months nearly destroyed civilian war spirit, as well as military efficiency, with tales of magnificent northern fortifications and of soaring airplane production and of how a war could be won without losing lives or spending money. The twenty-three days of the German offensive have got the French and English really fighting, as they have not been since 1918.

The Allied governments, realizing that gloomy frankness is a spur, have done a masterly job of anticipating the next German move. The English press proclaims with certainty that when the battle of Flanders is over, the Germans are going to attack England, and the French newspapers, with the same positive note, announce that the Germans will turn toward Paris. The effect is to get people on both sides of the Channel ready for anything that may happen.

THERE has been no mass evacuation of Paris, but during the last twenty-three days more and more people with children or without any definite reason for staying here have moved out—until things settle down, they say. A good many restaurants and small businesses that struggled along through the winter are closing for lack of patronage and their proprietors are joining the emigration. The blackout at night is complete, and cinemas and cafés close at ten-thirty. A few night clubs in Montmartre and one or two music halls gamely struggle on, finding their main difficulty not so much the early closing hour as the preoccupation of their normal public with other things. Luckily for the spirits of the moody, nights are extremely short, since, under daylight-saving time, twilight lasts until nearly ten.

The heart of the city doesn't appear deserted, and never in history have so many police been in evidence, all of them now carrying rifles for use against parachutists. Except in its very centre, however, Paris at present suggests a quiet neighborhood in Washington. Practically all the Belgian refugees have now been moved south from Paris. Their last days here were not so filled with cordiality as the first. Most of them, of course, completely disapproved of the King's surrender, but Parisians, while trying to be fair, couldn't help thinking of their friends in the Army of the North.

People who have arrived from the provinces lately report that the western and southwestern parts of France are so crowded with Belgians and northerners that it's hard to find a bed in towns formerly known only to commercial travellers. If Italy enters the war, there will be another great migration into the southwest from the southeast. "Up here," Parisians who remain reassure each other, with winks, "there is plenty of room. Perhaps we will run the Grand Prix this year after all—in the Métro."

THE intervention of Italy, if it comes, will be embarrassing but not fatal. The Italian air force may raise hob with the south of France, because the French will be able to spare few planes from the northern front, but the Duce's army is not particularly feared and his fleet is clearly outmatched by what the Allies have in the Mediterranean. Even now, few Parisians are earnestly angry at Italy. The average Frenchman's conception of the average Italian may not be flattering to Fascist dignity, but it is not unfriendly, either. "I always think of an Italian," the night porter in a hotel here recently told a guest, "as a man who eats a lot of tomatoes and plays a mandolin."

The bravest Frenchmen are sometimes dismayed, though, when they think of Paris being bombed from the air, because, they say, there is no city in Germany worthy of reprisal. "Berlin, viewed from an architectural and historical standpoint, is a rolling dirtiness," a Parisian remarked the other day. The feeling about Italian cities is different. Nobody here wants to think of bombing Florence or Rome, whose lovely aspects French artists have studied for centuries.

THE danger of Italy is less in the thoughts of people here than the shortage of Allied planes. If the Allies had a few thousand more on hand right now, they could win the war this summer, say the French, or if they were assured that several thousand planes would be delivered to them over the period of the next few months, they could hang on and win later. This war is beginning to recall the old nursery lines about the kingdom that was lost because of the lack of a horseshoe nail. Only this isn't a nursery kingdom.

14
The American Golconda

THE first and, as far as history records, the last American to salt a diamond mine was a man named Philip Arnold, who died of shotgun slugs as a sequel to a business argument in Elizabethtown, Hardin County, Kentucky, in the year 1873. Arnold was the man who set a limit to American optimism, realistically revising the nation's ideas about its future and its resources, and it is a wonder that historians have not as yet given him his due. Arnold was a banker worth a mere $300,000 when he died, but it was as a creative prospector in the West that he made his impress on his country's imagination. An ordinary prospector merely tries to find deposits of precious minerals; a creative prospector places them in the ground for others to find.

Arnold was born in Hardin County (which gave Abraham Lincoln to the nation) about 1830. When a young man, he inherited a small farm there and married. Shortly before the Civil War, he left his wife and a couple of children on the Hardin County place and went out to California to look for gold. Several times, after making small strikes, he returned to Kentucky. In the early sixties, with a partner named John Slack, he developed a claim near Marysville, California, that the two sold for $50,000. Arnold took most of his share of the money home to Kentucky and placed it in a large safe on his farm. By 1869 he was back in California, looking for something to do. Since no new gold fields had recently been reported, he took a job as assistant bookkeeper with the Diamond Drill Company of San Francisco. This firm sold diamond-pointed rock drills to mine-owners. The foundations of the great West Coast mining fortunes had been laid; men like George Hearst, James Fair, Darius Ogden Mills, and William Chapman Ralston, chairman of the board of the Bank of California, controlled the best properties. The haphazard days of Forty-nine were long over, but their tradition lingered in the form of a chronic optimism. An army of disappointed miners was still billeted on the Coast, ready to march at the first report of a new field. In the East and in England, investors, despite a number of unfortunate experiences, were still willing to put money into Western mines. The bonanza business needed only a new stimulus. The first hints of what this stimulus was to be came in the form of newspaper stories about the discovery of the diamond fields in South Africa, the third great source of diamonds in the world's history. The mines of Golconda, in India, had supplied most of the world's diamonds until the eighteenth century, when the Portuguese had discovered deposits in Brazil. South Africa eclipsed both these older fields. American prospectors almost immediately began to look for diamonds in Arizona and New Mexico Territories, where there were said to be geological formations like those in the African diamond lands.

Arnold, still at his job with the drill company, displayed great interest in diamonds. He explained to the head bookkeeper, another ex-miner, named Cooper, that he wanted to learn all about precious stones before he began looking for them. The company kept a considerable stock of diamonds on hand, of the flawed or discolored sort used for pointing drills, so Arnold had a chance to handle a variety of the stones and perhaps secrete a few. He used to question Cooper about tests employed to determine if diamonds were genuine and about the differences in appearance of diamonds from the three known fields. When he had pumped Cooper dry, he bought books about diamonds and studied them. By the spring of 1871 he knew as much about diamonds as anybody on the Coast. Reports from South Africa, ever more glowing, maintained the excitement in America. None of the prospectors in America had found any diamonds, but some of them had come back from Arizona with garnets, which they thought were rubies. To doubt the eventual discovery of diamonds here seemed like selling American short. The public was prepared for a diamond rush.

ARNOLD took a leave of absence early in 1871. He returned to San Francisco two months later, saying he had been into eastern Arizona with his old mining partner John Slack, and he showed Cooper the result of their prospecting: a handful of desert sapphires and rubylike garnets, with a few small uncut diamonds of the type that the Diamond Drill Company used. Arnold said that they had obtained the diamonds by trading with an Indian, to whom they had promised a gallon of whiskey if he would get them some more stones. The two prospectors had then followed the Indian and thus had found where the field was. The field lay within Apache territory, Arnold said, where it would have been dangerous for two white men to remain, so, after killing the Indian, the partners had marked the site of the field and headed back for California, to get help in developing them. Arnold and Slack took their stones to Asbury Harpending, a flamboyant San Franciscan who had once been a filibuster in Nicaragua and was at the time dividing his energies between land speculation and the promotion of wildcat mines. Harpending had known Arnold for a long time, for which reason, perhaps, he took no stock in the story. If the partners returned to their field and found a really impressive lot of stones, he suggested, they would have no trouble getting financial backing. Arnold and Slack then announced they were going back to the Arizona desert, and left town.

The two men reappeared in San Francisco several months later, worn and weatherbeaten. They called on George D. Roberts, another mining promoter, and asked permission to deposit a sack in his office safe, as it was after banking hours and they couldn't place it in the vaults of the Bank of California. This naturally made Roberts curious. He engaged Arnold in conversation—Slack seldom had anything to say—and learned that the sack contained diamonds, rubies, and emeralds, all from a mysterious region that the partners refused to locate specifically. Roberts was in no position to know that Arnold had just made a trip to London, embarking at Halifax, a port where he had been tolerably sure to meet no other Californians, and returning the same way. Arnold had brought back from this expedition about $12,000 worth of imperfect precious stones, uncut. On his return trip, Arnold had been met at St. Louis by Slack, who had remained in this country. They then had traversed the part of Arizona where the Indians traded garnets and had bought a peck or so of the red stones to give their collection bulk and foster the idea that the diamonds and garnets were found in the same general region. The bad feature of their strike, the partners told Roberts, was that it was situated in a section full of hostile Indians. To work it, they would have to organize an expedition strong enough to fight off the redskins, and they hadn't enough money for that.

Arnold and Slack did not ask Roberts to help them; Roberts insisted. Feeling that it would be too big a proposition for one man to swing, he went to the house of William Ralston, the banker, that night and let him in on the secret. Roberts and Ralston sneaked the stones out of Roberts' safe and submitted samples to San Francisco jewellers for appraisal. This was what Arnold had expected them to do, and he had correctly calculated the jewellers' reactions. He knew that there was no jeweller in San Francisco who had any large experience with uncut stones. All of them were familiar with tests by which to prove a stone was genuine; after the tests they could be counted on to set an arbitrary average price per carat, assuming that some of the stones in any given collection were good and others not so good. If they had known that the stones were all malformed culls, they would have named a much lower figure, but they didn't, of course, have that knowledge. The San Francisco jewellers set a value of $100,000 on the prospectors' $12,000 worth of flawed beauties. The stones looked like excellent samples, especially as Arnold and Slack said the lot represented only a few hours' digging. Under no conditions, the partners said when Roberts approached them, would they part with a controlling interest in their claim, but they would sell a good part of it in order to obtain working capital.

Roberts introduced Ralston, who said that he would put in some money if the partners first convinced him by taking a personal representative to the site of the field. Arnold agreed to take a man there on condition that the man should be blindfolded from the moment the party left the railroad. "Otherwise," Arnold said, "our secret is out and he can lead you back to the claim without us." Ralston took command of the promotion. He sent as his agent a satellite named General David D. Colton, a cool, sensible gold miner, not given to enthusiasm. Colton, however, had never seen a diamond field. Arnold and Slack took the agent by train to Rawlins, a station on the Union Pacific, in Wyoming Territory, where the three alighted. This rather surprised Colton, as he had assumed the field was in Arizona. Arnold told him that they had purposely given that impression to throw possible claim-jumpers off the track. Rawlins is not far north of the Colorado line, and the diamond field seems to have been in what is now Jackson County, Colorado. Arnold blindfolded Colton and put him on a horse. The three men rode for four days, the partners taking the hoodwink from Colton's eyes only after sundown, when they encamped. On the fourth day, when Arnold whipped the bandage from Colton's face, the agent found himself blinking on a mesa 7,500 feet high, which he supposed to be deep in the wilderness. The men dismounted and began to walk about the mesa, and before long Colton saw a great anthill sparkling in the sun. Approaching the mound, he found that it was powdered with diamond dust. Arnold came up and dug into the anthill with a knife and soon pulled out a small diamond. Colton then began digging and in a few minutes discovered a diamond for himself. During the day he got forty or fifty diamonds and emeralds, most of them in a gulch which intersected the mesa. Next day, Arnold told Colton they would have to move on, as he feared they had been observed by Indians. After another long, hard journey, during which Colton was blindfolded, they got back to the railroad. The gems which Colton brought in his pocket proved real, like the first batch. They were worth only a few hundred dollars, a jeweller told him, but it seemed a fair assumption that if a man digging with a pocketknife could find that many in a day, the deposits were of unexampled richness.

IT appeared to Ralston, after he received Colton's report, that he had stumbled upon a big thing, perhaps the greatest promotion of his life. He believed he might need operating funds of several million dollars, and that meant he would have to enlist Eastern capital. Speed was essential, because some trapper or independent prospector might at any moment find what Ralston was already calling in conversation the American Golconda. Since Ralston's own money was pretty well tied up in investments, he admitted a few more of his West Coast friends to the cabal. One was General G. M. Dodge (the country swarmed with generals for twenty years after the Civil War). Another was a promoter named William M. Lent, and a third was the dashing Asbury Harpending. Each, on being approached, expressed skepticism. Each, on learning of Colton's trip and the high valuation set upon the gems, became convinced. General Dodge, who, Harpending said long afterward, "had a low opinion of his fellow-men," talked to Arnold for a while and then said that he would stake his life on the fellow's integrity.

The promoters decided to go to New York, taking with them Slack, Arnold, and a bag of gems from the American Golconda. On the way East the financiers wrangled a bit with the two discoverers. Arnold and Slack now appeared suspicious and said they wanted some tangible guarantee of the promoters' good faith. Lent gave them $100,000 as earnest money. It was not hard for the Westerners to get a hearing in financial circles here, especially as the head of the Bank of California had retained General Samuel L. M. Barlow, the most distinguished New York corporation lawyer of the day, to act as intermediary and legal adviser. General Barlow had engaged as associate General Benjamin F. Butler, an influential congressman. Barlow had bespoken the interest of a group of New York bankers, including August Belmont and Henry Seligman. Before proceeding with the deal, however, the New Yorkers insisted that Charles Tiffany, the founder of the great jewelry house, be permitted to appraise the samples from the diamond field. In the event that Tiffany's appraisal was favorable, Belmont and Seligman wanted a mining expert of national reputation to go out to the site and make a report upon it. Arnold agreed to both tests, but said that his partner and he were not going to lead an expert to the mine until they had some sort of written contract protecting their rights. He signed an agreement with the promoters providing that if Tiffany and the mining expert endorsed the samples and the mine, the promoters would pay to the prospectors $650,000 in cash as the full price of their claim.

IT is impossible, in retrospect, not to marvel at Arnold's composure as he went to the meeting with Tiffany, reputed to be America's greatest judge of gems. The rendezvous was at General Barlow's mansion at 1 Madison Avenue. Horace Greeley, the editor of the *Tribune*, soon to be an unsuccessful Presidential candidate, was at the house when the Californian party arrived, as were the Eastern financiers and General George B. McClellan, former Commander in Chief of the Union Armies, who had been an unsuccessful Presidential candidate in 1864. Greeley liked to be in the know even though he had to pledge secrecy. McClellan was slated for a job on the board of directors of the projected mining company. He had a fine mustache and made good window dressing.

Tiffany, as Arnold must have been aware, knew no more about uncut stones than most other American jewellers. He had begun life as a Yankee notion peddler and had never served an apprenticeship on the Continent. He knew that the diamonds before him were real, and that several presumably competent experts on the Coast had made flattering estimates of their value. After a brief glance at the gems, followed by a regal wave of his hand, the whiskery jeweller said, "I cannot fix an exact value until my lapidary has had a chance to inspect each stone, but I can assure you that they are worth at least a hundred and fifty thousand dollars." Arnold, watching him, never blinked.

The meeting, although supposedly secret, was the chief talk of hotel bars and Wall Street offices the next day. That night, Arnold came to the Western promoters and said Slack was fed up with the whole business and would sell his share for $100,000, chargeable against the final purchase price. They got the money for Slack by morning. The two miners now had $200,000 between them. The Easterners who had witnessed the appraisal were feverishly hot on the enterprise and a struggle for the control of the corporation began before it officially came into being. Since it appeared that the financial and technical negotiations, including the selection of a mining expert to examine the property, would take several months, Arnold announced that he and Slack were going back to the West, and that they would leave their precious stones with the promoters as security.

Instead of going West, the prospectors travelled up to Quebec and took ship for London, carrying with them most of their bank roll. They needed more gems with which to resalt the mine. Arnold was not the man to jeopardize a $650,000 deal by skimping on a few quarts of niggerhead diamonds, as the dealers called imperfect South African stones. The pair bought about eleven hundred diamonds in London and then made a business-and-pleasure trip to the Continent, where they bought many of the worst diamonds in Amsterdam and Antwerp. Altogether they spent around $50,000. After their shopping spree in Europe, the partners returned to Colorado and installed the props. The mesa where they had fooled Colton was in fact only about fifteen miles from the Union Pacific railway tracks; they had led him there by a carefully circuitous course. It was near the north end of a pine-clad ridge that ran east and west, to the north of Brown's Hole in Colorado and eight miles below the Wyoming line.

THE Eastern and Western promoters in the combination agreed on Henry Janin, the leading mining engineer of his time, to make the inspection. The mine expert's fee was to be $2,500, plus an option on a thousand shares at $10 each. Only a Philip Arnold would have led a Janin to a salted mine. The prospector had the intuition of a great poker player for an opponent's foible. For the fact was that Janin had never in his life seen diamond land, and he was disarmed in advance by the high appraisal of the sample stones. Surely, he must have felt, if a sample from a mine was worth $150,000, the property was bound to be valuable.

Janin went out to the claim in the spring of 1872. Lent, General

Dodge, General Colton, and several other Californians who had remained in New York for the winter went out with him. Arnold and Slack met them at Omaha. The party got off the train at a station in Colorado Territory late one night. Horses were waiting; the men mounted and rode off into the unknown. Arnold and Slack, leading their companions by roundabout trails, made the journey long and difficult, as they had done when they had convoyed Colton. Janin and most of the promoters were physically soft, and the prospectors kept them riding for several days. When the money men got to the mesa they were dead tired and the provisions were low.

Within a few minutes after their arrival, Colton found the anthill shining with diamond dust he remembered from his first visit. Almost instantly the men started spading into the ground, shouting with pleasure like children at a picnic as they turned up their shining finds. Many of the stones, it appeared, were near the surface. Arnold and Slack pointed out places for their backers to dig, and whenever a promoter followed their advice he found a diamond. The party remained eight days on the ground. During that time, Janin reported, working only with spades and knives, the men turned up 256 carats of large diamonds worth $4,096 at prevailing rates, 568 carats of small ones worth $1,704, and four pounds of rubies worth $2,226. Since the party had dug up what was estimated to be about a ton and a half of rock and dirt, this indicated to Janin that the mesa assayed better than $5,000 to the ton, a figure unparalleled in mining history. He conservatively estimated that the land should yield $5,000,000 an acre. "With a hundred men and proper machinery," he told Lent, "I would guarantee to send out a million dollars in diamonds every thirty days." The mesa contained at least three thousand acres, and Janin said there was no reason the rest of it shouldn't yield as heavily as the spot they had started on. As for the surrounding land, that was of a conspicuously similar geological nature. It might yield billions.

The investigators went on to San Francisco, again led over a circuitous route back to the railroad by Arnold, leaving Slack at the diggings as a guard. Nobody ever reported seeing Slack again. It will never be known whether he lost his nerve and went off with the money he had already made or whether he died by violence. He simply disappeared. Janin sold his thousand-share option to one of the California men at $40 a share, making a profit of $30,000. He said that he did not wish to retain stock in the company, as his report would then be construed as a boost for his own prosperity.

IN SAN FRANCISCO, the promoters organized the San Francisco & New York Mining & Commercial Company, with 100,000 shares of stock. None were offered to the public. The shares were divided among twenty-five leading West Coast mining sharps, men like Ralston, Roberts, Lent, and Harpending. Each of them paid $40,000 into the company's treasury for initial expenses. One of the incorporators, a banker named Gansl, acted as the West Coast representative of Baron Rothschild. Janin released a favorable report and it appeared in the *Mining & Engineering Journal* and in the San Francisco newspapers. It caused a sensation. When Arnold saw the report, he pretended to be very angry. He said he had not realized the property was that good. Roberts and Ralston reminded him of his contract and virtually forced the $450,000 balance of the agreed purchase price upon him. They were glad when he left town. He said he was going back to Kentucky, where he would have a loaded shotgun always ready to welcome any San Francisco mining sharps who came to visit him.

The San Francisco & New York Company opened tremendous offices in the California city, featuring General McClellan and a permanent display of the largest diamonds from the diggings. Would-be investors besieged the place, but the fortunate shareholders would sell no stock. As always on the flanks of a great financial operation, a number of imitations had sprung up. These corporations claimed to have diamond lands of their own, but the public knew that they were only waiting for the big company to reveal the location of its holdings, when they would rush out prospecting gangs and file claims as near the company's diggings as was legally possible. In Paris, Baron Rothschild rejoiced that he had a finger in the pie, even though it was not a controlling interest. "America is a rich land," he sententiously told an interviewer. "It has given us many surprises. It reserves many more."

THE exposure came in a curious manner. To explain it requires the introduction of a character who had had no direct connection with the affairs of the San Francisco & New York Mining & Commercial Company. He was a thirty-year-old government geologist named Clarence King, a member of the first class to be graduated from the Sheffield Scientific School at Yale. King is credited with being the founder of the United States Geological Survey; readers of the "Education of Henry Adams" will remember him as one of Adams' closest friends. In 1872, King, with a party of assistants, had completed a survey of the fortieth parallel of latitude in the United States, which had led him through the salted-mine territory. It piqued him that in his painstaking inventory of mineral resources he had come across no trace of diamond lands. Feeling that his professional reputation was at stake, King went back over the ground he had covered to find, if possible, where he had slipped up. Any party travelling through that country at that time was conspicuous; King located some sheepherders who had seen the Janin party on the march. Guided by them, he set out with a small expedition and found the mesa. The aspect of the place aided him, for Arnold, well documented in diamond mining, had picked the sort of site where diamonds might well have been found.

"The section of the geological locality is so astonishingly considered," King reported later to the unhappy directors of the company, "that I can feel no surprise that even so trustworthy and cautious an engineer as Mr. Janin should have brought home the belief he did." This was much kinder to Janin than most of King's statements. Making his way to the top of the mesa, the government geologist found "in conjunction four kinds of diamonds, Oriental rubies, garnets, spinels, sapphires, emeralds, and amethysts—an association of minerals impossible of occurrence in nature." "The gems exist in positions where Nature alone could never have placed them," he wrote in his report. "They do not exist where, had the occurrence been genuine, the inevitable laws of Nature must have carried them." It was a polite way of saying that he found stones which had been obviously stamped into the ground by a man's boot and others placed in the crevices of rocks. There was even one in a tree stump. The most absurd discovery of all was made by a German in charge of King's pack animals. "Look, Mr. King," the German said, pulling a bright chip out of the ground near the anthill, "this is the bulliest diamond field as never was! It not only produces diamonds, it cuts them!" He had found a cut diamond, one which must have got in among the rough stones by mistake when a dealer in Antwerp or London was wrapping Arnold's purchases.

King rode to Laramie, Wyoming Territory, where he sent a telegram to Ralston, the most prominent director of the company, and then boarded a train for San Francisco. When he arrived in that city he sent the following note:

> To the Board of Directors of the San Francisco & New York Mining & Commercial Company:
>
> I have hastened to San Francisco to lay before you the startling fact that the new diamond fields upon which are based such large investment and such brilliant hope are utterly valueless, and yourselves and your engineer, Mr. Henry Janin, the victims of an unparalleled fraud.

Ralston persuaded him to hold off his announcement while the directors of the company considered what to do. King agreed to wait a fortnight on Ralston's promise to prevent trading in the stock. During this time, King guided a party of the directors back to the site and convinced them that their mine was worthless. Colton was one of the group and so was Janin. The fraud now seemed to them terribly obvious. On November 27, 1872, a long story appeared on the front page of the San Francisco *Bulletin*, embodying the text of King's report to the directors and a statement by Janin admitting he had been deceived. Most of the sharped sharpers felt too foolish to be angry at anybody; Lent was the only one of the crowd who was not ashamed to go after Arnold for his money. He had, it appeared, bought out several of his colleagues, and was hooked for more than $300,000.

SLACK had disappeared, but Arnold's whereabouts was no secret. He was home in Kentucky, where, in the short time following his return from California, he had become one of the local nabobs. He had bought himself an $18,000 house on a plot of thirty-two acres near Elizabethtown, moving into it on the day of the purchase and on the next day spending $4,000 for livestock. In the house he had a great safe, and in the safe, according to Elizabethtown gossip, he had at least $500,000 in cash. The late war was a fresh and rankling memory in Hardin County. Most of Arnold's friends were retired Morgan raiders, and indeed he is said to have ridden on a few raids himself during his holidays from the gold fields. Arnold did not fear whatever prosecution might be instituted by Yankees in Hardin County, nor was there any chance that the governor of Kentucky would allow him to be extradited. The governor had a prejudice in favor of Kentuckian defendants.

When Lent came to Louisville and instituted a civil suit against Arnold to recover $350,000, the Kentuckian played injured innocence. Arnold's attorney issued a statement that his client would fight the case to the bitter end "for the sake of suffering humanity, which has been robbed and swindled by these California mining sharks for the last twenty-five years." The initial difficulty in Lent's suit was that nobody could be hired to serve the attachment on Arnold. The retired prospector continued to live at Elizabethtown, but Hardin County people insisted he wasn't there. It seemed neither polite nor judicious to contradict them.

Lent and some California friends stayed at the Galt House in Louisville, drinking the wine of the country while they waited for the case to get under way, and every day or so the *Courier-Journal* carried a humorous story on the "search" for Arnold. One day, said the newspaper, a process-server announced that he had got to Arnold by disguising himself as a tramp and had pressed the papers on the miner and escaped before Arnold could get to his shotgun. This was immediately denied by Arnold's friends, whose version was that "a suspicious, seedy-looking man" had been seen by workmen to climb "out of the sewer leading to Arnold's privy." Arnold, they said, was ready with the shotgun and would have fired had not the stranger "dashed through a nearby creek and up the Louisville & Nashville tracks for about two miles" without leaving any papers behind him. The discouraged Lent at last went back to California, but his lawyers kept up such a running fire on Arnold that the former prospector agreed to compromise the case. He might have remained safe in Hardin County for the rest of his life without paying a cent, but he would have risked legal trouble any time he crossed the county line. So he settled Lent's claim with a payment of $150,000.

Of the first $200,000 that Arnold and Slack had received, they had spent about $50,000 on stones for salting and another $10,000 for expenses. If, as seems probable, they divided the rest, Arnold got $70,000, which, with the final payment of $450,000, brought his net receipts from the hoax to $520,000. After disgorging $150,000 to Lent and paying his lawyer $25,000, he remained a very wealthy man for Elizabethtown.

AFTER the settlement, Arnold acquired about five hundred acres of good farming land. He built the first store in Elizabethtown to be equipped with plate-glass windows. He announced that he had discovered a silver deposit in Kentucky worth $9,000,000 and that he would soon start work on it. He also entered the banking business, and that was a mistake. There was another bank in Elizabethtown, managed by two partners. The banks' interests clashed, and the odds, because of the code of Hardin County, were two to one against Arnold. The retired gold miner shot one of his competitors in the arm, but the fellow's partner sneaked up behind Arnold and let him have a charge of buckshot in the back. This was fatal to Arnold, a man who has left his mark on the American psyche. Arnold had found investors willing to believe absolutely anything. He left them willing to believe not quite everything. Their credulity never rebounded to the pre-Arnold level. The Age of Innocence was over.

15
The Colonel of the Ship

Men far apart in time and space fall back upon the same simple stratagems when they find themselves in similar predicaments. I know a White Russian colonel who, when taken prisoner in the Crimea in 1919, feigned madness and was sent to a hospital, from which a White Russian doctor helped him to escape. And only a couple of weeks ago a colonel of the Free French Air Force told me that he too had pretended to be mad when he was arrested in a city in Vichy France. "I had already been condemned in my absence to death for treason, twenty years for desertion, and twenty years for stealing a naval vessel," the Colonel said. "Not a joke, exactly, if they had gone through with it, you'll agree." He is a slim, elegant man who talks fast and slangy French; his gestures are very animated and he looks no more than forty. His face is not completely symmetrical, a bullet having rearranged the right half. We were having lunch in the Hunting Room of the Astor, in a corner that has windows on two sides, and sunshine and a great deal of happy street noise were coming in through the windows. The Colonel was here on a mission involving equipment, and would soon go to join the forces in Egypt. At a nearby table four men were talking to a thin, red-headed girl. I supposed it was about a play they wanted her to appear in, because two of them had typescripts, from which they read to her alternately. The other two just nodded and smacked their lips, looking at her each time one of the readers stopped, as if to say, "Isn't it terrific!" She looked as if it was god-awful.

The Colonel kept glancing over at the red-head, just as I did, and this detracted from the dramatic effect of his recital. He talked with the same good-humored *brio* he probably would have devoted to the account of a *steeple* at Auteuil. "There were a couple of officers I knew on the board that examined me when I was arrested," he said. "Good boys at heart, you know, but of the type who do not want to lose their promotions or their pensions. There were also two officers of the gendarmerie—blackguards by professional deformation. A few minutes before the session began, one of the officers I knew had the opportunity to speak to me without the others' hearing. He said, 'Act crazy!' " The Colonel looked at the actress, perhaps wondering what she would have done if asked for such an ad-lib. "It is very difficult to improvise the scenario of a psychosis in five minutes," he continued. "If you do not believe me, try for yourself sometime. My first thought was to perform an immodest act, at the same time calling my judges all the most violent names I could think of. But then I thought that they might take this as evidence of my sanity. I next thought of imitating Hitler—too topical. At last I had an inspiration. I shouted, *'Vive l'Empereur!'*

"A colonel of the gendarmerie howled, 'What are you trying to hand us there?' I howled louder than he, *'Vive l'Empereur!'* My great fear was that the president of the court, an officer I had known since the other war, would burst out laughing and give the show away. My only answer to the whole interrogatory was *'Vive l'Empereur!'* 'What is your name?' *'Vive l'Empereur!'* 'Married or single?' *'Vive l'Empereur!'* 'Titulary of what military grades and decorations?' *'Vive l'Empereur!'* In the end, you understand, it bored them. The president of the court said, 'I move that the prisoner be remanded to the custody of the superintendent of the local hospital for mental diseases for observation.' Even the gendarmes agreed to that. In parenthesis, they were two heads of cows such as you don't see twice in a lifetime.

"When I arrived at the hospital the superintendent did not put me in the great room with the lunatics who were already classified but in a room with two other new arrivals. One did all the time like this." The Colonel put down his knife and fork and started flapping his arms briskly from the elbows, as if he wanted to shake his hands off. "If you don't think that's contagious—" he said wryly, and went on, "The other lunatic believed himself Marshal Joffre. He kept on saying, 'Soldiers, we are at the Marne. The day has arrived,' et cetera, et cetera. The two lunatics were not on good terms. The one who swung his arms said to me, 'Don't believe him. He isn't Joffre.' But I was neatly for Joffre. He was more amiable. I called him *'Monsieur le Maréchal'* and he put matchsticks in my buttonholé and said they were the Médaille Militaire. I had a diverting life for a couple of days, and then the superintendent of the hospital, who was not a collaborationist, discharged me and told me to get out of town. He said he would tell the military court I had been transferred to a hospital with better facilities. This was the result that the president of the court had undoubtedly anticipated, so I suppose there were no embarrassing questions."

"Did you find many officials like that in Unoccupied France?" I asked him.

He nodded. "Yes. Most of them are against the Germans, as long as it doesn't cost them anything," he said. "Of course, there are some assassins, men pledged to Darlan and Laval. For example, a number of old sergeants of the professional Army who have been made captains and majors on condition they keep watch on their brother officers. One of that sort, a captain, murdered a boy I knew in Syria, a nice kid of eighteen. The boy was a motorcyclist with the Free French. One of our light detachments—armored cars and motorcyclists—met a couple of Vichy tanks. The boy rode forward alone to meet the tanks. They let him get close without firing. The boy shouted, 'Frenchmen! We are French too! Let us not kill each other! Come out and be friends!' The crews got out of the tanks—they wanted to surrender. Only the captain remained behind, unseen in the interior of one of the tanks. He had a revolver and he shot my friend near the heart. Then he emerged and finished the kid with three shots through the back as the boy lay on the ground. A brute! But his men were afraid that now, if they surrendered, our fellows would murder them in reprisal. So they climbed back in the tanks and made off."

The waiter took away the plates and we ordered black coffee and cigars. "Most of them are not like that, the Vichy officers," he said. "Only, they don't want to get into trouble. I spent six months in Marseilles last year recruiting aviators for the Free French. Hundreds of fellows knew I was in town, but nobody turned me in. A great many officers I met didn't even know I was wanted. There is such a confusion in France that the sentence of a court-martial in one district is sometimes not communicated to the authorities of the adjoining one. Nobody takes official cognizance of anything that isn't forced under his nose. But most of the fellows knew that I had been sentenced, and they did not mention it for fear it might embarrass me. Only, one night I had a little scare. I was sleeping in my hotel room. The night was very hot and I was lying on the bed naked, with just a sheet over me. At about four in the morning I heard a knock at the door and someone said, 'Open in the name of the law.' I went to the door and unlocked it and then jumped back onto the bed and pulled the sheet over me. It was a detective from police headquarters, a big, fat man with curly black hair and mustache and a breath, compounded of *aioli* and *pastis*, that I could smell across the room—a real Marius of Marseilles. He said, 'I have come to take you to headquarters.' I thought, I will make conversation to distract him; then, when we are going down the stairs, I will trip him and run. I said, 'What a curious choice of an hour to get a fellow out of bed!' He said, 'It isn't my idea, you know. It's the military police who want you.' He sounded ashamed of himself. I started pulling my clothes on as slowly as possible. 'I suppose I could just as well come back at about nine o'clock in the morning with two other inspectors and get you,' he said. 'Maybe you could beat it.' I was so happy that I jumped up and threw my arms about him, disregarding the *aioli*. 'But you must tell me where you are going,' he said. That puzzled me, but he explained, 'They will keep me busy looking for you, and it is necessary for my professional reputation that from time to time I find you. Always just too late, of course. I say to my colleagues, "I tracked him down, but he is a dangerous man. At least three of us must go together." We go, we arrive, the hotel clerk says, "It is exact. A type of the indications you give was here, but he has just departed." So drop me a line whenever you move. Address it to Inspector Bastantonio, Headquarters, and I can play billiards tranquilly when I am supposed to be looking for you.' He went away and I finished my sleep and checked out at half past eight. I moved three or four times after that and I always sent him a word. It worked to a marvel."

The red-head and the four men with the two typescripts had paid their check and were leaving. The Colonel looked after them and said, "She moves nicely. Of the theatre, without a doubt. It is a life that would have fascinated me. So full of sudden emotions!"

THE waiter brought our coffee and cigars, and I said, "I believe you mentioned that you once stole a warship? Was it a large one?"

"Only about five hundred tons," the Colonel said. "An armed trawler. I gave it to the English. They are sidesplitting, the English. They didn't want to accept the ship at first because I was not a naval officer."

"How did you happen to steal the ship, Colonel?" I asked.

"It is a little complicated," the Colonel said, and then, in the manner of a man who knows he has a good story but has told it so often that he is beginning to get slightly tired of it, went on, "In the last war I was an airplane pilot, but in this one I commanded a flying school. In a flying school one is continually impested by doctors, who deprive you of your best students by finding hidden defects in them. One day I said to one of these dirty doctors, 'For a joke, give me the impossible examination to which you subject these youngsters.' He gave me the examination. It lasted for hours. At the end he found that, with the exception of a slight stiffness of one knee, the result of a bullet in the other war, I was perfect. I was quite fit to pilot a fighter plane. The next day I went to the general of the Army of the Air who commanded the district. I said, 'Old boy, I am through with the rigmarole of conducting this species of boys' school. I have passed my physical examination and I demand to be incorporated in a fighter squadron.' He objected at first, but I insisted, so they posted me to a squadron. I took part in the Battle of France. There were six planes in my squadron, all old cuckoos. There were twelve pilots in readiness, so we used to roll poker dice to see which of us would get a plane. I was lucky. I had a lot of experience in rolling dice in the bars near the Trocadéro, so I had a plane very often. One day they sent our six planes to attack eighty German bombers accompanied by a flock of Messerschmitts. I was shot down somewhere between Arras and Amiens. I borrowed some civilian clothes from a peasant, hid my uniform, and started south, like the Germans. I had hurt my game leg in making the forced landing. I was a pitiable sight. The Germans were very chic; they gave me a hitch on a tank. I said my farm had been destroyed and I was going to join relatives south of Paris. When we got near the front line I thanked them and left. At heart they are very sentimental people—but also bloodthirsty imbeciles. When I got back to the territory we still held, things weren't going any better. On the contrary. I couldn't find my squadron or even get word of where it was. The personnel was probably someplace on the roads, in trucks, the planes long since destroyed. I made myself known to the Bureau of Military Circulation of the army with which I found myself. The colonel in command said, 'You must wear some sort of uniform, old man. I'm sorry that I have none of the aviation to give you.' So he loaned me the uniform of a captain of engineers. He said, 'I could give you temporary papers attesting that you are attached to that regiment, but they would not be official. You have just as good a chance to be shot with them as without.' I said, 'Don't worry, my Colonel, I always carry a rubber stamp with me and plenty of nice, purple ink. I understand our national habits of thought, which attach great importance to any paper with a stamp on it. I will make out my own papers.' He gave me some watermarked paper and said, 'Serve yourself.' I wrote out a dandy set of papers and stamped them. 'Thanks, old boy,' I said, and walked out onto the street. I didn't like to be a captain after having been a colonel—what the devil!—so I found an obliging woman and had her sew two more bars on my arm. That made me a colonel again. As a colonel, it was easy for me to stop automobiles and order the drivers to throw out a couple of other passengers and make place for me.

"I drove south in style, but I could not find my squadron, and by that time it was easy to see that the battle for France was lost. It never occurred to me that France would make peace while the English were still fighting. The problem, it seemed to me, was to get all the fighting men and all the matériel we could to North Africa and to England to continue the war. Soon I found myself in the south of France, in the very city where the school for pilots which I had once commanded was situated. I present myself at the gate of the field—not even a sentry. The staff of the school has packed off, the enlisted men likewise. In the barracks I find twenty-one student aviators, kids of seventeen and eighteen, their training almost finished, who do not know quite what to do. They recognize me, even in my uniform of a sordid engineer. We embrace mutually. I say, 'Follow me, my children. We will fly again for France in the sky of England! All we lack is a means of transportation.' They are enraptured. All of them have revolvers, and we go out onto the highroad and commandeer a magnificent truck, in which we all proceed. After a while we stop at a café by the side of the road. The proprietor has turned on the T.S.F.—the radio, you know—and the speaker is saying that Reynaud has resigned. From his tone we get the sensation that a surrender is imminent. We have not much time."

THE Colonel stopped and lit a new cigar. "It sounds insane when you tell about it now," he said, "but it was like that the last few days. All over France there were groups of men like us, who wanted to continue fighting but did not know exactly how. The administration of the Army did not exist. Certain vital officers had disappeared; without them neither superiors nor subordinates could function. It was as if you pull just a few important screws out of a machine; it throws the whole thing out of balance and the machine racks itself to bits. And yet life in some ways seemed normal. There was no trace of enemy action in the country around us. You could still go into a country hotel and order a whacking good dinner and get it, with the best wines in the world, for the same price as before the offensive started. In the south you could even buy all the gas you wanted at the gas stations. I said to my boys, 'It's no use going to Bordeaux. The city is stuffed with civilians trying to get out. It will surely be bombarded, and also those blackguards who will be in control now will try to hold all French troops in the city so they can hand them over to the Germans. Let's try one of the small ports further south.' So, the day before Pétain asked for the armistice, we arrived at Bayonne.

"Bayonne was like the rest of France—nobody knew what was going to happen next. People couldn't believe that it was so nearly over. They didn't feel they had been beaten. They hadn't even seen any part of the war. The *sous-préfecture* was surrounded by foreigners who wanted exit visas so they could cross the Spanish border at Hendaye. The local people looked at the foreigners as if they were part of a show that did not concern Bayonne itself. In the drinking places around the port there were a lot of drunks, and they were very patriotic. They sang the 'Marseillaise' and 'God Save the King' endlessly, at the tops of their voices. And an armed trawler, one of those that the Navy used to chase submarines, came into port with forty German prisoners! A destroyer had sunk a German submarine and rescued her crew. She had transferred the Germans to the trawler. I think they were the last German prisoners taken before the armistice. The trawler tied up and debarked the prisoners. A crowd gathered at the waterside and cheered like mad. One would have said, 'A triumph!' The Germans were landing as prisoners in a conquered country, but they didn't understand how bad it was with us. They looked frightened. And all around them on the streets were fellows from our Army looking for a way to get out of France, men who had lost their regiments and officers who had lost their men—here a group of eight from a tank regiment, there five Colonial gunners, there four *chasseurs à pied.*

"I had kept my twenty-one kids around me and when I had seen the trawler about to dock, I had said, 'Here's our chance. Look sharp,' and I led them down as close as we could get to the place where the sailors were going to put over the gangplank. As soon as the prisoners had been marched down the plank, I walked onto the ship with my twenty-one types. I presented myself to the commander, a lieutenant from the Naval Reserve, and told him that the Germans might arrive in Bayonne any minute. 'In that case,' I said, 'we would all be had like rats. You must get out of port immediately.' And I explained to him that twenty-one trained aviators could not be allowed to fall into the hands of the enemy. He agreed to go and to carry us with him. Then I saw a detachment of seventy Polish soldiers on the pier. The officer in command of them shouted to me, 'Can we come aboard? We want to continue the war, but if these blackguards of Germans catch us, they will shoot us.' I waved to him to come on, and in a minute the seventy Poles are marching up the gangplank. That did not sit so well with the commander of the ship. He said to me, 'I said it was all right for you, but seventy Poles in addition to your fellows and the crew—it's a little crowded, you'll admit. After all, it is I who command here.' 'It is you who command the ship,' I said, 'but I am the senior officer in command of the combined forces, military, aeronautic, and naval. A colonel in the Army has a rank equivalent to the captain of a battleship.' I was glad then that I had thought to have the fourth and fifth stripes sewed on my uniform. There was not much time for argument. I had implanted with him the idea the Germans were in close proximity, so although he grumbled, he gave orders to cast off. We put to sea with the Poles on board as well as my kids. They all crowded the deck. As we went out of the harbor, people leaned out of the windows of their houses and waved to us, howling, *'Vive la France! Vive l'Angleterre!'* There was no chill in their eyes, the people of Bayonne. They did not feel beaten.

"But on the next day, while we were at sea, the ship's radio picked up Pétain's broadcast speech asking for an armistice. Word of it got about the ship. The crew were a bad lot. They began to demand that we return to port. 'It's finished,' they said. 'We're knocked out. What's the good of remaining out here to be torpedoed uselessly?' I went to talk to the commander. I could sense that he was wavering. He said that the radio operator, an outstanding example of a mug, had received a message from the Admiralty ordering all our ships back to French ports. 'It must have been a German-controlled station,' I told him. 'I am your superior officer and I order you to steer a course for Gibraltar.' He grumbled and was undecided. I went out of his cabin, got half a dozen of my boys, and arrested him. I locked him in his cabin, put a guard with a drawn revolver at the door, and went on deck. The sailors were furious, but the Poles, most of whom were armed, were on our side. A few of the sailors who opened their mouths the widest against us I ordered put into irons and locked into a species of storeroom. Some of the fellows in the crew were all right. One petty officer said he understood navigation. My types also had learned a bit of navigation, for blind flying. It's not exactly the same thing, but it helps. So there I was, an aviator in the uniform of a colonel of engineers, in command of a warship. The first time in history, perhaps."

THE Colonel paused, puffing at his cigar. "It was not a big ship," he said, "but it was really not bad. The pier at Bayonne, I forgot to tell you, had been covered with casks of wine and *eau-de-vie,* waiting for transport to England. The sailors, seeing they would have no chance to take any other provisions in port, had rolled twenty or so casks on board in the short time we were tied up. After we put to sea everybody was half asphyxiated constantly. We had a twelve-pounder, a one-pounder, six machine guns, and no end of depth charges. Once I was in control of the ship, I said to my boys, 'In international law, for all I know, we may now be pirates. There is no use standing on formalities. Whether we get to Gibraltar a few days earlier or later is not important. Let us hunt submarines while the depth charges hold out.' So we did for a few days, but we didn't find any. Perhaps a special technique is required. It would have been chic, all the same, a band of aviators to sink a submarine with depth bombs. It would have been a world's record. After a couple of days I let the commander out of his cabin to direct the navigation of the ship, but we always had one of my boys with him in case he should start to act suspiciously. 'No nonsense, old boy,' I used to tell him, 'or we shall make you a good little hole in the head.' The eighth day out, he said, 'We will be outside Gibraltar early this evening.' 'Good,' I said, and I ordered him down into his cabin again and locked him up. I didn't want any scenes.

"We approached Gibraltar in the night. It was completely blacked out. Suddenly guns began to go off and shells to pass overhead. Lights appeared on shore, flashing on and off. They were signalling something or other, but since only the commander and the radio operator understood the signals and they were both stowed away, I didn't know how to answer. I ordered the engines stopped and after a while the fellows on shore stopped shooting. I concluded that I had done what they wanted. Presently a British destroyer headed out toward us and put out a motor launch. The launch came over and a young

British officer climbed aboard. When he saw my uniform he was puzzled. He said, in English, 'Are you the captain of this ship?' I answered, in my very bad English, 'No, I am the colonel of the ship.' He said, 'It's quite irregular. Where is the captain?' I did not want to say, 'I have locked the captain in his cabin.' That would perhaps have seemed more irregular. I said, 'What difference is it where is the captain? I give you the ship freely. Take it.' He said, 'I can't do that. It isn't regular.' So we got a bottle of Scotch and sat down to discuss the affair. I said, 'It is a most useful ship, with a twelve-pounder, a one-pounder, and six machine guns. Take it.' He said, 'I quite appreciate that, sir, but you can't hand over a ship unless you're the captain.' I tried to explain myself. In my very bad English I shouted," and here the Colonel, proud at the memory, half stood up from his chair, like a man rising in his stirrups, and cried, in ringing tones and in English, " 'I am not za captain of zis ship, but I am her *master!*' " He sat down and smiled happily. " 'Oh,' he says to me," the Colonel continued, " 'you are the master? Well then, that's quite regular.' And they accepted the ship. The English are side-splitting."

"And is the ship still in service?" I asked him.

"When I last heard of it a couple of months ago, it was," he said. "The British handed it over to Muselier eventually and it became part of the Free French Navy. It is good to know that the commander, when he realized what it was all about, joined the Free French Navy too, as an officer. He was a decent fellow. It desolated me to be so disagreeable to him."

AUGUST 10 (BY CABLE, DELAYED)

16
Letter from France

EVERYWHERE the Allied troops go in Brittany, the French wear smiles of pure contentment. They walk like happy lovers, smiling without shame and a little foolishly, knowing that the whole world understands. Even the Archbishop of Rennes noticed it on the first Sunday of liberation. "People had walked around every Sunday," he said to me when I talked with him, "but this Sunday everybody smiled. It is a commentary on the quality of a race when its mere absence can make other people so happy." The Archbishop, Monseigneur Roques, was a professor of German in a seminary before he was advanced to his prelacy, and he spent many of his student years in Germany, so he has some qualifications as a judge. "A race of men without individuality," he says. In the mind of a Frenchman, this is the ultimate condemnation. For four years the Archbishop, who is not a Breton but a Gascon, had the delicate task of dissuading his people from flying at the invaders with knives and stones, and being massacred for it, and at the same time of trying to temper the Gestapo's fury against Bretons whom it knew to be intransigent. His problem was complicated by the German-supported and German-financed Breton separatist movement. Leaders of the small but loud separatist sect, who had been forced into discreet obscurity when France went to war, came into the open when German troops occupied Brittany, and they denounced the Archbishop as a Frenchman who was antagonistic to a Nazi world order. Now, like many other varieties of quislings, they are discredited. Some Breton priests were active in the Maquis, who made attacks against isolated groups of Germans all through the four years of occupation. "It was better not to know of these matters—officially," the Archbishop says. Certain Nazi officials told him that Germany was not anti-Catholic, that there were Catholics in the Nazi Party. "But the Catholics had no influence on the Party, of course," he said. He sometimes found officers of the army of occupation amenable to reason, but officials of the Gestapo were almost impossible to deal with. Whenever priests were arrested because of articles they had written for diocesan publications, the Archbishop succeeded in getting them released only by assuming the entire responsibility for their acts and by challenging the Germans to arrest him. They never did.

In milieus less exalted than the Archbishop's palace, I found similar sentiments. One evening, in a dark little café near the ancient house of Bertrand du Guesclin, I heard a sergeant in the resistance forces, which have now come out into the open under the name of the Forces Françaises de l'Intérieur, or F.F.I., telling how the Germans had "interrogated" his wife after he had gone off to join the Maquis. She had been seven months pregnant and they had beaten her until she had lost the child, but she had not told them anything. The sergeant, a lanky, good-natured man with a turned-up nose, didn't speak of this as if it were an exceptional event. Two middle-aged men at the next table told him that they had been imprisoned for six months for no stated reason. They presumed that an anonymous letter had denounced them as patriots. They had at last been released, still without being told why they had been arrested. They didn't seem excited; they were slightly apologetic about even mentioning it, like Londoners in a pub diffidently exchanging bomb stories. After they had finished their reminiscences, all three of them began to laugh. They slapped their knees, they bent double, they choked, they wiped their eyes, and finally one of them sputtered, "And to think, we are rid of the bastards for good!" Then they all had another glass of wine.

The proprietress, joining the group, said that the German military had imposed a curfew hour and that the German soldiers would come after hours and insist on being served. "They would break the lock on the door, throw chairs at the waitresses' legs, and threaten to have the place closed for good if we didn't violate their own rules," she said. One waitress at whose well-shaped legs some chairs had been thrown interrupted to say, "Once, when I said that the English who had been in Rennes in 1939 were not so bad, some German soldiers reported it and the place was closed for a month." A prostitute, sedately sipping an apéritif near the zinc bar, said, "Once I called a German soldier a Jew just to make him angry. He reported that I had called Hitler a Jew. The Gestapo arrested me, and I had thirty-three days in prison on bread and water. They were great talebearers." The day Rennes was liberated, crowds in the streets mobbed some women who had been mistresses of Germans, and shaved their heads, but full-time prostitutes were by common consent exempted from this treatment. "A prostitute is a prostitute and a German is a German, and each acts according to his nature," a resistance sergeant explained to me.

IN NORMANDY, whose great agricultural output was badly needed by the Germans and whose rich farmers they thought they could win over by appealing to their greed, the Nazis made some efforts, during the early days of the occupation, to conciliate the people, but in Brittany they did not attempt to be "correct." They knew it was hopeless. The Bretons started to kill German soldiers eight days after the invaders arrived, in June of 1940, and the ambushes and reprisals, the attacks on German road convoys and executions of hostages, never ceased. Now Bretons of the F.F.I., armed in part with Sten guns dropped from Allied airplanes and in larger measure with captured German rifles and machine pistols, scour the woods and side roads, rounding up bands of German soldiers who have been out-distanced by the rapid American advance along the main roads. Small parties of Frenchmen are bringing in scores of prisoners. The fight has gone out of these Germans. They hide in the woods not because they have any hope of rejoining the German forces, by now many miles to the east, but because they are afraid that if the French capture them they will be killed. This fear is unfounded, because the F.F.I. detachments are now officially a part of the French Army and observe the Geneva conventions as carefully as the American and British troops.

In the fighting for such places as St. Malo and Lorient, the patriots have frequently been able to cut German communications before the Americans arrive. They also take a considerable part in any sort of fighting in which straight shooting and a knowledge of terrain can offset heavy weapons, which the patriots do not as yet possess. Sometimes the resistance soldiers capture a town before the Americans get there, and our armored column arrives to find the local garrison already under lock and key. In one such town, I talked to the only avowed collaborationist I have met. He was a pot-bellied little man of fifty-six, with a face that was puffed from a beating some women had given him. "They were widows of men he betrayed to the militia," a resistance man who had brought me to see the collaborationist in his prison informed me. The pot-bellied man was locked in a cell of the Gendarmerie. He lay on a concrete dais, which was the nearest thing to a bed the cell contained, his grotesque, almost feminine figure wearing a dressing gown and blood-stained pajamas. Some resistance men had gone to his house and dragged him from his bed at night. His head was swathed in a turban of bandages; he looked like the self-portrait of Hogarth wearing a nightcap. "No, no, I didn't betray them!" he cried to me. "I never betrayed them! It's a lie!" He added, surprisingly, "I'm willing to be shot as a collaborator, but not for having betrayed those men. Somebody told the women I had betrayed their husbands, but it isn't so." In the cell with me, the collaborator, and my guide, who was a small, nervous fellow with the three slanting gold chevrons of a sergeant on the lapel of his civilian jacket, were a young gendarme in a tan uniform and black leather leggings and a great, heavy-set farmer armed with a German rifle, who was serving as the prisoner's special guard. All three Frenchmen began to argue with the prisoner at once.

"You know that you talked to the militia the day before they jumped those fellows!" cried the sergeant. "And then, animal, the night after they murdered our men, you had the officers of the militia to dinner at your house!"

"Shut up, thing of filth!" the gendarme thundered, from professional habit, even though the prisoner wasn't speaking.

"It wasn't you who always had a good word to say for the Boche, *hein?*" the farmer rumbled.

"Yes," the man on the concrete dais said, "I was pro-German. I acknowledge it. I worked for them. I took money from them. It is finished for me. I want to be shot."

"Let me get this straight," I said. "You want to be shot?"

"Yes," he said.

"*Il n'est pas difficile, vous voyez,*" the gendarme said to me. "A curious mentality."

The sergeant said, "He's an architect. He built barracks and blockhouses for the Germans. Aren't you ashamed of yourself, miserable object—you, an educated man?" he howled at the prisoner.

The pot-bellied man looked fixedly at the wall without replying.

"Why did you work for the Germans? Did you think they could win?" I asked.

"Not after the Allied landing," he said, "but then it would have been disgusting to change. I could have run away, but I stayed. I am willing to be shot."

We walked out into the courtyard of the Gendarmerie. Seven gendarmes and their families were living in the barracks. All of them had been active in the resistance movement and they were very happy now. The Germans had not trusted them; they had taken away all their ammunition except nine bullets apiece for their old-fashioned revolvers. "They were right, of course," one of the gendarmes said to me. "We were all against them. Any time the Gestapo told us they wanted a man, we warned him. They told us as little as possible after the first few months of the occupation. The militia did their dirty work. Once a band of militiamen even attacked the Gendarmerie and we had to beat them off with our nine rounds apiece. They have no guts." The militia, the Germans' only reliable auxiliary in the effort to keep France down, was recruited from French convicts, who were released from jail and given what amounted to a full license to pillage and torture in a society that had rejected them. They particularly hated the gendarmes because the gendarmes had their records. "We had a Maquis group of about eighty men here," the sergeant told me. "Here, in northern Brittany, there isn't cover for large groups of resistants, as there is in the wilder regions. But these were men of quality, most of them noncommissioned officers in the old Army. On the night of June seventh, one day after the American landing in Normandy, the men of the Maquis were going to attack a German road convoy moving north toward Normandy. The man you have just seen betrayed them. He knew that everybody in the countryside hated him. Children made fun of him. Women spat at him. He hated us all. That evening two hundred militiamen and Gestapo agents attacked our fellows. They had machine guns, mortars, and grenades. We had a German machine pistol, perhaps twenty rifles, and one revolver. We killed twenty-one of them. They took only fifteen prisoners. The militiamen loaded them into two trucks and started toward Rennes, where they intended to take them to Gestapo headquarters. But one of the trucks turned aside and drove to a quarry near here. It had eight prisoners in it—seven Frenchmen and one American. The American was a parachutist who had landed here on June sixth. The Maquis had fitted him out with civilian clothes, so that he would not be spotted. The militia refused to admit that he was a soldier, although he had his identity discs. They were found on his body later. They stripped him and the other fellows and tortured them—tore out their fingernails, crushed their most sensitive parts, that sort of thing, so that they would give information about the

Maquis. Then they took them to the edge of the quarry and shot them, so that their bodies fell over the cliff. Then some of the bastards climbed down and finished off one or two survivors with pistols. They told nobody. A farmer who saw the shootings informed the gendarmes, and they climbed down next day and got the bodies. Now you understand why this man will not admit he gave them the information and why he wants to be shot. He does not want to be released from jail, Monsieur. It would be the worst thing that could happen to him."

This town had been able to muster a hundred and fifty armed men the moment the American armor swept down through Avranches and headed toward Brittany. The Maquis proper were now being helped by all the other active resistants, men who had continued to live in their homes and work at their trades under the eyes of the Germans. The local chief of resistance was a sly, merry man with a double qualification for his rôle. He was district tax collector, so he knew everybody's business and had a good excuse to circulate everywhere and correspond with everybody, and he was the greatest poacher in the countryside, so he knew all the trails through the woods. He was also, as I subsequently found out, a discriminating collector of old Calvados and Armagnac. His principal aides were the town's leading physician—an elegant, youngish man, clean-shaven and wearing shell-rimmed glasses to indicate his modernity, but retaining the black worsted jacket and striped trousers that symbolize the professional man—and a florid, smiling, thick-fingered man who owned a local bus line. They, like the tax collector, had perfect reasons for travelling a great deal and seeing many people. The couriers between the district organization and the regional headquarters in the nearest city were several pretty young women of good families who rode their bicycles along the highways, as it has become normal for young women in France to do when they want to go anywhere. The leaders used to meet in the shop of the town milliner; they were constantly taking hats there for their wives—"God knows it's impossible to get anything new in France and the only way for women to freshen up a little is to have something done to an old hat." The Germans, as soon as they took over the town, had ordered the surrender of all firearms on penalty of death, but the local F.F.I. had assembled a small stock, mostly by killing German soldiers and militiamen who were carrying particularly tempting items.

In the town there was a large hospital, which before the war had been a tuberculosis sanatorium. When the Americans began their advance, it had a couple of hundred German wounded, and the German field commander had sent a detachment of troops to protect their evacuation. The resistance men captured both the hospital and the protecting detachment, mostly by bluff. Other F.F.I. patrols lay in ambush on the side roads off the Avranches-Rennes highway because they surmised that small detachments might try to escape along these byways and make their way to a German port garrison. They captured three hundred and fifty men in all. It was a clean-up job that would have occupied a couple of infantry companies for a week. "We were very anxious the night before the Americans reached this town," the tax collector told me. "There we were, with all these prisoners, in the dark, only one guard to each twenty prisoners, and we were afraid that some fanatic among the Germans might talk the others into attacking us. But nothing happened." Then he showed me a receipt an American M.P. officer had given him for a hundred and seventy-five unwounded or slightly damaged prisoners.

The seriously wounded Nazis and the German doctors were still in the hospital the day I went to see the place. I was taken to the office of the chief surgeon. He was a swarthy, square-shouldered Bavarian in his middle thirties, with a decent enough face. He had taken good care of several wounded resistance men, I was told. I asked him why the German soldiers had let themselves be disarmed by a handful of French with a few guns. He insisted that all the Germans had been seriously wounded and bedridden. I asked him if he thought the war was over, as far as Germany was concerned, and he said yes, the war was lost. "Three million Germans have been killed or wounded to save Europe from Bolshevism," he said, assuming that martyred look which the Germans always used to put on when, as "reasonable men," they discussed the last war with Americans they took for suckers. I could see a new myth—which would replace the "stab in the back" and the "English plot"—building up in the muddy, Teutonic mind, and I felt just like kicking the doctor in the seat of the pants.

SEPTEMBER 22 (BY WIRELESS)

17
Letter from Paris

PARIS has been liberated for only four weeks, but an American arriving now would find it hard to believe that the Germans had been here for any considerable time. The Germans build nothing. In Paris, because of the fortunes of war, they were also prevented from destroying anything. Culturally sterile, they have left no imprint on thought or on manners here, except that people still laugh when they recall how the Germans used to shout at each other in cafés and how the privates would twist themselves into knots and quiver in ecstatic terror at the approach of a corporal. They have left one other reminder—the memory of the hundred and twenty thousand Parisians they tortured and killed. But other Parisians will be born to replace the mutilated dead and the horror will be forgotten. The Beauty, in Ludwig Bemelmans' last book, said, "I will tell you how I feel about Germans. In time of war I detest them. In time of peace they don't exist for me." It is perhaps the most dangerous quality of Germans: they are so easy to forget and, after a few years, so hard to believe in. Perhaps the French government should preserve the torture chambers of the Gestapo as national museums; for example, that shooting gallery in Issy-les-Moulineaux, where prisoners were placed barefoot on metal plates, which were then charged with electricity. Each time a charge was shot into the plates, the victims leaped high into the air, galvanized into human bounce balls. They dug their fingernails into the walls at heights never achieved even by Olympic jumpers. The marks are still there. But if the government preserved this establishment, twenty years from now the intellectuals would be saying that the museum was a chauvinist fake.

THE physical conditions of life in the city are slowly approaching normal. The subway is running about half its normal service, electric light has been restored for a few hours each evening, and the food supply has definitely improved, though belts are still fairly tight. The fighting front is now as far from the city as it was in May, 1940, but whereas the front was then moving toward Paris, it is now moving toward Berlin, which makes the war seem remote. As the war recedes, people think and talk more about the future of France. Many of them feel that General de Gaulle has an opportunity, never offered to any other man, to make sure that this future will be a bright one. France, these people say, has oscillated between revolution and excessive legalism for the past five hundred years. Written law is a fetish in France; the French worship it. It defines the political rights of the individual and the privileges of property, and most Frenchmen think of themselves as small property owners, or at least as potential ones. This passion for law alternates with a passion for social justice, and the two are sometimes in conflict. The revolutionary terror of the First Republic was a triumph of justice over law, and the suppression of the Commune in 1871 was a triumph of concrete code over abstract justice. Many resistance leaders feel that de Gaulle's opportunity is unique because he can, if he wishes, reconcile these two tendencies and seal the rift in the national psyche. They say that he could proclaim what they call an "economic revolution by due process of law."

The broad political problem is closely linked with the more specific problem of punishment for collaborators, a subject that obsesses the public. De Gaulle's popularity is possibly unequalled in French history, and therefore what many people call his slowness in approaching these problems is being blamed on everybody but himself. Editorial writers have been criticizing his ministers and suspect that there has been foreign interference in France's internal affairs, but none of them has yet presumed to attack the General himself. One popular theory is that he wants to get full recognition of the Gouvernement Provisoire and a good seat at the peace table before he sets up an internal program that will very probably antagonize certain British and American elements. The orthodox government line (in politics, orthodoxy is a quick-growing weed), as expressed in the newspaper *France Libre,* is that external affairs must take precedence over everything else at this stage and that internal disputes must be deferred until after the return of the prisoners of war, the general elections (which are not to be held until these men are home again), and the signing of the peace treaty. The detractors of this line say that by that time the traitors—those among the industrialists and bankers, at least—will again be protected, physically and financially, by phalanxes of lawyers and a labyrinth of interlocking directorates and Swiss holding companies, and that the inevitable whitewashing of these collaborators will be followed by an equally inevitable revolution. It is true that General de Gaulle, as a professional soldier, took no part in internal politics before 1940 and that in his incarnation as statesman, which began so dramatically on the twenty-third of June that year, he at first confined himself to foreign and colonial affairs because his government had no control over France itself, but only a year later he was saying that "bold ideas" were needed in shaping the social and economic structure of the France of the future. He spoke of his debt to the working people, who were at that time the chief support of the Free French cause in France. There is little reason to think that his fundamental conceptions have changed or that he has forgiven the men of Vichy; he seldom forgives anybody. In any case, instead of the blood bath confidently predicted by certain people in Washington and London "if that man de Gaulle gets control in France," Paris is now witnessing merely the desultory interrogation of a few hundred putative collaborators picked up here and there and the incarceration of some of them to await trial in calmer times.

THE *roman feuilleton*, or continued novel, was always an important feature of the French press, and Parisian newspapers are fortunate now, when space is so limited that few of them can print a real *feuilleton*, in having the daily running story of the investigation of the Lafont and Bony gang. Lafont and Bony, former inspectors of the French Sûreté Générale, opposite number of the F.B.I., were broken before the war because their corruption exceeded anything ever known even in the Sûreté, the organization which blandly protected Stavisky while the Paris police were looking for him. This denoted a remarkably high level of dishonesty. When the Germans came in, this precious pair of cops were highly recommended to Laval's partner-conquerors. Both acquired German citizenship and received commissions in the Gestapo, and then, gathering a nucleus of administrators and stool pigeons, they organized the French section of the Gestapo. Their milieu, as reconstructed during the investigation, is reminiscent of both Chicago gangland and the milieu in which the Lonergan affair had its being. They had magnificent houses in the Etoile-Elysée district and mistresses who included a White Russian princess, a night-club marquise, and a German film star. There were fake Baltic barons, pastiche French vicomtes, and in general a café-society hoopla. In addition, on the fringe, there were characters like the little man who picked people's eyes out with a fork and another who specialized in cutting off noses and fingers, and the German art expert and fence known as Manuel Flatfoot.

The police who are conducting the investigation have the true *feuilleton* manner of developing a story; every day they introduce one or two new characters who make good reading. Yesterday it was a man called Jo La Terreur, whose relevancy seems to depend entirely on his being a friend of Violette Morris. Violette was an English-born auto racer who was supposed to have killed men for calling her a woman and who had a surgeon remove her breasts so that she would look mannish. Violette, being a sadist, was quite at home with the Gestapo. Three months ago, while she was stalking a man in the Maquis who was to be arrested and tortured, some Patriots shot her to death. The police freed Jo La Terreur, but not until his name had made a fine headline and the details of Violette's personality had given the newspapers a walloping good *Daily News* story. The Lafont and Bony gang specialized in fake raids and arrests. They would rob the apartments they raided and kidnap the occupants, and then torture the "arrested" people until a ransom was paid. Since the gangsters held cards in the Gestapo, they could not be prosecuted. Naturally, the victims of their raids were always carefully selected—a corps of finger men did this work—and the hauls were magnificent. They had to split the take with the German Gestapo men to hold their franchise, and Manuel Flatfoot saw to it that they didn't hold out the good items and pass along the shoddy ones. The French and German Gestapos maintained a joint marketing organization to dispose of the varied loot: securities, specie, jewelry, paintings, antiques, and vast quantities of more commonplace but valuable objects like felt hats and groceries. They were businesslike. To keep in good with the more earnest elements in the German parent organization, Lafont and Bony sometimes had to forego big profits and arrest or liquidate real Patriots. For instance, Lafont kidnapped the head of the Belgian Intelligence in France and delivered him to the Germans, who tortured him to death. On another occasion, Bony pretended he was an R.A.F. pilot who had bailed out of a plane, and, when some Patriots took him in, informed on them to the German Gestapo. The gang also recruited North African thugs to fight against the Maquis. These chores they performed to prove their good faith. They didn't relish them, for there was little money in them.

The trouble with a story so full of horror and cynicism is that after a while the reader begins to follow it as if it were actually only a *roman feuilleton.* Lafont and Bony are becoming, in a perverse way, public heroes, like Landru—the Bluebeard of 1919—and Doctor Petiot, who, during the German occupation, killed and dissected a hundred and sixty people. Like Lafont and Bony, Petiot was welcomed to the bosom of the Gestapo. He is now somewhere in Germany. His game worked this way: he promised to get people out of France and into America. Naturally, a great many of them were de Gaullists and Jews. Petiot would impress them with the necessity of secrecy; they must tell nobody they were leaving or where they were going—just take all their money and come to his cottage in a suburb of Paris, where he would start them on the underground railway. When they arrived at the cottage, he would tell them that the American authorities insisted on inoculations and that, luckily, since he was a doctor, he could give them. Then he would shoot them full of morphine and start to dissect them before they came to. He kept their money and turned over their papers to the Gestapo, which was grateful for his aid in protecting Europe against the "Bolshevist peril." Men such as Lafont and Bony and Petiot are dangerous in the same way the Germans are—because nobody really believes in them. People read about them as they read about the Lublin massacres and say they're too bad to be true.

THE exuberance of the first week of liberation has died down. The children in the little park under my window who sang the "Marseillaise" all day every day that week and walked about waving tiny flags are now playing the French equivalent of hopscotch, as they used to in 1940, when I lived in the same room I live in now, overlooking the same park. The small *gardien* in the green uniform who stood by the fountain in the park on the day I went away is there again, his hands locked behind his back. The fountain, with its four allegorical female figures (the rivers of France), plays on and I am once again tempted to throw peachstones into the navel of the fat stone woman who represents the Loire. A fat flesh-and-blood woman in a flowered wrapper comes out on a sixth-story balcony of a house fronting on the park and waters some geraniums. I recognize her; she is the woman who came out on the same balcony early in the morning of May 10, 1940, when German planes first appeared over Paris, and waved at some frightened pigeons and cried, "Confidence!" And I remember how people at other windows on the square laughed and waved, too. She was wearing a flannel nightgown then. The children have forgotten the Germans already, I am sure. The rest of us will forget too soon.

18
Colonel Baranoff and the Newspaper "PM"

EVERY now and then I read that Russian mistrustfulness is lacerating the sensibilities of some contemporary journalist. For example, the Russians approached the San Francisco Conference, it appears, like a small boy who would willingly pick a dime off the sidewalk if he weren't afraid that the coin had just been heated and left there by a practical joker. I feel guilty when I read such a lament, because I fear that I am in part responsible for this Russian attitude. The Russians have long had at least a couple of excuses for being leery of the capitalistic world, such as the press campaign against them that began at the time of the Revolution and has never stopped. However, I sometimes think that I poured into the ebullient brew of Russian feelings about America the last little drop of doubt that made the mixture overflow. It happened late in April, 1943, while I, then a correspondent on the American front in Tunisia, was sharing a tent with a Colonel Baranoff. Baranoff—that is not his name, but it will do—was a correspondent for Tass, the Soviet news agency. He was also a colonel of artillery on the active list of the Soviet Army, which gave him enough rank to impress the hell out of the American and British public-relations officers in the field, who seldom topped major. Not long ago he was put on one of those joint Allied commissions that run countries in the Mediterranean, and since many of his colleagues on the new beat are colonels, he has been upped to major general.

Baranoff had been with the British Eighth Army in Libya for several months before he came over to look at the Americans. I had heard a lot about him when I was in Tripoli earlier that month, but I had never chanced to meet him until he came with us. The British have a system of assigning what they call accompanying officers to correspondents, which in practice often means that the correspondents have to accompany the officers. The Eighth Army correspondents travelled in parties of three newspapermen to one accompanying officer, plus a couple of drivers who doubled as batmen. Each party was also provided by His Majesty's Gov with a couple of lorries equipped with cots and typewriter tables. Eighth Army Public Relations, operating with its customary felicity, had placed Baranoff under the protection of a particularly fluttery ex-member of the Duke of Windsor set. Baranoff, British newspapermen had told me, got a bit of innocent fun out of this situation. Every evening, when his party started to pitch camp, Baranoff would, if any artillery was at all audible, turn to the accompanying officer, who was a baronet, and say something like, "Sir Papa [a form of address of his own devising], that last salvo was not far from us. To the north a little only." Then he would listen again, and after the next salvo he would say, "*That* one was to the south. We are bracketed. On my honor as artillery officer, Sir Papa, next one will land here. Perhaps on the table where you are about to have tea." So the little caravan would pack up and move elsewhere. If Baranoff and the other press men felt lively, he would do this two or three times in an evening, and it cheered everyone, except Sir Papa, immeasurably. On the whole, Baranoff held himself rather apart from his colleagues; only once, they said, had he seemed to feel himself really in rapport. That was during one of the engagements that punctuated the Eighth's long advance from El Alamein to northern Tunisia. A British brigadier had not only failed to get some guns across a wadi but, what was worse, he had reported to his divisional commander that the guns were across when they weren't. This had, of course, balled up ensuing operations. On the following morning some correspondents, including Baranoff, called at the brigade command post to investigate the incident and found that the brigadier was no longer there. "The brigadier!" Baranoff inquired. "Where is he?" "They bowler-hatted him," an officer said, meaning that the brigadier had been relieved of his command—in obsolescent American slang, "handed his hat." "Ah," said Baranoff, smiling with quick comprehension, "I understand. You have shot him." When he learned that they had not shot the brigadier, he looked puzzled, and you could see that he felt he was up against the inscrutable Occident again.

TRIPOLI, early in April of that year, was already several hundred miles behind the front lines; the Eighth Army had pushed west across the desert and then north along the shores of the Gulf of Tunis until it was up around Gabés and Sfax, in Tunisia. Tripoli had supplanted Alexandria as chief supply port for the British forces and was rapidly acquiring the more obvious characteristics of a base: an Army newspaper, theatricals and "flicks," tall, impractical-looking Sudanese sentries wearing green turbans, and swarms of rear-echelon officers competing for the de-luxe quarters. There was actually something to compete for in Tripoli, since the Italian government, fond of operatic magnificence, had built fine houses for even minor colonial officials. All the littlest vermicelli, as well as the biggest macaroni, of the Fascist hierarchy there had departed in a hurry, leaving their *palazzi* ready for the British. The Eighth Army public-relations officer at the base was a captain who wore the shoulder flash and cap insigne of the Grenadier Guards, because as a youth he had served with them for a year in London. He had sensibly preëmpted a villa in the suburbs, a mile or two from the port itself, which still drew occasional bombardments from enemy planes based in Sicily. The villa, although it had housed only a minor Italian official, a street-cleaning superintendent or the secretary of a Fascist club, was imposing—a long building of Italian-Arab architecture, with two wings of bedrooms separated by a suite of dining and living rooms. The Guardee reserved one wing for himself; he allowed the correspondents, of whom, it is true, there were seldom more than ten or fifteen, to use the other. There was a bathroom in each wing. The one in the captain's wing worked; the one in the correspondents' didn't. While I was there, a band of British correspondents came back from the battle of Wadi el Akarit. One of them had been conked by a piece of a shell and had just spent a few days in a field hospital. They couldn't get a bath. There was a deep artesian well that supplied the villa with water. Another well, nearby, supplied the native Jews and Arabs of the surrounding suburb. Both wells were pumped by stationary engines. The engine that worked the neighborhood well broke down, but the Guardee wouldn't let the Jews and Arabs draw water from the villa well because he didn't like to have them tramping across the lawn. He would lurk among the orange trees on the grounds at dusk, and when he saw little girls sneak up on the well, he would wait until they had filled the gasoline tins they had brought for water and would then rush out and hit them across the backside with his swagger stick. The girls would drop the tins and run away, howling. "If they really needed water, the beggars could draw it from their own well by hand," the captain would say.

In the mornings the captain would sit swilling tea, on the open terrace that ran the length of the villa, until the wasps trying to get at his marmalade became too numerous, which usually happened at about ten o'clock. He didn't try to hit the wasps with his stick, because he was afraid of them. When he had had enough of them, he would take his cap and his stick, blow hard through his nostrils until the ends of his long brown mustache fluffed out, and go off in his motor. It was only a Humber; he was pained that he had not succeeded in pinching an Isotta-Fraschini from a departed Italian. "The chaps who arrive in the first fortnight snaffle everything good," he used to complain. He always was secretive about his morning missions, implying that it would be a breach of censorship to tell us what they were about. One morning I was talking to Major Robb, a Scotch agronomist, at the Tripoli Agricultural Research station, when our captain arrived there on one of these missions, his chest pushing the front of his battle dress, mustaches floating on his breath, "hrrrumph"s rising in his throat, a gruff, manly condescension in his voice. He introduced himself and then tried to cadge an electric fan and a quart of cream. For lunch, a meal that he tried to make the best of the day, because fewer correspondents were at the villa than at breakfast or dinner, the captain would customarily eat a bit of fresh mutton bought at the public market, and then perhaps a treacle tart. The mutton was openly bought, not black-market. Only bread was rationed in Tripoli, since the British argued, reasonably, that the Arabs didn't have money enough to pay for meat and weren't used to it anyway. Replete, the captain would retire to his office, a room in which no correspondents were allowed, and compose letters to his superiors in Cairo asking for more enlisted men and vehicles. He already had sixty-four men when I was there, though he needed no more than five, but he felt that having more men under his command would add to his dignity. He put up the ones he had in a couple of villas across the road, to keep them from getting underfoot.

The captain's solicitude for his dignity reacted disastrously only once while I was in Tripoli. When I arrived, he had a soldier cook who, for the British Army, did quite a decent job. However, the soldier was rated merely as a driver and he had learned cooking by experimenting on correspondents in the field. The captain thought that a man of his consequence should have a graduate of an Army Catering Corps school. Negotiations had been proceeding, I discovered, for months, and a Catering Corps alumnus, a sergeant, arrived on the sixth day of my stay. We expected the correspondents from Wadi el Akarit to come in that evening, and knowing how hungry they inevitably would be for fresh meat, I went to the market and bought eight pounds of lamb chops for the equivalent of nine dollars—not too bad a price, it seems in retrospect. (You would pay that much for one portion in Paris now.) I turned them over to the Catering Corps sergeant and he boiled them, with the fat on, until the meat broke down into tiny shreds, which floated about in the greasy water. We drank our lamb chops out of cups—all but Willie Forrest, the fellow who had been hit on the head. He got sick, in the full British sense of the word. By the time I left Tripoli, the captain had started negotiations with Cairo to take the wretched sergeant away. It was a delicate subject because the captain had already raised so much hell with Cairo to get him. It was these boys from Akarit who told me the first yarns I heard about Baranoff.

I WENT up to the Eighth Army front after my stay in Tripoli and spent a few days with the Fourth Indian Division at the beginning of the battle of Enfidaville. Then Lieutenant Colonel Tealeaf Stevens, the public-relations officer of the division, lent me a lorry, with a driver named Whitaker, from Hull, in Yorkshire, to take me back to the American Second Corps. The front by that time was continuous from the Gulf of Tunis to the Mediterranean shore west of Bizerte, and Whitaker and I travelled along back of it, passing through the zones of the Eighth Army and the French Nineteenth Corps and the British First Army before we got up to where the Americans were preparing to jump off. Whitaker was a bearlike, hairy man, and the Desert Army shorts and the shirt open at the neck made the hairiness conspicuous. He had high cheekbones and narrow eyes. Both his parents, he told me, were Polish, but he had been born and reared in Hull; Whitaker was an Anglicized approximation of the Polish family name. He had been out in Africa for three years and had attained the rank of corporal. He was also one of the most accomplished foragers I have ever met in any army. When he wanted eggs, which we boiled hard and carried with us as a supplement to our rations, he would stop the lorry, even in an apparently uninhabited waste, and, standing on the running board, hold out some tea leaves on the upraised palm of his right hand. Then he would shout, "Eggis! Eggis!," a word which he fondly believed was Arabic for eggs. (The tea leaves were a special product. They had already been boiled out when he was making tea for his own use—he liked his tea strong—and then had been dried in the sun so that they could be used for barter.) Instantly dozens of Arabs would appear with eggs, and Whitaker always got as many as he wanted.

The only notable event that occurred on our journey was a miracle. When we started out, there was hardly a drop of liquor left in the entire Eighth Army area. British officers were entitled to buy a certain amount of spirits from the N.A.A.F.I. (Navy, Army, and Air Force Institute), an organization maintaining stores like our Army Post Exchanges, and there were N.A.A.F.I. shops, under canvas, scattered all the way from Cairo to Enfidaville. But the stocks of liquor west of Tripoli were exhausted. So Whitaker's chief had provided him with a couple of thousand francs and ordered him to keep an eye open for French farmers who might have brandy or, failing that, wine, to sell, which he could take back to the chief. Whitaker and I drove some three hundred miles without traversing any wine-growing country. Then, as we approached a road intersection behind the extreme left flank of the British First Army, only a couple of miles short of the American zone (where we could be *sure* there would be nothing to drink), the motor stopped. This it had done once before—on a road under mortar fire, near Enfidaville—and Whitaker and I had had to get out and push. This second time, Whitaker fiddled with all the buttons and levers within reach, then muttered something about "bloody water in the bloody petrol line," and got out to have a look under the lorry, taking some tools with him. He stayed there for a couple of disgusted minutes, crawled out from under, probably to get more tools, looked at a low, mud-walled Arab granary by the side of the road, and stood transfixed, pointing at a paper placard over the granary door. The placard said, "N.A.A.F.I." Whitaker said, "Fate works in mysterious ways." Watching his face, I could see him size up the situation. "They be First Army," he said. "Happen they'll have liquor. They get it through those Algerian ports." Whitaker's desert shorts and the lorry, with its sand-colored camouflage, marked him as one of the Desert Heroes that people at home in England had been reading about. The First Army had not come out until 1942, and this part of the First Army was so far from the Eighth that it was possible the N.A.A.F.I. clerks had never seen a Desert Hero. Whitaker was from outside the territory that the First Army N.A.A.F.I. was supposed to supply, but the clerks might give him a break. "I'll have a try," he said, wiping some extra dirt across his face with the hand that he had

had in the machinery while he was beneath the car. "I'll tell them that we're dying of thirst, *all* of us." He went into the granary and came out in a couple of minutes, grinning. "It worked," he said. "The sergeant told me to fill out a requisition for the total number of officers and men we've got in our unit. They don't give much for each one, of course." He took a well-chewed pencil stub from the breast pocket of his shirt, chewed on it some more, and said, "There's just four officers and eleven men, to be truthful. But we have sixteen other officers at Cairo, and about seventy-eight men." I could sense, when he got to the "about seventy-eight," that he was beginning to improvise. Then he said, "And we have hundreds more at Calcutta. Do you think it would be wrong to draw for them?" I reminded him that he had just one lorry, so he compromised by adding only the Cairo lot to his own group. He got seven bottles of Scotch, four of gin, and some beer. One of the pale, lately-from-England soldiers in the N.A.A.F.I. store carried it to the lorry for him. When Whitaker got back into the driver's seat, the motor started instantly. Neither of us was able to figure it out.

THE American press camp, which we found after a bit of trouble, was on top of a narrow, pine-covered ridge near a town called Béja. It was all tents, ranged in single file along the crest of the ridge. The trees afforded pretty good cover, but, as we were soon to find out, there wasn't much need for it, because the German air force in Africa was by then almost non-existent. There was a large cook tent and an even larger tent that served as a mess and newsroom. The correspondents lived in small wall tents so well provided with black-out flaps that you could burn an electric light inside them at night. A mobile generating plant supplied the power. Each tent was big enough for only two men. When I reached camp, there was just one vacancy, and that was in the tent occupied by Colonel Baranoff, who had arrived a few days before. He came home that evening after supper. He had eaten at the First Division headquarters, which he had been visiting. Our artillery particularly interested him; it is an arm well developed in both the American and Russian Armies. He had a set speech he used whenever he was presented to a divisional commander. He would say, "How do you do, sir? You have a magnificent army here. You are teaching your teachers. You should begin immediately a Second Front. You have nothing to fear."

Baranoff was a straight, slender man in his early thirties. He had fair hair, cut very short, a narrow, blond mustache, two gold teeth in the front of his mouth, and a precise, almost staccato manner, as if the first phrase he had learned in English was "Count off!" He was not undersized, as W. L. White says Russian officers are, or oversized, like Feodor Chaliapin or the late Grand Duke Nicholas or a wrestler I used to know named Matros Kyrilenko, all of whom grew up before reading Mr. White's book. I would say that Baranoff was a legitimate welterweight. Senior residents of the camp had cots, but there weren't enough to go around, so I slept on the floor that night. But I knew that a lieutenant in the camp was going to Algiers the next day, and that meant he would have to get up before dawn to drive out to the nearest airfield. I arose early, stumbled around to the lieutenant's tent, and came back to my tent with the cot before any of the other cotless correspondents were awake. When Baranoff opened his eyes and saw me, across the tent, in the cot, my head on the same level with his, he grinned. "Very good capture," he said. "Example of primary acquisition."

It was hard to think of things to talk to Baranoff about. When you asked him about anything Russian—the Soviet air force, for instance—he just said it was wonderful and stopped. You felt that you offended him a little by inquiring, as you would by asking a waiter at a good restaurant if the fish was fresh. The press camp had been in one place for ten days, which was unusual, and quite a lot of mail, including several bales of newspapers, had caught up with the fellows there. There were about twenty copies of The Newspaper *PM,* in sequence, dating, as I recall, from February. I thought Baranoff might like something to read, so one night, after the camp poker game broke up, I carried half a dozen copies of The Newspaper *PM* back to our tent with me. Baranoff was a light sleeper. He woke when I came in.

"Turn on the light!" he said. "It is O.K."

I said, "I have some copies of one of our more liberal New York newspapers here. I thought you might like to read them. It might help you to understand what people at home are thinking about Russia." I hoped he would never see a copy of the *News.*

"Oh yes," Baranoff said. "Thank you. How interesting! I will look." He took The Newspapers *PM* from my hand and looked at the top one. He glanced at it casually, and then turned over on his stomach, holding the newspaper close to his eyes. He was silent for several minutes. "It is a series of articles entitled 'Foes of the Soviet Union in America,' " he said after a while, in explanation of his silence. "It appears that your State Department is honeycombed with them. What a fine expression! How interesting! Also the universities and labor unions. The banks, of course—that was to be expected!"

And when I fell asleep he was still reading.

For a couple of nights after that, I got no conversation out of Baranoff at all, because he was always reading The Newspaper *PM*. "How interesting!" he would say now and then. "I had no idea we have so many enemies." I looked at a couple of the papers one afternoon when he wasn't in and found just one of the usual series about Fascists and reactionaries that named a fairly large percentage of people in the telephone book. But it was no use trying to tell Baranoff. "How interesting!" I would hear him say. "How interesting!" Then I would fall asleep. "These people they talk about," I once ventured, "of course, they may really be enemies of Russia, but they don't represent the Administration's views."

"No?" asked Baranoff. I decided that he was trying to figure out why, in that case, the Administration didn't shoot them. "How interesting!" he finally said, and I could see that he was not convinced.

Then came a day when I went jeep-riding over what seemed most of northern Tunisia, getting in and out of the machine a score of times to scramble up to observation posts. I had with me an old gold Waltham watch that had belonged to my father. This was foolish, because I had no pocket to put it in that it couldn't slide out of. When I got back to camp that evening, I became aware that the watch was missing. I had had it in the pocket of my field jacket. I searched the back of the jeep, where I had been sitting, but it was no good. I was annoyed, because my father's mother had given him the watch when he was twenty-one years old, and he had always bragged that he had never dropped it hard enough to break the glass, and he had been accustomed to say that I lost everything. Now, although he couldn't say "I told you so," because he had been dead six years, I *had* lost it, and it made me angry. When I returned to the tent, I said to Baranoff, "I had tough luck today. I lost my watch." I washed up and went to the mess. When I came back, he was lying on the dirt floor, looking under my cot. "What are you looking for?" I asked him.

"I look for your watch," he said.

"But I know I didn't leave it in the tent," I said. "I lost it getting in or out of the jeep, on the road."

"How can you be sure?" he said. "I do not like such things should happen when I am sharing the tent with you, you know. Have you looked in your bedding roll? Perhaps it is there. I will look."

It was then it occurred to me that he might think I suspected him of stealing my watch. You can't say to a man, "I know you didn't take my watch" or "I don't suspect you for even a minute," because that would be an admission that you had considered the possibility. And he couldn't conceivably have taken it, of course; I was frightened by the notion that he might consider me capable of suspecting him. "I know I had the watch with me at an O.P. this afternoon," I said. "I looked at it several times." Baranoff did not seem impressed, and I thought, "Maybe he believes I'm framing him. He has probably seen a movie in which an agent of a foreign power falsely accuses a Soviet officer of theft." Baranoff said nothing more then, but he looked unhappy. I thought he might visualize himself as an Inter-Allied Dreyfus. I could imagine a montage of headlines flashing past behind Baranoff's eyelids: "Soviet Officer Steals Watch," "Soviet Officer Falsely Accused of Stealing Watch," "Red Army Man Denounced by Propaganda Liar," "*PM* Unveils Another Anti-Soviet Plot." I tried to be especially cordial to him in order to show him that the watch was a bagatelle, already forgotten. As I fell asleep, he was again reading The Newspaper *PM*—probably an account of how evidence had been faked against some labor leader in a Southern state. I wished I had never seen the watch or that I had left it in a safe-deposit vault in New York.

When I went into the news tent for breakfast next morning, one of the soldiers who worked in the cook shack came to tell me about the second miracle figuring in this rather brief narrative. An Arab had found my watch in the dust where I had dismounted from the jeep the night before at the camp, right at the foot of the hill the camp was on. He was one of the Arabs who helped with K.P. in return for scraps of food, and he had been either honest (a fantastic hypothesis), or too unsophisticated to know how to dispose of a watch, or afraid that if the French gendarmerie found him with it they would shoot him. The odds against a Tunisian Arab's returning a gold watch are, I suppose, about equal to those against my now picking the winner of the 1955 Kentucky Derby. "We knew it was your watch," the soldier waiter said to me, "because you been hollering your head off, and besides it has your name inside the case. The Arab is out in the kitchen now." I went to the kitchen, got my watch, and gave the Arab two hundred francs, which was four dollars. That was as much as he could have earned in four weeks on a road gang, so he was pleased. I didn't bother about breakfast, although I was hungry. I jogged right back to my tent, with the watch in my hand. Baranoff was sitting on his cot, looking at the floor. "Hey, I found my watch!" I said. "An Arab found it. I was getting out of a jeep—" Baranoff sprang up. He was obviously a man discharged of a heavy load. The two gold teeth flashed like the headlights on a two-and-a-half-ton truck coming against you at night. He placed his hands on my shoulders and looked at me with emotion. "Colleague!" he cried. "How glad I am to hear this! How happy I am that you have found your watch!"

After Colonel Baranoff had left the camp for the day to make his speech about the second front to another general, I hurriedly gathered all the copies of The Newspaper *PM,* took them out in a field, and burned them. In the evening, I told Baranoff that their owner had insisted on having them back. I said that the owner had been one of two correspondents who had left camp that day to go over to the British zone.

"I am very sorry," Colonel Baranoff said, "but fortunately I have taken interesting notes. Documentation, I think is the correct word. Few people, even among the highest Soviet officials, have an *idea* what goes on in America. They should read The Newspaper *PM.*"

19
The Whole Story

ELECTION or no election, one of the important books of our generation bears the title "Hearings Before the Committee on Un-American Activities, House of Representatives, Eightieth Congress, Second Session: Hearings Regarding Communist Espionage in the United States Government" (United States Government Printing Office, Washington, 1948; 878 pages, numbered from 501 to 1,378; $1.75). Covering the period from July 31st to September 9th, it has been printed in an edition of only a thousand copies, for the use of the members of the Committee whose deliberations it records, newspaper correspondents, and others with a special interest in the proceedings, such as, presumably, the two witnesses who are now suing two other witnesses for libelling or slandering them on the radio. There is not a person in the country, however, who, consciously or otherwise, has not a special interest in the record of these hearings, and a first edition of a million copies would have seemed to me moderate, since this record gives the story of the Committee's hearings a continuity, and thus a shape, that newspaper presentations of isolated tidbits from day to day almost completely failed to convey. Perhaps some book club might still be induced to send out "Hearings" in place of the customary historico-mammary bargain offering. The text is bulky enough for a book-club selection, and in a dust jacket featuring a *World-Telegram* reporter's concept of a beautiful blond spy, it might well be acceptable to a high proportion of subscribers. Certainly none who began reading it would send it back, for it is a book difficult to lay down, a sequence of dramas that are Shakespearean except for the poverty of the idiom. In this Shakespeare, however, the Shallows and Dogberrys are the protagonists; other characters appear only transiently, leaving the drolls to apostrophize each other. In recognition of the preponderant parts they play, the book bears on its flyleaf a roster of the nine Committeemen and of the two principal investigators, like a Dramatis Personae. The witnesses are listed later, like Lords and Ladies of the Court, or Citizens of Verona. Two of the nine featured players, Congressmen John McDowell, Republican, of Pennsylvania, and Richard B. Vail, Republican, of Illinois, have since been withdrawn from the cast by the decision of their constituents, who voted them out of office. Mr. McDowell, at least, will be hard to replace.

"Mr. Chairman and members of the Committee," says Mr. McDowell, in the record, in a tribute to Miss Elizabeth Bentley, the initial witness, "here is an American citizen who delved into this business and now has the courage to walk through the valley of the shadow of publicity." (At the time this statement was made, photographs of the beaming Miss Bentley had appeared on the front page of nearly every newspaper in the nation. In them, she seemed happy to escape from what Mr. McDowell would probably call the glare of obscurity.) Mr. Fred E. Busbey, Republican, of Illinois (another election casualty), testifying as a guest expert, says, "Now, anybody that knows anything about the Spanish situation knows that the Loyalists in Spain and the Abraham Lincoln Brigade were definitely one-hundred-per-cent Communist outfits." Mr. Robert E. Stripling, the chief investigator, says to Alger Hiss, a witness, "You are an intelligent person and not naïve enough that you wouldn't know a Communist if you saw one." (This simple visual test for political belief may well prove invaluable to future poll takers.) The lamented Mr. Vail says, "In the interest of the accuracy of the record . . . the picture to which I refer was a picture of Karl Marx instead of Joe Stalin." Mr. F. Edward Hébert, States' Rights Democrat, of Louisiana, says, "It is interesting to note that every time we talk about Communism we hear about Columbia University . . . and I think General Eisenhower has a big thing to do to clean that place up." Mr. John E. Rankin, States' Rights Democrat, of Mississippi, is one of the first members of the cast to establish his character in the mind of the reader. He says to Miss Bentley, in extracting from the shadow-walker an anatomy of Communism, "In other words, it is nothing but a system of abject slavery, dominated by a racial minority that has seized control, as members of the Politburo; is that correct?" Miss Bentley balks slightly. "I am not clear about the racial minority," she says. "I am," says Mr. Rankin.

Rankin continues, at every opportunity, to shake his particular bauble. "I know the Senate is busy now nagging the white people of the South, and all of the F.E.P.C. and all this Communistic bunk," he says. When he hears from Whittaker Chambers, a witness, that Hiss is head of what the witness called the Carnegie Foundation for World Peace, Rankin, under an evident misapprehension about Hiss's origin, says, "Under the New York F.E.P.C. law you can't ask this man whether he is a Communist or not, or where he came from, or what his name was before it was changed. [Hiss comes from Baltimore and his name has always been Hiss.] You can't even ask for his photograph. Of course, he can get into an institution of that kind in New York, but he couldn't in Mississippi." Rankin receives some coöperation from the chief Dogberry of the Committee, Mr. Stripling. "I have a document here which shows the employment history of Lee Pressman," Stripling says. Mr. Karl E. Mundt, Republican, of South Dakota (he has since been promoted to the Senate by the voters of his state), says, "Will you identify the document, please?" Mr. Stripling answers, "It is *Who's Who.*" Rankin, rising to his cue, then asks, "*Who's Who in American Jewry*, isn't it?," and Mr. Stripling responds, "Yes, *Who's Who in American Jewry,*" after which he reads approximately the same list of Pressman's jobs that he could have read from an ordinary *Who's Who in America,* the natural place to look for such information. (It is likely that if the Committee continues to function, Rankin will be its dominant figure.)

Mr. Hébert has his own pet thought, to which he returns often—the value of stool pigeons. For example, at one point he says to Chambers, an ex-spy by his own admission, "Isn't it a fact that there are many saints in Heaven today who were not always saints?," and when Chambers replies devoutly, "I believe so," Hébert continues, "We would not take their sainthood away from them after they have become saints and repented, not saying, you understand, that you are a saint, now mind you." Chambers replies, modestly, "I am not a saint, indeed." The regretted Mr. McDowell, striving to understand the unproved depravity of Mr. Hiss, says, "Well, this Mr. Hiss has a very similar background to my own. . . . He was a brilliant young man." The comics scuffle a little among themselves, seeming to give away a bit of the plot line when Mr. Rankin objects to a turn the inquiry is taking, and Chairman J. Parnell Thomas, Republican, of New Jersey (more recently himself under investigation by the Department of Justice, for simony), says, "We have been unearthing your New Dealers for two years, and for eight years before that."

I WAS a fairly assiduous reader of the newspapers all during the Committee's hearings, but I do not remember seeing any of the above excerpts from the stenographic transcript except the crack about *Who's Who in American Jewry,* which made the Q.-and-A. section of a *Journal-American* story. Some of the quips, to be sure, were offered in executive sessions and so were not at the time available to the press, but this official printed record has been out for a couple of weeks now, and I have not seen in any newspaper an attempt to re-create the atmosphere of the hearings as a continuing performance. This lack of continuity, I think, is one of the grave flaws in newspaper presentation of almost every kind of happening.

The most arresting statement in all the hearings, to my notion, never, I believe, got into the public prints. It is conceivable that because it was uttered in a closed session, on September 8th, it did not reach any of the newspapers immediately, although information about what went on in closed sessions was steadily leaking out. I suppose that by the time it could have been officially made common knowledge, by the publication of the record, editors regarded something that happened on September 8th as ancient history. At any rate, the statement, which may be ancient and certainly is historic, was made by Chairman Thomas to a lawyer named Maurice Braverman, who was appearing before the Committee as counsel for a witness. The Chairman ordered the attorney to become a witness himself, on the spot. Braverman said, "I have a right to be represented by counsel, if I appear here as a witness. I have not been subpoenaed." Mr. Thomas then said, for the ages, "The rights you have are the rights given you by this Committee. We will determine what rights you have got and what rights you have not got before this Committee." Braverman declined to be bluffed. His testimony, which he offered next day, after having been duly subpoenaed, had small importance. But Thomas had tipped his hand.

An alert editor reading Thomas's lawless declaration might have contrasted it with another passage in the record, on page 926, in which Frank Coe, a former Treasury official charged by the publicity-anguished Miss Bentley with belonging to a Communist group, asked if he might question his accuser. Congressman Mundt, acting as chairman in Thomas's stead, told Mr. Coe, "Had we the full authority of a court, certainly it would be easier to get down into the disputed evidence in this particular case. Since we do not have, we cannot adapt ourselves to part of the rules of a court without having the authority that goes with being a court. Unfortunately, we cannot accept your request . . . we do not have the authority." These pronouncements would seem to represent what it is now fashionable to call a dichotomy. The confusion of a newspaper editor—and of his readers, to whose attention, one would think, he would feel bound to call this contradiction—would be intensified by reading certain remarks of Mr. Hébert, recorded on pages 846 and 847. Addressing A. George Silverman, another witness, Hébert said, "Dr. Silverman, you are now before the greatest open court in this country, I believe, beyond the confines of any limited courtroom in this country." Silverman, a witness who, when he refused to answer the investigators, said that he did so "in the exercise of my constitutional privilege against self-incrimination under the Fifth Amendment," asked advice of counsel before responding to a question. Upon this occasion, Mr. Hébert said, "You didn't ask advice of counsel before handing these documents to Miss Bentley, did you? [The problem before the Committee, of course, was whether Silverman *had* handed over documents to Miss Bentley.] Miss Bentley has made these charges, and you are familiar with them. Now you have your opportunity in open court." (Mr. Thomas, incidentally, appearing before a Federal Grand Jury in Washington on November 4th in connection with the Justice Department's charge of corruption against him, refused to answer questions on the ground that he might incriminate *him*self. The United States District Attorney's comment on this tactic is not available.) The anomaly of a committee that describes itself as the greatest open court in the country on page 846, no court at all on page 926, and omnipotent . . . might fairly have been considered worthy of bringing to the attention of a bemused public.

THE tangled story of the relationship of Alger Hiss and Whittaker Chambers probably resulted in more headlines than did any other development of the inquiry. Nevertheless, an examination of the files shows that even this was erratically reported. (Again, the dailies might well point out that their reporters could not be expected to know what was occurring in closed sessions, and I, in turn, again point out that that is all the more reason for clarification after "Hearings" was published.) The newspapers, for example, gave me the impression that Hiss had not indicated that he recognized Chambers until the evening of August 17th. Then, as I got it from the press, Hiss walked into a closed session of the Committee at the Hotel Commodore, here in New York, looked at Chambers, and said, "That is the man I knew by the name of George Crosley." According to Chambers, Hiss had known him simply as "Carl." Chambers' story sounded fantastic; as the late Harry Dexter White, also accused by Chambers, had phrased it, "I doubt very much whether I would have known any man by just the first name. It would have been very peculiar." But the tale of Hiss's lightning-flash recognition of Chambers as "George Crosley" seemed even less plausible. The record shows, however, that Hiss had already, on August 16th, at an executive session in Washington, told the Committee that he thought Chambers might be a deadbeat he had known by the name of George Crosley, and had told them why.

The transcripts of the August 16th and August 17th hearings are, I should say, the best theatrical material in the book (with the possible exception of White's triumphant appearance before the Committee on August 13th, when that old government servant, dying of heart disease, handled the Committee men like a Border collie maneuvering sheep). "I have written a name on this pad in front of me of a person whom I knew in 1933 and 1934 who not only spent some time in my house but sublet my apartment," Mr. Hiss tells the Committee on the sixteenth. "If I hadn't seen the morning papers with an account of statements that he knew the inside of my house, I don't think I would even have thought of his name. I want to see Chambers face to face and see if he can be this individual." There follow a couple of pages of dialogue in which Hiss protests at the balancing of his evidence with that of Chambers, whom he refers to as "a confessed former Communist and traitor to his country." Hébert produces a variant of his familiar speech about stool pigeons and saints. "Some of the greatest saints in history were pretty bad before they were saints," he says this time. "Are you going to take away their sainthood because of their previous lives?"

Then on the same day, page 955 of the record, Hiss says, "The name of the man I brought in—and he may have no relation to the whole nightmare—is George Crosley." Hiss goes on to tell the story of his acquaintance with an unsuccessful free-lance writer who lived for a couple of months in 1935 in an apartment in Washington that Hiss happened to have on his hands. There follows a considerable amount of question-and-answer, all of it amicable, about Hiss's domestic arrangements circa 1934, and a discussion of lie detectors (it was proposed that Hiss submit to a test by one), which Hiss says he has been informed have no sound scientific justification—that they show "emotion, not truth, and I am perfectly willing to say that I am not lacking in emotion about this business." Chairman Thomas tells him that the Committee has decided to hold a public hearing on August 25th, at which Hiss will be given an opportunity to confront Chambers. Hiss says, "May I ask a question about the press?" Thomas says, a little incoherently, "Yes. I want to tell you something. Every person in this room with the exception of yourself has stood up and raised his right hand and taken an oath that he will not divulge one single word of testimony given here this afternoon, questions asked, so I am going to ask you to take the same oath." Hiss agrees to make no public statements about the hearing, although there is no effort to make him take a formal oath to that effect. The New York *Times* the next morning reported, "Mr. Hiss left the committee room this evening refusing to comment on his long session with the committee."

The next session of the Committee was not a public meeting, nor was it on August 25th. It was the closed session at the Commodore, in New York, late the following day, August 17th. The transcript of it reads like the second act of a taut play. Hiss enters, obviously furious. "I would like the record to show," he says, "that on my way downtown from my uptown office, I learned from the press of the death of Harry White, which came as a great shock to me." (This, by the way, is the only mention, in the whole of the record's eight hundred and seventy-eight pages, of Mr. White's death three days after his appearance before the Committee. The Committee took no official cognizance of it.) "I would like to make one further comment," Hiss continues. "Yesterday I think I witnessed—in any event I was told that those in the room were going to take an oath of secrecy. . . . I would like this record to show at this stage that the first thing I saw in the morning paper, the *Herald Tribune*, was a statement that the Committee yesterday had asked me if I would submit to a lie-detector test."

The dialogue of the Commodore session is decidedly acrimonious. For example, Mr. Richard M. Nixon, Republican, of California, says, "I think Mr. Chambers should be sworn." Hiss says, "That is a good idea." Nixon says, "Mr. Hiss, may I say something? I suggested that he be sworn, and when I say something like that I want no interruptions from you." Hiss then says, "Mr. Nixon, in view of what happened yesterday, I think there is no occasion for you to use that tone of voice in speaking to me, and I hope the record will show what I have just said." Farther along, Nixon asks Hiss to tell about the lease he gave Crosley. Hiss says he told about it the day before, when Chambers was not present. Nixon says, "We are repeating it for his [Chambers'] benefit as well as to see if he can recall this incident." Hiss says, "I am glad he has no other way of finding out about it, Mr. Nixon." Later, Hiss says, "The ass under the lion's skin is Crosley." Chambers says, "I was a Communist and you were a Communist." As the men positively identify each other, the record notes, "At this point Mr. Hiss arose and walked in the direction of Mr. Chambers." Hiss says, "May I say, for the sake of the record at this point, that I would like to invite Mr. Whittaker Chambers to make those same statements out of the presence of this committee without their being privileged for suit for libel. I challenge you to do it and I hope you will do it damned quickly." To judge from the dialogue (there is no stage direction here), Mr. Louis J. Russell, a Committee investigator, gets between Hiss and Chambers, and Russell and Hiss have an argument about who is touching whom—a near scuffle, apparently. McDowell, Nixon, and Stripling try to persuade Hiss that Chambers need make no statement outside the hearing room. Nixon says, "You will recall that he [Chambers] testified that he did make these statements to Mr. Berle in 1939 concerning you, and he testified also that he made them to Mr. Levine. Those statements, both to Mr. Levine and Mr. Berle, would not be privileged." In point of fact, Chambers' statements to Mr. Berle in 1939 were so much milder than his statements to the Committee in 1948 that they would have afforded no possible basis for a libel suit, even if they were not by now outlawed by the statute of limitations. Berle testified on August 30th that in 1939 Chambers "did not make the direct statement that any of these men were members of the Communist Party" and that "there was no espionage involved in it." For a person reading the record merely as a play, the statements of the Committee people in their attempt to stall Hiss should stimulate a certain amount of curiosity as to their motivation. Chambers, on a radio program, has since repeated a part, although not all, of his original charge against Hiss, and the latter is now suing him for seventy-five thousand dollars.

Chambers testified before the Committee that Hiss was a Communist and a member of a group that had espionage as "one of its eventual objectives." On the radio, he made no mention of espionage.

THE proceedings in these two executive sessions—as rattling good, meaty scenes as any playwright could turn out—were made available in full to the press on August 25th, at the suggestion of Hiss. But no New York newspaper printed them. One gathers from a reading of this volume the impression that a reputable witness before the Thomas Committee is in the position of a man spattered with dirty water by a passing taxicab on a rainy day. If he is angry enough, he may run after the taxi, but by the time he gets to the corner, it is five blocks away, splashing somebody else.

It was poor Mr. White, the most sympathetic character in the Committee's drama, who commented best on the newspapers' handling of the hearings. Congressman Mundt said, while White was on the stand, "In the best court of this country, which is the court of public opinion, which—"

White cut in, "If it is properly presented, Congressman Mundt. If the whole story is presented, I agree with you."

The Congressman said, "Now, I am referring, you understand—"

Mr. White, completing his own thought, said, "And the public could read something beside the headlines, Congressman Mundt, you know that, as well as I."

Until newspapers and public adopt Mr. White's program, books such as this record are indispensable to an understanding of our time.

20
London Terrace and the Wild West

I DO NOT REMEMBER any other two people who posthumously became so thoroughly well known in so short a space of time as Norma Holt and her husband, Emory, who shot and killed her and a man named David Chambers Whittaker and himself in Whittaker's sixteenth-floor, one-and-a-half-room apartment, in the southwest corner of London Terrace, at nine-thirty on the evening of March 9th. By this, I do not mean merely that the names of the couple suddenly popped into headlines because of the spectacular nature of Mr. Holt's crime, word of which reached police here by way of a telephone call from Mrs. Holt's mother, in California. My point is that the public learned, almost simultaneously with the news of the killings, what the Holts' last weeks of life had been like—what occupied their minds, what sort of place they lived in, where they ate and what they drank, what Mr. Holt believed Mrs. Holt was doing, what a private detective reported to him that she was doing, and what Mr. Holt wanted done with his body. Both the Holts belonged in a category that is perhaps larger than one supposes—that of people who keep diaries. Mr. and Mrs. Holt's diaries, together with the detective's reports, an angry note the wife had written to her husband, and the latter's instructions about the disposal of his body were all found by the police in the couple's apartment, at 145 Henry Street, in Brooklyn Heights, after the shooting. Only Whittaker was inarticulate in death. From time to time in the past, there has been some dispute about whether newspapers should publish stories of homicide in minute detail (*Izvestia* and the *Christian Science Monitor* agree in not mentioning crimes of passion at all), but, as a fascinated reader, I should have regretted any omission from the story of the Holts.

The shooting happened within a couple of hours of a train robbery on the Baltimore & Ohio Railroad, near Martinsburg, West Virginia, and the result was a brief domination of front pages by crime news, as I became aware when I picked up the late city edition of the *Times* on the morning of March 10th. The headline over the first column at the top of the front page was devoted to the battue at London Terrace, while another, over the second and third columns, called attention to the train robbery. The first headline read:

3 DIE IN "TRIANGLE";
ALARM GIVEN HERE
FROM CALIFORNIA
WIFE SHOT DOWN BY HUSBAND AS SHE
TALKS TO MOTHER IN HOLLYWOOD
HE THEN SLAYS FRIEND
FINAL SHOT ENDS HIS OWN LIFE IN
APARTMENT IN LONDON TERRACE—
POLICE BAFFLED

This was a pretty complete synopsis of the story, except that the police, for once, had had nothing to be baffled about. An anonymous *Times* rewrite man, after saying in his lead that police thought the crime "an astonishing version of the hackneyed theme of 'the eternal triangle,'" evidently felt that he had been too concise and, a few paragraphs down in his story, stated, "The tragedy, so far as the police could put it together, had some unexplained aspects, on which they could only speculate. . . . One of the speculations was that perhaps Mr. Holt had been enraged over some sort of relationship between Mr. Whittaker and his wife."

The *Times* headline introducing the railroad story read:

4 ROB ALL ON B. & O. TRAIN
IN WEST VIRGINIA AND ESCAPE
CHEF OF THE AMBASSADOR IS SHOT,
OTHERS ABUSED IN "WILD WEST"
HOLD-UP—BANDITS TAKE ALL
MONEY BUT SPURN JEWELRY

This again was a fairly good summary of what had happened, although it later turned out that there had been only two robbers. I think, however, that most New Yorkers reading the subhead probably assumed that it was the chef of the Ambassador Hotel, on Park Avenue, who had been shot, and not, as happened to be the case, a cook on the train called the Ambassador, which runs between Baltimore and Detroit and is practically unknown here.

In dealing with the Holt case, the *Mirror* displayed no *Times*-like doubt about the murderer's motivation. Its headline, spread all across the front page, read, "ENGINEER SLAYS WIFE, LOVER, SELF." The policemen to whom its reporter had talked were of a more forthright breed than the *Times*' informants. "Police said Holt shot his attractive brunette wife and Whittaker at the end of a futile 'showdown' discussion," the *Mirror* declared, "and he fired the first three shots as he stood at the phone, with his mother-in-law, Mrs. Elsie Thomas, at the other end of the line in her Hollywood home." The *Times* headline and story had the wife at the phone when the shots were fired. The *Times* reported that Whittaker and Mrs. Holt had each been shot once, and Mr. Holt twice. The *Mirror* reported that each of the victims had been shot twice and that the husband had killed himself with a single bullet. "One lifeless hand held a .38 calibre pistol," said the *Mirror*. "Five shots had been fired from it." The *News* headline read, "SLAYS HIS WIFE, RIVAL AND SELF," and the story, agreeing with the *Mirror* that Holt had been at the phone when he began to shoot, said that he had fired six shots into his wife and Whittaker, then one into himself—a total of seven. The *Herald Tribune* story ("KILLING OF 3 HERE HEARD ON PHONE IN CALIFORNIA"), written by John H. Durston, took a midway position between the *Times* and *Mirror*. Mr. Durston reported that police only "guessed" that the meeting had been arranged by Holt for a showdown, but he used the expression "triangle tragedy" *without* quotation marks. He, too, was a five-shot man. The *Times* and *Tribune*, in identifying the weapon, respectively, as a .38 calibre pistol and a nine-millimetre Luger, were in agreement as to its size. The *Journal-American* made it a .59 millimetre pistol, which would have a muzzle about as big as a hypodermic needle—or, if the decimal point was a mistake, the size of a small cannon. Such discrepancies, real or apparent, add to the excitement of a first-day crime story, making you feel as if you were learning about an event from an excited crowd in the street.

The story of the small massacre, as set forth in the four morning newspapers, was essentially simple, but it had one extraordinary feature—the telephone calls. Toward nine o'clock on the evening of March 9th, in Whittaker's apartment, Holt, a North Carolinian by birth who was an officer in the merchant marine during the war and had since then been a chief engineer on large ships, presumably produced the pistol and announced to his wife and Whittaker that he was going to shoot them. All three were nice-looking people in their early thirties. Mrs. Holt and Whittaker sat side by side on a sofa, and Holt evidently confronted them, covering them with the pistol. (On the day after the shooting, a woman reporter on the Post recorded that it was a rose-colored sofa, that the room had gray walls, and that Holt was found slumped in a blue lounge chair. The morning papers hadn't tried to be chromatic. None of the papers, I noted in passing, described Whittaker's place as "chic," "swank," or "lavishly furnished;" the story had no need of a buildup.) Before Holt opened fire, he put in a telephone call, or permitted his wife to put in a call, to his mother-in-law, Mrs. Thomas, in Hollywood, where it was still afternoon. Husband and wife spoke to her, explaining the situation. According to Mrs. Thomas, as quoted in a United Press dispatch from Hollywood, Holt spoke last. She tried to talk him out of killing her daughter, but he said, "It's too late, Mama," and then, according to the United Press, she heard three shots, or, according to the *Times*, four. She could get no further response from Holt, so she telephoned to a Mrs. Githens, a friend in New York who she was sure would know Whittaker's address. The Holts, it seems, had told her that they were at Whittaker's but hadn't told her where Whittaker lived. The *Tribune* and *Mirror* said that Mrs. Thomas's next step was to call New York Police Headquarters; the *Times* and *News* had the detail of the call to Mrs. Githens. Later, it was established that Mrs. Thomas had called Mrs. Githens, found out Whittaker's address from her, and *then* called Headquarters and told the police to go to London Terrace.

There was no explanation of why Holt had called Mrs. Thomas, and I still catch myself wondering about that. Had he something against her, too, or did he simply need an audience for what he may have thought of as the great, Wagnerian finale of his until then obscure life? And suppose, in the latter case, the long-distance operator had reported "no answer." Would he have postponed the execution or called up somebody else? Mrs. Thomas's resourceful presence of mind also impressed me.

In view of the morning papers' performance, I was not surprised to find the afternoon *Journal-American's* Latest News Edition (on the streets at 10 A.M.) giving its entire first page to crime, with the exception of a quarter of a column about a lockout of ten thousand Railway Express workers and a front-office box advertising three features in the following Sunday's paper. The features were articles entitled "Heartbreaks of Society," "Case of the Broadway Butterfly," and "My Faith," the last by Bailey Willis, professor emeritus of geology at Leland Stanford University. I am sorry to say I missed them. The *World-Telegram* had the killings and the train robbery all over the upper half of its front page, except for one column that was given to the trial of Axis Sally for treason. The expressmen's-lockout story got onto the lower portion of the page, and so did the scratches at Gulfstream Park, Sunshine Park, Oaklawn, and New Orleans. The *Telegram* carried an eight-column streamer reading, "BARE TRIPLE KILLER'S LOVE VIGIL," and followed this up with two stories under the subheads "Diary of Vengeance Noted Fatal Trysts" and "Jealous Husband Kept Tabs for Weeks on Wife."

The accent by this time was, of course, all on the documents the Holts had left lying about their Henry Street apartment. (Incidentally, it was in the first-day story in the four-star edition of the *News,* which goes to press an hour later than any other morning newspaper but still appears before daylight, that I first read about the couple's diaries.) Reporters also discovered there a pen-and-ink portrait of Mrs. Holt of the kind that rapid-sketch artists make at open-air art shows. It displayed the face of a young woman with a square jaw, a cupid's-bow mouth, and shoulder-length hair. Both the *Journal* and the *World-Telegram* used it. In the *Post's* description of the Holts' home, I read, "The apartment, in a well-kept building in a fashionable neighborhood, was filthy. Mrs. Holt's clothing was strewn about the place. Twenty pairs of her shoes were heaped in a closet. There were numerous jewel boxes. Dust was thick. One of the two bedrooms had been used to store long-emptied beer bottles, newspapers, trash." The *Journal* drew its own conclusions from the appearance of the place. "That Holt arrived at the decision to have a showdown with Whittaker and his wife only after days of drinking was indicated by the bottles that cluttered the 4½ room apartment," it said. "There were four empty whiskey bottles and 20 empty beer bottles in the littered kitchen. Dirty glasses stood everywhere. . . . Police deduced that either Holt or his wife had been preparing to leave from the fact that one room, empty of furniture, was piled with suitcases that were fully packed."

It appeared that in this disintegrating household, inhabited by two people too preoccupied to heed their surroundings, Holt had sat writing in his diary, playing classical records on the phonograph, and waiting for reports from the private-detective agency he had retained, all the time working away on the whiskey. His wife, his diary entries indicated, came home only when she needed a change of clothes or a few hours' sleep. In the apartment building, afternoon-newspaper reporters found a communicative doctor and his mother, who had been close friends of the Holts for six years. (The Holts married in 1943 and immediately moved into the Henry Street building.) Until this year, the doctor and his mother said, the couple had appeared to like each other. It was only after Holt's return from a voyage in January that he had become suspicious that his wife might be having what the tabloids call an "office romance." Mrs. Holt was secretary to the president of a camera company on West Twenty-third Street, or, according to the *Mirror,* was in its "stenographers' pool." Mr. Whittaker was that stock figure of tabloid *feuilletons,* a handsome executive in the same company. "Office romance" is one of those terms, like "stenographers' pool," of white-collar language, which is now a recognized form of sub-speech, along with ballpark or automobile lingo. As for "showdown," originally taken over from poker, it now has a distinctly sexual connotation in this patois. It is what couples have when they decide to "break up."

The reports of Holt's private detective may well have been the direct cause of the slaughter. It costs forty dollars to engage a private detective for an eight-hour day. The operative assigned to the Holt case had a habit of knocking off around midnight, leaving the "subject" (Mrs. Holt) and the "male subject" (Whittaker) in potentially adulterous situations. Holt, reading the detective's reports, wandered vicariously about the city with his wife and the other man—from the camera company to the faded, turn-of-the-century grandeur of the Prince George Hotel, and from there to the dimly lighted, *schmalzig* atmosphere of the Penthouse Club, on Central Park South—always remaining on the pavement outside the places they went to and going home before they emerged. He stood vicariously outside a telephone booth in a restaurant at 182 Fifth Avenue while Mrs. Holt made "a ten-minute telephone call." The call, reported by the detective in the clipped, ominous style of an agent who wants to show he is doing something for his money, may have been to a friend of Mrs. Holt's in the camera firm's stenographers' pool, but to Holt, reading the report in the dirty apartment, it presumably had only one meaning. The detective never gave him anything definite enough to get a divorce on, merely enough to make him feel sure that he was right.

Some of the newspapers mentioned that the detective signed his reports with a code number—S-12—but none of them used his name or that of the agency whose bill or letterhead must certainly have been on Holt's person or hidden someplace around the apartment. Nor did any of the papers give the reason for this discretion. To an outside observer, it would seem that a commercial detective agency has no more right to protection from possibly unfavorable publicity than, let us say, London Terrace or 145 Henry Street. Personally, I should like to know whether the police withheld the name of the agency or whether the papers knew it but didn't use it, and, in either case, why.

COMPARED to the Holt-Whittaker affair, the Great Train Robbery, as the *World-Telegram* headlined it, turned out to be rather lightweight stuff, but it afforded a nice study in automatic word association, and also in the unreliability of witnesses when something happens in a hell of a hurry. All four morning newspapers on March 10th referred to the Wild West in their leads on the robbery. All four, moreover, reported that there were four criminals, although it soon developed that there had been but two. There were in fact, however, only three accounts of the robbery in the four papers, since both the *Herald Tribune* and the *Mirror* used an Associated Press dispatch from Martinsburg. This began, "Two gunmen in a melodramatic holdup reminiscent of Wild West days robbed everybody aboard a Baltimore & Ohio express train near here tonight, shot one person, and slugged several others. . . . They were joined by two accomplices and escaped in a car stolen from a nearby night club." The *Times* carried a special story from Martinsburg, which started off, "Four young men, waving pistols in the fashion of the old Wild West, held up the Ambassador Limited of the Baltimore & Ohio Railroad here this evening. . . . Two of the gunmen were said by passengers to have boarded the train as coach passengers at Washington. . . . These were the only men who took part in the holdup of the cars, the other two robbers not joining in the operation until later, when they held up the engine crew." The two gunmen, it was subsequently determined, had in truth boarded the train at Washington, but they were the only two in the robbery, having held up the passengers and then the trainmen. The Martinsburg correspondent, having committed himself to the four-man theory, explained the presence of the third and fourth men by writing, "Where the second two of the four bandits boarded the train was not certain, but it was believed that they had awaited the others at Martinsburg, or perhaps had been beside the tracks at Warm Springs, about two miles from Martinsburg, where the train was finally halted on a grade crossing and delayed for an hour and forty minutes." The story had its four men staying together as, upon leaving the train, they continued their depredations. "All four men appeared to have taken part in the holdup of the Clover Rail Night Club," the correspondent reported concerning this phase of their activities.

"Four gunmen employing the old Wild West technique held up the Baltimore & Ohio's Ambassador Limited near here tonight, shot one person and slugged five others," the *News's* special story from Martinsburg began. It was so close a paraphrase of the lead in the *Times* that I thought it possible that the two papers might have been relying upon the same West Virginia correspondent. "F.B.I. agents said the desperadoes, brandishing .45s, got between $800 and $3,000 from the passengers," the *News* continued, without explaining how the F.B.I. men got into the case. "The four gunmen escaped in a stolen car. . . . Not long after this robbery the quartet held up the Clover Rail Night Club." If the correspondent was the same, he favored the *News* with one bit of information he did not give the *Times*. "The careful planning of the gunmen was evident," the *News* story said, "when James Graham, B. & O. agent at Connellsville, Pa., explained that there are three trains which arrive at Martinsburg within a half hour of each other, all going west. The Capitol gets in at 7 p.m., the Columbian at 7.10, and the Ambassador at 7.24. If either the Capitol or the Columbian had been held up and stopped, the next train would have crashed into it. But after the Ambassador there is no other westbound train until 10.19. The fellows who held up the train had studied their schedules." On the day after the holdup, the *World-Telegram* ("Great Train Robbery") correctly reduced the quartet to a duet, calling them "Jesse James-type bandits." This was in a U.P. story. An A.P. story in the *Sun* made the atmospheric point twice by reporting that the train "was robbed in true Wild West fashion. Jesse James and his cronies would have been proud of the technic." The *Sun* also quoted a railroad-police official as saying that there hadn't been a train robbery like that since frontier days—anyway, not in the thirty years he had been in service—which was probably correct.

By the time the early-afternoon papers were on the New York streets, the two young hoodlums who had robbed the train had been arrested, and not without a bit of trouble. Two policemen caught them in a pawnshop in Washington, whither they had travelled from Martinsburg by bus, having first wrecked an automobile that they had stolen. One showed fight, and a policeman shot him. This gave New York papers new leads on the story, but it was still Wild West stuff to two of them. "A Washington cop with a Destry-quick draw today shot one and collared the second of two badmen who held up a B. & O. express in the 'Wild West' country near Martinsburg, W. Va., last night," the *Post* story began, and the *World-Telegram* lead spoke of "Two zoot-suited train robbers who held up a Baltimore & Ohio streamliner in Wild West style." Later in the day, the hoodlum who had not been shot admitted that he and his friend had held up the train, netting less than six hundred dollars. He explained that they had been drinking in the club car and had become angry at the steward because they didn't like the way the liquor tasted. So they had opened their suitcases, taken out the revolvers they apparently carried as standard equipment, like hairbrushes, and held up the train, entirely without premeditation. I thought it made a much more amusing story that way, but the newspapers apparently felt let down. The *World-Telegram* ran an editorial complaining about the quality of our only two contemporary train robbers, and the *Herald Tribune* said they were just roughnecks.

21
Another Parable

JEAN PAULHAN, the French critic, wrote for a clandestine paper during the Resistance a short parable called "The Bee." The bee that stings dies, Paulhan observed, but if individual bees could not be depended upon to sting when attacked, their species would have become extinct long since. The mystique of the apparently useless act of courage is a subject that has, naturally enough, preoccupied postwar French writers more than it has their colleagues here, where the most severe test normally put upon a writer's fortitude is a request to let his name be used on the letterhead of an unpopular committee. When Will Cuppy, the humorist, died last September, one of the obituaries reprinted some lines he had once written about a fish called the stickleback: "The three-spined stickleback . . . when swallowed by a perch erects his sharp spines and kills the swallower. This does not help the stickleback much. He is still swallowed." This dismissal of the stickleback's sacrifice is an example of unreflective individualism run riot. The stickleback in killing its swallower helps all other sticklebacks by maintaining the ratio of sticklebacks to perch in a given pond. My familiarity with apiaries and ponds being negligible, I do not presume to say whether any bee or stickleback ever thought the problem out and set a course for its co-specimens, but there seems never to have been any doubt on the part of the respective beasts that their reactions are all for the best.

The problem for the French intellectual between 1940 and 1945 was less easily resolved. The very clarity and good sense that had been celebrated for centuries as the hallmarks of French thought acted to hinder him from risking his life when there was no prospect of immediate resulting gain to anybody. The decision was harder to make than any a soldier is called upon to make in formal war, because the individual was free to refrain entirely from the struggle without incurring any penalty, even that of social disapproval. His participation or non-participation remained secret in any case. The dilemma, sometimes explicit, sometimes in the form of parable, has left its mark on the most distinguished French writing of the forties. Camus has treated it three times, at least—once negatively, in "The Stranger," a novel about a man who couldn't feel any rapport with other people; once philosophically, in "The Myth of Sisyphus," in which he extolled, a trifle mystically, the man who is impelled to keep on pushing the rock, although he knows it must roll back; and, finally and most impressively, in "The Plague," in which the decent men of a city band together to fight a plague against which they can do nothing effectual. In "The Plague," the journalist, trapped by the quarantine on the city, symbolizes the quandary of the intellectual everywhere. He plans to escape to his love in the outside world; then, when he has perfected his plans, he changes his mind and remains to assume his share of quixotic responsibility. In one of Vercors's more notable stories, a man returns from a German concentration camp at the end of the war, broken in spirit. He confides to a friend that in the camp he was forced to dump corpses into an incinerator. Once, wheeling a dismal burden along, he saw the apparent corpse move. Under the revolvers of the guards, he dumped the living man anyhow. He could not have saved him; any gesture of protest he might have made would have resulted in his own death. Nevertheless, he feels himself soiled forever. The assumption or refusal of responsibility, when it means torture and death, is also one of Sartre's most frequently repeated themes. The dilemma has become almost a convention of modern French writing, but it has so far proved unacceptable here. Read in this country, a story of a man who hates himself for his failure to die seems practically as academic as the motivations of the characters in "The Cid" or "Antigone."

Sidney Hook, writing in a recent issue of the *Partisan Review,* even denies that there was such a dilemma. "Despite the myths and legends which sprang up after the liberation, there was not much of a Resistance movement to the Nazis in France," Hook says. "The Resistance consisted of a handful around De Gaulle, the Jews, and, after June 22, 1941, the Communists." This imputes to the writers of France a mass hallucination, and also a disproportionately high casualty rate. If there really was "not much of a Resistance movement" in the country at large, it is surely odd that Marc Bloch, the historian; Jean Prévost, the most brilliant of Stendhalists; and Jacques Decour, the novelist, suffered death for their parts in it.

Hook's reluctance to accept the postulated situation is symptomatic, however, and it is unlikely that "The Witness" (Pantheon), a brief novel by Jean Bloch-Michel, effectively translated by Eithne Wilkins, will impress even as many American readers as did "The Plague," which was aided by a Defoe-like paraphernalia of macabre realism. Bloch-Michel's exposition of the common dilemma is a parable that is so bare of sensual images that it seems a trifle disembodied. His reply to this probably would be that such "furniture" (to use Stendhal's term for unessential detail) merely gets in the way of thought. But even Stendhal admitted that he sometimes underfurnished a story.

The narrator and chief figure in the tale, a young intellectual who grew up between wars, has permitted himself to survive first his brother and then his wife, neither of whom he could have saved but with either of whom he could have died had he so wished. He tells his story in the form of a long letter to a casual acquaintance, with this prefatory explanation: "If I turn to you, it is precisely because you don't know anything about me, and so I shall have to explain what I am." He tells how he let his brother Michel drown in a choppy sea three-quarters of a mile offshore. He attempted to bring Michel in, but, realizing that if he did not leave him, both would drown, he left him. He became the lover and then the husband of Claude, Michel's old sweetheart. They made their home in Lyon, where he taught history in a secondary school. He tried to shut the outside world from his consciousness and live only in the love of Claude, who mothered him. The Munich crisis, the *drôle de guerre,* the juvenile patriotism of his pupils seemed to him only so many aggressions of society against him.

The writer of the letter gave up his school post to take a job as a publisher's translator, so that he could escape from his pupils. But Claude, much as she loved him, could not withhold herself from life. She took part in the Resistance. One evening, the narrator arrived home at their suburban cottage and found two men who were plainly Gestapo agents leading Claude away. On a previous occasion, he had seen Gestapo agents brutally arrest two Frenchmen, and the sight frightened him. "I saw her turn her head in my direction," the narrator records. "I had a vague glimpse of her face. I could have been with her in a few minutes, have done something for her, protected her or shared her lot. Terror stopped me. At the time I thought I knew what the reason was: I was afraid of seeing the two men hurt

Claude, as I had seen them beat the two men they had arrested at Lyon. I believed that I simply wanted to avoid seeing something unbearable—and perhaps that really wasn't the reason why I didn't go to join Claude. If it was that, I don't think I have any cause to conceal it or be ashamed of it; but once again, among all the contradictory reasons driving me to act or preventing me from acting, the one I decided to choose was the one that justified my cowardice. And so not only did I not run toward her, I turned suddenly to the left, to hide behind our neighbor's cottage. A few seconds passed, and then I heard the car driving off."

After the war, the narrator tells his correspondent, he learned that Claude had died in Ravensbrück, the concentration camp for women, and he received a letter she had left with a woman friend to be given to him upon confirmation of her death. He had already condemned himself. Claude's letter concurred with his verdict. "What you hated in others was their virtue," she wrote. "And when that virtue actually took the form of courage, of choosing danger and accepting death, the sight of it was as loathsome to you as though it had been meant to convince you of your own cowardice and make you ashamed of it." At the end, the narrator writes that he is going to suppress "the last and most implacable witness" against himself—himself.

Bloch-Michel, according to the novel's jacket, was born in 1912, in Paris. He became a prisoner of war in 1940, escaped, joined the Resistance, was arrested, in Lyon, in 1944, and was imprisoned, tortured, and finally released. He is a friend and obviously a disciple of the even younger Camus. A review cited from *L'Aube,* the newspaper of Georges Bidault's Popular Republican Party, calls "The Witness" "a sober, chaste, immensely moving confession, of astonishing keenness of perception." It is chaste, despite a couple of sparse, explicit descriptions, and to me, at least, it is indicative of "an astonishing keenness of perception." Whether it proves "immensely moving," however, will, I fear, depend upon the reader's own conditioning, which means that it isn't a really first-class book, but just a good one.

There is a rather large group of Americans who will understand to the full the pain of the letter-writer in Bloch-Michel's tale. They are the men who in the stress of combat failed to do the impossible and have had trouble forgiving themselves. Others landed in Army psychiatric bases, shattered because, through no fault of their own (or through some minor fault, such as overstaying leave), they had not been in planes in which their everyday crewmates perished. They are like the blessed tank sergeant pulled out of the Channel on D Day, whose amphibious tank had been swamped, and whose first remark was, "If we hadn't mucked up, those other kids [the infantry on the beach] might not of been killed." The assumption of unlimited responsibility is a form of madness, but one to be admired. And rationalization is a fine thing, but easily susceptible of abuse. There was too much rationalization in France before the war ("Why die for Danzig?"), and now there is—among writers, at any rate—an exaltation of Sisyphus, the bee, and probably, if he exists in France, the stickleback.

22
Pyle Set the Style

LESS than three months ago, a four-hundred-and-twenty-eight-page biography of Ernie Pyle would have seemed as outdated as the word "foxhole." Yet the appearance now of "The Story of Ernie Pyle," by Lee G. Miller (428 pp., Viking), seems the result of a miracle of publishing prescience—a prescience our intelligence services unfortunately did not match. For there has been in the interim a revival of Pyle's subject matter.

This is an example of Pyle, from a 1943 column, quoted by Mr. Miller, who, as managing editor of the Scripps-Howard Newspaper Alliance, was the late correspondent's editor and one of his greatest admirers:

> The men are walking. They are fifty feet apart, for dispersal. Their walk is slow, for they are dead weary, as you can tell even when looking at them from behind. Every line and sag of their bodies speaks their inhuman exhaustion. On their shoulders and backs they carry heavy steel tripods, machine-gun barrels, leaden boxes of ammunition. Their feet seem to sink into the ground from the overload they are bearing. They don't slouch. It is the terrible deliberation of each step that spells out their appalling tiredness. Their faces are black and unshaven. They are young men, but the grime and whiskers and exhaustion make them look middle-aged. The line moves on, but it never ends. All afternoon men keep coming round the hill and vanishing eventually over the horizon. It is one long, tired line of ant-like men. There is an agony in your heart and you almost feel ashamed to look at them. They are just guys from Broadway and Main Street, but you wouldn't remember them. They are too far away now. They are too tired. Their world can never be known to you, but if you could see them just once, just for an instant, you would know that no matter how hard people work back home they are not keeping pace with these infantrymen in Tunisia.

Pyle Set the Style

The thin, old-looking reporter who was killed by a Japanese sniper on Ie Shima in April, 1945 (he was only forty-four, but to enlisted men he seemed as old as a senior admiral), contributed a stock figure to the waxworks gallery of American history as popularly remembered. To a list that includes the frontiersman, the Kentucky colonel, the cowboy, and Babe Ruth, Ernest Taylor Pyle, to give him the full name nobody ever called him by, added G.I. Joe, the suffering but triumphant American infantryman. The portrait was sentimentalized, but the soldier was pleased to recognize himself in it, and millions of newspaper readers recognized their sons and lovers in Pyle's soldiers and got some glimmer of the fact that war is a nasty business for the pedestrian combatant. Through millions of letters from home enclosing clippings, the soldiers learned that their folks read Ernie Pyle. He provided an emotional bridge. When he died, something like seven hundred papers were buying his column. I have no figures on Homer's syndication in Hellas, but he is reputed to have begged his bread, which Pyle, had he survived, would never have had to do. A substantial fraction of the readers of the seven hundred papers read nothing about the war but Pyle and the headlines. He was the only American war correspondent who made a large personal impress on the nation in the Second World War.

Ernie, whom I knew in Africa and France, had a profound capacity for self-pity—for which he had more reason than most—and a knack of projecting it. You could have been sleeping on the ground for a fortnight without thinking much about it, but when you read that he had slept on the ground, your bones ached. In 1940, before he had been to war, he wrote to a friend whose parents he had just visited, "Seeing my own folks—so old, so disappointed, so eager and helpless—and seeing your folks so exactly like my own—it kind of throws me. There is no sense to the struggle, and there is no choice but to struggle." He had intimations of goshawfulness.

Ernie took his writing seriously. I was about to say he sweated over every sentence when I remembered that he was never warm enough to sweat and complained almost continually of cold. He suffered acutely when he read clippings of his columns and noticed the editorial excision of a phrase. On such occasions, he damned the transatlantic Mr. Miller, who handled his copy personally. He had frequent doubts about the quality of his stuff and often demanded reassurance. After he was killed, near the end of the war, he became a fixed part of a historical period that appeared to have come to a close with the dropping of the first atomic bomb. The prototype of what was evidently to be the war correspondent of the future emerged in the person of William L. Laurence, the science expert of the New York *Times,* who rode in the plane that dropped the second atomic bomb, on Nagasaki. Mr. Laurence's erudition contrasted strongly with Ernie's highly emphasized simplicity, and it looked as if anybody who wanted to cover a future world conflict would need a degree from M.I.T. or Carnegie Tech. (Laurence is a Harvard man, but he has filled in the gaps in his education by extensive reading. Ernie, incidentally, was not so innocent of formal education as his folksiness implied; Miller says he got as far as the middle of his senior year at the University of Indiana, when he quit after he had been turned down by a coed. I would never have thought him so romantic.)

As of today, however, Pyle is the most imitated writer in America, just as he was in 1945. The newspapers are again full of G.I.s, front-line quotes, M-1s, and bazookas, and more than ever the individual combatant fights under the glaring light of publicity, since the ratio of correspondents to combatants in Korea is without parallel in the history of warfare. The Pyle influence was evident in the early dispatches of the men doing straight news stories of the Korean fighting; even while fleeing through rice paddies with invading tanks close behind, the correspondents found time to get the name, rank, and home town of every soldier they talked to. For example, a story by Tom Lambert, of the Associated Press, on July 12th quoted Lt. Edward James, of Columbus, Ga.; Pvt. Freddy Pickens, of Columbus, Miss.; Pvt. Robert Reed, of Michigan City, Ind. (who said he had had a carbine and then a rifle shot out of his hands); Pvt. Edward Rounds, of Thurman, N.Y.; Pvt. Tommy Bishop, of Quitman, Miss.; Pfc. Leon Wilson, of Sullivan, Ind.; Sgt. W. F. Wociechowski, of Chester, Pa.; and Pvt. Edwin L. Rowland, of Paducah, Ky. (who "nodded assent"). On July 5th, Marguerite Higgins, of the *Herald Tribune,* saw a "blond G.I." die and gave the occurrence intimate coverage. There was a general disposition to report war through the eyes or, more often, the spoken recollection of the soldiers themselves; this was, perhaps, inevitable at a time when there were only five hundred Americans in combat, according to our Korean headquarters. In such warfare, each soldier had the importance, in relation to the whole force engaged, of a war-strength regiment in the American Army of 1945, and the blond G.I.'s death was approximately equivalent to all the American casualties on the Norman D Day.

It was not until the last part of July that the more formal aspirants to the Pyle role began to arrive. Pyle's copy was aimed primarily at afternoon papers and was never spot news or "big picture." He wrote almost always about individual soldiers—including, sometimes, generals—and, most importantly, about himself. The afternoon-paper field in New York is limited and has been even more so this summer; if Pyle had been covering the Korean campaign, he would have had no New York outlet during the first nine weeks of the fighting, because he worked for the Scripps-Howard Newspaper Alliance, and the Scripps-Howard paper here, the *World-Telegram & Sun,* was closed down by the Newspaper Guild strike during all that time.

The two afternoon dailies to which this city was temporarily reduced—the *Post* and the *Journal-American*—have been represented by an average of one and a half Pyle-type war correspondents: the *Post* by Jimmy Cannon and the *Journal-American* by Frank Conniff and Bob Considine. Cannon, Conniff, and Considine, besides being alliterative, have a number of other qualities in common—they are Celtic, knowing, and representative of the Toots Shor, or man-about-town, school of journalism; Cannon is a sports columnist and Considine used to be. Their backgrounds place them at an initial disadvantage in the Pyle stint, for Ernie had spent six years before the war building up a reputation as an Average American. During that time, he produced a column that dealt mostly with subjects like the beauty of the Grand Canyon and the human qualities of human beings in all parts of Nebraska. But an even more serious handicap for his successors has been the repetitiousness of situations. This, for example, is Cannon, who got to Korea on July 18th, writing about soldiers coming around a bend there on August 2nd:

> The farther forward you go, the younger the troops are, but the older they look. All men age with fatigue, but these combat soldiers seemed abruptly deprived of their youth and stricken with crippling maturity just before they turned the bend in the road and came, stooped and shriveled with weariness, toward trucks which would transport them to a more dangerous sector of the front. . . . The act of dragging themselves on trucks seemed unbearably difficult for them, as though the blood in their young bodies had been frozen by the years. They were round-shouldered under the burden of their arms. Dirt turned to mud as sweat clotted on eyelids. Their ears were foul caves. Some of them wore goatees which didn't seem incongruous on their trouble-pinched faces but gave them the wizened

look of wise, sleepy, year-drugged old men. They were quiet—the very old are silent—transfixed by memories. . . . But they belong where you are. . . . Remember them not as dedicated men but as kids similar to the ones you know who are hurt by nothing more than the sickness of first love.

It is plain that Cannon is confronted with a problem. The last war ended only five years ago, and we are all in danger of becoming callous. But Cannon's soldier dialogue is more accurate than Pyle's, who was really good only on old draftees. (Cannon was an enlisted man, albeit a correspondent for soldier newspapers, for four years during the Second World War.) And on August 5th, he produced a column that shows he is not incapable of emotion.

Put this down as an hysterical piece written by a 41-year-old adolescent whose adult life has been concerned with games [he wrote]. Sports journalists are permanent residents of boyhood and we reject middle age to dwell as frightened aliens in a country of youth. . . . It is inconsequential now if a fight manager is a scoundrel, if Notre Dame will ever play Army, if Jake LaMotta will fight Ray Robinson for the middleweight championship. . . . What does it matter who got loaded in Shor's and what comedian they're knocking at Lindy's? . . . Remember this is not a USO war with actors telling their gags especially written for the occasion. It is a war in which generals use bazookas.

Conniff, as the campaign has worn on, has turned out some good columns, particularly one cowboy-and-Indian-style yarn about how tanks were menacing Pohang airfield, which the Air Force was soon to quit. But on August 7th, by which time he had arrived in the classic Pyle situation—"Conniff in a Fox Hole," the *Journal-American* labelled his story of that date—he was acknowledging the common difficulty. "Now that I have read this over I realize that it is just another shelling story," he wrote, "a story of something that happened again and again during the last war."

Considine, a late starter, had, as of last week, advanced only as far as a regimental headquarters, and had then returned to Tokyo for a breather. The fateful headline "Considine in a Fox Hole, Too," has, as I write this, not yet appeared.

But none of the current correspondents is likely to replace the subject of Mr. Miller's biography, who appears in its pages as a more complex man than I had supposed. When I first met Ernie, in the fall of 1942, he seemed jarringly like the character he had created for himself in his column, then only moderately successful. He had complained in a letter to his wife, quoted in the book, because his column, which he was then writing from England, had only forty-five newspaper clients. (Miller, measuring success by the number of clients, notes that by January, 1943, it had sixty.) Ernie in those days was abstinent and resolutely Philistine. He would have been the last to admit that he had ever read a book. Since he disliked wherever he found himself, I took it for granted he was homesick. I also assumed, without definite knowledge, that he was devout. He was quiet, friendly, and obliging in the small details of communal life in cramped quarters. We travelled to Africa together aboard a transport, and during the campaign there I used to run into him in places like Tébessa and Gafsa and Béja, and wherever it was he was always coming down with a cold or recovering from a mild attack of dysentery. He was invariably worried because he had not prepared a sufficient supply of columns in advance—at that time he was writing them three weeks ahead of publication date. It was not until rather late in the African campaign that he made his first prolonged stay in the front lines, going out from Béja to spend a week with a battalion of the First Division that was fighting its way toward Bizerte in what was to be the last, decisive battle of the war in Africa.

When I met up with Ernie again, in the press camp at Vouilly, in Normandy, in 1944, he was at the height of his vogue. He was drinking more than a bit, and his nerves were not too good. I evolved a theory to account for the change in him. The success of his frontline series from Africa, I deduced, had caused his home office to needle him into increasingly frequent trips into real danger, on the ground that readers of the column, once blooded, would never again be content with stories about poker-playing officers in quartermaster depots who missed their friends in Merchantville, N.J. Ernie, under this pressure, I figured, had abandoned his Hoosier abstinence in order to keep up his nerve, and the remedy was not a complete success.

This theory, I learn from Miller's book, was far too simple. Ernie's African phase had been atypical in that it marked about his longest stay on the wagon. He was a heavy drinker and in the twenties had been a conventional Menckenian rebel against stuffiness, mixing gin in the bathtub and living in fake sin with his legally wedded wife, Jerry. ("For years they made a fetish of insisting they weren't really married," Miller records.) He was an agnostic: Miller quotes a letter he wrote to his ailing wife in January, 1945, in which he told her,

"You say you want to learn to pray. That has to be up to you, of course, but it is so different from anything you or I have ever felt. I want you to get well, but I wouldn't want you to get pious—for then you wouldn't be *you.* I don't think you can get well by any mystic device or even willing it so. . . ." The simple Hoosier shell had been an induced accretion of Pyle's column-writing years.

I also learn that most of the time Pyle was overseas he was in a terrible emotional tangle; his wife, whom he had married in 1925, when both were twenty-five years old, had gone mad in 1941. Pyle had written to Miller then, "For more than ten years Jerry has been a psychopathic case. In the past few months it has reached a stage in which you would have to turn your back to call it anything less than a form of insanity. She is a dual personality, you might say a triple personality—one side of utter charm and captivation for people she cares nothing about; one side of cruelty and dishonesty toward the few people she does care about; and another side of almost insane melancholy and futility and cynicism when she is alone, which is her true personality." In the years since 1941, she had shuttled between institutions and the outside world.

Far from being homesick, Ernie appears on Miller's showing to have been terrified at the prospect of going home. He must have felt guilty at his knowledge that he didn't want to go. While he was certainly afraid of being killed, he must often have wished he would be. The trips to the front were perhaps a kind of Russian roulette that he played with himself. (I must say that he never seemed to me a reckless man; he protracted the game.) His constant illness now appears to have been largely hypochondria. Miller says Ernie often had himself examined by doctors, and they never found anything much the matter. In short, his appearance of placid, pawky normality seems to have been as deceptive a dickey as ever covered a troubled breast, and I like him a lot better for it, and for keeping his troubles to himself.

Miller was under no obligation to make these troubles public now, but after all Ernie is dead and so is Mrs. Pyle (since November, 1945), and it is better for Ernie to be remembered as a man than as a hick character in a movie.

23
The Mustang Buzzers

THE Pyramid Lake Guest Ranch, where my wife and I stayed for a while early this winter, is thirty-three miles north of Reno, on the only road that follows the west shore of Pyramid Lake. The road ends, it is said, some ninety miles farther on, at a town called Gerlach, which has five bars and a general store. I have never been that far. The guest ranch and the lake lie within the Pyramid Lake Indian Reservation. Inside the reservation, the road is pocked with potholes, since the county has no obligation to maintain it and the Bureau of Indian Affairs doesn't. After it emerges from the reservation, at the head of the lake, it gets really rough, being covered with a species of gravel the size of turkey eggs, a piece of which has been known to fly up from under the wheel of a car and kill a coyote a hundred yards away. A man named Hugh Marchbank told me he saw it happen.

An appendage of the ranch is the only bar in the hundred and twenty miles between Gerlach and Sparks, a suburb of Reno. It occupies a separate building alongside the road, and in a country where the dust is conducive to particularly powerful thirsts, everybody driving the road knows about the long dry stretch coming, and almost everybody stops to take prophylactic measures, or at least booster shots, at the bar. There are practically no travellers from afar, because there is a much better road between Gerlach and Reno on the east side of the lake, and anybody with sense would take it. Just about all the people who stop by the bar during the week live on ranches up the line and know Harry Drackert, the boss of the Pyramid Lake Guest Ranch. On Sundays the bar is likely to be filled with family excursionists from Reno, who come up to look at the lake, and usually just buy pop and use the washroom. Harry has a telescope mounted on the bar and a picture window behind it, through which nature-lovers may look over at the other shore and at the roughly pyramidal tufa islands that give the lake its name. An especially enraptured gazer sometimes buys a postcard.

In summer, most of the guests at the ranch are women establishing residence in Nevada to qualify for a divorce, and they give the bar a pretty good play. A lot of them have children, who are always nagging because Red Snow, the ranch wrangler, won't let them ride some particular horse, or else are always trying to drown each other in the swimming pool, and by sundown the mothers need a snort. But from early fall to late spring you never know who is going to turn up in the bar. There are busy evenings when the place fills up with Mexican laborers working for the Southern Pacific, a branch of which intertwines with the road, crossing it a dozen times as it heads north, and finally shoots off in the direction of California. This line brings a lot of lumber down from Klamath Falls, in Oregon, and you seldom see a train on it that has fewer than a hundred freight cars. Naturally, there are work trains, too, and when one happens to be on the siding back of the ranch on a weekend, the men come in and cash their pay checks in the bar. They mostly drink beer and play the three slot machines—nickel, dime, and quarter. Harry carries tequila for the sportier Mexicans. Other nights, there may be a dude up from California to hunt with Harry, or a secretive old gentleman sweating out an off-season divorce, or just a couple of Indians playing Paiute poker with their wives. (Paiute poker is a three-card game in which you play for the ante, but as it warms, players challenge each other with side bets, until you find yourself with stakes on high card, low card, high spade, low spade, high heart, low club, and anything else that occurs to anybody.) The people who stop in off the road furnish the diversion. A nice feature of the picture window at night is that you can spot headlights a long way off. One night in late October, for example, there was an illumination up the road like a locomotive headlight, and a sound like an oncoming train, except that whatever it was wasn't on rails. It turned out to be a truck and trailer of gleaming aluminum, each section about thirty feet long and looking like a block of solid metal. A man got out of the front end smoking a big cigar and came into the bar for a drink. He said the outfit had cost fifty thousand dollars and would carry thirty-two head of cattle a trip from Elko County, Nevada, down to southern California. He worked the whole rig himself. He said that he had made a mistake and taken our road down from Gerlach, and had nearly had a fifty-thousand-dollar wreck. Then he climbed back into that gleaming chariot, and we never saw him again.

Later that same night, in came this fellow Hugh Marchbank, who is a mustanger. There are herds of wild horses in the mountains north of the lake, and a mustanger catches them for the horse-meat market. The increasingly passionate devotion of the American people to pet dogs has put up the price of horse meat—a Great Dane will eat several pounds of it a day—and consequently mustangs bring fours cents a pound on the hoof instead of five dollars a horse, which was the standard price before the First World War, when dogs' and cats' appetites were less discriminating and the horse's hide was the only thing of value. The wild horses of Nevada are not members of any aboriginal species but simply ranch horses that have escaped and bred among the canyons for horse generations. Sometimes, coming down to graze on the cattle range, they mix with herds of tame horses—"gentle" horses, as Hugh calls them—with disastrous effects on the conformation of the foals the ranch mares subsequently throw. The wild studs are ardent but scrubby. They have to survive without hay or grain, digging through the snow to get at greasewood or sagebrush during the winter and sometimes nibbling one another's manes and tails to help out. This does not make for size or bone. In cowboy opinion, therefore, the wild horses are more trouble to break than they are worth. The wild horses of the Smoke Creek area up north of the ranch are of a particularly profitable strain, however, Hugh told me, because the feed is pretty good by wild-horse standards—the country is only semidesert—and also because back around 1914 the government opened the country up there to homesteaders who came over the California line to attempt dry farming. Some of the homesteaders gave it a good try; you can see their abandoned houses and corrals. But none made the grade, and when they quit, many turned loose their farm horses—big draft types with a lot of meat on them. These went to join the wild herds, and now and then you find descendants of the mixed blood who weigh a thousand pounds. Putting a twenty-dollar bill down on the bar, Hugh said, "You can get two of these fellows for one of them big horses. Now, down south around Tonopah, where it's real desert, the mustangs won't average four hundred and fifty pounds apiece; they're breeding down to kangaroo mice. And you got to run just as far for them. I know it's a sin and a shame for anybody who likes horses to run them mustangs, and a dude woman once said to me why didn't I get a honest job stealing cattle, but somebody's going to get that money, and it might as well be me."

The night I met Hugh, he had been to Reno with a truckload of horses and had stayed a week for recreation. He was on his way back, tired but contented, to the tent he shared with his partner, Bill Garaventa, up in the Smoke Creek country. Hugh, a lean man with a long, lean face and a long nose turned up at the end, had a lock of dingy-blond hair falling over his right eye, which was of as honest a blue as Pyramid Lake in chilly sunshine. His left eye was hidden by the forward deck of a long-shaped white hat with a high, cleft crown. The back of the hat stuck up from his head like an Indian's feather. When he took off the hat and put it on the bar, you could see that he was mighty pleased with it. "There's two and a half horses in that hat," he said, "and them blue sort of feathers in the band is chukar partridge, which I ate." He rolled the eye that had now become visible and went on, "I been catching up on my romancing, and I drunk enough Seagram Seven to kill a Mexican, but I come of hard stock. They had to rope my mother up in Idaho and hog-tie and blindfold her so she'd let me nurse."

Before Hugh left, he explained his simple *modus operandi* for mustanging. He and Bill Garaventa had their tent and outfit by an abandoned but still functioning artesian well forty miles up the road from Harry's. On the lower slope of a mountain that paralleled the road, they had built a long, V-shaped corral and camouflaged its sides with brush. Bill owned a Cub plane, which he kept at a nearby ranch, and on clear mornings he would roll it out onto the road at dawn, take off, and fly up into the mountains farther north. He would cruise through the canyons until he spotted a band of mustangs—usually an old stallion with some mares and young horses. Then he would buzz them and start them off in the general direction of the corral, steering them from the air and firing a shotgun at their tails when they seemed disposed to dally. In the end, after a run of from fifteen to twenty-five miles, he would edge them toward the open end of the corral. There they would see a couple of gentle horses grazing peacefully. The distraught wild horses would look to the self-possessed strangers for a cue. But the presence of the gentle horses was not fortuitous; these shills had been trained to act as padres, a mustanging allusion to the priests who walk a condemned man to the gallows. They would trot into the corral as Garaventa made a final pass, and the wild ones would follow. When the mustangs were well within, Hugh, who had been hiding behind an outer wing of the V, would mount a fast horse and chase them far down toward the point, the padres efficiently leading the rout. He would shut the first of a pair of gates behind the main body of mustangs and then take out after any that had doubled back and bolted. "You got the plane to help you, buzzing the mustang and turning him," he said. "So even though your horse has got all your weight on him, you lass' the mustang sooner or later."

When Hugh went out into the night, the light shone on the intelligent eyes of a sorrel horse standing in the back of his pickup truck. "That's Billy," he said. "He's a thoroughbred I bought cheap at the Washoe County Fair a while back when he couldn't win. He may not be no Native Dancer, but I've made a damn smart horse out of him. I can use him as a padre or rope from him, either one, and on a long, straight run he's better than any short horse." A short, or quarter, horse is of a strain bred for quick turns and sudden bursts of speed, essential in working cattle; you see them riding in pickups and trailers behind their cowboy owners every time you go down the road. Hardly a horse in Nevada walks to work.

DURING the next several days, Hugh stopped off frequently at the bar, and every time he would ask Joan Drackert, Harry's wife, in an elaborately casual manner if there were any new women boarders at the ranch who might be interested in seeing how wild horses were run with an airplane. Joan told me that during the high divorce season he had initiated more women into mustanging than Aly Khan had been photographed taking to the races. Joan is a blonde with a good figure and an inquiring mind, and her wide gray eyes are slightly keener than a chicken hawk's. In default of more exciting company, Hugh asked me to come along, but since I am not an early riser, I was content with his description of what mustanging was like.

That was before Lamberti, a short, sallow man who is a correspondent for an Italian picture weekly called *Tempo,* came to Pyramid Lake in search of the Far West. When I told Lamberti about the wild horses, he immediately insisted we go on an expedition. "*Cavalli selvaggi!*" he erupted, and then, in French, which was our usual medium of intercourse, "*Des chevaux sauvages dans cet âge de la réfrigération et de la bombe atomique!,*" and finally, in English, "To 'unt the wild 'orse!" I remarked that it was refrigeration that made wild-

'orse 'unting a commercial proposition, but Lamberti was lost in the theme of his *grande inchiesta,* or investigation, for his magazine. The title of this was "The Far West of the Cinema—It Exists or No?" and he had been inspired to undertake it after sitting through three showings in Rome of an American film he called "Eegnun," which I identified from a musical phrase he supplied as "High Noon." One of Lamberti's chief arguments in inducing his publisher to send him on this expedition had been that since he had never visited the United States, everything would be new and fresh to him. Arriving in Washington, he had asked an attaché at the Italian Embassy the way to the Far West. The attaché had referred to him to the Library of Congress, and a folklorist on the Library staff, who may have been thinking in the past tense, had directed him to Virginia City, Nevada, which is now inhabited almost exclusively by writers and painters, and closely resembles Provincetown impaled on a mountain. The Embassy had promptly made a *démarche* to the State Department to obtain the Secretary's benevolent intervention with Senator Pat McCarran, of Nevada, for a *laissez-passer,* or *permis de séjour,* within the State of Nevada, and the Senator had furnished Lamberti with a letter bespeaking the good offices of all Nevadans on behalf of a distinguished foreign journalist who was in favor of free silver, no federal tax on gambling devices, and universal recognition of Nevada divorces.

One look at Virginia City had convinced Lamberti that the Far West of the cinema was a myth. But he had found what he considered one good story in a nearby mining town called Yerington, which still has a legalized red-light district: " 'A Brothel in Puritan America—What Is It Like?' Sensational reportage of our special correspondent Lamberti." Lamberti had presented Senator McCarran's letter to the town's only madam, who, clasping the communication in one large fist, led him through every bar in the place, buying drinks for the house at each stop and then bidding the bartender read her nice letter from Pat. After that, Lamberti felt himself at a dead end in Virginia City, particularly since his English was rudimentary. A sympathetic woman painter had suggested he look me up, since I speak passable French, as he does, and could therefore interpret the Far West for him. What she hadn't said was that I knew nothing about it; she subsequently explained to me that she had counted on my powers of improvisation. So he had come to Pyramid Lake.

My story of the wild horses and the aviator-cowboys reignited his passion for the *grande inchiesta,* and it burst into a conflagration when Bill Garaventa stopped in at the bar the night after Lamberti's arrival. Bill's big head, big torso, and wide-set blue eyes make him look like a Dutch sea captain down to his waist, and below that his thin legs, bowed from buckarooing, make him look like a cowboy. His clothing expresses the same duality; he wears an Army fatigue cap and a leather flying jacket above Levis and high-heeled cowboy boots. He dresses this way for both flying and riding. What gave Lamberti an extra *Tempo* angle was that Bill, although born of a squatter family on the reservation, speaks pretty fair Italian, because his parents were Genoese. Bill said that he would be glad to take us mustanging, but that Hugh had gone to Reno earlier in the week and hadn't reappeared, and then on Sunday he himself was going over to California for some pheasant shooting. "But we ought to be all set to run some horses next Tuesday, if the weather's good," he said. "Why don't you come up then?"

By the time Monday night rolled around, the *grande inchiesta* had grown to a four-man affair. Harry was coming along to drive the ranch's station wagon, for fear Lamberti and I would not be able to find the horse-runners if we went alone, and a fellow-guest called Bob was coming for fun. I hate so to get up early that I wake long before the execrated hour, shave and dress, and walk about for ages before the alarm clock goes off, by which time I feel drugged and want to go back to bed. The morning of the rendezvous, I fumbled in the dark for my clothes, and my wife, half asleep, murmured, " 'To hunt the wild horse'—sounds so poetic." I asked her if she wanted to come, and she buried her head in the pillow again. I went out and looked at the mountains across the lake. The sun was as yet only a golden flame behind them; their western faces were in black shadow. There was no light in the kitchen. I thought of sawing firewood to keep warm, and I congratulated myself on having a wife who knew when she was well off.

Pedro, the Filipino cook, came down to the kitchen and started work. I was drinking my second cup of coffee when Harry Drackert, not relying on the alarm clock to get me up, walked over to my cabin. He knocked on the door and shouted. This awakened my wife, and she decided to come along after all. Lamberti, olive green in the gray light and wearing a blue beret and a tweed topcoat, since he felt the cold, emerged from his cabin. He hates early-morning rising as much as I do, because he spent the last year of the war in the concentration camp at Mauthausen. "Sleep was our only escape," he once told me. "When we awoke, we remembered where we were." When he is in Rome now, he never dresses before noon. In our first conversation, he informed me that he had been a convinced Fascist until the second year of the war in Spain, which he covered as a correspondent. There he had begun to hope Fascism would fail. In the big war he had served as a correspondent with the Italian troops on the Russian front. With disabused eyes—he detested the Germans—he had detected the deterioration of the Reichswehr and counselled Ciano to abandon ship. The Germans, learning of his views after Ciano's execution, had clapped him into prison. He survived—only because he was forgotten, perhaps. "It is painful to form part of an alliance whose defeat you desire," he once said. But he added with pride, "We were more of a liability than an asset to the Germans. Without us they might have won."

Bob arrived in the kitchen a moment later, and in about half an hour more my wife showed up and sat down to breakfast. Our provisions for this dash into the unknown were bologna sandwiches and two bottles of whiskey—one of a popular blend, for trade with the natives, and one of Scotch, for drinking purposes. As an afterthought, Harry stuck two shotguns in the back of the station wagon. They would be of no avail against wild horses, he explained, but we might just happen to see some wild ducks or geese.

By eight o'clock, we were on the road. Harry said that if we got up to the corral in an hour we would be all right. "Bill starts flying through those hills looking for horses as soon as the sun comes up," he said, "and it usually takes him two, three hours to drive them down." But just as we hit the top of the first rise going north, we saw a jeep coming toward us with Bill Garaventa driving. The peaked cap and leather jacket were unmistakable in that big-hat country. When we met, Bill yelled, "Glad I got you before you wasted your day! Hugh *still* ain't come back from town. Either that widow shot him or he run off with some other woman. So I'm on my way over to Nixon to ask Levi Frazier will he ride for me tomorrow." Nixon is the village on the reservation, and Levi Frazier is a Paiute who is supposed to be the best roper in the state.

Harry said, "Have you checked the jails and hospitals for Hugh?"

Bill said—unfeelingly, I thought—"No, I ain't. If he's too drunk to get word out to me of his own accord, he ain't no use to me anyway."

"I would if I was you, Bill," Harry said, in a conciliatory tone. "Anybody can get throwed in jail nowadays."

Bill drove off down the road, waving back to us with his left hand and yelling "I've had a *jillion* partners!" as he disappeared into the dip.

This cancellation suited me, but I expressed polite condolences to Lamberti, who was sitting with his elbows on his knees and his head in his hands. I imagine he had already composed his lead, and could visualize the title over his article in *Tempo:* " 'Conqueror of Wild Horses in the Region of Wild Indians.' Our colleague Lamberti lives a saga of the plain." Personally, I wanted to go back to bed. Harry spiked that hope. "As long as we're on our way," he said cheerily, "let's keep on going and see if we can get a couple of wild geese." The suggestion appeared to console Lamberti. "Wild 'orse, wild goose," he said, "*che importa?*" My wife, who reacts to the West like a teen-age dude, promptly began to sing an old song of Frankie Laine's:

> "My heart knows what the wild goose knows
> And I must go where the wild goose goes."

"Explain me what it mean," Lamberti said.

She did so, and Lamberti said, "Is very beautiful. I will make a translation in Italian. The man will not stay by this woman who love him."

"Fly away, fly away, fly away!" honked my wife, flapping her arms. By that time, we were near the northern end of the lake, and Harry said the song reminded him of Joe, who used to live on a ranch up there. The ranch is owned by Joe's former wife, Letty, who wears Levis, has a man's haircut, and does all the outside work around the ranch—riding, mending fence, and branding. She is handicapped in her branding, though, by the fact that she is not a top roper. For twenty-two years, that was Joe's only complaint about Letty. "My wife can't rope," he used to say when he got to exchanging domestic confidences with some stranger at Harry's bar. "But don't you ever get to shooting with that old coyote for money. She can shoot a running antelope's eye out at a thousand yards." Letty's marksmanship might have been expected to keep Joe straight, but it didn't. He was a big man, and so strong that he once picked up a two-hundred-pound ranch dinner bell with one hand and set it on a table, and everybody between Nixon and Gerlach knew the story of his courtship of Letty. Joe had been thrown off a freight train in front of the ranchhouse one day, and Letty and her mother had carried him into the house and soothed his lacerations and reduced his contusions. Letty's brothers had already moved away to towns—they were tired of having nobody but their siblings and coyotes for company—and wranglers were hell to find. So Letty married Joe as soon as he got back on his feet, and it worked out all right for twenty-two years. It was a small ranch, on which the two of them kept about a hundred head of cattle, but there was good irrigated land around the house and they had chickens and a truck garden, and Letty ran a fourth-class post office. Letty was shy of the city, so it was Joe who would make the periodical trips to Sparks with a steer or a crate of chickens to sell. On one trip down, he stopped by Harry's bar and ran into a pretty woman named Ellen, about thirty, who was married to a fellow working at a marl pit not far away. She asked Joe for a lift to town. A month later, they were saying they had never known what true love was like before. So they got divorced and then married each other. Joe received half the cattle, but Letty kept the ranch and the tractor. Letty didn't complain any, but it was common knowledge her feelings were hurt, and she hired a woman to come out from town to keep house for her while she did the wrangling. A little later, a fellow Harry knew stopped by there and found Letty alone again, so he asked what had happened to the hired woman. "The damn fool went off and got married," Letty said.

"The funny part of it is," Harry said after telling the story in terms he thought Lamberti might understand, "this Ellen that Joe married, she can't rope, either."

About fifteen miles north of our starting point, Harry took the station wagon off the road and onto a rabbit path that led out toward the Big Slick, a flat plain of alkali land that is entirely submerged during the spring, when the snow water runs down off the mountains, but is dry the rest of the year, except for a couple of shallow ponds. The ground looks like white linoleum with a million fine cracks in it, and when it rains, it is as slippery as a rink, which is how it got its name. Harry hoped there would be ducks on the ponds. It had been decided that Harry and Lamberti would do the shooting; Lamberti said he had been a sharpshooter as a *Bersagliere* in the First World War. But there weren't any ducks. After inspecting both ponds, Harry said it looked as though we would have to go over to

Art Heller's, at Fish Springs, where irrigation ditches kept the fields green and there were usually wild geese.

BEFORE hunting on a ranch, even a friend's, it is protocol to call on the proprietor, so we headed for Art's house first. It is a long, low building made of old railroad ties painted white. The corrals and barns are of white railroad ties, too; there are probably enough condemned ties at Fish Springs to build a railroad across an Eastern state. The rear of the house is protected from the weather by a mountain, and in front of it the fenced fields, intersected by flowing ditches, look almost like Iowa or Illinois. Where there is no water, the land is just sagebrush again; Heller has a hundred and twenty-five square miles of range, most of it under lease from the government, on which he runs around a thousand head of cattle.

It didn't take much sleuthing to find geese on Heller's place; a group was feeding among the Herefords at the back end of a pasture within a quarter mile of the corrals. This presented a problem. If we started toward the geese, they would either take off before we got within shotgun range or force us to fill Heller's choice stock with buckshot. There was little chance that the geese would move if we didn't disturb them; they obviously liked their surroundings. We drove on up to the front door of the ranchhouse and got out among a crowd of dogs that would be socially unacceptable in a town pound. Mr. Heller, Harry said, was a great dog-lover, and his test of a man's affection for a dog was the animal's uselessness. "He says even a Basque sheepman will feed a sheepdog, but that's just for what the Basque can get out of him," Harry said. "Art won't hire a man to ride for him unless the man has at least one worthless dog of his own."

Heller, a chunky, fair-skinned man in shirtsleeves, came to the door to greet us. After telling the dogs to shut up, he asked us in and motioned us to seats around a long, bare table. Mrs. Heller, a woman with carefully waved gray hair, offered to make coffee. We told her not to trouble, and produced our two bottles of whiskey and the bologna sandwiches. The Hellers said they had already had lunch—it was almost noon—but to go right ahead, and Mr. Heller said he had never refused a drink of whiskey in his life. He chose the raw article.

Lamberti was always looking for a big ranch, like the one in the movie "Red River." He asked Mr. Heller if he had many cowboys.

Heller said he had two—three, counting himself—and during the roundup he would have to hire a fourth, to replace his daughter, who had moved up to Ravendale. "I lost my best cowboy when Bonnie got married," he said.

"The whole country choosed up sides about Bonnie," Harry volunteered. "Most wanted her to marry Dan, the head cowboy here."

"I lost Dan, too," Mr. Heller said, looking glum. "He went away to forget. But I got nothing against Bonnie's husband, mind you. He don't drink, or gamble, or nothing like that. He's a hard-working fellow." His son-in-law's virtues seemed to have a dispiriting effect on Mr. Heller, who poured himself another drink of the blended whiskey.

"Pancho stopped by the bar the other night," Harry said, to change the subject. Pancho had been the Heller's second-string cowboy until Dan left, and was now their No. 1 man. "He saw me mixing a Tom Collins for one of the guests and wanted to know what it was. I told him, and he said mix him one, and he drank three. Then he said it was all right but he wanted some liquor, and he took to whiskey until he got kind of tired. After that, he saw a girl having a Moscow Mule, and he drank a few of those, and then a half case of beer because he said the vodka made him thirsty. Then he asked was champagne good for a hangover and I said yes, so he said he would drink a few splits right now, because he knew he would have a hangover in the morning."

Having made enough general conversation, Harry now thought it proper to mention geese, and did so.

"Why don't you just take a rifle and pick a couple of them off?" Art asked.

Harry, who is really keen on hunting, said he didn't think it was sportsmanlike to kill unsuspecting geese with a rifle.

"Well," said Art, "either you want a reputation as a sportsman or you want a goose."

I asked him if he used a .22 and shot the goose in the head.

"Hell, no," Mr. Heller said. "I use a 30-06 and aim to hit him in the belly. That way I don't have to clean him."

Harry said that if we saw a few on another part of the ranch on our way home, we would try them with the old shotguns. Art said that would be fine and please come again.

When we got outside among the dogs, Harry said he had a plan of campaign. "If somebody put these geese up in the air, I think they'd come down in the next place they thought there was water and good feed," he said. "They're not going on south any more today; they broke their trip here to get some groceries. The next good place is that little sump about two miles back, just this side of the edge of the Big Slick, where there's a haystack. I'll put out some decoys in the grass, and Lamberti and I'll get into the stack and wait. When we get set, you two fellows can scare the geese off the ground, and if they fly over to look at the decoys, I'll call them in." Harry always carries items like duck calls and goose calls in his pocket, and packs two or three kinds of collapsible decoys in the rear of the station wagon, along with the shotguns and ammunition.

The plan seemed pretty farfetched to me, and when I translated it for Lamberti, he was bleakly skeptical. In French, he said to me, "Harry pays himself our heads. These geese, even, are as tame as pigs. Regard them. And the whole story of the wild horses," he continued, with an access of unbelief, "is a mystification." In English, he said, "All right, 'Arry. I come."

Bob said solemnly, "Let's synchronize our watches." Harry replied, "That's a good idea," and the five of us put our left wrists together and decided that it was twelve-thirty-one. "I want you to put the geese up at one-fifteen," Harry said after we had made the watches agree. Then he and Lamberti and my wife started out in the station wagon, leaving Bob and me, both city fellows, feeling slightly idiotic. We wandered around in back of the ranchhouse, where we found two salad-oil tins to use as tomtoms and a couple of beef bones to pound them with. We looked into all the pens and coops on the place, killing time. In one pen was a sow that must have weighed as much as most horses, and in another a steer that had lost the lower half of one leg. There was a rich disorder about the place that reminded me of one of Chichikov's visits. The geese stayed where they were, grazing among the cattle.

At ten minutes past one, my wife returned in the station wagon to tell us that Harry and Lamberti were in position. She was the only member of the party except Harry who took the ambush seriously. Bob and I swung ourselves up on the pigpen fence with our percussion instruments. At precisely one-fifteen, we ran past the sow's snout and debouched into the pasture, shouting and banging on our salad-oil tins as we advanced on the Herefords. As I ran, I chanted, "Ah-o, ah-o," a Paiute song that means "He's thinking, he's thinking," which you sing to rattle opponents in the Paiute version of the match game. The geese, however, were unrattled.

As Bob and I charged, first the Herefords and then a band of ranch horses took off at a gallop. But the geese waited until we were within fifty yards of them before languidly rising. Once airborne, they lifted slowly, formed a loose V, and flew off. When we rejoined my wife, she said that from her perch on the pigpen fence she had seen the geese sit down two fields farther over. We climbed into the station wagon, and she drove us along a trail in back of the ranchhouse to the new goose pasture. There we got out with our timpani again, and this time the geese caught on quickly. They took off and disappeared.

We climbed back into the station wagon and drove off toward the haystack. The road was bad, and it took us six or seven minutes to get to a point where we could see the haystack from the car. Lamberti and Harry were standing out in the open, apparently with live geese all around them. My wife whooped "Shoot! Shoot!" before she remembered the decoys. Harry and Lamberti were looking away from us, and we couldn't tell whether they had had a shot or had given up their posts in the stack because they were disgusted. Bob and I got out of the station wagon, and when Lamberti saw us coming, he brandished his shotgun in the air three times. We ran the rest of the way down the slope, and found that they had killed three geese, all right—big graybacks, with black heads and white faces. Lamberti was sobbing with contrition. " 'Arry," he said. "I didn't believe. I didn't believe. 'Arry, you are the Eisen'ower of the goose!" In French, he said that there was no such bird as a wild goose in Italy, so he had thought the whole deal was a spoof. He said Harry had fired four shots and killed two geese. He had fired twice and killed one. "I was falling asleep in the haystack when I heard Harry blow the goose caller," he said. "I thought he was trying to wake me up. I look at my watch. One-fifteen. I look up. Whuh, whuh!" He imitated the noise of wings and flapped his arms like a goose. "The geese arrive, in military formation. *Pouf! Pouf!* I forgot my gun was a pump-action or I would have descended six."

We lugged the geese out to the road—they weighed eight or ten pounds apiece—and Lamberti, who wears a camera around his neck on safari, and illustrates his own stories, took pictures of my wife with a goose, Bob with a goose, me with a goose, and Harry with three geese. I suggested that Bob and I black up as native beaters and that Lamberti pose between us as the Italian Robert Ruark. The gag fell flat because he had never heard of Ruark.

On the way back, Lamberti, only half joking, asked Harry if he could always make game run on schedule, and Harry said, "Sure." Then, apparently acting on a hunch, he said, "Would you like to see some deer?"

Lamberti said, "No tree 'ere, 'Arry. 'Ow can be deer?"

Harry turned the station wagon around and headed off into a valley lined with a shrub called buckbush. When there are deer around, they like to browse on the buckbush, but only the previous week Harry and a dude from Los Angeles who was staying at the ranch had gone out on three successive days without sighting even a single doe. Harry would have liked to get his customer a shot, naturally.

We drove for about ten minutes and then came upon a hillside with so many deer going up it that they seemed to be on an escalator. We counted fifty or sixty—all does and fawns and young bucks except for one big old stag, who was standing, with antlers on the skyline, reviewing them. The deer season had just ended, and maybe the old stag was counting casualties. I don't suppose I'll ever see anything like it again. Lamberti just sat there with his mouth open, and finally he said to Harry, "'Arry, if you tell me tomorrow there is a golda mine, I believe!"

Harry said afterward that he was sorry it was too late in the day to take Lamberti up to see old Loco Jack, the only surviving prospector around.

BACK AT THE RANCH, Lamberti retired to his cabin to write about the *oca selvatica,* or wild goose, and about the noble savages of Pyramid Lake and the utility of Nevada divorces in Italian society. They wouldn't be legal, he told me, but they might become chic. " 'Six weeks' residence in the seducing surroundings of the Far West of the cinema, pimentoed with the life of the casinos of great luxury and the presence of beautiful blond awaiters of divorce who are enfamished of love'—that's the way I'll write it, of course," he said, adding that though he was not, as a matter of fact, much impressed with American women, there is in Italy a convention, nurtured by the movies, that a reporter must respect. "Within the year after my article appears," he said, "there will be from two hundred and fifty to five hundred Italians here to obtain divorces. And many of them will come to Joan and Harry's guest ranch, preferred of the richest, most beautiful awaiters of divorce, cuisine incomparable." Lamberti was a great rooter for Harry. Eventually, he finished the tenth installment of his *inchiesta,* which he entitled "The Far West of the Cinema—Exists!" Then he heard the wild goose calling him to San Francisco.

The night before Lamberti's departure, we gave a big dinner for him in the bar. Pedro roasted the goose Lamberti thought was his personal victim, Bob bought six bottles of the best Chianti available in Washoe County, and my wife presented Lamberti with three records to take back to Rome: "Wheel of Fortune," to remind him of the roulette wheel at the Riverside Hotel, in Reno; the ballad from "High Noon;" and, of course, Frankie Laine's "The Cry of the Wild Goose." Lamberti said he wanted to learn the words of the goose song, so my wife played the record about a thousand times in the bar. Lamberti drank whiskey during the whole process, and tried to turn the words into Italian verse as she wrote them down. I got pretty tired of Frankie Laine before it was over, and sat in the corner farthest from the juke box playing Paiute poker with a party from Nixon. When Lamberti had read all the verses, my wife told me afterward, he put his hand on hers and exclaimed, " 'Ow could this man 'ave known my secret? 'E 'as written the 'istory of my life."

Next morning, he was gone.

24
Letter from Glasgow

WALKING through the deserted streets of the center of Glasgow one Sunday morning not long ago, I came upon a message neatly lettered in chalk several times on the sidewalk of George Square, which is the Glaswegian equivalent of City Hall Park. It read, "Clyde Socialist Group. Hear Hugh Savage on NO NEWSPAPERS—NO LIES. Drury Street, Sunday 7:30 P.M." The message, I knew, must refer not to the Glasgow papers, which were appearing regularly, but to the so-called national press—the London daily and Sunday newspapers, ordinarily circulated throughout Britain, which had been closed for more than three weeks by a strike of maintenance men. The square was yellow with potted daffodils and forsythia, rushed outdoors at the first coming of fair weather, which, miraculously, was prevailing that day. But the weather had brought nobody out into it. "Scotland greets the sun with the fervor reserved for a long-absent friend," I had read in an editorial in the Glasgow *Citizen.*

Alone in the middle of the square, I gazed at the inscriptions on the sidewalk with the interest of Crusoe discovering the footprint. It was the only visible evidence of recent human activity. It was also the only promise of anything to do until Monday, because Glasgow on Sunday is shut tight—no football games, no cinemas, no pubs. I had read in the *Citizen* that morning that not even Billy Graham, the crusading evangelist from North Carolina, then on tour in Britain, would buck the Glasgow Sabbath. He was taking the day off, possibly in order to let the resident clergy save a few souls on their regular workday. The Crusade had played Saturday matinée and evening performances, the paper had informed me, to audiences totalling 33,100, of whom nearly a thousand had opted for Heaven. I pictured Drury Street as a lane in a proletarian quarter of town. From the porter at the Central Hotel, however, I learned that it was a short one-way street leading off Renfield Street, which is one of Glasgow's main shopping thoroughfares, and that it was set aside on Sunday nights for public speaking. I decided I would go there that evening and listen to Mr. Savage.

As a guest at the hotel—a traveller—I could have all the drink I wanted, but it was a glum place on the Sabbath; commercial travellers have apparently learned to avoid Glasgow on Sunday, and there were none of the military who, with their fraudulent claims of tenancy, had kept the Central a gay and turbulent place during closed hours in wartime, when I was last here. The sole human sounds in the dining room during the midday meal, besides those of mastication, were the "'nkya," "'nkya" that constituted the running dialogue between an Englishman and his waiter, enlivened by an occasional big line, such as "Do you recommend the calf's liver?" In the war days, the lounges of the Central—an interminable succession of them, with ceilings forty feet high and names like Ailsa Craig, Montrose, and American Bar—were caves of mystery and joy, where, among uniformed men and women, you could get into any kind of near-trouble you preferred, from an almost-fight to an almost-affair. The despot who prevented any of these enterprises from reaching maturity was an old bar waiter named Myles, who controlled the flow of liquor. Myles was no stickler for seeing room keys. He was usually willing to bring a drink to any officer who belonged to a regiment he approved of. The Cameronians and the Highland Light Infantry were his favorites, and he had a prejudice against the Brigade of Guards. He would serve Poles and Americans if he thought the Scots had enough whiskey in sight to get through the evening. Stocks were short. When he felt that a customer had had enough, he would shut off the supply. For doing this at precisely the right moment, Myles had an ameliorated instinct, like a wire walker's sense of balance, or a jockey's sense of pace. His order was like a hand on a man's chest, keeping him from falling on his face. "Colonel," he would say, or maybe it would be "Major," "ye've a wee thingie on." And Colonel or Major would rise and march. It was not only that he knew he would never get another drink from Myles if he didn't. He also knew that if Myles said he couldn't hold another drink, Myles was right. I think Myles' objection to the Guards was lack of discipline. When I asked for him on this visit, a barman said he had been retired from his command and was now washing glasses in the pantry. I could not bring myself to call on him. It would have been like visiting Marius among the ruins of Carthage.

An American officer I knew served most of the war in the lounges of the Central Hotel. There was a theory that he had made his way here straight from a troopship and had lost contact with the unit to which he was attached. Since its destination was top-secret, he had never dared ask questions about it. I half expected to find him still at the Central, perhaps working as a lift boy, when I returned. But he had departed. It was at the Central, too, that I once heard a Highlander denounce another as a fraud because he had not "the faceel appearance of a Macneil of Barra," which the chap claimed to be. Thinking on these things made me sad, and I went out glummer than I had come in.

MY frame of mind improved during the afternoon, for I discovered where the people of Glasgow go on Sunday, and I joined them there. The riddle had harrowed me, because I could not believe that even the children were home nursing hangovers. The Glaswegians go to a part of the adjoining county of Renfrewshire that is not included within the Glasgow city limits. There *they* are travellers, according to the merciful Scotch law, which does not demand that in order to prove he is *en voyage* a man must hire an expensive room. Each inn maintains a registration book, and by signing it and deposing that he is a resident of another town a man may drink in peace. Bus fare from the center of Glasgow to the city line is only one-and-four, and the more popular landlords provide free transportation back. "Boswell Arms keeps five boosses running all day," my taxi-driver told me on the way to Renfrewshire. The men take their women and children with them; the scenes along the Renfrewshire roads are like rural fêtes by Breughel. I invited the driver to become a traveller at my expense. "That thing will keep on ticking," he warned me, nodding toward the meter. I told him that would be all right.

My two pints of black-and-tan (ale and stout mixed) stood me two pounds seventeen, including cab fare, but it was worth it, because we did a lot of sightseeing on the way. For example, the driver showed me the National Art Gallery, with a large sign on it advertising a national exhibition of children's art. I waved him wildly on. After a considerable lapse of time—we were in a far less posh part of town—he waggled a hand toward a house bearing the date 1451 and said, "Lord Darnley's hoose. He slept there th' night befure Queen Mary hod him ossossinated, or something like thot." After that, we fell silent, both thirsty. He was not an avaricious man. He stopped at the very first licensed house on the free side of the border, instead of driving on to the Boswell.

Our haven of liberty was the Eglinton Arms, in the village of Eglinton, and a bright, prosperous inn it was, crammed to the doors with refugees from the urban Sabbath. My driver and I entered by a rear door, and before being admitted to a bar we were conducted to the Book, which lay on a lectern in the front entrance hall and was about the size of a Webster's New International Dictionary. I noted that not many blank pages remained. A sergeant of the Renfrewshire Constabulary, in a blue uniform with red-and-gold chevrons, stood at my elbow to see that I gave an address at least as distant as Glasgow; he had no doubts about the driver. Having regularized the procedure, we went on to the bars—a succession of rooms opening one into another and all packed with very merry people, as the lounges of the Central had been during the blackout. Nothing, apparently, pleases a Glaswegian more than getting the better of a tyrannical, self-imposed sumptuary restriction. The *ambiance* brought to mind the universal good will among men that had reigned in the United States during prohibition. The excursionists, weary from greeting the sun—an occasional peeled nose or wilted wildflower indicated that several actually had volunteered a greeting—lolled about tables in family groups, the children consuming and upsetting orange squash, the parents partaking of healthful beer and spirits. Dashing couples, who had arrived in sports cars or on motorbikes, held free hands with the old speakeasy ardor. Single types stood, though not straight, with the bar firmly mortised under an armpit.

The driver and I found space between a wall and a man who had a brother in Yonkers. He divulged this bit of family history as soon as he heard me speak. The man with a brother in Yonkers said he himself was an enthusiastic pedestrian who loved to take a bus out from Glasgow and ramble in the braes of a Sunday. On the way home, he would stop in at this pleasant inn for a pint. I observed to the man behind the bar who drew our pints that it seemed a shame people had to travel so far for a drink. "It's because the Glasgow chaps canna han'le the stuff," he said. "They go ma' wi' drink. It wou' be a disoster to permi' drinkin' there o' Sobboth."

"There'd be no inducement to exercise," the pedestrian said.

I bought the driver a pint and he bought me one, but he wouldn't split the fare.

I REACHED DRURY STREET in the dusk, after a stop back at the hotel for tea. I was a bit early, as one often is when alone, and a meeting was in progress that was obviously not that of the Clyde Socialist Group. Nine or ten persons were singing "This is my story, this is my song," a hymn that is a theme song of the Billy Graham Crusade. A young couple stood holding the hands of an impudent small girl in a red dress. When the notion occurred to her, she would lift her feet from the asphalt and swing from her parents' arms. Two preachers, red-faced men wearing flat hats, short jackets, striped trousers, and black gloves, stared out across Renfield Street without expression. A small, pale boy in a kilt furtively handed out tracts, looking ashamed of what he was doing. Three or four faded, triumphant females stood in the background, rolling impending dust and ashes on their tongues as they scrutinized passing infidels. There were people on Renfield Street now, but where they were going I don't know. In any case, few stopped.

When the singers had finished what seemed to me a great number of verses, one of the preachers held up his hand, and they were silent. He began talking, with considerable self-satisfaction, at and about the unheeding promenaders. "There are two ways before you!" he shouted. "The broad way to Hell"—he pronounced it "Hale," and when he said it, he looked up Renfield toward Sauchiehall Street, where there are music halls, although they are closed on Sunday—"and the norrow poth thot leads to salvation." He looked up in the air to indicate where *thot* led.

A pair of girls tapped by on loose heels, and the preacher reflected with complacency, "During this week, there are pairsons who ov posst, not heeding, and who ov since lopsed into etairnity."

Some young men walked past, arguing loudly about football, and the man in the flat hat shouted, "Jesus retairns! Not as a shepherd"—he said "shaiphaird"—"but as a judge!"

When the preacher had finished, they sang again, "This is my story, this is my song."

The child in red, who had slumped to her knees between her parents, began to cry. I took a walk around a couple of blocks, and by the time I returned, the godly people had been succeeded by the Clyde Socialist Group. These appeared a snappier lot, or at least a snappier handful, than their predecessors. They had a professional-looking portable stand, like a metal stepladder with a shelf on top of it, for their speakers, and a couple of young men in sports jackets and slacks, and with their hair cut in duck tails, were moving about, bent double, to reletter some chalked "NO NEWSPAPERS—NO LIES" inscriptions, which had been scuffed about by the army of righteousness. They even had an audience: nine men, including me. The eight others wore caps.

The Group was coquettish about getting under way. Seven-thirty had long passed, but the young men still fussed with the chalk marks, hoping to attract more of the curious. Finally, with the audience apparently stable at seventeen, the first speaker opened the meeting. He was a little egg-shaped man with the pink, round face of an angry baby. When he began to speak, however, he made it plain that he believed in full-grown actions. "The Clyde Socialist Group-a believes-a in the forrcible overthrow-a of the goovermint-a," he said. The "a" he appended to almost every polysyllable and to some monosyllables was evidently an oratorical device calculated to make his words more impressive. He had begun using it, I suppose, as a break to permit him to take breath, but it was now sheer ornament, and he loved it. "The Labour Party-a has betrayed the doctrine-a of Carol Marex-a, who never-a envisaged-a the overthrow of the goovermint-a by democratic-a processes," he went on. The Glasgow accent is extremely varied, and I have no way of knowing if the fellow was a true Glaswegian or an émigré from some other part of North Britain. He didn't talk at all like the cabdriver, and the cabdriver hadn't talked like the man behind the bar. "Nothing could be farther-a from my thoughts than to take up your-a time-a when you are-a waiting impatiently to hear our comrade Hugh Savage on-a 'No Newspapers—No Lies-a,' " the speaker continued. "But I feel-a im*pelled*-a to say a few worrds-a about the Great-a Crusade-a of Mr. Billy Graham—the old copitalist-a soporific of-a Pay in the Skay. The Crusade is financed-a by copitalists who want the worrkers to forget their legitimate-a grievances here-a below-a. But it os collopsed-a! Among the hoondreds-a of convairts—larrgely the same ones-a who come forward every night—there os been not one lad from the shipyards! Not one worrkingmon!" We of the audience, our backs flattened against the shopwindow of Dunn & Co., hatters, received these remarks in dead silence. The young men mutely peddled copies of an innocuous four-page newspaper called *Revolt.*

When the little man had shot his bolt against Pay in the Skay—forrcible rrevolution-a was *his* norrow poth to salvation—Comrade Savage mounted the stepladder. He grabbed the ends of the shelf as if they were the handle bars of a powerful motorbike on which he was taking off for immortality. Comrade Savage was a young man, short even in his elevator shoes, with a sullen, handsome Celtic face—high cheekbones, straight forehead, curly hair, and a profile that he appreciated. The capitalist press, he said, was a conspiracy against the worker to beguile him with stories of saix and distract his attainshun from the main eessues. The late Labour Government had, indeed, appointed a Commission of Enquiry into the press, but the chairman had been an Oxfurmon. How cou we expect conclusions of volue from an Oxfurmon? He spoke of Oxford in the tone Joe McCarthy uses for Harvard. The workers had shown what they could do by payralyzing this monster (the strike was destined to end three days later, but he didn't know that, of course), and sairtain sayctions of it might never recover. "The *Noo Skronikel,*" he shouted, referring to the London *News Chronicle,* "is reported to be on its laist laigs!" There was one national newspaper, he continued, that cou na be sayed to be copi'alist controlled—the *Daily Worker*—but that ha betrayed the Breetish workingmon by constituting i'self an instrument of Soviet foreign policy. He cited no specific instances of how the press had deceived the workingman; its chief crime, evidently, was that it "made the workingmon feel infeerior," and here, I felt, the recollection of some childhood snub echoed in the conceited, dogmatic voice. The men in caps listened silently. "Wain vaisted interaists os becoom the foonction of the praiss, we're be'er oaf wi'oot it!" he stormed, and subsided. There was a dead stillness. The men in caps dispersed. The boys with the duck-tail haircuts folded the stepladder. The meetings had presented two faces of old-fashioned intolerance, but the people on the street had paid hardly any attention to either. By the time they were over, though, I had heard so much about Billy Graham that I determined to see what went down nowadays.

NEXT EVENING, accordingly, I set out for the Kelvin Hall—across Argyle Street from Glasgow University—which is the Glaswegian Madison Square Garden. Monday is a more cheerful day than Sunday in Glasgow, if perhaps a less animated one in Eglinton. Pubs are open from noon until two-thirty and from six until nine-thirty, and bookstores all day. The weather continued grand.

As my cab approached the Kelvin Hall, I could have no doubt that the Crusade was big business. A row of nineteen tall masts with cross spars and banners gave the vicinity of the hall a nostalgic touch of the New York World's Fair Grounds of 1939, and the people flocking toward the great doors from their chartered charabancs, marked with names like Glackmannan and Argyll, had the scrubbed, sightseeing look of Fair visitors. "You're going to have a rare pleasure this evening, sir," the taxi-driver said as he let me out.

I almost didn't. Walking gaily in—it had never occurred to me that I needed a ticket to be saved—I was halted by a man of such righteous mien that I broke into a sweat of spiritual inferiority. Without a ticket, he told me, I could not enter the hall, from which I could already hear the strains of a smart potpourri of celestial music. "You may join the overflow in the sheeppen," he said. (The hall, I deduced, is sometimes used for livestock shows. I was glad he had not classed me among the goats.) The situation was redeemed by a uniformed attendant, who slithered up behind my back and pressed a slip of paper into my right palm. "Tha'll gait you a guid place," he whispered.

I reached into my pocket for a florin and then decided to begin my regeneration by declining to give a bribe. The fellow looked disappointed, but I felt a rewarding glow as I let the coin settle back in my pocket. It was a relatively good seat, at that—in what at the Garden would be the last row ringside. Behind me rose a high bleacher covered with clean people. There were similar bleachers on the three other sides of the rectangle; the services were conducted on a raised stage in the middle of the floor seats. A young man with mild acne and a badge marked "Steward" presented me with a Billy Graham songbook, bound in a Graham tartan. (The Crusade is always on the alert for local tieups.) I could return it at the end of the service, he said, or buy it, for three-and-six. I paid him three-and-six. A choir of women, which filled one bleacher, sang. There was a trombone solo and then a baritone solo, and then a slick fellow came onstage and asked those who were there for the first time to please stand. While we were in a distinct minority—the Crusade was beginning its fifth week—we constituted about a third of the house. "Well, how do you do?" the slick fellow asked, and got a laugh. "Where have *you* been?" he asked, milking it, and got another. "This great hall is filled to ca-*pass*-idy again," he cooed. "'Sa miracle." He then explained that it cost a lot to put on a Crusade—this one was costing forty-seven thousand pounds. The members of the Billy Graham party were not receiving one penny of this amount, he said, leaving us with a problem in the logistics of manna. Then the organ played and the collectors passed among us. I went for five bob.

After that, we all sang to ease our hearts, and presently the great evangelist began his broadcast discourse. He began slowly, with folksy-homesy remarks aimed at distant listeners, especially in places he had visited during his previous Crusade, in England. After that, he got onto goodness. Jesus had been good, he said; how many of his listeners thought they were good? He looked boyish, modest, and like the Glasgow concept of Hollywood. "Oh, compared to *me* you may be good," he went on, provoking a murmur, almost a titter, of horrified disclaimers. "But compared to *that* standard are you good?" Clearly, nobody was. The only way to start being good, then, he said, was to acknowledge one's sins and come to God. It wasn't good enough to have been good yesterday or the day before yesterday—you had to keep on starting all over again. From the faces around me, I could see that the audience thought it a discouraging prospect. But what happened if you put off the start? Well, the soul was the most *val*uable thing there was. The Devil wanted it because it was so *val*uable. God wanted it because it was so *val*uable. (He accented the first syllable strongly and sucked the liquid "l" lovingly.) Jesus had said, "For what shall it profit a man, if he shall gain the whole world, and lose his own soul?" That proved *one* soul was more *val*uable than the *whole* world, with all its countless mountains of precious metals, its great natural resources. The only way to be sure of not losing it was to come to God. It sounded to me like an argument for putting money in the savings bank, but it was apparently effective. Women around me began to betray uneasiness, as if walking up a narrow alley in a bad neighborhood at night with the rent money in their bag.

Mr. Graham now seized the opportunity to do a bit of cost accounting. "Yes," he told his listeners, "you may say, 'Forty-seven thousand pounds is a lot of money,' but *God* says the whole *world* is not so *val*uable as one man's soul. Forty-seven *million* pounds would be cheap if it meant saving one man's soul. Oh, the body is a wonderful institution, but it deteriates." I could see the more elderly auditors around me wince. "You may say, 'Oh, Billy, I don't have to make my decision today. I'll make it tomorrow. There's *always* time.' You remind me of the story of a great juggler, who juggled in vaudeville—in the music halls, as you would say."

Mr. Graham himself—tall, limber, and dressed in sports clothes—

looked like one of the suave-talking jugglers who used to appear second or third on the bill when there was vaudeville. He went into a juggling pantomime. Thirty thousand eyes were on him—at least if the attendance figures later issued by the Crusade's publicity department were right. For some of the congregation, I suppose, it was the nearest to a real music hall their principles would allow them to get. "This juggler was a European," Mr. Graham said, "and when the time came to go home—after years of hard work in the theatre—he took all his savings, his earnings of a lifetime, and invested them in a single *val*uable pearl. He thought he could sell it for a great deal more money when he got home. He put the pearl in his pocket." Mr. Graham put his hand in his pocket. "He got aboard the ship. He waved goodbye." Mr. Graham waved goodbye to somebody in the top tier of the bleachers. "*Bon voyage!*" he cried. ("Don't be frightened," I felt like telling the woman next to me. "He's not going yet.") "All went well," Mr. Graham said in slow, deep accents, "until the day before the end of the voyage." Here he began picking up speed. "It was the captain's dinnuh. The passengers gave an entertainment on deck. The juggler did his tricks. He was superb. He was marvellous. He was at the top of his form. His fellow-passengers applauded. The wine at dinnuh had gone to his head. He cried, '*Wait!* I'll show you something.' He ran to his cabin. He returned. He had his *pearl,* his *whole* fortune, in his hand." This sounded logical; he was wearing a tuxedo for the captain's dinner, and he had left the pearl in the pocket of his other suit. "He rushed up on deck, followed by the other passengers. He took the pearl." Mr. Graham held out his right hand, palm up. We craned forward to look, although we knew the pearl wasn't there. " 'This is the fruit of my life's labuh!' " Mr. Graham shouted, impersonating the possessed juggler. " 'I'm going to show you I'm the greatust juggluh in the world!' " North Carolina grew on him as he became more dramatic.

Mr. Graham pulled his arm back and swung it upward, as if throwing a high fly in a game of catch. "He threw it way up into the ayuh!" he cried. Then he turned away, to the evident alarm of his audience. Would the pearl fall behind him, and bounce into the sea? They need have had no fear. Mr. Graham is not the man to miss an imaginary catch. After a few seconds, he put out his hand again, palm up, and the imaginary pearl fell right into it. (He must have thrown it about a furlong.) "They apploaded," Billy said. "It intoxicated him. He took the *val*uable pearl again." Billy leaned over backward, cocked his arm, drew a bead on the ceiling of the Kelvin Hall, and threw the imaginary pearl right through it. "They all cried, 'You shouldn't have done *that!*' " he said. " 'Your pearl is lost!' " Ten seconds passed, and the people around me looked uneasy again. "But the juggluh reached out his hand," Mr. Graham said, supplying the gesture, "and there was his pearl again." (That time he must have thrown it a quarter of a mile.)

Fifteen thousand diaphragms relaxed in unison. But Mr. Graham continued his relentless recitation: " 'I'll show you!' the juggluh said. 'I'll throw it still further—out to sea—and it will return to me.' " The diaphragms contracted again, the eyes turned upward in horror as Mr. Graham started his windup. They could sense the dénouement. But this time it was a balk. "There was a woman in the crowd," the evangelist recalled. "She cried, 'Don't do that! We *know* you're a great juggluh! Don't imperil your most *val*uable possession!' But the juggluh"—Billy resumed his windup—"*threw* the pearl. It went high in the sky." This time he followed it with his eyes. "It seemed lost irrevocably. And then"—here he went through the routine of an airplane spotter taking cognizance of a hostile aircraft just before it goes into its dive and becoming more certain of its identity with every five thousand feet it drops toward him. There was an expression of foolish vainglory on his face as he stepped forward, almost to the edge of the platform, his hand outstretched for the catch. Then he staggered. The expression turned to horror, fading into despair. "Just as he reached out for his pearl, the ship gave a lurch," he said. "The pearl fell past his outstretched fingers—down, down, into the sea!" He knelt despairingly at the edge of the platform, peering down into the ringside crowd. A number of impressionable auditors ducked their heads to help him look for the pearl.

After that, Mr. Graham made the turn, as the pitchmen say, urging the converted to come forward before, like the juggluh, they stretched the Lord's patience too far. The organ played slow, Radio City Music Hall, celestial-type music, and by twos and threes the thrifty came to place their valuables in the heavenly safe-deposit vault while Mr. Graham wheedled. They were for the most part women, with mother-and-daughter combinations numerous among them, but there were men, too, most of them with their wives. Men unaccompanied by women were fewer, but there was one in clerical garb, with a Roman collar, who looked the way a real clergyman should. As the angry man on Drury Street had said, there were no workingmen to be seen among the converts. In Glasgow, a workingman dresses differently from a clerk. These were all white-collar people. Some of the women were sniffling, but none appeared to be undergoing any violent emotional crisis, like converts in the old camp-meeting tradition. Many looked as if they had been through the process before, and, indeed, if you are going to keep a high polish on your salvation, you must renew it regularly, as the evangelist had been at pains to explain in the first part of his address. (The attendance at the Kelvin Hall meetings, regularly supplied to the press by the Crusade publicity department, averaged around fifteen thousand—or near capacity—and the number of "decisions" just as consistently averaged a little under five hundred. Since two-thirds of the audience on that particular evening were recidivists, it is logical to suppose that two-thirds of the converts were, too.)

Others patently hesitated in their seats. When the human flow toward the platform appeared to have ceased, several young men went forward, among them my acquaintance, the steward who had sold me the songbook. The employment of this small strategic reserve appeared to have a stimulating effect on the undecided; a few more mother-and-daughter pairs made their way to the front. The most distressed persons in the audience near me were two adolescent girls, sitting about ten yards apart, who couldn't quite bring themselves to get up—either too self-conscious, I suppose, or clinging to a sinful preoccupation with boys. They probably took away from the hall with them a sufficient load of guilt to make them unbearable for years. The effects of the Crusade on the saved are quite possibly less lasting than the traumata sowed among the almost-saved.

The reclaimed souls, after huddling a while in prayer around the pastor, were herded off to a detention pen, where, I was given to understand, their names and addresses would be placed on cards that would be mailed out to resident ministers for follow-up treatment. (Some of the ministers, I also understand, consider this a great bore, since they are unprepared to maintain the standard of showmanship the crusaded expect.) We were enjoined not to leave the Kelvin Hall until all of them had been checked in. When the last had disappeared from the public ken, I looked at my watch—a gesture that becomes a reflex after a few days in Glasgow. It was precisely nine-thirty, and too late to buy a drink.

25
The Case of the Scattered Dutchman

THE afternoon of Saturday, June 26, 1897, was warm and moist in New York City, and it is probable that boys were swimming off every idle dock in the North and East Rivers. James McKenna, thirteen years old, of 219 Avenue C, and John McGuire, fourteen years old, of 722 East Twelfth Street—both addresses within a few steps of the East River—were among those who at three o'clock were swimming in the slip on the south side of what was then a disused dock at the foot of East Eleventh Street.

I will lift the next five paragraphs bodily from a story at the top of the first page of the Sporting Edition of the *Evening Telegram* of that date, because I cannot think of any sound way to amend them:

> They saw an object slip into the line of vision past the edge of the dock, and the cross current gave it the appearance of trying to enter the slip. It looked much like a package of merchandise, but the article in which it was wrapped looked like a bright piece of bunting or a flag, with the sun striking it.
>
> The two boys swam eagerly toward what they thought would prove a prize. The bright covering they found to be oil-cloth, and the package was carefully tied up with good strong string.
>
> McKenna got on one side and McGuire on the other and between them the package was brought inside the slip and one of the boys pulled one end of the string from around the oilcloth and dropped it over the edge of the stringpiece.
>
> There was a general rush on the part of the dock hangers-on to furnish a knife, and McGuire slipped back over the edge of the dock and dug the knife in the oilcloth covering.
>
> The knife stuck and refused to come out, and the boy gave it a wrench. Then he tried again, and succeeded in working a small hole in the cloth. He saw something white, and the sticky feeling of the knife blade sickened him.

The *Telegram*, which specialized in sporting news, had a later final edition than the city's other afternoon papers, since its readers counted on it to report the winner of the last race at Sheepshead Bay. (The race that day was a steeplechase, won by Mars Chan, at 2–1.) On Saturdays, the *Telegram's* Sporting Edition was even later than on other days, because there were seven races instead of six. The story of the discovery in the East River was the only important non-sporting item on the first page, and over it were these headlines:

MAN'S TRUNK
FLOATS IN RIVER
HEADLESS AND LEGLESS BODY WRAPPED
IN OILCLOTH GETS INTO EAST
ELEVENTH STREET SLIP
FOUND BY SWIMMING BOYS
THEY THINK THEY HAVE A FIND, BUT
MAKE A GHASTLY DISCOVERY
IS THE WORK OF AN EXPERT
CUTS LOOK LIKE THOSE OF DISSECTING
TABLE—MAN WAS IN PRIME

The other top headlines on the page dealt with a bicycle race at Manhattan Beach, the victory of the New York Giants over the Washington Senators (both in the National League then), and the triumph of a two-year-old named Blueaway in the Zephyr Stakes, twenty-five hundred dollars added. (A well-played second choice, he also paid 2–1.)

After telling of the sickened boy, the unknown *Telegram* writer continued:

> It was not until a half hour later that someone reported the matter to the Union Market police station [this was on First Avenue, near Tenth Street], saying merely that something securely wrapped in cloth was knocking against the end of the dock.
>
> Policeman Winter was detailed to take care of the matter. With the assistance of some laborers, he got the package upon the boards.
>
> The policeman cut the cords and rolled back the oilcloth, disclosing to view the trunk of a man, in an almost perfect state of preservation.
>
> The neck had been severed cleanly from the body, almost on a line with the shoulders, and the work was done in such a manner as to lead to the

conclusion that it was that of someone accustomed to handling amputating instruments.

The work of amputating the legs had not been done so cleanly. They had been severed from the trunk just below the abdomen, in a rather slovenly fashion, not at all like the work of a dissecting table.

The chest had been marked and scarred in a peculiar manner. The flesh had been lifted from the bones just below the left breast and cut off cleanly all the way across the chest to a point almost on a line with the shoulder. The cut was even and laid open to view several of the ribs.

This, in connection with the clean amputation at the neck, inclines the police to the theory that the trunk was fresh from the dissecting table when found.

The only drawback to this is the unprofessional work on the lower half of the trunk.

The possibility that the dissection had been performed by two persons working in great haste—the more professional member of the team on the neck, the other on the torso—had not occurred to the *Telegram* man.

A district reporter for the *Telegram* may have been in the police station when the tip came in, and accompanied Policeman Winter to the dock, or he may have learned of the find from the station blotter and hurried to the dock while the parcel was being dragged from the water. In either event, he—or a police surgeon he may have talked to—was clearly an excellent observer, and the further development of the case was to confirm not only the details he phoned in to the rewrite man but many of the rewrite man's immediate deductions from them. It may be, of course, that my own deductions about how the *Telegram* story was put together are in error, and that the city editor, apprised by telephone of the interesting nature of the find (he could hardly have been informed of it before four o'clock), dispatched a star reporter straight to the scene in a hack. Even with the prevailing speed limit of twelve miles an hour, the reporter could have got from the *Telegram* office, in Herald Square, to the foot of East Eleventh Street in twenty minutes, made his notes from his own observation, and returned to his desk by five, after which he could have written his story between the fifth and seventh races. This would have been drawing it fine, however, even for the newspaper titans of 1897, when, according to an old journalistic friend of mine named

Ned Brown, "what they call a porterhouse now wouldn't have counted as a chuck steak."

The rewrite job, as I therefore judge it to be, continues:

The trunk is that of a man who was evidently in the prime of life. He must have weighed fully 180 pounds, and the arms are big and powerful. The chest is that of a man accustomed to unusual exertion and regular calls for increased lung power.

The flesh is clear and white, and indicates that the man was in perfect health, and the muscles of the body show plainly that their possessor was a giant in strength.

The hands are small when figured in proportion to the evident weight and height of the man. The fingers are small and well shaped and do not resemble in any way the fingers of a man accustomed to manual labor.

On the inside of the left palm is a small blue mark, evidently extending deep into the cuticle. It looks as though it might have been burned in with powder. There are no needle pricks to indicate it is a tattoo mark, nor is there any regular formation to it.

The oilcloth in which the body was enclosed was brand new. It had never been placed on a floor as a covering, the underside bearing no mark. It was of good quality. The pattern was red squares with small gilt stars.

The string was white, very heavy, and after the knots were tied had been cut cleanly with a sharp instrument. Scissors or a small pocket knife would not have been able to cut it so cleanly.

A curious crowd surrounded the object as it lay on the Eleventh Street dock. A messenger was sent to the Coroner's office.

The police are taking an extraordinary amount of interest in the case, owing to a great extent to the signs of refinement and the fact that the body had been but such a short time in the water.

Between the oilcloth and the spine of the trunk was found a sheet of new cheesecloth, a little heavier than the ordinary kind, more like that used in hospitals, but in no way resembling absorbent cloth.

This discovery has served to strengthen the theory of the police that the work is that of a band of medical students from the dissecting table of a hospital.

In substantiation of the rumor of foul play, its adherents point to the peculiar wound on the breast, claiming that the strip of flesh may have been taken off to destroy tattoo marks or other marks that would help toward an identification.

They also claim that the legs may have been marked in some way, and they too were taken off and disposed of in some way.

None of the other afternoon papers—the *Evening World,* the *Evening Journal,* and the *Evening Sun*—had so complete and incisive a story. Their city desks had been put off by the first reports from the police of the precinct, who, the *Evening World's* brief story said, "incline to the belief that the body may be that of a medical subject." The police claimed later that they had taken this position in an effort to keep the newspaper sleuths out of their way while they got started on the serious business of investigation, but the *Journal,* having been caught flat-footed, continued for weeks to charge that the police had tried to squelch the story just to save themselves trouble. The *Journal's* implication was that Lord knew how many other crimes had been shrugged off in this fashion; only the enterprise of newspaper reporters—the *Journal's,* of course—had forced the police to revise their attitude in the torso case.

The next morning's *Sun,* on behalf of its teammate, the *Evening Sun,* attributed the medical-subject theory to pure stupidity on the part of the police, and the *World* of that Sunday morning took the same position. The paper was on to the possibilities of the story and gave it two columns on the first page, under the headline "BOY'S GHASTLY FIND." In the course of its account, the *World* observed, "It does not appear that the police made any attempt at investigation, but jumped at and accepted the theory that the portion of the human being had been cast into the river by the students of some medical college who had been studying anatomy." According to the *World,* the discovery that it was probably a case of murder had been made by doctors at the morgue, after the torso was removed there.

None of the Sunday papers had anything substantial to add to the *Telegram* account, although they padded it out with direct quotations from the coroner, a Dr. Tuthill; the medical examiner, a Dr. Dow; and the Superintendent of Bellevue, a Mr. Murphy. (First names of such well-known civic characters were evidently considered superfluous in news stories of that golden age.) Both the *World* and the *Herald* were skeptical about the likelihood of a solution. "The finding of the upper portion of the headless trunk of a man in the East River yesterday furnishes a mystery that will not easily be solved," the *World* reported, and went on, "All indications point to an atrocious murder. There is, however, no apparent clue by which the identity of the victim may be discovered, or his slayer brought to justice." The *Herald* stated, "There is nothing to tell when or where the crime was committed, whether on land or on sea, and there is not one chance in a million that the identity of the victim will be discovered." The suggestion that the man had been murdered and dismembered aboard a ship evoked the romantic possibility that he had been a Spaniard spying on Cuban gunrunners. The police said he could not have been a sailor, because there were no calluses on his hands.

THE morning *World* and the *Evening World* had different staffs but shared the eleventh floor of the proud new Pulitzer Building, on Park Row, and dovetailed their coverage of running stories. The Pulitzer Building, with its sixteen floors, was the tallest building in New York, and from their city rooms the men of both *Worlds* could look over to and beyond the North River or out to sea, as well as at Brooklyn, across the only bridge there was over the East River at that time. All Manhattan lay visibly at their feet, and it accentuated their cockiness. The *World* had a circulation of 370,000, which was almost as much as the four other morning papers had among them. These were the *Herald* and the *Sun, ex aequo* with 120,000; the *Times,* with 75,000; and the *Tribune,* with 76,000. The *World's* predominance had been achieved within a few years after Joseph Pulitzer came to New York from St. Louis and bought the paper from Jay Gould, in 1883. The *Evening World,* founded by Pulitzer four years later, had overshadowed its afternoon contemporaries just as decisively until it was challenged by a newer newcomer—young William Randolph Hearst's *Journal,* which made its appearance in 1895. Hearst was trying to take over Pulitzer's afternoon field by imitating all Pulitzer's circus tricks and then adding an extra elephant for the clowns to jump over. By 1897, despite brilliant retaliatory strokes on the part of Pulitzer, Hearst was beginning to show results. The *Evening World* still led the afternoons, with a circulation of 360,000, but the *Journal* claimed 309,000, and was gaining. The *Evening Sun* and the *Evening Telegram,* with 100,000 each, were out of the hunt; Edwin Godkin's *Evening Post,* with 25,000, had become a symbol of the unpopularity of virtue.

The Hearst-Pulitzer feud made for virulent competition, and in its course reporters became direct rivals of the police. A *World* or a *Journal* man finding a useful clue at the scene of a crime would bring it back to his newspaper, in which it would appear as a chalk-plate illustration over the vainglorious line "Made from a photograph taken in the *World* [or *Journal*] office." Had reporters reached the East Eleventh Street dock before the police on the day the torso was found, the officers would have attached no significance to the chunk missing from the victim's brisket. They would have been sure that a *World* or a *Journal* man had carried it away.

Reporters developed their own leads in solving crimes, outbidding the police for stool pigeons and at times outbidding the detective branch for details observed by uniformed men. Then they would follow through in person, "arresting" suspects, if the latter didn't appear dangerous, and extorting confessions from them. These they would publish as scoops. The practice sometimes proved momentarily awkward when it developed that a reporter had abducted an innocent party, but there were few such mistakes a ten-dollar bill couldn't square. Neither the *World* nor the *Journal* begrudged outlays occasioned by excessive zeal. In making "arrests," the reporters, who had shiny badges and pistol permits, usually represented themselves as detectives, but when printing the story their papers invariably said they had "made the arrest as citizens." Some of the reporters, as one might expect, became better detectives than most city detectives, and when a big case broke, the Police Department would put tails on the leading newspapermen, while the newspapers would put tails on the more resourceful detectives. This was a form of recognition the latter enjoyed to the point of sticking to familiar disguises in order not to throw the journalists off their track. Naturally, there were exchanges of information between friends in the two professions, by which cops helped reporters to discredit rival reporters and reporters helped cops to discredit rival cops.

The *World* and the *Journal* assumed airs of independent sovereignty. In headlines as well as editorials, the rival sheets gave themselves credit for defeating candidates they had opposed, rectifying conditions they had deplored, stopping outbreaks of leprosy they said they had detected, setting fashions, making slang, and, above all, solving crimes. Even the sportswriters conveyed the impression that they were not merely reporting games but coaching both teams and refereeing. "Being a newspaperman gave you stature then," says Ned Brown. "Everywhere except in society. It didn't cut any ice there. But elsewhere a first-string reporter on any recognized paper—especially one of the *Worlds*—had a lot of prestige. *Civis Romanus erat.* He was a citizen of no mean state."

TODAY, Ned Brown, a small man, is as spare and brisk as a whippet, with a sharp, inquisitive profile and lively blue eyes. He prides himself on his penetrating *coup d'oeil*, which makes him a master at rapid chess and crossword puzzles, and at sizing up situations. Mr. Brown has worked for only one newspaper in his life—the *World*. The job lasted thirty-four years, until the paper ceased publication in 1931. During most of his service with the *World*, he was a boxing writer, but he didn't begin as one. When the mysterious torso was fished from the river, Ned was a very junior member of the *World* staff; he was working there during the summer vacation following his first year at Bellevue Hospital Medical School, which was then situated at Twenty-sixth Street and First Avenue, across the street from the hospital, with its wards and morgue. He did small assignments, mostly legwork, at space rates—five dollars a column if he telephoned the stuff to a rewrite man and seven dollars and a half if he wrote it himself. The bits he wrote personally were for the most part humorous items he picked up at night in the Tenderloin—the bright-light district that, by his definition, ran from Thirtieth Street to Forty-second, between Sixth and Eighth Avenues. He liked the Tenderloin beat because it permitted him to spend his nights in saloons—looking at people, listening, and fancying himself a young man about town—without having to disguise the fact from his father, who was Frederick Sherwood Brown, the telegraph editor of the *World*. The elder Brown had established his family in Flatbush, a remote *faubourg* of the independent City of Brooklyn.

Ned found Flatbush slow. His official hours were from two in the afternoon until midnight, but often when he was covering the Tenderloin he worked an extra hour or two, business merging with pleasure. On such occasions, the long journey home to Flatbush—by steam elevated train to Brooklyn Bridge and then by trolley car into the dark interior of Long Island—frequently seemed too dismal to endure, and then he would spend the rest of the night in the Murray Hill Baths, on Forty-second Street. The Murray Hill Baths were not on Murray Hill but between Broadway and Sixth Avenue, and, like all the other Turkish-bath establishments of the region, they stayed open all night. Turkish baths were infinitely more popular and numerous then than they are now; men on the town for the evening regularly wound up in one or another of them. An individual cubicle cost a dollar, a bed in the dormitory fifty cents; the ticket for either one included a scrubbing and use of the steam room and the plunge, universally esteemed specifics for overindulgence; an alcohol rub cost an extra two bits. There was always a tip for the rubber, who would not scorn a dime. The baths all favored a fanciful Oriental décor, like the tiled interior of a mosque. The Murray Hill was one of the largest and most ornate.

In those days, Mr. Brown says, few medical students went to a liberal-arts college; he himself entered medical college straight from Erasmus Hall High School, in Brooklyn, and in 1897 he was still in his teens. He was a hard-liquor drinker, but not when he was working; on those nights, he would buy a beer or two in each establishment he visited, "just to hold the franchise." When he retired to the baths, therefore, his mind would still be clear and his curiosity active; he would engage the rubbers in conversation and sometimes land a boulevardesque anecdote worth a dollar and a half at space rates, or a bit of information that might come in handy someday as background. He was keenly interested in anatomy, which was then, as it is now, the principal subject of the medical first year. At the baths, he had before his eyes a living exhibit of anatomical and dermatological peculiarities, and he was accustomed to discuss these with the rubbers; at heart every masseur is a doctor *manqué.*

Ned doesn't recall being in the *World* city room when the torso was first reported, and he is sure he wasn't sent uptown to the dock. But when he read the Sunday papers the next morning he was fascinated—both as a medical student and as a newspaperman. Coroner Tuthill, he noted, had told reporters at the morgue that the disaggregated man could not have been dead more than twenty-four hours when his chest was taken out of the river; Dr. Dow had said "ten hours at the most." Even if one accepted the longer estimate, and added a few hours for possible error, the man could not have been killed earlier than Friday. The conclusions different doctors reached as to his height and heft varied a bit—one doctor explained that his estimate of five feet ten inches depended on the premise that a man's height is equal to the reach of his outstretched arms—but all agreed that he had been taller than average. Every newspaper account mentioned the solid but unworkmanlike hands. He had been a man who kept himself in good physical trim, but not by hard labor. A wealthy sportsman? A college athlete? An Army officer? Any one of them would make a corking good victim from a newspaper point of view. Ned had a special family interest in this kind of murder, because his father, while a reporter on the Cincinnati *Enquirer,* had cleared up the murder of a girl named Pearl Bryan, whose severed head had been thrown from the suspension bridge over the Ohio River between Cincinnati and Covington, Kentucky. The guilty wretch may have hoped thus to create a conflict of jurisdiction; the elder Brown, however, proved that the actual crime had been committed on the Ohio side of the river. It is a spiritless son who would not like to outdo his father, but Ned, as he rode the trolley over the bridge to work that Sunday afternoon (like all young and single men on seven-day newspapers at that time, he worked Sundays and had a weekday off), had small hope that he would be assigned to the Ghastly Find story. The Ghastly Find would be in the competent hands of Gus Roeder, the *World's* homicide specialist, and of Bill Reitmeier, who covered Police Headquarters, on Mulberry Street. They would need no help in keeping the story fresh for a day or two, after which, if it was as hopeless as the morning-paper stories indicated, it would lapse and be forgotten.

When Ned stepped off the elevator on the eleventh floor of the Pulitzer Building, he had no need of his peculiar gift to recognize that something extraordinary had happened. The day staff on Sunday was always light, but on that particular afternoon the city room was perfectly empty except for one early copyreader and the man on the desk—a Sunday substitute for Edward J. Casey, the *World's* assistant city editor. The man on the desk was telephoning, and as he saw Ned come in he put his hand over the mouthpiece and beckoned him with a sweep of his arm. When other reserves are exhausted, even the summer soldier is welcome. The man on the desk took less than a minute to tell Ned that a second parcel wrapped in oilcloth with a pattern of red squares and small gilt stars had been found, this one on the Bronx side of the Harlem River, at about the latitude of 176th Street, or ten miles from where the torso had turned up. Two boys out berrying with their father had come upon it in a sylvan setting, into which it had apparently been tossed from Undercliff Avenue, a winding carriage drive on the side of a hill. When the parcel was opened at the High Bridge police station, in the Bronx, it had yielded another section of the cadaver. The captain there had dispatched it to the morgue to be matched up with the East River bit. "If the pieces fit, it's the same stiff," the man on the desk said. "If it's part of a different stiff, then the guy with the red oilcloth has murdered them both." He spoke, Ned remembers, with the pleasure of a man who cannot lose. From the moment the first tip about the second bundle came in from Reitmeier, the Sunday city editor had been calling every member of the staff he could reach by telephone—directing those who lived uptown to the region of the find and ordering the downtown fellows to converge on the morgue or Police Headquarters. He had also been sending out the regular Sunday men as they reported for duty. He told Ned to hustle up to the morgue and report to Gus Roeder, who was running the Pulitzer operation there. "Do whatever Gus tells you," he said, unnecessarily. "The *Journal's* probably got forty guys there already." Mr. Brown recalls his emotion on being assigned to his first big story, even though he anticipated only a legman's role (for which he was well fitted, being a tireless runner and weighing precisely a hundred and nineteen pounds). The field of his début could not have been better chosen, for, owing to his year at medical school, he was familiar with the morgue, and if there was one subject on which he would back his own opinion, it was a cadaver. The steam elevated bore him to the vicinity of the morgue in quick time, and he ran the rest of the way at a quarter-miler's pace.

Gus Roeder, the homicide man, was a red-faced German-American, already in his forties and therefore, to Ned, a hoary veteran. He could express himself well in English but spoke the language with a perceptible accent. (He worked from pencilled notes, which he surrounded with rhetoric as he dictated his stories to an office boy who, unlike him, knew how to run a typewriter.) He wore conservative dark clothes and a hard hat, and was not enough of a bohemian to be popular with his fellow-reporters. He was on good terms with a powerful faction of the detective force, however, and exchanged information with his police friends, to their advantage and his. He was also a friend of Frederick Sherwood Brown's, and knew that Ned was a medical student. The Bronx portion of torso had by this time been brought downtown, and the two fragments, put together, matched as neatly as pieces of a jigsaw puzzle; so did the cut edges of the two sheets of oilcloth. The second piece of victim included everything from the abdomen to a point above the knees, where the saw or knife had been employed again to detach the legs. These hadn't turned up yet. Ned found the juxtaposed segments of great interest. "The gaping ends of the blood vessels at the neck, where the head had been severed, and the thighs, where the legs had been cut off, indicated that the man had lost a considerable amount of blood before expiring," he says now, relapsing into his freshman patter. "In other words, the guy had been alive while they were cutting him up. That knocked out the medical-school idea." Ned also had a long look at the highly publicized hands. When he finished, he told Roeder what he suspected, and Roeder instructed him to follow his hunch. Roeder already had a score of men out working on even longer shots.

SOME indication of the number of paths Roeder's men explored was to be found in the *World* of Monday, June 28th. A five-column top head on the first page thundered:

THE FRAGMENTS OF A
BODY MAKE A MYSTERY

Under it, in lines three columns wide, was:

A PIECE OF A MANGLED TRUNK FOUND
YESTERDAY IN HARLEM FITS AN-
OTHER PIECE FOUND SATURDAY
IN THE EAST RIVER
BOTH WRAPPED IN RED
AND GOLD OILCLOTH

Then, in single column:

A MAN OF THE MIDDLE OR BETTER
CLASS HAS EVIDENTLY BEEN
BRUTALLY KILLED
MANY STABS WOUNDS AND BRUISES
PORTIONS OF THE BODY, WHICH MAY
HAVE CONTAINED MARKS OF IDEN-
TIFICATION, CUT AWAY
THE POLICE ARE AS
YET ENTIRELY AT SEA
CARL WEINECKE, WHO DISAPPEARED
MAY 17, HAD MARKS WHICH
WOULD FIT PLACES CUT
AWAY ON THE DEAD
TRUNK
CORONER TUTHILL HAS
A THEORY OF HIS OWN
THINKS THE VICTIM WAS ATTACKED
AND KILLED IN A FIGHT AFTER A
HARD STRUGGLE

The text of the lead, set in bold type, was exclamatory and consecrated to the obvious. "Somewhere in Greater New York or near it since late Friday afternoon an awful crime has been committed" is a fair sample.

The layout of pictures on the front page illustrated the peculiar attraction of the great Pulitzer's journalism. Nestling under three columns of the top headline was a chalk-plate reproduction of the "Hand of the Headless Murdered Man—Exact Size (from a flashlight photograph made in the morgue last night by a *World* photographer)." The hands of the victim had been described in various accounts as large, small, and medium-sized. When I first saw the "exact-size" illustration in a bound volume of *Worlds,* I could not resist an impulse to put my hand over it and compare the two, and I suspect that three of every four readers of the paper in 1897 did the same thing. (From my comparison, I judge that the victim, like me, wore a size-8½ glove with a wide palm and short fingers.) The stubby thumb in the *World's* photograph was superimposed on a map showing "Route headless shoulders would take in floating from spot where other part of body was found." This had been drawn in accordance with a theory, enunciated in an interview granted by a former Chief of the United States Secret Service named Andrew L. Drummond, that the murder had been committed in the Bronx and part of the body thrown from High Bridge into the Harlem, which leads into the East River. "It would be foolish for a man to carry the body from the Battery, say, to High Bridge in order to throw it into the water," Mr. Drummond had told a *World* reporter. Next to the upper, or Bronx, end of the map was a sketch of "where the trunk of the body was found," and, next to the Eleventh Street end, a sketch of "where boys found the headless shoulders." The layout was completed by illustrations of the oilcloth ("reproduced from sample brought to the *World* office") and of the "clumsy knot with which each bundle was tied" (also "photographed in the *World* office").

Inside the paper were a dozen stories on assorted angles of the case. The wife of a Dane named Weinecke—an unemployed lumber inspector, of 82 East 115th Street, who had disappeared on May 17th—thought the installments might be of him. The *World* had to take some account of her views, although it did so with patent unenthusiasm; he would have made an anti-climactic victim, despite a half-hearted effort on the part of the editors to supply him with a mysterious past before his arrival in this country. There was a long story on efforts that were being made to trace the red-and-gold oilcloth pattern through jobbers to retailers, in order to question everyone who might remember selling any recently. Police authorities had wisely refused to theorize about the murder, and in revenge the *World* and the other morning papers said they were incompetent and "all at sea." The medical men had allowed themselves to be drawn more easily, and the reporters had induced Dr. Philip F. O'Hanlon, the coroner's physician who performed the autopsy, to venture a surmise as to how the man had been killed. "From what I can learn from the condition of the body, I should say that this is what occurred," the *World* quoted Dr. O'Hanlon as extrapolating. (It was the decade of Sherlock Holmes, and every physician felt that Dr. Watson had been unfairly dealt with.) "The man, who was a big, powerful fellow, was attacked. He made a strong resistance, but I should say he was overpowered by numbers. That he was knocked down I think is proved by the imprints of the toe and boot-heel on his arm. Some of the other bruises on his body may have come from kicks. I should say that he struggled to his feet and was standing erect when someone, who must have been very muscular, stabbed him in the collarbone with a big knife. This was followed immediately afterward by another wound—that which cut the heart. That caused death immediately. The blood under the thumbnail shows that he struggled hard or else that he clasped his hand to his bosom after he had been stabbed."

A *World* story on the autopsy itself reported:

> A close inspection was made of the hands with a view to determining the man's position in life. They were long and broad, the fingers were well formed, and while the palms were not callous, yet they indicated that the man had done some work, not recently, perhaps. The nails were cut down almost to the quick, evenly rounded, as though their owner had taken some care of them.
>
> The fingertips of the left hand were smooth and even; on the forefinger was a scar extending from the nail back to the second joint. It was an old one, and in the opinion of the examining physician, might have been caused by an operation. . . . There was little hair on the body, the arms, or the hands, and the latter showed little of the effect of the sun.
>
> Not a man who could live without work, was the judgment of those who examined the trunk, nor yet a man whose livelihood was earned by hard manual labor; he might have been a policeman, a carpenter, a bartender.

The most romantic reconstruction of the crime was furnished by Drummond:

> Andrew L. Drummond, for twenty-two years Chief of the Secret Service of the United States Government, and now head of a great detective agency in this city, with offices at No. 1 Park Row, is greatly interested in the developments in the murder case [the *World* reported].
>
> "I read the account in Sunday's *World*," said Mr. Drummond last night, "and from what you tell me now of the finding of another part of the body near High Bridge and of the result of the autopsy, I believe that this most atrocious murder was committed by a foreigner.
>
> "In the whole history of crime in this country murders which were done with like ferocity as this have always been committed by foreigners, usually those of a warmer climate than ours.
>
> "I should judge, from what I have heard of this case, that the murderer is a Sicilian, or possibly a Spaniard or Cuban. Maybe a Spanish spy has been put out of the way by Cubans.
>
> "But the theory of the murder which strikes me as the most likely one is that it is the result of a family feud among Sicilians. I know the ways of the Mafia so well that this strikes me as the most plausible theory. The red oilcloth points to Sicilians, who love bright colors. . . .
>
> "Probably the murdered man was invited to a friendly game of cards at the home of the murderer, who had sworn a vendetta against him for some wrong to his wife or sweetheart. Then, in an unguarded moment, the man was killed and his body cut up for disposal by one or several men."

The Drummond story was the last on the murder in the *World* (it brought the total space the paper devoted to the case to eight and a quarter columns, not counting pictures), and was followed by this plug, in boldface type: "Further developments in New York's great murder mystery will appear in the editions of the *Evening World*."

NED BROWN, reading the story about the hands in the Monday-morning *World*, may have feared that a couple of the details would set somebody else to thinking along the line he was already following. But if so, there was nothing he could do about it, and he had a full program for the day. Ned was searching for a kind of soap called Cotaspam, or Kotaspam—he is no longer sure of the exact spelling. Not that he looked as though he needed soap; that morning Ned was probably the cleanest man in Greater New York. His naturally pink skin was now positively translucent. He had in a pocket ten dollars that he had drawn from the *World* treasurer, on the authorization of Gus Roeder, to use as expenses. Cotaspam was expensive soap—twenty-five cents a cake. Ned had to walk over to Broadway to find a druggist who stocked it, and when he did, he bought two boxes containing a dozen bars each, for a total of six dollars.

The reason Ned wanted Cotaspam specifically, he says, was that once, before having dinner at the home of a wealthy boy he was tutoring in Brooklyn, he had washed his hands in the bathroom there and had been so impressed with the fragrance of the soap that he asked the name of the brand. "It smelled Elysian to me," Mr. Brown says now. "Sandalwood, verbena, geranium, Sen-Sen, and Ed Pinaud's Eau de Quinine all in one." With the two boxes under his arm, Ned took a Broadway car as far as Herald Square, where he transferred to a westbound Thirty-fourth Street crosstown and rode to Ninth Avenue. Then he walked half a block north and entered a tenement at 441 Ninth Avenue. It was a family neighborhood of working people, mostly respectable and chiefly German or Irish. During the years after the end of the Civil War, brick tenements had replaced frame houses as the city marched north. They were mostly small buildings, three or four stories high, with two families on a floor, and sometimes a store on the street level. A parking lot occupies the west, or odd-numbered, side of the block now, but some even-numbered houses still standing on the east side of the avenue in the next block north give at least an idea of what the neighborhood must have looked like. Ned climbed the stairs to the top floor of No. 441 and worked his way down, knocking at each door in turn. There was a woman in practically every flat, and to each Ned presented a cake of soap and delivered a little spiel. The company he represented was trying to find a larger market for its soap, he said, and so was making a special introductory offer. Each recipient was to use the soap for a day, just to experience how good it was. If she liked it, she could give him a nickel for it when he returned in the evening; if not, she was privileged to return the soap without any obligation. "One smell and they fell for it," Mr. Brown says. "They could tell it was expensive soap. Some of them wanted to give me a nickel right then, but I said no dice. 'The company wants to get your opinion of its product after you have used it,' I would say. 'I will be back at six o'clock.' " Such door-to-door canvassing was more common then than it is now; Ned had heard the routine scores of times in his own home. His appearance was plausible; he was young and thin, and wore a cap and a shiny second-best suit. He got rid of half a box of soap in No. 441 and then went through the same performance in Nos. 439 and 437, omitting only one apartment. This was on the second floor, above a drugstore, in No. 439, and a nameplate on its door bore the legend "Mrs. Augusta Nack, Licensed Midwife." When Ned had finished with No. 437, he had only a couple of cakes left, and he stuck them in his pockets. It was nearly noon, and he walked out of the neighborhood to a café near Herald Square to eat lunch and look over the afternoon papers as they came out. Talk about the elegant soap would spread through the three tenements, he knew; the women visited across the halls or from their fire escapes in warm weather, and in the afternoon there would be knots of them on the sidewalk getting a breath of cool air.

"There is nothing like a sweet smell to catch a woman," Mr. Brown says. "I know it from experience now, but at the time I had to figure it out for myself. I was what you might call precocious." Ned read the afternoon papers with apprehension, which turned to smugness as he found more and more signs that they were off what he felt was the right track. Monday morning's papers had had a big new development to report—the discovery of the second segment. All the afternoons could do was ramify speculation.

RIVER'S MURDER MYSTERY
GROWS STRANGER AND DEEPER

the three-o'clock edition of the *Evening World* proclaimed, listing Clues (no new ones) and Theories (same) in its lead. It had on its front page a portrait of the missing Weinecke (which it spelled Weincke), three columns wide, with question marks at either side of his head, but he bore an unexciting resemblance to a testimonial writer in a patent-medicine ad. "Is he the murdered man?" the caption writer asked, and most readers' reaction to Mr. Weinecke's photograph must have been "Who cares?" The *Evening World* had balanced its front page with an equal display of a story headed "JOHN L. SPARS WITH WORLD MAN," written and illustrated by the *World* man, W. O. Inglis; his account of this terrifying experience took the form of a letter addressed to Bob Fitzsimmons, the heavyweight champion, to fight whom the thirty-eight-year-old John L. Sullivan had announced his emergence from retirement. (Sullivan's advertised comeback had a patriotic motive. On losing his championship to

James J. Corbett, in 1892, he had said, "I am glad I was beaten by an American." On March 17, 1897, Corbett had lost the title to Fitzsimmons, a New Zealander born in Cornwall.) "Friends tied on our four-ounce gloves," Inglis wrote. "I could not have tied a knot in a two-inch hawser, much less in the laces of a boxing glove. You will feel that way, Mr. Fitzsimmons, when you are getting ready to go into the ring with Sullivan." It was the true *World* tone, and it amused Ned, who correctly suspected that the comeback would go no further than the first time Sullivan raised a thirst.

In the *Evening World,* the exact-size picture of the victim's hand had been moved back to page 2 and reinforced with a diagram of the body, in which the recovered portions were printed in black and missing areas in gray. "The inhuman, fiendish manner in which the butcher cut up the remains of his victim seems to suggest that it was the work of a maniac," a hard-pressed rewrite man had ventured, and there were a couple of sidelight stories on the Jack-the-Ripper murders in London and other unsolved mysteries. "The superb handling of this interesting case in the *World* this morning, both as regards writing and illustration, made all other morning papers look like second-rate provincial sheets," a house plug at the bottom of the page announced. "If there is anything left to tell about the mystery when today's *Evening World* is done with it, the *World* tomorrow morning will again show the little imitation morning papers how to handle a big local story. From the *Evening World's* last night extra the thread of the strange crime will be taken up and carried on by the morning edition. The *World* is a continuous performance of newsgiving—morning, noon, and night. It never stops. It has no rival. Remember that." Despite this advertised unity, there was hot rivalry between the staffs of the *World* and the *Evening World.*

The *Evening Sun,* which had lost the dash of its Dana days, took a thoroughly dim view of the case and assailed the police. "Indications in Mulberry Street this morning pointed to the conclusion that the police had not yet waked up to the serious import of the case," it grumbled. "Chief Conlin wasn't there. . . . Chief Conlin is a man who has no taste for murder mysteries. . . . Capt. O'Brien [the chief of detectives] has even less than Conlin. Like every other policeman not possessed of distinct detective genius, his one wish is to get rid of a case of that kind, and, consciously or unconsciously, the wish will take the form of pooh-poohing it at first and letting it slip out of sight and out of mind as soon as the excitement about it dies out."

The *Telegram,* its field forces out-numbered by the hordes of *World* and *Journal* reporters, tried to sell papers with the headline:

DR. WESTON SAYS BODY WAS BOILED

"Coroner's Physician Weston has advanced a most important theory in regard to the great murder mystery," a *Telegram* reporter had written. "He was at the morgue this afternoon on another case, and while he was there he examined the mutilated, headless, and legless trunk. He said to me afterward: 'It appears to me that an attempt has been made to dispose of this body by boiling it. The flesh of the stump of the legs appears to have been dipped in boiling water. It is probable that the murderers thrust the legs into a kettle, hoping to boil the flesh off, but found they could not do it quickly or easily enough, and that they then cut up the remains.'" The doctors made decidedly better copy than the detectives.

NED moved along to other bars as the afternoon wore on, avoiding those most frequented by newspapermen. Had he been one of the *World's* stars, he would have had to take precautions against being trailed, but he knew he was too inconspicuous for that. All he had to avoid was a chance encounter. The dark interiors, cooled by electric fans, offered escape from the afternoon sun, and each time he changed saloons he bought a later batch of papers to read over his next nickel beer. The Late Edition of the *Evening World,* which went to press at four o'clock in the afternoon, headlined a typical Pulitzer stroke—a five-hundred-dollar reward. "The *World* will pay $500 in gold for the correct solution of the mystery concerning the fragments of a man's body discovered Saturday and Sunday in the East River and in Harlem," an announcement read. "All theories and suggestions must be sent to the City Editor of the *World,* in envelopes marked 'Murder Mystery,' and must be exclusively for the *World.* Appearance of the solution in any other paper will cancel this offer of reward." There followed a "suggestion" of what the solution should include: motive, identity of the criminal or criminals, time, place, and method of the crime, actions of the criminal or criminals after commission of the crime, and, last but not least, identification of the murdered man.

This was the final regular edition of the *Evening World,* and it ordinarily coincided with the *Journal's* final, but within minutes of its appearance the latter paper hit the street with an extra run of its

Night Edition, in which a three-column head on the right-hand side of the first page read:

$1,000 REWARD
THE NEW YORK JOURNAL WILL PAY
$1,000 FOR INFORMATION OR
CLEWS, THEORIES OR SUG-
GESTIONS WHICH WILL
SOLVE THE UNIQUE
MURDER MYSTERY
OF THE EAST
RIVER.
IF NONE OF THE THEORIES OR
SUGGESTIONS IS PERFECTLY EXACT
THE $1,000 WILL BE DIVIDED
AMONG THE TEN THAT COME
NEAREST TO SOLVING
THE MYSTERY

It was the familiar Hearst technique, infuriating to *World* men, of waiting for Pulitzer to think of something and then raising his bid.

The *Journal,* Ned noted with distaste, had followed the *World's* example in its play of the striking hand picture. The first page of the *Journal* bore detailed illustrations of the unknown's right hand, his left hand, his injured finger, and his broken fingernail. "The *Evening Journal* has the Most News, Latest News, Best News," the left ear of the paper's masthead boasted, and the right ear stated, "The *Evening Journal* Prints the Best Local, Telegraph, Cable News." It was enough to raise the hair of Ned's blond, James J. Corbett pompadour haircut.

The *Journal* was also playing up its own favorite candidate of the moment for corpus delicti, with a slashing first-page head:

LOUIS A. LUTZ THE VICTIM?
NEPHEW ALMOST SURE HE RECOGNIZES
THE REMAINS AT THE MORGUE

The missing Mr. Lutz, a carpenter in a piano factory, had not been home for five days, the *Journal* said, and while he had no known enemies, and no money on his person when he left his house, his nephew was sure he had been killed, because he didn't think he would have committed suicide. (No other possible explanations of his absence were considered.) The *Journal* presented a boxed, signed, and undoubtedly paid-for statement by the nephew, who was named Louis E. Lutz, in which, as a clincher, he remembered that his uncle had once hit himself on the left hand with a hammer, injuring a finger. Stephen O'Brien, the Chief of Detectives, had furnished a signed statement to the editor of the *Journal* to the effect that until they found the missing sections of the body, his detectives had little to work on. "LITTLE TO WORK ON" was the headline. Dr. Nelson A. Conroy, of Bellevue, still another medico out to vindicate Dr. Watson, had given the *Journal* a personal statement, in which he declared irrefutably: "It is hard to say just what the man's face looked like." Apparently something of a palmist, Dr. Conroy added, "The conical hand of the man indicates a practical temperament. This man must have been engaged in some useful art—an artist of some sort—for it is evident he had not done any hard work for some time." All references to the dead man's hands had a special interest for Ned, and he was relieved to see that Dr. Conroy was as far off the track as the rest.

If the *Journal* ventured gingerly into palmistry via Dr. Conroy, the *Evening World*, in a Night Extra that shortly followed the *Journal's*, went all the way.

$500 REWARD TO ANYBODY WHO
UNRAVELS THE MURDER MYSTERY

a headline across the first six columns bellowed, and then:

THEORY OF WOMAN
AND A PALMIST

A four-column cut under the reward line showed the "Hands of the Murdered Man," and under this was a two-column cut of "The Broken Nail."

"An analysis of the hand of the dead man of the river mystery was made this morning for the *Evening World* by Queen Stella Gonzales," the first-page story began. (The paper's editors brushed off the *Journal's* Mr. Lutz with a one-paragraph sneer under the lower-case line "Alleged Identification." "The morgue people take no stock in the identification," the item ended.) "Queen Stella and Cheiro are the two most famous palmists of America, Queen Stella's drawing-room reputation excelling that of Cheiro." Queen Stella, the story went on, admitted that she was handicapped by having only a photograph of the back of the hand to work from. "She said it impressed her at once as a tragic hand," the *Evening World* reported. "'... Having square nails, that denotes ruling power. His little finger, pointed and reaching above the third phalange, denotes business capacity in a higher degree.... Through his domineering disposition and rashness in speech he must have made one or more deadly enemies.'"

Queen Stella's analysis was the beginning of a complete coverage by the *World* of the occult aspects of the case, which included appeals to another palmist (a man, who was smuggled into the morgue), a phrenologist (slightly handicapped by the absence of the head), a clairvoyant, a physiognomist (working from a photograph of the supposed victim after his identity became fairly certain), a handwriting expert, and, finally, a spirit medium.

The woman's-angle theory mentioned in the *Evening World's* head got equal play with Stella's. It was written by a Mrs. McGuirk, not otherwise identified and possibly invented. It wasn't a woman's work, Mrs. McGuirk ruled, and continued, "There is just one thing in the whole business that might suggest a woman's hand. The knots with which the parcels were fastened are the clumsy, uneven ones which women are prone to make." Mrs. McGuirk thought the victim might have been a peddler and the oilcloth part of his stock in trade. "Women poison," she concluded. "It is easier. They seldom use knives, unless very hot blood runs in their veins." The *Evening World's* Night Extra had a total of thirteen masterly columns on the case, which make good reading even after fifty-eight years. They included a remarkable collection of mystery-solution letters, which the editors claimed had been written by readers and delivered by hand between four o'clock, when its reward offer appeared, and about five, when the Night Extra went to press. A biting bit next to the reiterated reward offer contrasted honest and dishonest journalism and accused the *Journal* of snitching the letter-contest idea.

By the time Ned had finished with the evening papers, it was nearly six o'clock, and he accordingly made his way back to the west side of Ninth Avenue between Thirty-fourth and Thirty-fifth Streets. One reason Ned chose the time he did to return was that in such a neighborhood it was an hour when the man of the house was almost sure to be at home, except on Saturday night or unless something had happened to him. The women with whom Ned had left soap that morning and who had their nickels ready to clinch their bargain must have been doubly delighted, because he never came back to collect.

Instead, he went directly to No. 439, climbed to the floor above the drugstore, and rang the bell at the door—slightly more pretentious than the others—of Mrs. Augusta Nack, Licensed Midwife, which he had skipped a few hours earlier. He waited in hot-and-cold anxiety. It was possible, of course, that Mrs. Nack wasn't at home, or that if she was, she wouldn't come to the door. These were the longest days of the year; it was full daylight, and he hadn't been able to tell by a lighted or unlighted window whether anyone was in. The greatest blow to his hopes would have been the heavy tread of a man coming to answer the doorbell, but, instead, he heard the slupping sound of the advance of a woman in house slippers. Then the door was ajar and Mrs. Nack stood in the aperture. She was just about Ned's height—five feet six—but she must have weighed at least two hundred pounds. Her face was wide and flat and lardy white, with small eyes, not much of a nose, and what Mr. Brown still remembers as an extremely sullen mouth. She was wearing an apron over her house dress, and there was a smell of cooking sauerkraut that has left Mr. Brown with a permanent distaste for the stuff. Ned would have given anything to see into the room behind her, but she was a hard woman to see around.

Before Mrs. Nack could ask what he wanted, Ned began, "Good evening, Madam. Have you enjoyed your trial bar of Cotaspam soap? Hasn't its fragrant lather left your hands feeling as if freshly kissed?"

"You didn't giff me any!" Mrs. Nack replied angrily, and Ned understood immediately why she had looked sore from the moment she laid eyes on him. The other women had described him while telling her about the wonderful soap, and Mrs. Nack felt she had been slighted, as usual. (Feeling slighted is a characteristic of especially high incidence among Germans and unattractive women, and Mrs. Nack was both.)

"I would have sworn I'd been to every flat in the house," Ned said. "But I guess I wasn't, or I would have remembered you sure."

It was coquetry lost on Mrs. Nack, who said merely, "Giff me the soap now."

"I'm sorry, Madam, but I'm afraid I can't," Ned said. "You see, I have to get a report for my company on what each lady thought of the soap. That was the purpose of our special offer."

"Leaf it and come back tomorrow," Mrs. Nack commanded.

"I'm sorry, Ma'am, but I can't do that, either," Ned said. "Tomorrow I'll be working up in Yonkers." Then he tried to look as if he had just had a bright thought, and went on, "But I happen to have a couple of bars left over. If you could give the soap a trial now, while I wait, I'd be glad to let you have one."

After thinking this over for a minute, Mrs. Nack said, "All right. Giff me the soap." Ned moved toward her, fumbling in a pocket and being careful not to give her the soap until he was inside the apartment. He knew she wouldn't shut the door in his face before he came through with the special introductory sample. As she pulled back from the door, he went through it as if in the suction set up by her big body.

"Here it is, Ma'am," he said after he was safely inside. Mrs. Nack took the soap in her pale, shovel-like paws, raised it to her nose, and sniffed it. She looked mollified. "As a matter of fact," Ned continued, "I've got just two left, and since I'm putting you to all this trouble, I'm going to let you have both of them, if you like the first one. But I get awfully thirsty, climbing stairs all day in this heat, and I wonder if I might ask you for a glass of water before you start washing your hands."

"I guess so," Mrs. Nack said. "Sit down on the chair there while I get you the water."

Ned sat down in a black leather upholstered chair and looked around him while the woman went to the kitchen, in the rear of the flat, to get his drink. Within a few days, the newspapers were to describe the contents of Mrs. Nack's apartment in much more detail than Ned was in a position to take in, but his eyes fell on one item that subsequent newspapermen were destined never to see. "Leaning against a lamp, on a kind of a knickknack stand, there was a studio photograph of a big blond guy with little turned-up mustaches under his nose—a kind of Dutch version of a sport," Mr. Brown recalls. "The minute I saw it, I was sure I had seen him around, without ever knowing his name." The floor was bare, and Ned noticed that the rug was rolled up and tied, as if Mrs. Nack were getting ready to move. When Mrs. Nack brought the water, he downed it thirstily, just as if he hadn't been drinking beer all afternoon.

"Now, Madam," Ned said after thanking her, "you will have the rare pleasure of making the acquaintance of the world's most luxurious hand soap. Do not hurry it, but run a basin of warm water and then work up a creamy lather. Let your hands soak in it! You will feel each finger separately caressed. When you withdraw your hands, hold them to your nose! The fragrance is a secret formula, copyrighted by the makers of Cotaspam. You have beautiful hands, Madam. They deserve Cotaspam!" The midwife slupped away again, and as soon as Ned heard water running in the rear of the apartment, he grabbed the photograph and slipped it under his jacket. He now passionately desired to leave at once, but he knew that to do so, if his suspicions were correct, would be likely to frighten Mrs. Nack into immediate flight. He also had a hunch that the longer he waited, the more he would learn. All Mrs. Nack's actions indicated that she was alone in the apartment, but the apparently substantial nature of the meal she was preparing hinted that she expected company for dinner. If it was the man in the photograph, all Ned's theories would come tumbling down and he would probably feel obliged to invite the fellow out to the nearest saloon and buy him a seidel of beer. But if it wasn't the man in the photograph, it might be Mrs. Nack's accomplice in his murder. Ned had formed a most unfavorable impression of Mrs. Nack; she looked capable of murdering an infant—and probably had, for midwives often doubled as abortionists. But he was not physically afraid of her, despite her lardy bulk. He was an athletic young fellow, who, with his brother, had rigged a trapeze and flying rings in the attic at home in Flatbush; Ned could chin himself innumerable times with one arm, and fancied himself as an amateur boxer. The dinner guest, however, would almost certainly prove to be a large adult male, armed and with a nasty taste for fragmentation. While Ned was pondering this prospect, Mrs. Nack returned, a smile for once suffusing her desk blotter of a face. "It is nice soap as possible," she said. "Very elegant."

Ned whipped out his reporter's notebook and started writing in it. "May I quote you, Madam?" he asked. "We intend to publish testimonials in the newspapers, and a testimonial from a midwife would have double value. It would be a good ad for you, too."

"I don't need ads," Mrs. Nack replied. "I am going soon anyway back to Germany." For a moment, she seemed sorry she had said so much, but Ned's look of bland innocence evidently reassured her. "Now you give me the other soap also," she said. "Here is a dime." Ned felt sure she had been told by other women that the soap regularly sold for twenty-five cents—that they knew it did because they had priced it in the drugstore downstairs. "It is wonderful how with any woman the idea of a bargain will obscure larger issues entirely," Mr. Brown says. "She was looking at me and talking about the soap, and it never occurred to her to look around the room and notice that the picture was missing."

Ned gave Mrs. Nack the second bar of soap, took her dime, said goodbye, and walked through the doorway. Then he stopped, because a man was coming up the narrow stairs. "He was a husky man—no giant, but a full-sized middleweight," Mr. Brown says. "About thirty years old, I should guess. He was wearing a derby hat, although it was summer—only the dudes wore straw kellies—and he had long black mustaches. I remember them as black, although the papers said afterward they were light brown. Maybe he had dyed them. Still later, he shaved them off. What I particularly remember about him, though, was his eyes. They were deep-set and glaring, and they shone like a cat's. At his trial, the artists had a field day drawing those eyes. He was furious at seeing me there—the door to the apartment was still open—and he grabbed me by the shoulder. '*Wer ist's?*' he yelled in German—'Who is it?'—and then he started giving the woman hell. I could see she was frightened—he had her buffaloed. I had learned enough German at Erasmus to understand that he was bawling her out for not keeping the door closed. He said he had told her not to let anybody in. She started explaining who I was, and telling him if he made so much noise the neighbors would come to see what was the matter. Finally, he took his hand off my shoulder—I certainly didn't look dangerous—and went inside. 'Donkey-head!' I heard him call the woman, in German, and then the door slammed, and I heard a slap you could hear right through it. I ran down the stairs and kept going. From the way those two had acted, I was sure that I had the right man's picture and that they were the ones who had killed him."

THE reason Ned's skin had appeared translucent that Monday morning was that during the previous evening it had been buffed to gauzy thinness by successive pairs of large, powerful, clean, untanned, uncallused, well-kept hands with nails trimmed extremely short in order not to scratch customers. He had spent a good part of that night, after leaving the morgue, in a series of Turkish baths, making discreet inquiries about rubbers who might be missing from work.

"The minute I saw the hands on the mystery stiff at the morgue, I noticed that the skin on the tips of the fingers was crinkled, like a baby's sometimes after a hot bath," Mr. Brown says. "I remembered

I'd seen the same thing recently on an adult's fingers, and then I remembered where it was—on a fellow named Bill McPhee, who was giving me an alcohol rub at the Murray Hill Baths. And I'd asked McPhee, 'Do your hands get that way permanently from the hot water and soap, or do the crinkles go away when you go home?'

" 'Oh, they stay that way for a couple of days, maybe a week, if you aren't working,' he said. 'But then they go away and the skin looks just like anybody else's.'

"I sized the stiff up. Good muscular development—massaging twenty or thirty customers a day is hard work, and some of those fellows used to pride themselves on how hard they could grip. Clean, white skin—where could you keep cleaner than working in a bath, and where would you get less sun on you? Carefully trimmed fingernails, but too short for a dude or a society fellow. The big fuss about the 'extraordinary refinement' of the hands was cleared up in a minute. I told Gus Roeder that Sunday afternoon in the morgue, 'This guy was a rubber in a Turkish bath,' I said, 'and he must have worked not long before he was killed, or the crinkles on his hands would have smoothed out.' Then I explained what McPhee had told me about the crinkles' lasting only a few days. 'If we check the Turkish baths in the city and find one that has had a rubber missing for less than a week and more than a day, we've got our man,' I said. Gus was a hard fellow to get excited. He pointed out that there were hundreds of baths in the city; they were popular on the East Side and in Harlem as well as in the Tenderloin, and you'd have to check those in Brooklyn, too, and anyway the man might have been lured or shanghaied from out of town. The *World* didn't have enough men to spare for that kind of quick check, Gus said. We had a dozen hot crime men—real sleuths—but they all wanted to try out theories of their own. If we passed my idea on to the police and they thought much of it, some detective would be sure to spill it to the *Journal* and we would get no credit for it. 'But if you want to work your hunch yourself, kiddo, go ahead,' Gus said. 'I assign you to it. All the baths you take you can put on the swindle sheet, but more than a quarter tip the auditor won't believe, so don't try to get away with it.' "

Thus admonished, Ned hit out straight for his favorite district, the Tenderloin—first, because the biggest establishments were there, and, second, because he thought the rubbers in that area were more worldly types, and so more likely to get in trouble, than their confreres elsewhere. He did not begin with the Murray Hill, his habitual retreat—probably because we never expect the strange and mysterious in surroundings that are familiar to us. He began, instead, at the Everard, on West Twenty-eighth Street, and tried three more before he arrived at the Murray Hill, at about nine Sunday evening. By that time, he had been scrubbed until all his surfaces felt like Jimmy Valentine's sandpapered fingertips. In each place, he had asked the attendants to put him through fast because he had a heavy date and wanted to get rid of a hangover before he picked her up. He began his quest at each bath by asking where the big fellow was who didn't seem to be on the floor that night. In each, he was told that the staff was at full strength, and upon hearing this he mumbled that he must have been thinking of some other Turkish bath. At the Murray Hill, since he was known there, he varied the approach slightly by remarking to the rubber, McPhee, that the place looked kind of shorthanded, and asking him if anyone was missing. McPhee, an irascible type, said there damn sure was. Bill, the big Dutchman, who always had Sundays off, had taken Friday that week, trading days off with a man who normally would have been working Sunday. The other man had worked Friday and Saturday and then stayed home, but the big Dutchman had failed to show, leaving them one man short. Naturally, there had been more of a rush than they expected. The previous night had produced an unusually heavy crop of bad heads; it always happened that way when you were short a man. "He took Friday off because he was going to look at a house in the country with his girl—or so he said," McPhee snarled. "Saturday, some Dutchman called up to say Guldensuppe wouldn't be in to work Sunday because he was sick. Guldensuppe is his name," McPhee added in a tone of distaste. "Drunk someplace, of course. Today, when he didn't show, the boss said he was fired." Ned submitted to his fifth scrubbing in five hours without feeling any discomfort. He was anesthetized by preoccupation. "About how big is this big Dutchman?" he asked. "I must have seen him around here, but I can't place him in my mind."

"Oh, probably around five eleven," McPhee replied. (That was taller for a man in those days than it is now.) "And he's built big—big shoulders and a fine big chest on him. He's just built like a big Dutchman. You must have noticed him. He has the upper half of a woman tattooed all over his chest—used to be a sailor on one of them Heinie windjammers when he was a kid. He has one of those trick mustaches like two half-moons on his lip. Not a bad Dutchman," McPhee conceded, "but skirt-crazy."

When McPhee mentioned the tattoo, Ned's heart jumped. "I remembered the torso I had looked at that afternoon, with a slab of integument—of whole skin—removed from the chest, apparently to get rid of some distinguishing mark," Mr. Brown says.

Stopping at the cashier's desk on the way out to pay for his massage, Ned asked the cashier where Bill Guldensuppe lived. "I borrowed a dollar from him last time I was in here, and now I hear he's not coming in any more, so I want to send it to him," he explained. The cashier looked at a list and said that he didn't know where Guldensuppe lived but that he got his mail at a saloon on Ninth Avenue, near Thirty-sixth Street—not an unusual arrangement. "And if you're going to write to him, you might add that he's fired," he said. "That'll save us a stamp." When Ned got out of the Murray Hill Baths, he didn't write. He grabbed a hack and told the driver to get down to Thirty-sixth and Ninth and not to spare the horse on the way. He felt like Richard Harding Davis, who at that moment was covering a war between Greece and Turkey, after attending the coronation of Czar Nicholas II in St. Petersburg.

THE saloon on Ninth Avenue was quiet that summer evening. It was a Raines Law hotel, with the ten bedrooms upstairs and the petrified sandwich on every table that entitled it to remain open on Sundays, under the statute passed not long before to appease the Sabbatarians upstate. (The bedrooms established its status as a hotel; the sandwiches represented the food that was legally required to be served with every drink.) The Irish bartender had the cowlick center part in his hair and the handle-bar mustaches that were tonsorial caste marks. The sandwich man, on hand in case anybody wanted one that could really be eaten, was an old German. Ned sized the saloon up as a neighborhood headquarters—the most pretentious place for a hundred yards in any direction. He ordered a schooner of beer and knocked it off with unaffected enthusiasm; the baths had dehydrated him until his shoes felt large. He ordered another and bought one for the bartender, at the same time ordering a ham-and-cheese on rye, for he had not eaten since noon. Having established relations, he asked the bartender if he knew big Bill Guldensuppe, the Dutchman who worked at the Murray Hill Baths. Acquaintance with a masseur in a flashy Turkish bath was a social reference over on Ninth Avenue. The bartender said he knew the big Dutchman who worked in the baths, but the last name didn't sound right. He thought it was Nack. The sandwich man, arriving with the ham-and-cheese, said the name was Guldensuppe, all right; he and the rubber belonged to the same Low German death-benefit society. "He even gets mail here under the name Guldensuppe," he said. "He goes by Nack in the neighborhood because he lives with his sweetheart—Mrs. Augusta Nack, the midwife, right over Werner's drugstore." The sandwich man winked. "She got plenty of cash," he said. "She treats him good."

Ned, trying to seem casual, said that he'd happened to be in the neighborhood, so he'd stopped by, hoping to meet Guldensuppe and have a beer with him, since he knew Sunday was the rubber's night off. "He always talks about this place," he said. "He's a hot sketch!"

The bartender said he hadn't seen the big Dutchman for a couple of nights. "Maybe they've went to Coney for the day—him and his lady friend," he suggested. Come to think of it, he added, he hadn't seen him around since late Thursday night. "He usually be in for a few beers after he gets through at the baths," he said. "The work takes the moisture out of them. I hope he isn't deserting us, because he's a good customer." Ned felt like a poker player who, peeking at the second card dealt him, sees it is another ace. If Guldensuppe had been on a protracted drunk, as McPhee had supposed, it was inconceivable that he wouldn't have once poked his nose into his favorite barroom in seventy-two hours.

"He's a hot sketch!" Ned said again, to dissemble the depth of his interest in Guldensuppe's absence. "Always after dames."

"You bet!" the sandwich man said. "You should see some of the letters he gets here. Pink envelopes! No wonder he don't want Mrs. Nack should know."

Ned said, "He's got a hell of a build. If he had been born in this country, he might be fighting Fitzsimmons."

The bartender said he had heard the big Dutchman could handle himself pretty good, at that. "There was a fellow trying to beat his time with some dame, I heard, and the Dutchman give him a good going over," he said. "The fellow pulled a gun and the Dutchman took it away and kept it."

Walking down Ninth Avenue, after a valedictory beer, Ned had a good look at the building that housed Werner's drugstore—No. 439. There were no lights in the windows on the second floor. Back in the

World office, he found Roeder just finishing off his lead story on the mystery—the one declaring that an awful crime had been committed. After Roeder had dictated and sent away the last take of his two-and-a-half-column story, which would earn him $18.75, he consented to listen to Ned. Roeder was still not overly impressed by Ned's theory. "The fifth place you visit, you find a man missing," he said. "Maybe if you went to all of them you would find two dozen. The tattoo sounds good, all right, and the jealous dame and the fellow with the gun he took away from him. What you got to do tomorrow is have a talk with this Mrs. Nack and get a good look inside the flat. Maybe there are signs of a struggle—bloodstains. Maybe the head is still in the apartment. And get a picture of Guldensuppe."

Ned thought up the soap scheme on his long journey home to Flatbush.

WITH Guldensuppe's picture under his jacket and the other man's glare still vivid in his memory, Ned made his way down to the *World* again on Monday evening. He was now dead certain he had the solution of the mystery. The sequel was inglorious. Colleagues of greater prestige had turned up what the city desk thought was a better bet. When the Early Edition of the next day's *World* came off the presses Monday night, the front-page headline on the murder read, promisingly enough:

WORLD MEN FIND A CLUE

But the story under it was a letdown for Ned.

> The most interesting discovery of the day was made by reporters for the *World* [it read]. It was that a wagon, in which were two men and which contained two packages, crossed to New York on the ferry from Greenpoint, L.I., on Saturday afternoon, a short time before the finding of the headless shoulders in the East River at Eleventh Street.
>
> The Greenpoint ferry landing on the New York side is at Tenth Street, and a bundle thrown from an incoming boat would have been carried towards the Eleventh Street pier, with the tide running as it was that afternoon. . . .
>
> That a saloonkeeper from that very section was reported missing last night, having left home on June 2 with a considerable amount of money, makes this phase of the case especially interesting.

All day Monday, while Ned was making the rounds with his soap, the *World's* torso campaign was being run by Casey, the assistant city editor, under constant inspirational prodding from the front office. Roeder, Reitmeier, and a platoon of other reporters were working with the police, and Ike White, the *World's* famous lone-wolf star reporter, was working against them, with a squad of special undercover agents. Fred Sturtevant, a celebrated rewrite man, was welding the gross crude output into an artistic whole, and the circulation department was having such a picnic that there must have been a substantial psychological resistance to Ned's story, with its possibility of putting an abrupt end to the frenzy. Roeder, however, was beginning to think well of it, and that Monday night he told Ned to hand over his precious photograph to the art department, so that it could have an engraving ready. "It was a good day's work, kiddo," he said. "Thanks."

Ned was so full of his story that even though it was after midnight, when he got home to Flatbush, he awakened his father and told him about it. "Why didn't you grab the fellow and bring him in?" Frederick Sherwood Brown said. "That's what I would have done." He then went back to sleep.

THE mystery continued to sell unparalleled multitudes of newspapers all the next day—Tuesday, June 29th. A *World* editorial that morning stated that in offering a reward the paper was acting simply as a minister of justice, without ulterior object. The *Journal* editorialized in the afternoon, "The only reason why every crime is not detected is that society does not employ the best order of brains in its work. . . . The *Journal's* offer should bring to the investigation of this mystery intellects and intentions not usually given to this kind of work." To offset the *World's* two-men-on-a-ferry story, Tuesday's *Journal* splashed a report by one Charles Anderson, of No. 7 Bowery, that he had seen two men on a Mount Vernon trolley car on Sunday afternoon loaded down with bundles wrapped in the fateful red oilcloth with gold stars. The resourceful *Telegram*, ever on the lookout for a sporting angle, promoted the candidacy of "a heavy bettor named McManus, who has not been at the track for five or six days," under a headline that read:

RACING MEN WILL VISIT THE MORGUE

The *Evening World,* in its Night Extra, which was relatively safe from Hearst plagiarism, offered a stimulating speculation by still another medical man, under the headline

WAS IT CANNIBALISM?

DR. FRANK FERGUSON, THE PATHOLOGIST,

IS INCLINED STRONGLY

TO THAT BELIEF

The same paper also presented an exclusive interview with former Police Inspector Alexander S. Williams, who said, *inter alia:* "The motive was revenge.... More than one person committed the crime.... It was probably done by a German."

Ned felt that the former Inspector was getting warm. But there was nothing more he could do about the case himself. Ike White and Roeder had vetoed the idea of going straight to 439 Ninth Avenue and "arresting" Mrs. Nack and the man with the black mustaches before somebody had positively identified the torso as Guldensuppe's. It would have been easy to visit the Murray Hill Baths, collect a couple of the big Dutchman's colleagues, and take them to the morgue, but this would have been hard to keep quiet from the competition. Roeder therefore waited until Tuesday night and then got a man named Joseph Kavenagh, a Murray Hill rubber who was off duty, to accompany him to the "storehouse," as the gay police reporters called the morgue. In consequence, the Late Edition of Wednesday's *World* had a technical scoop—a brief story on the second page with the headline

ANOTHER IDENTIFICATION

DEAD MAN SAID TO BE WILLIAM

GILDENSUPPER, A TURKISH

BATH ATTENDANT

The story under this reported that two detectives had left Police Headquarters at one-thirty that morning looking for a suspect; they were "acting on information given by Joseph Kavenagh, of 229 Madison Street, Hoboken." At the Murray Hill Baths, some cautious person in charge had informed the *World* that Gildensupper (the name was spelled a half dozen ways in the newspapers when the story first broke) had not worked there in three months.

The *World* of Thursday, July 1st, proudly claimed credit for this first revelation of the torso's identity, which it had printed with little display and less conviction. The reason for its original lack of enthusiasm was that on Tuesday night, while Roeder was squiring Kavenagh to the morgue, another identification of the torso had been made, this one seemingly more plausible and circumstantial, and the directors of the *World's* board of strategy had fallen for it. A cabinetmaker named Theodore Cyklam, who, like the already forgotten Mr. Lutz, had injured the index finger of his left hand (an occupational disfigurement, since a cabinetmaker uses it to hold every nail he drives), had disappeared from his home in College Point. (The locale jibed beautifully with the *World's* pet exclusive story about the two men and the wagon on the Greenpoint ferry, which carried traffic to and from College Point.) Louis Zimm, the superintendent of the factory employing Cyklam, and three fellow-workmen had appeared at the morgue and sworn, after looking at the torso and its scarred forefinger, that it was Cyklam, or part of him. It was therefore Cyklam's picture, sketched by a *World* artist "from full and detailed description given to the *World* by Louis Zimm," that appeared on the first page of Wednesday morning's paper, instead of Guldensuppe's, reproduced from the photograph snatched by Ned Brown.

Wednesday morning's *Herald*, although it didn't have the murdered man's name, profited by a quick tip from its man at Mulberry Street to head its main story:

MURDERED BY JEALOUS HUSBAND

"It was reported early this morning that the victim of the murder had been identified . . . and suspicion pointed to a jealous husband," the text below this stated. "It was said that the man was a shampooer in an uptown Turkish bath house, who has been missing for a few days. This man, it is said, had been living with a baker's wife."

Mrs. Nack's legal spouse, Herman Nack, was, in fact, the driver of a bakery delivery wagon, but he had not particularly resented it when his wife left him, and after the identification of Guldensuppe he considered himself lucky to be all in one piece. He nevertheless enjoyed the eminence of a putative master criminal for at least one day.

MURDER MYSTERY SOLVED
BY THE JOURNAL

an eight-column streamer across the front page of that newspaper bragged on Wednesday, and more headlines dropped away beneath it:

MRS. NACK IDENTIFIED;
HER HUSBAND HELD
BY THE POLICE
MRS. MAX RIGER RECOGNIZES THE
MIDWIFE AS THE WOMAN WHO
BOUGHT THE OILCLOTH IN ASTORIA
STOREKEEPER FOUND BY EVENING
JOURNAL REPORTERS AND
TAKEN TO POLICE
HEADQUARTERS
WHERE SHE
TELLS HER
STORY
MRS. NACK IS AT ONCE ORDERED
UNDER ARREST BY THE AUTHOR-
ITIES WHEN MRS. RIGER'S
STATEMENT IS
COMPLETED
HERMAN NACK IS RUN DOWN AND
HANDED OVER TO THE POLICE
BY TWO JOURNAL REPORT-
ERS WHO FIND HIM
ON HIS BAKERY
WAGON NEAR
HIS WIFE´S
HOME

The *Journal*—by its own account, at least—had unravelled the whole mystery; it had had the body identified by Guldensuppe's colleagues, had interviewed Mrs. Nack and scared the devil out of her, and had put the police wise to the whole solution, all on the previous day, but had refrained from saying anything about it at the time, for reasons it didn't go into. Nearly half of its Wednesday front page was given over to an idealized sketch of Mrs. Nack's head, which made her look rather like Pallas Athena. The caption under it read, with what papers would now consider reckless disregard of the law of libel, "Mrs. Nack, Murderess!"

> After tracing the bakery wagon driven by Herman Nack all night, *Journal* reporters overtook it at 11:15 this morning at the corner of Fortieth Street and Ninth Avenue [part of the *Journal* eulogy of the *Journal* ran].
>
> It bore the sign of the Astoria Model Bakery, owned by Joseph B. Schaps, of Astoria, L.I.
>
> Nack was on the driver's seat. The two *Journal* representatives tried to climb up on the steps of the wagon, but Nack pushed them off.
>
> He then whipped up his horse and dashed through Fortieth Street to Tenth Avenue.
>
> He turned down Tenth Avenue, with the two *Journal* men in close pursuit. They watched for a policeman, but saw none until they reached the corner of Tenth Avenue and Thirty-third Street.
>
> They managed to attract the policeman's attention, and he joined in the pursuit.
>
> The wagon was overtaken in another half block, and then another struggle ensued.
>
> Nack was desperate, and with his whip beat off the two *Journal* men.
>
> He was ghastly white and seemed determined to escape arrest at all hazards. He fought with desperation.
>
> Finally the policeman, who belonged to the West Thirty-seventh Street station squad, climbed up on the opposite side of the wagon and subdued Nack.
>
> The two men from the *Journal* helped the policeman to overpower the desperate driver, and he was at once taken to the West Thirty-seventh Street station in his wagon.

There he proved to know nothing at all about the murder.

The *Evening World,* chronicling "The Arrest of Supposed Murderer of William Guldensuppe (Nack)," gave all the credit to detectives, and didn't even mention the horsewhipped *Journal* reporters. It published a picture of Mrs. Nack and one of Guldensuppe, which, Ned was delighted to see, it had reproduced from his trophy. It also carried a long, if not entirely veracious, story of Mrs. Nack's love life, obtained by detectives from her and from neighbors of hers on Ninth Avenue. She said that she had quarrelled with Guldensuppe and that he had gone away, but that she did not believe he was dead. She had had telegrams from him on Sunday and Monday, she said. The name of a third man, known familiarly as Fred, crept into the stories of both the *Journal* and the *Evening World.* He was the man who had had the fight with Guldensuppe.

Guldensuppe's legs turned up on the same day, Wednesday, floating into a dock at the Brooklyn Navy Yard. And on the following day a notice appeared on the bulletin board in the *World's* city room announcing an award of $5 to E. G. Brown, for outstanding work on the Guldensuppe murder case.

DURING the next few days, it became clear that Fred, and not the complaisant husband, was the man in the case. Fred's real name was Martin Thorn, the police learned, "Thorn" being a Germanization of "Torzewski." Thorn was born in Posen, in German Poland, and was a journeyman barber—a silent, moody kind of man, whom other men shunned and who, like Guldensuppe, lived in part off women; the rubber had been a genial *maquereau,* the barber a sombre one. Guldensuppe had driven Thorn away, but the latter had sneaked back to see Mrs. Nack during the rubber's working hours. Once Mrs. Nack's picture had appeared in the newspapers, a woman in Woodside, Long Island, identified her as the stout woman who, with a male companion, had rented a house from her in what was then a sparsely settled neighborhood. The companion matched the description of Thorn. The house had outside drains, which leaked, and the neighbors' children now recalled that for two days the pipes had run "red water," which ducks had drunk with avidity.

Mrs. Nack was under arrest, but she refused to admit anything. Every policeman and every reporter in town, including Ned Brown, was out looking for Thorn, but nobody turned him up, and there was a report that he had got safely away on a ship to Germany. Actually, he was living in a cheap hotel on money he had obtained by pawning Guldensuppe's watch and clothes. He felt that his revenge on Guldensuppe would be incomplete if he kept it to himself, so within a few days of the identification of the fragments he walked into a barbershop where a man he knew was working, and told him the whole story—swearing him to secrecy, of course. The other barber, a man named Gartha, went home in a cold sweat and told his wife, who went straight to the police. Gartha made a date with Thorn at the corner of 125th Street and Eighth Avenue for nine o'clock on the evening of Tuesday, July 6th. Inspector O'Brien, disguised as a farmer, and about a hundred of his detectives, in various other disguises, kept it—each detective, to judge by subsequent newspaper accounts, trailed by a reporter. Thorn was waiting, and O'Brien arrested him.

The *Sun* of July 8th summarized the story Thorn had told to Gartha more or less as follows: Mrs. Nack had got tired of Guldensuppe (in the *Sun's* version, Gieldsensuppe) and Thorn hated him. It was not long before they decided to get rid of him for keeps, and for that purpose they rented the house in Woodside, because it was a place where nobody knew them. Guldensuppe had been after Mrs. Nack to open a house of prostitution, so when the time came to do him in, she told him that there was just as much money in baby farming, and that, moreover, taking care of illegitimate children was a legitimate business. Then she said she knew of a good spot for a baby farm in Woodside, and lured Guldensuppe over there to look at it. It is a safe bet that Mrs. Nack packed a picnic lunch for the excursion.

Thorn was at the house when the couple got there, but Guldensuppe didn't know it. Thorn had bought a new revolver. He had a razor, too, and on the way over to Woodside he had bought a saw. The lovers had also laid in a supply of plaster of Paris, oilcloth, cheesecloth, cord, and other supplies they thought might come in handy. When Mrs. Nack and Guldensuppe arrived at the Woodside house, Thorn was hiding in a closet near the second-floor stair landing. He had taken off, and neatly hung up, his outer garments, because he didn't want to get blood on them, and he was standing in his undershirt and socks. When he heard the gate outside the house click shut—a prearranged signal—he made ready. Mrs. Nack suggested to Guldensuppe that while she went and had a look at the outhouse, he go upstairs and see what he thought of the arrangement of rooms; she was familiar with it already, she said. Guldensuppe went upstairs, and when he looked into a bedroom by the landing, Thorn opened the closet door behind him and shot him in the back of the neck. The rubber fell, almost certainly mortally wounded but still gasping—"snoring" was Thorn's word. Thorn dragged him into the bathroom, put him in the bathtub, and cut his throat with the razor; Ned Brown's deduction that the man in the morgue had been dissected alive was correct. After the butchery, Thorn ran hot water into the bathtub, washing a good deal of blood down the drain and making the puddle for the ducks. Then he encased the head in plaster of Paris, so that it would sink when he threw it in the river, but he failed to do this with the other pieces, an omission he later regretted. He and Mrs. Nack together tied up their neat bundles, lugged them to a trolley line, and took a car to the Long Island slip of the Greenpoint ferry. The head sank beautifully, but when they saw that the parcels containing the legs and the upper torso were floating, they decided to hold on to the one with the lower torso. The day after the murder, they hired a hack from an undertaker near Mrs. Nack's flat and drove to the Bronx, where they got rid of that bundle. They meant to live happily ever after, in a flat Mrs. Nack had rented at 235 East Twenty-fifth Street, but the excitement over the serialization of Guldensuppe disconcerted them.

Thorn and Mrs. Nack were indicted for murder by a New York County grand jury on July 9th, but the indictment was found faulty, because the crime had been committed in Queens County. They were reindicted there, and in November Thorn was found guilty of murder in the first degree. He appealed, and was granted several stays, but in August, 1898, he was electrocuted in Sing Sing. Mrs. Nack, who had turned state's evidence against him, was permitted to plead guilty to manslaughter in the first degree. In January, 1898, she was sentenced to fifteen years in state's prison, which meant, with good conduct, nine years and seven months. The District Attorney defended this leniency on the ground that without her testimony it might have been difficult to establish a corpus delicti, since Guldensuppe's head had not been found; William F. Howe, of Howe & Hummel, who was Thorn's attorney, was prepared to contend to the last ditch that the pieced-together headless body could have been that of anybody at all. Mr. Howe said that Mrs. Nack reminded him of Lady Macbeth and all the Borgias rolled into one, and that she had hypnotized his client. "Martin Thorn is a young man of candor," he said. "From my first interview with him I found him saturated with chivalry—ready, if necessary, to yield his life as a sacrifice to the Delilah who has placed him in his present position."

Mr. Howe said this on November 11, 1897. By then, the Bellevue Hospital Medical School had been in session for a good month. But Edwin Gerald Brown, better-known as Ned, had not reported for his sophomore year. In fact, he never has.

26 Hippoprognosis in England

A MAJOR joy of English racing, for an American with a fancy for belles-lettres, is reading in the newspapers about what is not going to happen before it doesn't. Another joy is reading in the next day's papers about what should have happened after it hasn't. And there are other joys in between, if the reader goes to the races and is not obsessed with a sordid desire to make money. For example, there are jellied eels and the cries of the chaps who sell them—a wedding of gustatory and lyric delights. The fellow who sells them at Ascot, at the foot of the hill by the railroad station, calls, "Eels here, lovely eels—cold and beautiful!," making me think of the corpse of Marie Antoinette. At Lewes, in Sussex, the eel seller cries, "If you're wantin' good food, here's eels! Ten eels for two bob!" This is conventional hyperbole, like the old New York beanery sign "A Thousand for a Dime." You never got nearly a thousand, but you got enough. It is that way with the eelman. He means possibly ten neat segments of thin eel, each an inch and a half long, set in their own jelly and served in a tin cup, called, by another convention, a "bison." The British bison-eel is of a Bismarck-herring blue, like the rainwashed sky over a British racecourse when it isn't raining, which isn't often. With each helping you get a spoon, a hunk of bread, and access to unlimited vinegar. It's no good trying to bone the eel with the spoon; that is as hard as bobbing for apples in a pail of water. The proper method is to lift the segment of eel to your mouth with the spoon, suck the flesh from the bone, and convey the bone to the soil by the most expeditious method that occurs to you. A couple of days ago, when I last saw Lewes, the Sussex turf was starry with lacy filigrees of eel vertebrae. Nothing is better for soil, and as I jammed myself into a taxi for the ride to the station, I thought of the lovely green color the turf would be when I returned next spring. As an anonymous poet has said,

I sometimes think the grass grows ne'er so green
As where some buried eelman's cart hath been.

The taxi loaded six passengers, at three bob a head, and the driver sealed us in by passing a furled umbrella, seven feet long, through the rear windows, like a skewer. The umbrella belonged to three of the passengers—bookmakers in the Silver Ring, where betting, traditionally, is in less-than-paper money. They used the umbrella as business premises; it afforded them shelter from cloudbursts and shade from the sun on the infrequent occasions when shade was needed. Their slate, easel, duckboards (for standing on in the mire), and cash-and-ticket bag were in the front seat, next to the driver.

When he had us pinned, the driver, a poetic chap himself, said, "I'll take yer for a ride across the Sussex Downs." It would have cost him two-and-six to use the private toll road that leads out of the racecourse, so across the Downs we literally went, lurching along the sides of hills at a forty-five-degree angle, and eventually picking up a footpath, on which the driver had to temper his speed to that of a horse who had reached the path ahead of us. He was a tired horse, who looked like the one I had bet on in the last race, and he was being led by a stable lad with a lot of age on him. A "lad" in England—or, for that matter, in France, where they use the same word around racing stables—may be a grandfather. In *Paris-Turf* last spring I read the obituary of a lad sixty-eight years old.

The path was just horse width, so we trundled along at the horse's pace. Pedestrians, able to scramble up the sides of the hills and go around lad and horse, passed us continually. At length, we came to a comparatively level stretch, where the path wound past a collection of high, bleak, crenellated stone walls. The bookies, who had been wolfing sandwiches of cold fried fish, stopped eating, as if they had suddenly lost their appetites. They threw their crusts out the windows and wiped their hands on their trousers. "Lewes Prison," the driver called back over his shoulder, for my benefit. He knew I was an American, and he did not want me to miss any landmarks. The Silver Ring boys looked put out, as if they thought the reference vulgar and redundant. Then one of them, a fat chap—aware, I suppose, that I had noticed their change of mood—said with forced cheerfulness, "I wouldn't 'arf like to 'ave the bookmaking privileges in there."

"You mean the prisoners bet?" I asked.

The three bookies laughed. "I'd like to lay a fiver that if there's a race at three o'clock, every bloke inside knows the winner by three-five," the youngest one said.

"They 'ave a surprising number of winners, too," the third man said, but I was bright enough not to ask him how he knew.

THE newspaper fellows who write about horses are less succinct than the eel sellers. In fact, they are less succinct than almost anybody else I read constantly. English racing—including, unfortunately, the horses I bet on—is unhurried, and the practitioners of hippoprognosis are among its least hurried features. Even with the excitement over Suez, dailies like the *Express*, the *News Chronicle*, and the *Herald*, which normally have eight pages, devote a full page and sometimes part of another to racing. They use another page for football-pool news and forecasts, and still another for non-investment sports. The *Express*, analyzing one of its own issues recently, announced that it had run three hundred and sixty column-inches of general news and three hundred and twenty-eight of sport. The allotment of so much space to the turf is not capricious. Hippoprognosticators are public figures, ranking midway between cricketers and members of the Royal Family. "Ajax Goes Through the Card at Lewes," the *Evening Standard* boasted on the day I met the bookmakers, when its No. 1 seer got all six winners. "The Scout Gave Ten Winners Out of 22 Selections on Saturday, So Follow the Man in Form," the *Express* announced and exhorted on another occasion. All circulation groups play the races.

Tipsters affect journalistic history. Siegfried Sassoon has written that during the early, difficult days of the *Herald*, the Labour Party paper, a tipster who was "in form" held on to enough readers to keep the paper going. Today it has a circulation of around two million—a figure that is merely substantial in England but gigantic by American standards. The *Herald's* stable of swamis has increased nearly in proportion to its readership. This represents a new, almost Conservative reluctance to put all the Eleusinian eggs in one basket.

The *Express*, which publishes eight different prognoses, usually has at least one tea-leaf peruser "in form" every day. The reader's problem, of course, is telling which of them it will turn out to be—the Scout, Peter O'Sullevan, Bendex, Course Correspondent, Newmarket, Easy-As-ABC Form Guide, the Con Tip (daily doubles only), or Riddle-Me-Ree. The last gives one best bet a day in the form of a runic couplet. The other day Riddle-Me-Ree propounded:

My first might suggest exact to you,
My second "by twelve men good and true."
My whole may win Nottingham's 2.30 race.

Turning feverishly to the Nottingham Zip-a-Long Race Card in the next column, I ran my right eye down the entries for the two-thirty race. (I needed my left eye for the Con Tip; it would take me all day to read the *Express* if I used two eyes for each tipster.) I saw that there was a horse in the two-thirty named Just (suggesting exact) Verdict (by twelve men). It seemed a flatteringly easy way to turn brain power into money. Unfortunately, my right eye travelled on for a bit, and I noticed that the Zip-a-Long had designated a thing called Great Birnam as the probable betting favorite. As for Newmarket, he announced for a horse called Fresh Air, and said that he considered him one of his Best Three bets of the day. (Late Racing Special: Quorum, 10–1, won the two-thirty. Not tipped in the *Express.*)

The *News Chronicle,* a comparative sobersides of a newspaper, with a Liberal, Quakerish tradition, makes do with six extrapolators—Capt. Heath, Uno, Bookworm, Mr. Tyme, the Picquet, and a wag called A.T., or the Amateur Tipster, who is said to pick horses with a pin. The tabloid *Daily Mirror,* which has the biggest circulation of all (nearly five million), offers only four lines of medicine—Newsboy, Bouverie, Course Correspondent, and Form in a Flash—but in compensation it runs a table showing what your profit or loss on the season would be if you had made a flat play on all the mounts of any of the eleven leading jockeys. Only two of the eleven would give you an appreciable profit.

The *Express* is in competition with the *News Chronicle* for middle-middle-class readers and with the *Mirror* for lower-middle-class ditto, but the *Times* enjoys a lordly freedom from such preoccupations. Its circulation stays down and its advertising revenue stays up. It can afford to limit itself to two conflicting lines of prophecy, furnished by Our Racing Correspondent and Our Newmarket Correspondent. Our Newmarket Correspondent is stationed at that great training center and is supposed to get his information from the feedbox; Our Racing Correspondent leans more heavily on bloodlines and metaphysics. Although by London standards the *Times* is short on prediction, it is long on analysis and description. Our Racing Correspondent, like the chaps who write the obituary notices and the editorials, is a stayer.

The *Times*, the *Express*, the *Mirror*, the *Herald*, and sometimes the *News Chronicle* are the only papers I take at all regularly, but on the eve of a race as important as the Stewards' Cup at Goodwood, which I attended recently, I tell the night porter at my hotel to order *all* the morning papers. This adds the *Daily Mail*, the *Daily Telegraph*, the *Daily Sketch*, and the *Daily Worker* to my prognostic pabulum, and I have a fair wallow in prophetic prose.

"Why do you want to read all that?" Devlin, the night porter, asked me when I gave him the order prior to the Stewards' Cup. "Variety King is the ticket."

As a matter of fact, I had already come to a decision myself, but I wanted to feel the pulse of the *tout ensemble*, which is a French phrase meaning all the touts. Besides, Devlin might not understand how much pleasure I get from just reading the stuff. All he wants is a winner.

ENGLISH racing prose has its conventions, like the sonnet, and its meanders, like the essay. One convention is that every horse in a race must be mentioned in the course of the incantation. This is done, I imagine, to propitiate the spirits of its ancestors and prevent them from scrambling the dope. In the case of the Stewards' Cup, a handicap at three-quarters of a mile, the twenty-four probable starters insured a long, happy read over the kippers. Another convention is that the horses must be mentioned in inverse order to the magician's estimate of their chances, or the charm won't work. He sets forth the claims of the bottom horse, evaluates them, gets in a bit of anecdote about the Derby of 1937 or lovable characters long dead, explodes the pretensions of the horse's apologists, and finally lets the animal drop like a jellied-eel vertebra. He then takes up the horse he considers next least likely to succeed, praises it mildly, expresses a few reservations on the score of its second dam's family, concedes that it might be dangerous if it had more than one sound leg, and then discards it. As soon as the reader sees the next name, he knows that it won't do, either, but the field is narrowing and suspense is piling up. By now, the reader realizes that somewhere among the twenty-one horses remaining must lie the treasure-laden beast the shaman will designate. Twenty, nineteen, eighteen—the tension becomes almost unbearable. But Rhadamanthus continues implacably, like a man eating an artichoke. He passes each leaf between his teeth and puts it by. Six, five, four horses remain. At this point, I lose control of my emotions and look at the headline to see what the guy has picked—for there *are* headlines, and until I became acclimated I used to look at them first pop. Then an English woman I know explained that it wasn't considered sporting to peek unless you felt the blood pounding too dangerously in your temples. "It's *jolly* good fun if you don't look," she said. "Like reading a bulb catalogue." I have since learned that the newspapers began incorporating their chaps' selections in the headlines after a royal commission published a report noting a great increase in cerebral hemorrhage among newspaper readers before important handicaps. "In my day, we had racing writers who went three columns without giving you the foggiest," an old racing man of my acquaintance told me, with some asperity. "If you couldn't stay the course, you damned well had to pick your own horse."

The ultimate test of a stylist's excellence is how long he can protract his strip tease before satisfying the reader's curiosity. This can be measured by counting the lines of type he consumes before exposing his selection, and by this standard the Scout, of the *Express*, and Our Racing Correspondent, of the *Times*, brought off an incredible *ex aequo*, which is Latin for a dead heat, before the running of the Stewards' Cup. Each man presented his choice on the sixty-fourth line down from his lead. Our Racing Correspondent might possibly claim the purse on a technicality, though, since his first mention of the filly he picked contained no hint that he was going to pick her. "Ephemeral has not had the sort of ground she likes this season, and has shown nothing" was the way he introduced his heroine. It wasn't until line ninety-eight that he broke down and admitted, "Ephemeral must be the selection." The headline had given the show away—"EPHEMERAL WELL HANDICAPPED ON HER BEST FORM"—but anyone not up on the tribal customs would have thought that the headline had got attached to the wrong story, since Matador was the horse Our Racing Correspondent appeared to favor as he left the post. "Matador would set up a record if he won the Stewards' Cup today with 9 st. 2 lbs. [128 pounds]" was how he put it. "In spite of all his weight, he seems the best of those near the top." You had to know your way around the course to understand that Our Racing Correspondent meant he preferred something nearer the bottom. He gave no hint of what it would be until you got down there, although, one after another, you knew it *wouldn't* be King Bruce, Jackie's Kuda, Trouville, Amber Glass, Golden Lion, Nonchalance, Orthopaedic,

Light Harvest, or Cockrullah—the one I fancied. "Cockrullah, with 8 st. 3 lbs. at Goodwood last year, was a long way behind, and he now has 8 st. 7 lbs." was how Our Racing Correspondent dismissed him. That was a couple of furlongs before the telltale point at which he began to disparage Ephemeral.

The head over the Scout's competing medicine dance in the *Express* was "KNIGHT VALIANT IS CUP HOPE." The Scout, like Our Racing Correspondent, feinted with his lead. An entry named Epaulette was the horse he seemed to be riding as he left the barrier, but he was going to change mounts a couple of dozen times. "Epaulette, who travelled to Goodwood last week-end and worked over the course on Sunday, and again in excellent style yesterday morning, will probably start favourite for today's ever-fascinating Stewards' Cup," the Scout began. "Owner Mr. Jack Gerber has made no secret of his belief in the chances of his horse, now apparently restored to health after a long illness which so nearly put him in the hands of the knacker. Remembering the hopes held for Epaulette in the Two Thousand Guineas in the spring of 1954, I am reluctant to oppose him from his handy mark of 7 st. 12 lb." I knew the Scout would overcome this reluctance, because the story stretched on for a Stewards' Cup distance after that, but I was eager to see how he would do it. He did it very neatly: "It remains to be seen, though," he wrote, "whether a horse whose constitution has been so seriously impaired still possesses the rugged fibre to stand up to such a tough, all-the-way struggle." After that, he knacked a whole herd of intervening possibilities, until I thought I finally had him when he confessed, "Kenmore, unlucky last year, looks the right type, and I prefer him to the less certain Ephemeral." But I underestimated my man, for I had forgotten that there was one more horse in the race. "My idea of the winner, though," the Scout acknowledged, at last, "is Knight Valiant (nap). ["Nap" means "best of the day."] Aly Khan's tough, handily built colt is the ideal type for this undulating course." The first furlong of the Stewards' Cup course is, in fact, uphill; the next four furlongs are downhill; and the sixth is on the level. Then, just beyond the finish, there is a truly huge hill, which serves to stop the horses.

The Scout was as cold to Cockrullah as Our Racing Correspondent had been, but I was cheered to see, in the middle of the *Express's* racing page, "BENDEX SAYS—COCKRULLAH LOOKS GOOD," and I paused a moment to warm myself at Mr. Bendex's congenial glow. "Rae Johnstone has a great chance of adding a Stewards' Cup to his many triumphs in our big races," he very sensibly wrote. Johnstone, who lives and rides in France, seldom comes to England unless he has a good reason—something I had forgotten when he came to Epsom to ride Lavandin in this year's Derby, which he won. I could have had eight to one against him then, and I was determined not to let another such opportunity pass. Peter O'Sullevan's headline, "EPAULETTE—IF IT'S ONE OF HIS DAYS," didn't interest me except as an example of how to prepare a line of retreat. Bendex was my man.

The *Express* offered its readers two other Cup winners—Amber Glass, who was Course Correspondent's selection, and Testament, chosen by Easy-As-ABC Form Guide. The rival *News Chronicle* submitted a shotgun pick of exactly equal proportions, touting Knight Valiant, Testament, Light Harvest, Matador, and Kenmore. The *Herald,* the *Telegraph,* and the *Daily Mail* triple-dead-heated behind the leaders with four conflicting selections apiece. The *Sketch* proposed three, and the *Mirror* and the *Times* two each. Only the *Daily Worker* took a monolithic stand, naming just one runner, as if to repudiate talk of a schism within the Party. The paper employs only one selector, Cayton, who, like Our Racing Correspondent of the *Times,* chose Ephemeral. The hippoprogs do not divide along class lines. Out of the twenty-four horses in the race, there were twelve tipped to win, and the *Sketch* offered a thirteenth—Storm Sail—as a likely long shot. Having read the lot, I felt overinformed, as if I had swallowed the Syntopicon. It was hard to foresee a profit if I played thirteen horses, even though odds are likely to be liberal in a handicap sprint with a field of twenty-four.

WHEN I went down to Goodwood, I remained loyal to Cockrullah. (His owner is A. C. Cockburn and he is by Nasrullah, which accounts for his unfortunate name.) I had savers on Testament, Variety King, and Orthopaedic—Variety King because I didn't want Devlin, the night porter, to crow over me if his choice should come in, and Orthopaedic because I was with three young American women whose feet hurt. Goodwood is on the ancestral estate of the Duke of Richmond and Gordon, and His Grace provides few seats.

My day began badly, with the collapse of the one small investment scheme I had concocted on my own. It hinged on the success of a two-year-old filly named Jini, who had been flown in from France for the race preceding the Cup. In France, Jini had beaten a colt that I had seen win by twenty-four lengths over a filly that had later lost by one length to a good English two-year-old at Epsom. If you believe in form, as a good hippoprog should, the line through the second filly gave Jini a safe margin of about a sixteenth of a mile. I dragged my three guests out to the paddock to see *la charmante pouliche* who was going to pay for our outing. Our betting on the Cup, I explained to the girls, would come out of the capital we accumulated when Jini breezed in. The only point necessary to observe was whether she had been made nervous by her airplane trip. This was a Tuesday, and the weather was just what the Duke of Richmond and Gordon would have ordered. On the previous Sunday, however, England had been visited by a near-hurricane, which had stopped all air traffic. Because of the storm, Jini had been flown in late, and might not win by more than ten lengths.

The filly looked calm—contemptuously calm, as I remarked to *mes jeunes amies.* When I contemplate winning money on a French horse, my mood becomes embarrassingly French. I blew a kiss to Jini, and a tall woman of excessive maturity blew one back to me. She may have been a duchess; in any case, the gaffer with her, duke or no, waved his shooting stick menacingly at me, and I was glad that it is impossible to move in any direction at the Duke of Richmond's place until the horses have left the paddock, whereupon it becomes impossible not to move back to the stand, because *tout ce beau monde* moves in the same direction. "She regards these English females and says, '*Elles n' ont pas du chic!,*' " I said to *mes jolies compagnons,* all of whom have had college French. By "she" I meant Jini, a small bay animal who would have reminded me, if I had not known her quality, of one of the ponies that children ride in Central Park. Like them, she appeared sleepy. She must have suffered atrociously from airsickness, because *le lad* leading her would not let her approach the paddock's guardrail too closely; looking back, I can see that he did not wish her to behave in a manner *pas convenable* in public. What I took for composure turned out to have been exhaustion. The *Daily Worker* man had given her out as the Best Bet of the day, but Jini let me and the Communist Party down badly.

In a moment of bitterness after the race, I said that this Comrade Cayton must have been a crypto-Stalinist, out to wreck the Party. On reflection, I take this back. The Stalinist was Jini. Fortunately, I did not witness her *débâcle,* which is French for how lousy she ran, because in trying to get into one of His Grace's bars for a drink eight minutes before the race I entered the wrong queue, from which I found it impossible to extricate myself, and arrived in the men's room just as the starter sent the field away. I got in the right queue to pay off my bookie, though, and by the time I reached the lawn, I was down ten quid. I didn't say another word of French all day.

Cockrullah did better for us. He ran third, but I had bet him each way, which is like our win and show. He paid three to one for running third, so the net outcome was like winning an even-money bet. Most of the profit, unhappily, was absorbed by the "savers"—a cogent argument for putting all your eggs in one basket. I was on the rail and had a splendid view of the race for two and a half strides, when the field was directly in front of me. My expectations were unduly aroused by a towering Guardsman type at my right, who bellowed, just before the horses came into view, "Come on, Cockrullah! Do it for England!" What he meant, of course, was do it for him, but he was a profoundly patriotic man and couldn't bear to ascribe selfish motives to himself. I agreed with him. What was good for Cockrullah bettors was good for the world. When I saw the horses, though, the grossly over-burdened Matador—a big, powerful chestnut—was half a length ahead and going away. Cockrullah was second, with Johnstone, in a tartan racing jacket, high off the saddle and whipping like a good one, but beaten. A third horse, the critically ill Epaulette, came past him as I watched. It was a photo finish between the overloaded horse and the invalid, but Matador held a neck of his lead. Ephemeral, Knight Valiant, and the rest were nowhere.

ON the road back to London, in a Rolls-Royce that I had hired in anticipation of the riches to be acquired, I explained to the girls that it wasn't picking winners that counted but the logic on which you didn't pick them. "Hippoprognosis is like Latin," I said. "Not of practical value, perhaps, but matchless training for the mind." The girls, who have just completed their freshman year at tactful colleges, were polite, as they damned well should have been, considering the difference in our ages. The one from Vassar and the one from Radcliffe said, with pretty blushes, that just before the Cup, while I was handing over all that money to the bookmaker so it would fructify, they had happened to be leaning against the rail, and a tall, handsome chap had happened to be standing next to them, a sort of Robert Mitchum type but with a Cockney accent, and he had suggested that they back Matador, at fourteen to one, so they had. I gave them a sharp lecture about talking to strangers on racecourses. To fix this advice in their malleable little minds, I allowed them to pay for the Rolls-Royce.

Not until the next morning did I discover how narrowly I had avoided opulence in my own right. Peter O'Sullevan, the hippoprog on the *Express* who had selected Epaulette, revealed that my horse, Cockrullah, had been "running minus one shoe, which had to be removed at the start." If this had come from Bendex, who had picked Cockrullah, I might have suspected that it was an excuse, but I was predisposed to believe a man who had disagreed with us. I remembered how high Johnstone had been riding, and I could now understand why. He had been holding one of the horse's legs a shoe's thickness off the ground, to keep it at the same level as the others. Under the circumstances, it was no discredit to either Johnstone or myself to have been on that one.

27
A Stranger in New York

NOT long ago, when I was in London, I bought myself a derby or dicer, a bowler or titfer or *chapeau melon*—in other words, a billycock or hard hat, although the shop where I bought it prefers to call it a coke. It was the first I had ever owned, and made me feel full grown for the first time in fifty-one years, because my father, like every other New Yorker of his day, always wore one when I was a boy. All I have to do now is learn to shave with a straight razor on a moving railroad train and I will satisfy my own time-obscured image of adulthood. I liked the clerk who sold it to me—so much, in fact, that I let him also sell me a hound's-tooth tweed cap. I was surprised at myself, since I seldom wear caps nowadays—I wasn't even tempted to buy one when they reappeared in the windows of the smart New York haberdashers a few years ago—but the purchase made me remember that there was a time when I considered caps the only virile form of headgear for a fellow of sub-derby age. All through high school, I had refused to own a non-rigid hat, and I persisted in this idiosyncrasy right on through the second time I was put out of Dartmouth for overcutting chapel. This was in the late winter of my junior year. I do not know why I went hatless so long; most of my college contemporaries wore flat hats when they went home for the holidays. Maybe I meant to show that I did *not* come from a smooth prep school, but nobody would have suspected me of that anyway. I professed a similar contempt for coonskin coats, but here, I think, I was motivated by the circumstance that my father was a manufacturing furrier. I knew that he would either refuse to buy me a fur coat or insist that I get something smart and durable, like a Persian lamb. I feared this might be conspicuous.

On the occasion of my expulsion from college—the first time they threw you out they called it a separation, which was retrievable, but the second dismissal, I knew, wasn't—I felt that I ought to buy an outer garment fit for city wear. The one I selected at Campion's, in Hanover, was an extra-pale-fawn gabardine trench coat with a belt. I was a premature Private Eye. I needed a new cap, so I bought one with large black-and-white checks. I was eighteen years old and pretty big, but I didn't look like a prizefighter, as I would have liked to, because I wore thick glasses. A professor whom I had had no opportunity to antagonize, since I took no courses with him, had got me a job on a small magazine called the *Granite Monthly,* in Concord, New Hampshire. The magazine was owned by Mrs. Robert Bass, the wife of a former Governor. She was wealthy.

The thaw had not yet come, and it was cold in northern New England, but I wore my new outfit down to Concord. It would have made a hit with the publisher of a scratch sheet, but Mrs. Bass was unimpressed. My employment didn't last long, because I couldn't get interested in Oxford sheep, a subject the *Granite Monthly* had chosen for me. I offered to do a paper on José María de Heredia instead, but we could come to no agreement and soon parted. After the de Heredia impasse, I went back to Hanover and found several letters from my father and mother, who were off on a Mediterranean cruise aboard the Rotterdam and were not aware of my unattached status, since I had concealed the carks of care when last in New York, at the short holiday after midyears. I won forty dollars in a crap game in South Fayerweather Hall, although winning was an unusual experience for me, and accepted promissory notes for my furniture and textbooks, which I sold at eviction-sale prices to other inhabitants of Sanborn, where I had roomed. I then bought a ticket for New York and departed, secure in the belief that my parents would not be home for eight weeks and that in the interim I could draw on any number of people for funds while I made a success as a short-story writer.

I HAD always wanted to live like a stranger in New York, where I had had a circumscribed, indigenous existence most of my life, and the next few days were about as near to it as I ever got. It isn't a hard thing to do, of course; there are neighborhoods in which one can live for years without encountering an acquaintance. It's just that it is such a hard thing for a New Yorker to explain. Friends will accept the idea of a withdrawal to Nantucket or Mallorca but not to, let us say, Thirty-fifth Street between Fifth and Sixth, where they would be less likely to see you. (That, in fact, is the block I am saving to disappear on when the need arises.)

I went to a hotel on Seventh Avenue, in the upper Thirties, because nobody I knew ever went there and I had heard it was fast. It was also reasonable. None of the bellboys offered to get me liquor or a woman on my arrival, and this surprised me at the time, but now, as I recall my appearance, it doesn't. Having checked in, I telephoned to my father's younger brother, a lawyer, to inform him I had left college in order to become a writer of short stories. He asked me to meet him for lunch at Mouquin's, at Sixth and Twenty-eighth, and there I told him that as my parents' home was closed and I saw no reason to impose myself on him and my aunt, I thought I might as well stay at the Lancaster, as I shall call the hotel, where, I told him inaccurately, I was getting a lot of material for stories. My uncle, as I had thought he would, temporized until he had had a chance to talk things over with his wife, in Bensonhurst.

He asked me where I was going to sell the stories and, as an afterthought, whether I had ever written any. I told him everybody had to begin sometime, and named several magazines I felt sure I could sell to, once I had written the stories. He was a kind, vague man, always slightly in awe of my father, who had worked since he was ten years old and supported all his siblings until they could get under way. My uncle let me have fifty dollars, and I walked away from the restaurant feeling like a man-about-town.

I do not remember where I went that afternoon—probably to a vaudeville show at Proctor's Fifth Avenue, which was at Twenty-eighth and Broadway. It was the evening that was to become the memorable portion of my day—the day, I like to think, that I became the last Manhattan boulevardier.

MOUQUIN'S, where I had lunched with my uncle and often before that with my father, was a French restaurant in a sound tradition. The street floor was a café with leather-covered banquettes, marble-topped tables, newspapers in wooden holders that hung on a rack, and all the accompanying amenities. (The café of the Lafayette, which disappeared in 1949, was the last place like it in New York.) There was a restaurant upstairs at Mouquin's, but we ate there only when there were no seats in the café. Mouquin's, in the early twenties, used to get a great luncheon crowd from the business district around it, which was much livelier then than now. It was the heart of the fur-and-garment district then, but has been abandoned to Greek wholesale florists and ground-floor furriers—sub-contractors who are also, for the most part, Greeks. "It isn't a fine restaurant, like Martin's," my father used to say—the Café Martin, at Twenty-sixth and Fifth, had closed before World War I—"but it's all right if you stick to standard things." By standard things he meant the *plats du jour—cassoulet toulousain, sole Duglère, pieds de porc grillés Ste. Menehoulde, bouillabaisse* (Fridays), and *canard aux olives.* Prohibition was a more serious matter in the early twenties than later, but Mouquin's waiters would serve wine or spirits to any customer they knew, and it was not hard to scrape up an acquaintance with them. There was even a printed line on the menu that said, "We will continue to serve our customers as we always have." That was not literally true except in the evening and upstairs. Liquor was served in the café at noon in tea or coffee cups, because in such a crowd the waiters could not be sure of the identities of all the customers.

Mouquin's at night was a relatively quiet place. This was due less to prohibition than to changes in the neighborhood. The restaurant, when it opened, had been in the center of a gay night-life district, the Tenderloin, and within a block or two of the best hotels in the city, centered on Madison Square. The region directly west of it had been a run-down lodging-house and brothel area. The fur and garment industries had since moved into this western area, filling it with big loft buildings and supplying Mouquin's with a new luncheon trade, but the Tenderloin and the smart hotels had vanished, leaving Sixth Avenue a dead street at night. It was this Mouquin's *à la veilleuse,* uncelebrated by the biographers of Diamond Jim Brady and Stanford White, that saw me enter with gabardine trench coat instead of opera cape, and checked cap in place of collapsible silk hat.

I found the marble tables in the café bare and only a couple of old Frenchmen playing dominoes for *vermouths-cassis* at one of them, but I heard music in the restaurant, so I walked upstairs. There were several parties dining and several men, whom I recognized instantly as Babbitts, dancing with women who weren't particularly young or smart. The band was playing "Why Did I Kiss That Girl? Why? Oh, Why? Oh, Why?" The captain, a small, bald fellow with gold teeth in the front of his mouth, and Roberto, my father's favorite waiter, a tall Piedmontese with a handle-bar mustache like a Napoleonic grenadier's, may have been astonished to see me there alone, but they didn't let on. All the senior waiters worked in the café at noon. They evidently moved upstairs at night, while the restaurant luncheon waiters either stayed home or had other evening jobs. There wasn't enough work to go around. I sat down at a window table, one of Roberto's, and ordered a drink. I was an enthusiastic and not unpracticed drinker, having spent the previous summer in Montreal conscientiously working my way through wine cards and Provincial liquor-store catalogues by trial and error, in order to acquire the Continental polish I felt the prohibitionists had denied me. I wanted to be like James Gibbons Huneker and H. L. Mencken. My tastes in mixed drinks, which had been unavailable in Montreal, were less formed. I had a few Orange Blossoms and a few Old-Fashioneds, alternating them to see which I liked better, and then ordered a whopping dinner, with, as I remember it, the *canard aux olives* as the main course.

I always talked French with Roberto, because it made me feel more knowing. With dinner, I had a pint of Sauternes, which I had decided in Montreal was subtler and more distinguished than champagne. Sparkling Burgundy, I thought, topped the lot, and I did not learn until two summers later, in France, that I had fallen into heresy. I tried to bury my taste for those wines like the memory of an embarrassing affair, and succeeded, but at the time I owned the checked cap they had a glorious effect on me. I therefore had the Burgundy—a full bottle of it—after my demitasse and cognac, and began to look harder at the women. I liked most of them no better than at first sight, and besides the company they were in showed they lacked discrimination. Most of the men seemed to be at least forty. One woman, however, had remained alone all evening, at a table so placed that I could not help watching her pretty steadily. She had been summoned to the telephone twice by the waiter captain, and had returned smiling both times. Now, I fancied, she was smiling at me. She had a short upper lip, pulled back off her teeth—one of them was gold—so I could not make up my mind, until I had finished the bottle, whether her expression was in truth meant for me or merely unalterable. She also had a snub nose and a thick, protruding underlip, like a movie star of those days, Mae Murray. I resolved the question by asking Roberto, when he turned up the empty bottle, whether he knew *cette dame avec la dent d'or,* and when he replied that he did, I asked him whether he thought she would be offended if I sent him to her table to ask if I might buy her a drink. He said that he was certain that she would not, and from a perceptible widening of her grin I could see that the movements of her facial muscles were in fact voluntary and that she had divined the nature of our conversation.

Roberto went to her table as gravely as an ambassador—I shall always remember him with gratitude for not having made fun of me—and returned saying that Madame would be most happy if I would join her.

"I have been noticing your nice table manners all evening," she said when I sat down opposite her. "Your mother really must have taken a lot of trouble with you." I couldn't think of a good answer, and asked her if she would like some wine. She said no, it didn't agree with her, but she would just have a little bourbon-and-water. "I've been waiting here all evening for a very nice man who owns a paper mill," she said. "It seems there's some kind of a paper millers' convention in town. The first time he called up he was an hour late, but he said he'd be down right away; he and some of the other millers were just having a drink at a place on Fifty-second Street. The second time he said he was sorry but he was too stiff to move. What business are you in?"

I said I wasn't in any, and she said she was glad, because she wouldn't have to listen to me talk about it. "It's all men ever talk about to us," she said, "and we have to pretend to be interested. About how they will fix the sales manager's wagon if they land something or other, because that will show the boss who is really the old he-coon, and if they quit the company, he may as well kiss off the medium-price market. Or sometimes golf scores." I told her I thought she was the only pretty woman in the place; I couldn't understand how any man would want to be with the others.

"They're all nice girls," she said, "and they're good listeners. Ninety per cent of the customers now just come because their wives won't listen to their troubles. The men who are used to sporting girls are getting old, and they don't want much more than a woman to talk to, even when they go home with her. Soon the whole town will be full of speakeasies and kept women, but that isn't the same thing as cafés and sporting girls. A sporting girl isn't trying to kid anybody." She said she lived in one of a row of brownstone lodging houses on Twenty-third Street, between Seventh and Eighth. They have since been torn down to make way for a small apartment house.

I paid her bill, which was considerable and left me with little of the money I had got from my uncle that day—so little that I began to sober up. She told me to double the fifteen-per-cent tip I started to leave, and I obeyed, trying to act as if I had just been distrait. I offered to take her home in a cab, but she said we could walk and she would take me into Cavanagh's, across from where she lived, and buy me a nightcap. Cavanagh's was more discreet than Mouquin's and survived the thirteen-year nightmare of prohibition. In fact, it is still going, although it is now under new ownership. Mouquin's abandoned the struggle against the accredited extortionists of the dry squad in about 1925.

My companion gave all the waiters an especially wide smile on leaving. "They take my telephone messages for me," she said. "You just say it's for Miss Griffin, and they'll give me the message. When I haven't much appetite, they coax me to eat. 'Miss Griffin, you must keep up your strength,' they say. 'Don't let the liquor get you.' "

ON the six-block walk from Mouquin's to Cavanagh's, Miss Griffin held my forearm, but without tenderness. Her conduct toward me was, if not maternal, at least elder-sisterly. After we had our drink at Cavanagh's, I did not know how to proceed further. I felt at this moment none of the ardor with which, an hour or so earlier, I had seated myself at her table, and I felt a trifle guilty for having taken up so much of her time. It was the same feeling I had had in shops where I could not find my right shirt size. In such cases, in order not to irritate the clerk, I had often come away with a shirt a half size too small or an inch too long in the sleeve. Now, I thought, remembering what I could of such situations in Maupassant, would have been the time to ease her disappointment by a lordly gift. But, thinking back hard, I could not recall whether I had four dollars and seventy-five cents or five and a quarter left in my pocket. She was going to be disappointed no matter *what* I did.

"I'm sorry," I said, "but I think I'll have to leave you. You see, I'm in training for a track meet, and I have to get up at six o'clock in the morning and run ten miles."

"It's perfectly all right, darling," Miss Griffin said. "You paid for my dinner, and you didn't tell me any stories about how you have the linen buyer at Strawbridge's in Philadelphia right in your pocket. Just don't get out of breath running."

The next day, when I woke up in my hotel room, I telephoned my uncle for more money, but he said that he had cabled to my father in Beirut, explaining the situation; unfortunately, he possessed an itinerary of the Mediterranean cruise, for letter-mailing purposes. He said my father had cabled back that I was to go and live with him and my aunt in Bensonhurst, where I would have more time for writing. In the meantime, I was to have only a waffles-and-coffee-size allowance.

ONE time when I was in Cavanagh's ten years ago, I thought I recognized a very old waiter as the one who had waited on me when I was a boulevardier for a night, and asked him if anybody there had ever heard from Mae Griffin—not her right name, of course, but near it—who used to live across the street in the early twenties. I was right, at least, about the waiter's vintage. He did remember her.

"That angel, Miss Griffin, do you mean?" he said. "That would never tip less than twenty per cent even when she was alone, and would cry if she heard a busboy's wife had been unfaithful? She married an old gentleman from Nashville, Tennessee, that died and left her enough money so she'll never have to draw a sober breath. She lives up in Scarsdale now, with her second husband."

I never saw my black-and-white checked cap after that night at Mouquin's. I think I must have left it in the upstairs restaurant.

28
Notes on a Distant Trial

When I was in Jerusalem, Israel, late last March, my bedroom window on the second floor of the King David Hotel looked out on the walled Old City in Jerusalem, Hashemite Kingdom of Jordan. It appeared to be just behind the tree border of the terraced hotel garden, although it was in fact slightly farther—something under half a mile. The walls were built by the Ottoman Sultan Suleiman the Magnificent in the first half of the sixteenth century, but he saved his magnificence for parts of his empire that concerned him more. The walls are a neat and ordinary job of military stonemasonry, and were sufficient to discourage the village Arabs of the surrounding country from trying to plunder the *souks* of a provincial city held by a small garrison. The architectural effect is that of a state prison, plus a dome and minarets. Still, the walls are more agreeable to contemplate than the new buildings in the center of the Israeli half of the city, and the King David rightly regards its rear bedrooms as those with a view. The King David is a wide-spreading building of stone, of the architectural school of the Museums of Natural History in New York and London, with a porte-cochère, a dark, panelled barroom like that on a transatlantic liner of 1906, a wide, flagstoned dining terrace, and a garden with a fishpool and cypresses. It is a monument of the British occupation of Palestine, as the walled Old City is a monument of the Turkish.

When I moved into my room, I gazed at the Old City for about ten minutes, wondering whether anybody on the walls was looking at the King David with equal apathy. After that, I ceased to be aware of the existence of the people of the Hashemite Kingdom of Jordan, except when the wind blew toward me and I heard the calls of the muezzins, who use public-address systems. They never failed to surprise me. There were also occasions when anti-aircraft fire indicated that somebody on one side of the border thought a plane from the other side was breaching the line. At other times, I felt as I used to feel when I inhabited an apartment on Riverside Drive and, from my bed every morning, shot my first look of the day at the houses atop the New Jersey Palisades, across the Hudson. The people who lived in them were abstractions, because there was no way of approaching them more closely without making a ridiculously long detour by way of the George Washington Bridge, a distance of at least ten miles. Between the Old City and me was a barrier three furlongs wide that was more formidable than the Hudson. It was the armistice demarcation line between Israel and Jordan—two flyweight nations in a pause between rounds that has lasted eight years without either combatant's once admitting that the fight is probably over. My shortest practicable route to the other side of the garden wall would have led from Jerusalem, Israel, to Cyprus; from Cyprus to Beirut, in Lebanon; from Beirut to Amman, the capital of the Hashemite Kingdom of Jordan; and from Amman to six hundred yards from my bedside—provided I could have got the three sets of visas involved.

If you cross from one side of the line to the other, you are shot or arrested. (There are some infinitesimal classes of exceptions, for certificated Christian pilgrims to the Holy Places, officers of the United Nations Mixed Armistice Commissions, and so on, but they do not affect Israelis, Jordanians, or journalists.) The same conditions apply along the whole length of Israel's terrestrial frontiers, making the country a long, narrow island, accessible only by sea or by air over sea. This has brought about a feeling of isolation that has paranoid aspects. For while Israel and the Arab-language states are, *de jure*, worlds apart, they are, *de facto*, cheek by jowl, and individuals cross the line without permission. Whatever the direction of the trespass or its purpose—Arabs going to attend a relative's funeral in Israel, for example, or Israeli students sneaking a look at the ruins of Petra, in Jordan—it is a sinister "infiltration" to the authorities of the country infiltrated. The border patrols shoot to kill.

Since these are the only personal contacts between the states, the people on each side of the line fall into the assumption that homicide is the chief distraction or business of their neighbors. I think that Israel, because it is so completely closed off, has a more acute feeling of persecution than any of its adjoiners except the refugees of the Gaza Strip, squatting in Egyptian captivity behind their United Nations guards.

My last week in Israel coincided with the opening of the trial of eleven Israeli Border Force soldiers who were charged with killing forty-seven Arabs—all Israeli citizens, like themselves—at the village of Kafr Kasim, near the Jordanian frontier, at dusk on the previous October 29th. That was during the Israeli attack on Egypt, which a great part of the Israeli Army thought would be accompanied by an attack on Jordan, and Jewish Israelis were obsessed by the reasonable apprehension that Arab Israelis living near the border would transmit word of troop movements to their co-linguals over the line. After the affair at Kafr Kasim, however, the Israeli Prime Minister had promised that the guilty would be punished, and now, five months later, I learned from the Jerusalem *Post* that the trial had begun.

PROSECUTION DESCRIBES ORGY
OF KILLING AT KAFR KASIM

was the headline I read in my room, after taking a morning look over into Jordan. It was a fine, sunny day. The *Post* quoted the State Attorney, Colin Gillon, who was prosecuting, as having said, in part:

> On October 29, the Israeli Army struck deep into Sinai. At this time, forces were stationed in the area known as the Little Triangle to repel possible attack from Jordan [a cosmetic alteration of the circumstances that I found natural, considering Mr. Gillon's office]. Border Force police were posted to Kafr Kasim and other villages. They had received orders not to interfere with the normal life of the villagers. To prevent any friction arising out of Army movements, a curfew was also imposed. In direct contradiction to the orders, [the defendants] . . . perpetrated . . . a bloodcurdling crime which has cast a dreadful stain on the entire nation and its Army. It was a crime without justification or explanation. . . .
>
> Late in the afternoon of October 29, a unit led by Segen [First Lieutenant] Dehan was sent to Kafr Kasim, a village 800 metres from the Jordan border. They reached the village about 4:30 P.M. A non-commissioned officer told the *mukhtar* [village headman] that a curfew had been imposed from 5 P.M. to 6 A.M. The *mukhtar* protested, saying that it was impossible to inform all the villagers. Some worked outside the village and would not return, nor could they be reached and warned before the curfew took effect. . . .
>
> The first villagers to return after the curfew came into effect were four men riding bicycles. Two were killed. The bodies were left at the side of the road. Then came a wagon driven by a man with his small daughter at

his side, followed by two men and a boy. The driver said his daughter had been frightened by the shots. Police sent the boy into the village with the girl. Two of the three men were killed. A flock of goats tended by a man and a 12-year-old boy approached. Both were killed. Minutes later, a truck arrived, carrying a passenger beside the driver and three men in the back. One passenger was killed and another wounded.

A wagon with two men approached. Both men were ordered to stand at the side of the road. Several groups of cyclists arrived. They were told to stand near the two men taken from the wagon. . . . Six were killed. Fire was opened on the wounded to kill them also. Half an hour later a truck carrying 19 persons arrived. . . . Ten were killed, among them a seven-year-old boy. . . .

At this time, Segen Dehan, his driver, and a squad of three, were patrolling the village in a jeep. Segen Dehan came to the western entrance to the village (where all the shooting had taken place) and saw another truck arriving with 20–30 persons. He took them to their homes and ordered them to stay inside. Another time, he met a group of men, women, and children returning to the village. The women and children were sent home. Three men were killed.

When news of the killings became known at battalion headquarters, an order was issued to the Border Force men in the village to shoot only if anyone tried to escape or forcibly refused to observe the curfew. . . .

The bodies were taken to Rosh Ha'ayin, identified, and prepared for burial. . . . The killings were carried out by men acting in groups, and every member of a group was guilty individually.

I shall omit Mr. Gillon's attribution of rôles to individuals, because that, of course, is what the trial was about. But all, he was quoted by the *Post* as saying, had acted "in execution of orders given by Rav-Seren [Major] Malinki," the battalion commander, who was not at Kafr Kasim himself. "Mr. Gillon said every policeman should have refused to obey an order which he knew was 'illegal and unreasonable,' " the *Post* reported. "The prosecutor asked that both Rav-Seren Malinki and Segen Dehan be found guilty of murder."

The prosecutor finished by saying that the defendants had acted of their own volition, and defense counsel asked that this be stricken from the record.

"The acts were to be deeply regretted," one of the defense lawyers said. "But the accused . . . acted under orders, not on their own initiative."

I thought that it reflected great credit on the government of Israel to bring so painful an affair to public trial and to permit so explicit a report. I recalled a similar affair in my own experience as a reporter, when, in the fall of 1944, I visited a village called Comblanchien, in the Côte d'Or, where German soldiers retreating from southern France had attacked the inhabitants and killed, among others, old men and old women. The survivors told me their stories, and I raged. An experienced form of outrage is like a recurrent disease. When you have an attack, you recall all the circumstances of the last time you had one. Particularly, I remembered the case of a shabby, thin old man at Comblanchien, a retired railroad worker, who was raising a rabbit in his yard so that he and his equally undernourished wife could have a good feed at last when the village was liberated. Soldiers he had never seen came to his house and blew his heart out in the rabbit pen, where he had tried to hide. At the time, I concluded that the Germans killed the people of Comblanchien because they themselves were on the run and frightened. But now I think they killed the villagers for wishing against them—an anticipatory revenge for their own defeat—and the old man was guilty of what they killed him for.

I also remembered how I saw a Frenchman kill a wounded German soldier on the road into Paris in the summer of 1944. The soldier lay there, and the Frenchman killed him, but the most shameful part of the recollection is that I wasn't horrified. "What a beastly thing to do!" would have expressed the limit of my emotion, as if the Frenchman had spit in a coffee cup in a restaurant. So I understood something of the optics of atrocities.

My breakfast at the King David included no bacon, because the hotel kitchen went kosher when the place opened again this spring with the aid of a government loan; the loan would not have been forthcoming otherwise. I mention the bacon only because its suppression is characteristic of a trend that Israeli "Westerners" either deny or profess to consider with amusement—the imposition of religious quirks on non-religious people. There are, as more striking examples, city ordinances in Jerusalem and Tel Aviv against the sale, possession, or consumption of pig meat; municipal inspectors are empowered to enter a suspect's house, seize the *porcos delicti* without a search warrant, and, I suppose, remove samples of grease from the skillet for laboratory analysis. While I was in Jerusalem, these laws were still in abeyance, because the Minister of Justice had ruled that the part about the inspectors was incompatible with guarantees of personal liberty. The bacon, in this towering old monument to the British way of life, was replaced in juxtaposition to the eggs by pink-and-white slabs of processed cheese made from American surplus powdered skim milk. Israel is no gastronomic paradise.

When I had finished my breakfast and the gloomy reflections on sumptuary legislation that it inspired, I went to the government public-information office and got a press pass for the trial. I told the taxi-driver who took me to the information office to wait, and when I came out with my pass and told him where we were going next, we naturally began to talk of Kafr Kasim. He was a German-born man—spectacled, middle-aged, and friendly.

"It is too bad," he said. "I have been a soldier. If you are a soldier, you do what they tell you."

The courthouse was one of a number of large converted Nissen huts at the edge of a military reservation in a quiet quarter of the city. Finding a young soldier sitting under a tree in front of them, I asked him which hut the trial was in, and he pointed it out. There were no guards outside, and no queue of spectators hoping for a seat, as might have been expected at so sensational a trial. My pass proved quite unnecessary; nobody ever asked to see it. When I pushed through the door of the court-hut, I felt as if I were coming late to a meeting of a country school board. It was easy to find a seat. There was a single aisle, and on each side of it were eight benches for spectators. The floor was of field stone, and the windows were cut high in the walls, which conveyed the effect of a rural house of worship. At the far end of the hut, against the left-hand wall, were a couple of tables and a bench for the prosecution, and, against the right-hand wall, a couple more tables and two rows of benches for the defense. The defense attorneys sat behind the tables, and the defendants sat behind them. Three judges were sitting on the case, and they faced the spectators; an Israeli flag, of Greek-blue and white, was hanging on the wall behind them. At the head of the aisle, facing the judges, were a witness stand and a lectern on which there were two swearing-books. I subsequently ascertained them to be a Bible, in Hebrew, and a Koran; the prosecution would surely present Moslem witnesses from Kafr Kasim during the course of the trial, and I had learned from the Jerusalem *Post* story that two of the defendants were also Moslems. These were Corporal Abdul Rahman Ismail and Private Said Zacharia Shaban, both Cherkesser (Circassians). The Cherkesser who live in Israel serve in the Israeli Army, although they are orthodox Sunni Moslems like most Arabs, and the Cherkesser living in Jordan serve in the Jordanian Army. They are the descendants of Mohammedans who left the Caucasus when the Russians annexed the region in the last century. The Ottomans settled them in paramilitary agricultural villages like the present-day *kibbutzim* to keep the nomad Arabs in order, and they speak their own Aryan language in addition to Arabic.

There was no jury, since this was a special military tribunal. Two of the three judges were magistrates in civil life who had been recalled to duty as reserve officers in order to sit here; the third judge was a serving officer. State Attorney Gillon, the prosecutor, was a specially recalled reservist, too, appearing here as a lieutenant colonel; outside the court he continued to be the chief prosecuting officer of the Ministry of Justice. The government had wished to avoid the secrecy of a regular Army court-martial, with the possible attendant suspicion of a whitewash if the accused soldiers should be acquitted. The absence of a jury made it a hard court for the defendants, since emotional patriotic appeal was presumably useless. Perhaps in recognition of this handicap, they had been allowed to provide themselves with a small army of reservist lawyers. Major Malinki, the ranking defendant, I had read in the *Post*, had two purveyors of counsel, Lieutenant Dehan had one, Private Shalom Ofer had two, three of the other enlisted men shared one, and the remaining five collectively had one, which made a total of seven defense lawyers working in what racing men would call five interests.

When I sat down on a bench beside a young man in a skullcap who had yellow fuzz on his face and lank side locks, one of the defending galaxy was cross-examining a government witness, a major in battle dress. The witness sat with his back to the spectators, but as his cross-examiner moved about in front of him, he shifted his position in a constant effort to keep the attorney in view, so that I could often see him in profile. He was a pink-cheeked, chunky man in his thirties, radiating considerable confidence. The cross-examiner was a walking lawyer—a type occurring in all jurisdictions. The walking lawyer paces from one side of the courtroom to the other, giving the impression that he is thinking up his questions between strides, although he has actually got them up as carefully as Sugar Ray Robinson rehearses combinations of punches. If one deceptively stray-looking shot goes in, the walking lawyer will nail his victim with a volley. He counts on hypnotizing the witness, as a mongoose hypnotizes a cobra, by making him pivot his neck on his shoulders until muscular fatigue joins vertigo to numb cerebral response.

It was gratifying to me that I recognized immediately what the lawyer was trying to do, although I did not understand a word—with two exceptions—of what he was saying. The exceptions were "*ken,*" Hebrew for "yes," and "*lo,*" for "no." To understand a cockfight, you don't have to know how to crow like a rooster.

The Israeli walker was a tall, black-browed man, with a small mouth, which he pursed between questions to express his distaste for the humiliating necessity of exposing the artless fabrications of an incompetent perjurer. (Most of this was lost on the judges, but a courtroom lawyer trains for the jury system and cannot discard his windup.) To the lawyer's brief questions, thrown over a shoulder as he walked away to look at a mote in a beam of sunlight from a window, the witness's answers would always arrive a little late, and the walker would react with a distracted "*Ken?,*" as if he were already thinking of something else. The major's words came thicker and faster. He would not be cut off; he *would* make the court understand the full nuance of what he was saying. Abruptly, the lawyer turned toward him (and the spectators), smiling widely with white teeth. He flung his right arm horizontally, palm open. "*Ken!*" he said, now concurring with the speaker. "*Ken, ken!*" I gave this the meaning of "What have I been saying all along?"

The major, sputtering, rushed to deny the admission the lawyer imputed to him; he hadn't meant that at all. But the lawyer now generously essayed to calm him down, to shut him up for his own good. "*Ken, ken,*" he said deprecatorily, magnanimously.

I could see that the major wanted to talk more about that point, but the walker, again acting out indifference, was on to something else. He drew the court's attention to a large map that hung on the wall over the prosecution table; without being able to see it, I surmised that it was a plan of the village of Kafr Kasim. The lawyer wore a pullover and slacks, over which he sported a legal robe that was open in front and pulled down below his shoulder blades in back, as if he couldn't decide whether to take it all the way off or put it all the way on. Now he got a pointer and began making darting pokes at the map, asking the witness questions based on topography.

At this point, a tall man rose from the middle of the prosecution bench. Bigboned, freckled, and bald on top, with reddish hair and eyebrows, he was reminiscent of pictures of Bob Fitzsimmons, the great Australian world heavyweight champion. This, I gathered, was Lieutenant Colonel Gillon, about to raise an objection. The prosecutor wore a black robe in the same informal way as his opponent, but over British-style battle dress. One of his arms was in a sling, the hand in bandages. He rested his good hand on the table in front of him and began his address in the slow, measured manner of a foreign-born New York rabbi speaking English in public. His voice was pondered and resonant, and I suspected that he was grappling with a language he was not completely familiar with. While the judges—two of them small and severe-looking, the third with a pink, good-natured face—listened to the prosecutor, the walking lawyer remained stationary and gazed up at them with adoration, as if sure that three such Daniels-come-to-judgment must give him the green light. The judges talked among themselves for a moment and then headed for an exit. A court attendant in battle dress uttered a rigmarole in court-attendant Hebrew that was as impossible to understand as court-attendant English or French. Since spectators, defendants, and attorneys all began to rise from their seats, stretch, and walk about, I took it that there was a break, and, since there was no general exodus, that it would be short.

I had been so quickly caught up in the legal sparring that until this moment I had paid small attention to the defendants. They were hard to see as individuals, because they sat along the right wall, behind their attorneys, and presented only a side view to the public. Even that was obscured by the military cop at the end of the row nearest us. The cop was a girl in khaki, British style. She looked like a future gym teacher. Beyond her I had occasionally caught the profile of a defendant as he leaned forward. They all had looked as amused by the duel between the cross-examiner and the major as if their own fates were not involved; when the examiner got the better of things, they laughed heartily. There was nothing special about these faces except that, as a group, they were uncommonly nice—all young and bronzed, whatever the color of the hair above them. They were Teutonic or Slavic faces for the most part; there are many Jews from Germany, Poland, and Yugoslavia in the Border Force, which is a career organization. The Borderers wear neat—by Israeli standards, almost dandified—uniforms of Royal Air Force blue, with green berets. They are a *corps d'élite.*

Now that it was all right to shift about, I made my way forward in the courtroom to where I had a better view of the eleven. From the front, they looked to be as decent fellows as they had looked in profile, and it was plain to see that they considered themselves the victimized parties. They were standing jumbled in among their lawyers and well-wishers—a good proportion of the latter female. They were not shut off from the rest of us in any way, and as I shoved forward, the most impressive of them—a tall young man with a first lieutenant's shoulder pips—moved out to meet me, shook me by the hand, and introduced himself to me in French. He was Segen Dehan—a handsome soldier, straight, narrow-waisted and wide-shouldered, with sleek black hair, a skin the color of a Siamese cat, and light-blue eyes. The Lieutenant had on his arm an almost elegant hawk-nosed lady of fifty, who might have been a great beauty once, in a semi-Oriental way. She looked up at him as if he were wounded in the hospital and she were bringing him some proper home-cooked food.

"My mother," the Lieutenant said.

I asked him where he had learned his French.

"I am a Moroccan," he said, and after he said it I remembered where I had seen hundreds of soldiers like him—the eyes, the high cheekbones, the carriage, the shoulders, and the stature. It was among the battalions of Berber *goumiers* who were attached to the American 9th Infantry Division on the Piste Forestière, in Tunisia, in 1943. Most Berbers are Moslems, but some are Jews. The *goumiers'* concept of war was merciless, and they expected no more mercy than they gave. In the twelfth century, there was a war between two great Berber dynasties—the Almohades and the Almoravides—and it is related in the history of Ibn Khaldoun that when the victorious Almohade caliph was about to kill the last Almoravide ruler, the Almoravide, an adolescent, begged his enemy to spare his life. At that, the young man's bodyguard, mortally wounded in his defense, spat in his face and said, "Is this man your father, that you should ask him to spare you?" The victor, who was toying with the idea of letting the boy off, was recalled to Berber propriety by these words, and cut the young

Almoravide's throat—not so much because he was an enemy as because he was obviously a worthless fellow. Since the *goumiers* were fine soldiers, and on our side, we found them useful and amusing.

One of the government lawyers had remained at the prosecution table to consult a book called "Phipson on Evidence." Taking Phipson itself as evidence that the lawyer understood English, I went over and asked him how long the recess would last. He said that it was ten-minute break while the judges heard argument on the admissibility of certain testimony. In less than ten minutes, the judges reappeared, accompanied by the lawyers who had followed them offstage, and after an announcement from the bench the people in the courtroom began to head for the exits. The attorney with Phipson said that they had decided to take a forty-five-minute break for lunch before deciding about the testimony, and that when court reconvened it probably would be with press and public barred. The gym teacher led the defendants away, and attorneys and spectators, companionably chatting, moved toward the main entrance, I among them.

There was by now a mobile canteen parked off to one side of the Nissen hut, and the people from the courtroom stood about in the sun on the wiry green grass drinking pop or tea and eating cakes as they discussed the morning's maneuvers. In mid-lawn I saw the State Attorney and the cross-examiner who had tangled with the major; arms akimbo, robes hanging off their elbows, they were talking together with high good spirits. I moved nearer. They were speaking English, in which both seemed more happily at home than in Hebrew, their breadwinning medium. So many a pair of medieval lawyers, interrupting their Latin wrangling at noon, must have relaxed in the vernacular while they munched their bread and cheese. When they parted, I went up to the defense lawyer and asked him if he would mind telling me what he had been giving the witness such a bad time about that morning.

He asked me who I was, and when I had identified myself and he had told me, with scrupulous reciprocity, that his name was Orren and that he was a professor of law, as well as practicing attorney, in Tel Aviv, he said, "That was a major who claims to have arrived on the scene just in time to have seen everything they want to prove but just too late to interfere. I was trying to catch him on the light conditions at that time of day—between five and six in late October—and on the lie of the land, to prove that he couldn't have seen what he thinks he saw unless everything happened earlier than they say it did, and at that time he wouldn't have been there."

"Exactly," I said, happy to confirm my notion that it is not essential to know the language a lawyer is speaking to grasp what he is getting at.

"Our contention is that the man responsible for this crime has not been put on trial—that the order came from much higher than Major Malinki's battalion headquarters, and that it was intended to be carried out as it *was* carried out," Mr. Orren said. "By the way, have you met the prosecutor? A high type of man—a gentleman. Come and meet him. I don't want him to think I am loading you down with my side of the case." Mr. Orren had a slightly accented speech, of a variety often heard in Manhattan and Brooklyn pleadings. On our way across the lawn, he told me that he was Russian by birth and had received his legal training at the University of Paris; he had learned his English in Palestine under the British mandate. His client was Lieutenant Dehan.

Colonel Gillon was drinking a citric-acid pop through a straw when we joined him. He had a deep, agreeable voice, and spoke an English English. He is a South African—a former cricketer of note, I later learned—and a British barrister. But he has never become glib in Hebrew, and his measured courtroom delivery is an effort to turn his weakness into an asset. He is, however, strong on English common law, on which Israeli law is principally based, and so has an excellent trial record.

There are about six thousand immigrants from South Africa in Israel, and they have had an influence on the new state out of proportion to their number, since they came to Israel not as refugees but as Zionist colonists between 1935 and 1948. Many of them had considerable capital, and even more had valuable technical training. They included not only members of the urban professions but agronomists and experts in the diamond industry. (Citrus crops and processed diamonds are Israel's two leading export money-earners; the uncut diamonds come from South Africa, which for decades has also had a well-managed orange and lemon culture.) Their emigration coincided with the rise of Boer nationalism in South Africa, which had rabid anti-Semitic aspects while Hitler flourished. Their departure was also, in great part, a reaction against the Nationalist Party policy toward the native races, which the Jews, as congenital liberals, deplored. All but a thousand of them arrived in mandated Palestine before the Arab-Israeli war of 1948. There they took a highly effective part in a more violent struggle than the one on which they had turned their backs. The Jews had to defend themselves, but the issue left the new state with an Arab minority that was at the mercy of the winners. Because he was a South African Jew, Colonel Gillon was especially sensitive to the implications of an assault on the weaker group. He also felt that the trial must establish the reputation of Israeli justice in the outside world. (I here claim more knowledge of his mind than I could possibly have divined on meeting him, but I had chances to chat with him afterward.) He knew, nevertheless, that he had to win his case in court, and that it would be a long and devious trial. He and Orren agreed that it would go on for months—perhaps half a year. There is no capital punishment in Israel, but Gillon said that he thought all the defendants would get stiff prison sentences.

"Don't be too confident," Orren said. "There is an old saying in the Bible: 'Let him not laugh who putteth on his sword, because he may laugh out of the other side of his face before he takes it off.' "

The two tall men had a lawyerly chuckle together. I did not think that Gillon had put on the sword of prosecution in a jocular mood, but there is an international tradition of intra-professional levity among lawyers and doctors—as in Lincoln's day, when prosecutors and defenders rode the same circuit and sometimes shared the same bed and drank out of the same bottle between duels over the neck of a backwoods homicide. The prosecutor, therefore, conformed.

Since I would not be allowed to return to court after the recess, I left the lawyers together and walked off in the direction of the King David and my kosher luncheon, which was sure to end with strawberries in syrup, because the dietary laws have it that after pot roast Heaven hates cream. I wonder what Phipson would say about the evidential proof of that; it seems to me hearsay without corroboration.

NOT many days later, I left Israel on a considerable journey that took me into countries where the Jerusalem *Post* was not available, but when I got to London recently, I began to think again about the Kafr Kasim trial in the Nissen hut, which by then must have been unpleasantly hot. I telephoned to the Israeli Embassy and asked the press attaché if the Kafr Kasim trial was still on, as Mr. Orren and Colonel Gillon had predicted it would be. He said that it was, and that there was a file of the Jerusalem *Post* at the Embassy that I might consult.

The Embassy is a countrylike mansion in Palace Green, the row within the park that leads to Kensington Palace. It was one of those days that the English think hot but that resemble warm May or Indian summer in New York. Within the chain of parks in the West End of London on such days, the harsher world outside seems remarkably unapproachable—as separate as the Old City of Jerusalem from the terrace of the King David Hotel, or the Palisades from Manhattan. It was that way even during the war, when the barrage balloons over the Rowlandson trees appeared to be part of the décor for a *fête champêtre.*

The press attaché who greeted me—a Mr. Savir—said, a trifle anxiously, that the English papers had carried nothing on the trial for months, and not a great deal even at the beginning. "It's just as well," he said, "because some of the prosecution's testimony has been gruesome. They've had Arab survivors testifying for weeks. But now the prosecution has rested and the defense has begun." He led me over to a stack of papers on a table in his office and turned me loose.

I began, naturally, with the latest copy of the *Post,* dated June 28th, to see how far along the case had got toward a verdict. The headline "MALINKI DECLARES: ALL BUT DEHAN FOLLOWED MY ORDERS" brought me back to the small courtroom abruptly. The *Post* said that Rav-Seren (Major) Shmuel Malinki, the senior officer on trial, had sensationally switched his line of defense. Previously, the effort of his attorney had been, or had seemed to be, to put the blame for the events at Kafr Kasim on the orders he had received from Aluf-Mishne (Colonel) Issachar Shadmi, his superior. Now the Major said that Lieutenant Dehan, alone of all his platoon commanders, had misinterpreted or disobeyed the orders that the Major had passed on to the lot. Only in Kafr Kasim, where Dehan had had his patrol, had there been a slaughter. The Major, with the concurrent plea of a long, good, and honorable military life, thus abandoned the next-ranking defendant.

I could easily imagine what Mr. Orren thought of that, but not what he would do. I wondered whether Dehan would now try to shift the blame lower down—to the two corporals and seven privates—or strike back at Malinki. And what would each of the others do? Would each say that he, personally, had not fired and had tried to restrain the others, or would all maintain their front against the higher-ups? The eleven buoyant men who, in March, had sat along their bench like a football team might now resolve into the likeness of combatants in a battle royal, that divertissement of Henry James's age in which as many blindfolded Negroes as were procurable were set to knocking each other about for a prize of a dollar.

As I was speculating on Mr. Orren's tactics, a secretary came into the room with two large envelopes stuffed with copies of the *Post.* "You're in luck," she said. "We just got in a new lot." From the latest paper in this batch, I learned that Orren had put on the stand as witnesses for his Moroccan lieutenant two brother officers of the same grade, who testified that Malinki's orders had been specific—that he had said that "it would be well if several villagers were killed," in order to impress them. The two lieutenants said that they had understood this severity was intended to frighten the Arabs into abandoning their lands and fleeing into Jordan when the curfew was lifted in the morning. They testified that Malinki was a strict disciplinarian, and that they, too, would have obeyed his orders to kill if their respective company commanders had not intervened and modified the battalion commander's orders. Dehan had received his orders direct from Malinki, with no intervening link in the chain of command. Both lieutenants strongly implied that they would have acted as Dehan did if they had been in his place; one even said that when he heard Dehan reporting by walkie-talkie that his men at Kafr Kasim had killed one, then three, and then fifteen civilians, he had been angry at his company commander for having forbidden him a like opportunity to "impress" his own Arabs.

Then a Mr. Levitzky, Malinki's lawyer, had cross-examined them—one defendant's lawyer cross-examining another defendant's witnesses. It gave me an idea of how virtually interminable so convoluted a trial could be. Levitzky, trying to shame the witnesses into denying that they would have been as ruthless as Dehan, asked all sorts of revolting hypothetical questions—whether, for example, they would have killed a pregnant woman running out into the street. The witnesses, trying to help Dehan and throw all the onus back on the battalion commander, said firmly that they would indeed have done so if their orders had read that way. "I am a professional soldier; I obey orders," one of them testified. How these hypothetical questions about a hypothetical situation could help Levitzky's client I found it impossible, at such a distance from the court, to understand, since

Malinki had already denied giving the sort of order that these outsiders testified they would have obeyed if he had given it.

As for Dehan, he had declined to testify but had consented to make a statement not subject to cross-examination—an option that, I read with astonishment, is open to a defendant in an Israeli military court.

When I had had enough of these dispiriting browsings, I told Mr. Savir that I still would like to know how any trial could last so long. To be helpful, he called in a fellow on the Embassy staff who is a member of the Israeli bar. The lawyer, a blond young man who informed me later that he had been born in Tel Aviv, is the only native of Palestine who figures in my story. Mr. Savir, a small, quick man with a sensitive, pointy face, had already told me, when I complimented him on his English, that he was a former German refugee. The young lawyer said, "We follow common law, and the burden of proof is on the prosecution. It must establish the cause of death of each of these forty-seven persons, and which defendants caused which deaths. Then each defendant must have a full chance to clear himself. It is not true, though, that he can do it by proving that he obeyed an order. As in the British Army, it is his duty to refuse to obey an order to commit a crime. But, naturally, they figure that if they can prove they acted under orders, it mitigates their offense and they will get a lighter sentence. I think cases in Israel have an added tendency to drag because our lawyers, although they pass the same bar examinations, have so many different legal backgrounds. On the Continent, as you may know, the judge runs the case. The official prosecutor has some of the authority of a judge, and the defense runs a poor third. When a lawyer with Continental training begins to practice in Israel, he is amazed at the latitude allowed the defense, and sometimes he begins to overindulge. It's like a fellow from a rationed country reaching a land of rich food. I had my own legal training in England, so I may be prejudiced. But they sometimes fill the record with superfluous objections—as if that will help their clients—just because they are allowed to object. They go over the same ground endlessly. And then there's an atavistic tendency to be too lenient. In the Diaspora, when Jews were the object of discriminatory laws, the state was the enemy. Evasion of oppressive laws was considered virtuous. Jews were not supposed to bear witness against one another. Now that the Jews *are* the state, there's no reason for that. But the attitude persists. We're too kind to the defendant. Since I know nothing at first hand about the Kafr Kasim case, I don't know if these generalizations apply, but I fancy they must."

"I left Germany in 1938," Mr. Savir said in his precise, English-sounding English. "So you know how I must feel about crimes of this sort. But I do not believe the Germans were sadistic. They were disciplined. Do not underestimate the force of discipline. It is easy for us to talk here in a park in London, but if you or I were in the places of those men when they received the order. . ."

29
Should (or Would) You Like Some Ve.getables?

ONE of my weaknesses as a travelling correspondent is that I like travel better than writing. Long before I have decided what to write about the place I am in, I want to be someplace else, and the call usually comes out of the ether when I am within a short head of broaching the political significance of something or other. This may have stopped me from becoming an Alsop.

I was just settling down to Athens last spring, for example, when I received through the mail an envelope forwarded from the hotel where I usually stop in London. It was marked in the upper left-hand corner with a printed "Private," so I opened it with distaste, although I couldn't remember anybody I owed money very badly. It wasn't a dun, though, but an invitation to get rich, from a London bookmaker. "Office Open from 10 A.M.," it read. "Ring [a telephone number that I shall not publish, because of our narrow postal regulations]. Full Comprehensive Service." On the back was a list of race meetings for March and April, and I could not help seeing that on that very day there were fixtures at Birmingham, Epsom, Chepstow, Uttoxeter, and Wetherby. The Acropolis was all very well, I thought, but I wondered what Chepstow, Uttoxeter, and Wetherby were like in the spring.

There are races in Athens at a course called Phaleron, against a background of the Acropolis and Mount Hymettus, on Thursdays and Sundays, but they are of an interest sufficient only to stimulate nostalgia. On the Sunday before my receipt of the friendly letter from the London bookie, I had gone to Phaleron, where I bet on a horse named Aeolus to place in a race for Arabs. I bet a hundred drachmas, which is three dollars and thirty-three cents, and Aeolus placed, all right. Then, when I went to the counter to collect, the mutuel clerk handed me back a hundred drachmas. I tried to tell him that I considered this an insufficient return on a winning bet, but since I have no Greek beyond the cardinal numbers, which are indispensable in buying mutuel tickets, I could not make my indignation explicit enough. Since I seemed angry, he called over a colleague who spoke English. I told him a small part of what I thought, and the two clerks engaged in a long colloquy. When it was over, the interpreter said, "He says you were lucky not to lose."

The friendliness of the bookie's letter and my recollection of the short odds at Phaleron set me to thinking about England, and in this mood I left my hotel for a walk. I strolled in the sun past the crowded terraces of Zonar's and Floca's, the two big cafés that are so stylish they will not sell thick, sweet Greek coffee but only *café au lait, café viennois,* and other foreign drinks, such as tea, for which they can charge as much as the equivalent of twenty-five cents without rousing public protest. A little farther on, I reached the intersection of Odos Panepistimiou (University Street) and Odos Asklipiou (Aesculapius Street). Here there are booksellers' stalls—the lockup type, like the ones beside the Seine—set up along the south wall of the university compound, and I crossed the street to see what books in languages I can read had stranded there. I am not really a rare-book hunter, but it wouldn't be half bad to turn up a dog-eared, tattered, yellowed copy of "Don Juan" in the original boards, and find on the flyleaf Byron's autograph and a long, affectionate, possibly erotic dedication to a Greek sweetheart, maybe with a short, hitherto unpublished poem in her honor. I might make enough on a thing like that to compensate for a lot of unwritten think pieces.

There was nothing of that sort in the display. Most of the English items seemed to be by Agatha Christie, unautographed, and the French books were almost all translations of American detective stories. I did see, at ten drachmas, which is thirty-three cents, a small green cloth volume published by J. Bielefelds Verlag, of Freiburg im Breisgau, and entitled "The Little Londoner," by an author of sex indeterminable from the name on the cover—R. Kron. When I turned to the title page, I found the subject so in accord with my mood of gentle *Heimweh*—for London has become a *Heim* away from *Heim* for me—that I bought it.

"The Little Londoner" describes itself as "A Concise Account of the Life and Ways of the English with Special Reference to London. Supplying the means of acquiring an adequate command of The Spoken Language in All Departments of Daily Life. By R. Kron, Ph.D." I did not buy it as a first. It said plainly on the title page, "Seventeenth

Edition, 1924." In the preface, the author states, "This little book is a parallel volume to my *Petit Parisien.* ["Le Petit Parisien" is now high on my list of desiderata.] I have called it *The Little Londoner* for two reasons; firstly, because it treats of almost every aspect of London daily life, London being generally recognized as the leading English city to which the foreigner usually goes first, and where he makes his longest stay; secondly, because the book is written in such English as the educated Londoner of the present day uses in his ordinary unconstrained conversation. . . . The old Chapter XXVI (Colloquial English, Slang and Cockney) has been left away."

When I got "The Little Londoner" to a café table—I couldn't wait to carry it all the way back to my hotel—I entered upon English life with R. Kron in the correct manner, by the front door. The first chapter is called "Calls,[1]" the footnote explaining that Calls means vi.sits. (The dot, in R. Kron's works, follows the stressed sy.llable.)

" 'An Englishman's house is his castle,' says the pro.verb," the book begins. "No one, not even a poli.ceman, is under o.rdinary ci.rcumstances enti.tled to pass (or cross) the thre.shold of an English pri.vate house. Thus a well-bred Englishman would consi.der it a bold intru.sion on his pri.vacy if a stranger were to call upo.n him without an invitation or a letter of introduction." There are quite a lot of footnotes here and throughout, but I shall omit them except when espe.cially rema.rkable.

"Persons who are provi.ded with a letter of introduction," R. Kron continues, "must, at their first call, leave that letter along with their card and addre.ss. It may be advi.sable not to go in on that day, but wait unti.l the lady or gentleman to whom the letter is addre.ssed sends an invitation. One (or A single) introduction from an English friend is worth more than a score of introductions from fo.reigners in high posi.tions.

"Sunday is not the proper day for making formal calls; week-days should always be chosen for that pu.rpose. The u.sual (or cu.stomary, proper) time for calling is between 4 and 6 p.m. (i.e. *post meri.diem,* in the a.fternoon). No call should be made at any other time, unless on a very i.ntimate (or close) friend. Strange to say, these calls, although made in the afternoon, are termed (or styled) 'morning calls.' They are, it is true, made before di.nner, the time for which is u.sually between six and eight (o'clock). Morning calls are made in morning dress, i.e. a dark frock-coat (do.uble brea.sted and with long tails), or a si.ngle-brea.sted cut-awa.y coat with tails, fa.ncy-co.loured trousers and gloves. A well-brushed silk hat (o.r top-hat) is now no longer the fa.shionable head dress."

Herr Kron—I took it that a lady would not be wearing a si.ngle-brea.sted cut-awa.y coat with tails—wrote of a London anterior to that with which I am familiar; I don't know anybody now who knocks off work at four to receive visitors. It is also, in the opinion of English friends I have consulted, a London before 1924—probably indicating that he revised each of the preceding sixteen editions only slightly. Anyway, it was quite a Little London.

"A gentleman should take his hat and stick, but not the umbrella, into the room, and keep them in his hands unti.l he is invited to put them down. The right-hand glove must be remo.ved." In the umbrella bit, I recognized a vestige of the old Druidical superstition about not opening an umbrella in the house, lest you draw rain through the roof. To retain the stick seemed to me to imply too great a lack of confidence in one's reception, though. It is a good social principle not to call on anybody with whom one cannot cope bare-handed.

Here Herr Kron, as I shall from now on presume to call him, switches into the first person, throwing off the slightly inhuman mask of the first paragraphs:

"When I intend (or wish) to go and see a friend, or any one that has asked me to pay him a vi.sit (or to call upon him, to look him up), I go to his house and ring the (vi.sitors') bell; or, as is more co.mmonly done in England, I give several (at least 4 or 5) raps[16] [Footnote: "knocks, blows"] with the knocker, a kind of iron or brass hammer, such as are (to be) seen on most English front-doors. A se.rvant (a footman or a maid) will come and open the door. In speaking to him (or her, as the case may be), I need not take off my hat. . . . Before announcing me to his master, the servant will reque.st me to step (or walk) in, and will show me into the drawing-room. Here I await (or wait for) Mr. —'s arri.val."

Mr. —, whose costume is not described, puts in an appearance, and "The Little Londoner" continues: "In the eve.nt of my not knowing Mr. —pe.rsonally, I bow when he e.nters the room, and say: *Mr. —?* (in a questioning voice), or again: *Have I the ple.asure of speaking to Mr. —?* Mr. — will then a.nswer: *That* (or *Yes, that*) *is my name; will you take a seat, please?* and pro.bably conti.nue: *What can I do for you?* I may perha.ps say in reply, *I hope I am not tre.spassing on your time.* He will assu.re me, *O (h,) certainly not.*"

From the house of the insincere Mr. —, Herr Kron continues his round of calls to that of an i.ntimate friend, who we.lcomes him by saying: "*Good morning, (afternoon, evening),* or *Hallo., old man,* or *old boy,* or *Fred, & c.*[27] [Footnote explains that *&c., &c.,* or etc. are abbrevia.tions of *etce.tera* = and so on.]; *(I'm) very pleased* (or *glad*) *to see you. It's ages since I saw you last. What's the news?. . . (Will you take a seat? Take a seat! Sit down!). . . Well, how are you? Well, how are you getting on? Well, how is the world using you? How are you all at home? I hope you are all well at home. How is your father (getting on)? &c.*

"My a.nswers may va.ry as follows: *Capital* (or *Very well, Quite well, To.lerably well, Pretty well, Fairly well*), *As u.sual, thanks* (or *thank you*). After these or si.milar preli.minary to.pics of con-versa.tion, we have a co.mfortable chat."

"The Little Londoner" also furnishes detailed instructions for get-ting away:

"The usual form of leave-taking is *Good-by.e,* or *Good da.y,* or *Good night,* and among friends sometimes *Ta-ta. . . .*

"When i.ntimate friends leave each other, no bows are made. They just shake hands and se.parate with some such rema.rk as: *Good-bye, old fellow, I must be off now; Now I must say good-bye; Then good-bye, till to-morrow, till Friday week; So long; (I shall) See you again, &c.,&c.,&c. . . .*"

IN Chapter II, "Shops and Shopping," Herr Kron reveals an aspect of his character that contrasts with his hat-in-hand civility to Mr. — and his careless joviality with the i.ntimate friend who called him *Fred, &c.* On entering the shop, he states, it is permissible to say "Good morning (day, a.fternoon, evening)," but "In most cases the English dispe.nse with a greeting." The shop(wo)man, however, is effusive. "Good morning, Sir (Madam. Mrs. Cox)," he (she) says. "What may (or can) I do for you?—What may I have the pleasure of getting you?—What can I show you?—What for you, Sir?—Are you being attended to?—Is any one attending to you?—Now, Sir?"

All he wants is a pair of brown kid[73] [Footnote: "young goat (La.tin: *capra*)"] gloves, but he asks several deceptive questions to arouse the shop(wo)man's hopes of making a more considerable sale, like *viz.*[9] [Footnote: (from the Latin *vide.licet*) is read *namely,* or *to wit.*] "Do you keep i.llustrated (or picto.rial, or pi.cture) po.st-cards with views of the town?"

The shop creature answers politely, "Yes, we have a very good asso.rtment. Will you kindly come to the other counter?"

Instead of going with him (her), Herr Kron, perhaps miffed (cheesed) at having been called Mrs. Cox, merely changes the challenge.

"I see you have advertised in to-day's (*Daily*) *Mail* the latest sci.agraphs[85] by Röntgen's X-Rays; may I have a look at them?"

At this point, I needed a footnote myself. It said, "[85]pi.ctures showing the inte.rnal structure of an o.bject."

The shop person, however, is not stumped. He (she) replies briskly: "Certainly, Sir. We have a very large colle.ction of ra.diographs (or X-Ray photos). Will you walk this way, please?"

"Do you sell French no.vels? Have you (got) any new ones?" Kron may have expected this to make the shop (I incline here to think wo)man blush, but it doesn't rattle her.

"No, we keep English books only."

"What is the price of that travelling trunk in the window?"

"Seven pound ten."

The succinctness of this last answer indicates that the shop(wo)man is tired of his nonsense. From then on, nothing more is said about the po.st-cards, the sci.agraphs, or the trunk. Herr Kron sticks to the gloves, which were what he came in for.

The next section of the chapter is headed, "*The purchaser does not care for the article shown (to) him; he expresses a wish to see others:*

"I don't quite care for (or like) this style (or these, those). Have you no others to show me?"

"This pair (of gloves) seems to be too tight (wide). May I try one on?"

"The bu.ttons are sewn on very badly; there's one coming off already."

The shop person is at first conciliatory. "Yes, it is a nu.isance; they *will* sew them on so badly. If you'll wait a mi.nute, I'll have it put on for you."

"What is the price of this pair?"

"This pair is twelve shillings. That's a cheap glove (or line, or a.rticle)."

"*The purchaser thinks the price rather high, but haggling not being the custom in good English shops, he takes the article:*

"I think that very dear," he says, but the shop(wo)man, knowing he (she) has won, hardens.

"Dear? It's dirt-cheap."

"That seems rather dear. I know a shop where I can get them for less."

"Excu.se me, Sir. That's the best glove sold at the price.... You won't find them cheaper a.nywhere."

"Well (or All right), I'll take this pair."

"Very well, Sir. Thank you, Sir."

The purchaser makes a last effort. "Do you allow any di.scount for cash?"

"No, 12 s. is the cash price."

"Good afternoon."

"Good afternoon, Sir."

IT is in Chapter III, "Food and Meals," that "The Little Londoner" comes most poignantly to grips with English life. "Everything that is eaten for no.urishment, is called *food*," the chapter begins. "... English ladies seldom interfere with the cooking.... All meals in England seem to be arranged very much on the same lines.

"In most English ho.useholds, four *meals* are taken a day (or *per diem*), *viz.*, breakfast (about 8 or 9 in the morning, an hour later on Sundays), lunch (or lu.ncheon, about 1 or 2), tea (about 5), and di.nner (about 6.30 or later on in the evening)....

"The *Dinner* is the pri.ncipal meal in well-to-do fa.milies. It is a very important matter, and a more or less so.lemn affa.ir; all members of the family ge.nerally dress for dinner. Pu.nctually at the fixed (dinner) hour (u.sually at 7 p.m.), the dinner bell, or the muffled sound of the gong (a me.tal disc, so.mething between a drum and a bell) is heard, and each gentleman 'takes a lady in (or down) to dinner,' and all sit down in their allotted places....

"A thick or clear soup, which is very strong, and often seems to be prepared after Spa.rtan recipes—e.g. o.xtail or mock[24]-turtle[25]—so.metimes, but not re.gularly, o.pens the meal." [The footnote on "mock" says, "false, not real," while that on "turtle" is "large sea-to.rtoise (Latin: *chelo.nia mi.das*)."]

"The Little Londoner's" description of the rest of the meal is pretty diffuse, because it is a catalogue (voca.bulary exercise) of all the kinds of fish, all the kinds of meat, and all the kinds of ve.getables that could possibly turn up, including items that are highly improbable, like carp and moor hen. The ve.getables, it says, "are distinguished by the a.bsence of se.asoning. They are simply boiled in salt and water, and then seasoned with salt, pepper, and vi.negar, or oil (to be found in the cru.etstand) by each pe.rson according to his taste. A bottle of hot, ready-made sauce, 'Wo.rcestershire Sauce' or 'Yo.rkshire Re.lish,' is on the table for those who requi.re a spe.cial seasoning."

However Herr Kron may sneer at simple, undeceptive English fare, he is quick to snap up an invitation when one offers—"To get an invitation to dinner is, of course, consi.dered a great honour"—and is Johnny on the spot (prompt) in his best bib and tucker (threads), eager to show his savoir-faire (know-how, *Waszutunwissen*).

"It must be understood that it is a breach of e.tiquette to come even a little before time to a dinner party; o.therwise you will run the risk of being mistaken for a waiter. [Particularly if you have a German accent.] It is the cu.stom to arri.ve a little late, but not more than a quarter of an hour. Therefore invitations are issued, no.wadays '. . . at 7 for 7.15,' i.e., you may come at 7, dinner beginning at 7.15. The invi.ted gentlemen as a rule appe.ar in evening (or full) dress, or dress-suit, i.e., dress-coat (or tail-coat, or swa.llow-tail coat) and black tie, black waistcoat, and black trousers, but without gloves. Evening dress is *de rigueur* (i.e., compu.lsory) unless the invitation tells you o.therwise. The top-hat, though not needed, may be worn, whether evening or morning dress or di.nner-jacket (at small family or ba.chelors' dinners) is expected, but it is left in the hall or cloak-room, or given to the footman or maid.

"Vu.lgar people have the ha.bit of eating with the knife, altho.ugh it is considered very bad form to use the knife instead of the fork; the knife is only for cutting the food, and no e.ducated person ever allo.ws it to touch his lips.—Using to.othpicks is shocking.—Bread or rolls should never be cut into small mouthfuls, but broken.—Clinking glasses strikes an Englishman as a fo.reign habit."

Once the meal begins, it is every (wo)man for him (her) self. This is what used to happen At Table in 1924, according to "The Little Londoner":

"*The ho.st(ess) asks the guest what (s)he would like to have:*

"What will you have (or take), tea, coffee, or cho.colate?"

"*The guest makes (or takes) his (her) choice:*

"Tea, please. I'll (i.e., I will) take a cup of coffee, if you please."

"Do you take sugar and cream in your tea?" This is clearly non-responsive, and from here on matters disimprove:

"Yes, please.—Only sugar, no milk or cream, thanks (or thank you)."

"Will you (or Won't you) eat (or take, have) some hot (or buttered) toast with your coffee?"

"No, thank you, I think. I'll have some bread and ma.rmalade."

"May I send (or offer) you some bacon and eggs, or some haddock?"

"Thank you very much, I don't mind which (it is). I'm not very particular."

"Here is ham, cold beef, and kippered herring; which do you prefer?"

"I think I'll trouble you for a slice of cold beef, if you please."

"What soup may I help you to (or send you), Mr. Darling, vermicelli[112], or gravy[113]?" [The footnotes read: "[112](Ita.lian = little worms) soup with long, worm-like noodles, or macaro.nies." "[113] beef tea, i.e., juice (or soup) of beef."]

"Thank you, I'll trouble you for some gravy soup, a very little, if you please; I rarely take soup at all."

"What wine do you prefer? Cla.ret, sherry, hock (or simply: Claret, sherry, hock), or mose.lle, Sir?"

"May I trouble you for a glass of hock? I'm rather partial to it."

"No wine, thank you, I'd rather have a glass of water."

The hostess ignores this regression and asks, "Will you not have a piece of ice in your wine?"

"I think I will. Hock must be iced to taste really well."

Now that the company is contentedly drinking diluted wine, "*The ho.st(ess) asks (or reque.sts) the guest to make a hearty meal, and offers other dishes:*

"Take some more pi.geon pie, Doctor! It won't do you any harm, I am sure. Have another (or a second) helping, will you?"

"You are very kind, Ma.dam (or Mrs. Berry, Miss Cox); I really think I'll take a little more. I'm very fond of pie."

"Allow me to send you some more meat, Mr. Cox."

"Just a tiny piece, (if you) please; it is very nice indeed."

"May (or Can) I offer you another cup of tea?"

"Thank you, I think I'll trouble you for a se.cond cup."

"I see you have crossed your knife and fork. What can I help you to (or send you) now? Won't you take some Welsh ra.bbit?"

"Welsh rabbit? I never tried it. Would you let me have a very small piece, just to try it (or to see what it's like)?"

"Help yourse.lf, Sir."

"Thank you, I will."

The guy has now taken tea, coffee, bread and marmalade, bacon and eggs or haddock—whichever Mrs. Berry or Miss Cox happened to have handy—two helpings of meat (beef and unspecified), a chaser of gravy soup, a glass of hock with a hunk of ice in it, two sendings of pigeon pie, another cup of tea, and a segment of Welsh rabbit sufficiently rigid to be cut in pieces, but the hostess is unrelenting.

"Any more beef, Sir? Have some more lobster, Mr. Shaw."

"No more, thank you.—No, thank you, not any more."

The second, apparently, is from Mr. Shaw, a favored guest who has been guzzling lobster while his convives made do with haddock and gravy soup. He is full up with it, or perhaps has a claw stuck in his throat.

"Now try some poultry with sa.usage, will you?"

Herr Kron spurs faltering appetites with a footnote on sausage: "(French: *saucisse*) se.asoned meat cut into very small pieces, and stuffed (or filled) into a gut (or intestine)."

"No more, thank you. I have done very well."

"I see your plate is empty, and you've placed your knife and fork side by side on it. May I not help you to some more fowl?"

"I am much obliged to you, Mrs. D. [Food is pressing against the backs of his eyeballs, and he is seeing multiple hostesses] but I have finished and would rather not have any more, thank you."

"Will you venture on some plu.m-pudding?"

"No, thanks, if you'll excuse me, I will not take any."

She becomes frantic. "*Do* let me send you a go.oseberry tartlet, one only!"

"I had rather not, thank you."

Now she gets spiteful. "You *are* a poor eater. I fear (or I am afra.id) you have made a poor meal."

"No, thank you. I've made an e.xcellent meal. I've done very well, indeed." But the reader senses that he fears he will never be invited again.

Even in England, a Freiburg im Breisgau appetite cannot depend entirely on the hostess to keep it stoked (the lady above is an ide.alized po.rtrait), so Herr Kron has added some "Other phrases (addre.ssed to one's neighbour)," which will usefully fill in gaps in the conversation:

"May I trouble you for the bread, please?"

"Will you pass the water, please?"

"(I'll) Thank you for the mu.stard. (Colloquial.)"

"Kindly (or Will you kindly) pass the vi.negar."

And, to keep the neighbors happy and coöperative:

"Should (or Would) you like some ve.getables?"

"Do you (or I suppo.se you) take Yorkshire Re.lish?"

Laying aside "The Little Londoner," I decided I might be able to stand the eastern Mediterranean for a while longer.

30
The Dollars Damned Him

THE AMERICAN LIBRARY ASSOCIATION, listing forty-six Notable Books of 1960 not long ago, left out "Stephen Crane: Letters," edited by R. W. Stallman and Lillian Gilkes, with an introduction by Professor Stallman (New York University Press), and "Cora Crane," by Miss Gilkes (Indiana University Press). This saddened me. Writer-researchers who clear up a tragedy sixty years old can hardly expect any of the prizes that fall so readily to authors of bad novels and books about the Civil War, but Professor Stallman and Miss Gilkes could legitimately have aspired to make the list of forty-six. The letters clearly show us that Crane was the victim not of self-indulgence or a death wish, as it has been popular among critics to assume, but of his situation, which was banal. He died, unwillingly, of the cause most common among American middle-class males—anxiety about money. This fear expresses itself most often now through thromboses and cerebral hemorrhages, but it operates just as lethally with tuberculosis, which Crane had. Maladies, like breeds of dogs, move in and out of favor, but money worry is constant in societies wherein the Western Nonconformist Protestant culture sets the pattern. (In England and the United States, Catholics, Jews, and non-believers take the same impress early in life as Presbyterians.) It is the fuse within the somatic bomb.

Artists are neither more nor less susceptible than Wall Street men or haberdashers. It is a matter not of temperament but of anthropology. Old Osawatomie John Brown, who feared no bullet, wrote to a friend that his creditors made him feel like "a toad under the harrow." Bankruptcy saddened the early life of Ulysses S. Grant, the otherwise imperturbable, and then the terror of bankruptcy came again and got him after his second term in the White House. He wrote his memoirs while dying of cancer of the throat, as Crane, twenty years later, was to grind out stories for magazines as he lay dying of tuberculosis. Crane, for all his irregular life and beliefs, was the son of a clergyman and the brother of a grasping lawyer. He was therefore peculiarly liable to the disease of his kind.

The turn of the century was a time when expenditure was accepted as the outward sign of Divine Grace. The steam yacht was the nimbus, reserved for millionaires, and while the author of "The Red Badge of Courage" did not set himself so high, he had an unrealistic view of how he rated. Cora Crane, it is plain from her biography, shared his illusions. A handsome woman, adept at hospitality, she complemented her moody writer husband perfectly. Writers' consorts are of two kinds—those who are indignant at society's treatment of their husbands, and those who are indignant at their husbands for being writers. Cora was of the first sort. She shared Crane's justified conviction that he was a great man, and another, related but beside the point, that a first-class writer had a right to live on the same scale as the second-biggest brewer in Nottingham, Notts., or the best obstetrician in Tacoma, Washington. This shared heresy was so radical that not even the daredevil Crane dared express it, but it was implicit in his train of life. He did not say he was as good as a stockjobber, but he acted as if he thought he might be. He could hardly be blamed for wanting to live like a member of a profession that society took seriously. His mistake was thinking he could afford it.

Miss Gilkes' solo effort is the first extended account of Cora, born Howorth, in Boston, and married successively to men named Murphy and Stewart, but known to the leading citizens of Jacksonville, Florida, as Cora Taylor. Crane met her in Jacksonville while that town was headquarters for the American filibustering expeditions that were continually setting off for Cuba to aid the rebels there against the legitimate, internationally recognized government, which was Spanish. The filibusters took along American arms and Cuban volunteers, as during an incident of more recent memory, and since their expeditions were semi-public—we have a long tradition of indiscretion in such affairs—Jacksonville was headquarters for the newspaper correspondents covering them. Cora was the *patronne* of a bagnio she called the Hotel de Dream. Since Stewart, from whom she was separated, would not divorce her, the Cranes could not formalize their union, but Stephen established her in England as his wife in 1897.

Crane left her the following year while he went to Cuba to cover the Spanish-American War, and when he rejoined her in England they leased—at a bargain rental, because the place was in such disrepair—a great rambling old country house called Brede Place, in Sussex, which they operated with a scratch staff of eccentric servants. Crane was broke, although the public thought that as the author of "The Red Badge," published three years earlier and already a classic, he was wealthy. He should have been, but he wasn't. American first-serial rights had brought him ninety dollars. The Cranes were, in effect, worse than broke. Cora had run up bills in England, and so they were seriously in debt, to the tune of nearly two hundred pounds—at the old rate of exchange, almost a thousand dollars. This, and not a patch on his lungs, was the first lesion of Crane's terminal disease. Leasing Brede, in the opinion of Crane's contemporaries, was asking for trouble. Cora, in excusing the Cranes' presumption, wrote to the critic Edward Garnett, "I hope that the perfect quiet of Brede Place and the freedom from a lot of dear, good people, who take his mind from his work, will let him show the world a book that will live." The dear, good people, as events turned out, followed Crane to Brede and sponged on him, for his public condition, in contrast to his private one, glittered. His comings and goings were chronicled in headlines. He was the ascendant literary star; the theory that he was already all through was not born until after his death. It was pure hindsight.

Crane was also the star war correspondent of Hearst's *Journal*, then in its most flamboyant period of self-advertisement, and Mr. Hearst was supposed to shower his stars with the wealth of the Homestake Mine. Crane had written that great book "The Red Badge"—and the critics had been right in calling it great—in 1893, when he was twenty-two, but it had not been published until 1895. The reverberations of its success were still in the air. When he was twenty-one, he had written "Maggie: a Girl of the Streets," which he published at his own expense and which had no sale at all. Brought out in 1896, after "The Red Badge's" triumph, "Maggie" had added to his fame. And, in the few years since, he had shown that he could grow. In stories like "The Blue Hotel," "The Bride Came to Yellow Sky," and "The Open Boat" he had written better than ever before. He had questionable lungs, but Dr. Edward Livingston Trudeau, a famous American specialist of the day, had examined him a year earlier and declared that his mild case of tuberculosis was arrested. Worry and work reactivated it, and at the end of a heartbreaking struggle of eighteen months to reduce his thousand-dollar debt by writing too much, he expired, owing five thousand dollars.

The disease, the bad doctors of the period, and the anxiety, acting synergetically, got him. The treatment for tuberculosis was so ineffective that even people without a worry in the world died of it in droves. The Duchess of Manchester lost two daughters to therapy; her experience made her, in the Cranes' circle, an authority on the disease. Crane, with his anxiety, was a pushover. Even a general practitioner could have killed him, but Cora exposed him to specialists. They aggravated the illness and increased his need of money, his efforts to get the money to pay them further aggravated the malady, and as he declined, his wife sent for increasingly costly consultants, who prescribed more outrageously destructive therapy. Had he in fact "burned himself out," as some of his literary biographers insist, or had he cared to die, he would have succumbed more rapidly. Only his will to survive and his tough baseball-player's constitution kept him alive.

The measure of his modest profligacy was that he liked to have a horse or two to ride. He had once written to a fan, "My idea of happiness is the saddle of a good riding horse." He also liked to have guests to dinner. And, like Herman Melville, he thought himself entitled to "the calm, the coolness, the silent grass-growing mood in which a man *ought* always to compose." But he could not resign himself to acknowledging, with Melville, that "that, I fear, can seldom be mine." He had not learned, as Melville had, that he could not hope to earn as much money as a brewer or a solicitor. (At the top of his fame, Crane got three hundred dollars for "The Blue Hotel," and as the market went, that was a good price, while my own father, a furrier in New York, could get five hundred dollars for an Alaska-seal coat.) In this failure of imagination, Crane resembled other men made overconfident by great native ability, such as John Henry, the steel-driving man in the folk song, who set himself to outhammer a steam hammer, or Roland, in "The Song," who saw a million Saracens come into the vale and said, "I will strike a thousand and seven hundred blows with my good sword"—a computation that left him nine hundred ninety-eight thousand and three hundred short. The knack of arithmetic does not always go with a gift for the higher mathematics of the soul. Crane, like Roland, was a chivalric figure, and he could not count.

The letters reflect the progress of the uneven conflict—Crane against skewed values. (The consultant whose advice finished him off got two hundred and fifty dollars for coming down from London to dispatch him. Yet doctors are turned out of medical schools by the batch, while only one man has lived who could have written "The Blue Hotel.") There is still outward confidence in Crane's letter of February 16, 1899, to his London agent, James B. Pinker, although it contains evidence that he could hear footsteps behind him:

Dear Pinker:

I send you a rattling good war story—I think 5330 words. Please send me a checque [*sic*] for £40 so that I will get it on Sunday morning. [He was already financing by the day.] . . . How am I going? Strong?

By February 19th, he had done another story, but the situation had deteriorated:

Dear Pinker:

I am mailing you at this time a whacking good Whilomville story—4000 words—and I am agitatedly wiring you at the same time. . . . I must have altogether within the next ten days £150, no less, as the Irish say. But, by the same token, I am going to earn it. . . . £40 of my £150 have I done yesterday and today, but for all your gods, help me or I perish.

Translated into statistics, this meant that Crane had sent up on February 16th a story potentially worth fifty-three pounds—he usually got ten pounds, or fifty dollars, for a thousand words. Simultaneously, he had wired for an advance of forty. This would leave him, after Pinker sold the story and deducted his commission (five pounds six shillings), about seven pounds to the good. With the second letter, he sent on a story worth forty, but requested an advance of a hundred and fifty. He was consequently at least a hundred and three pounds farther behind than when he started writing the first story. But since he had written the forty-pound story in two days (he did not count the days of gestation that must have preceded writing), he flattered himself that, if he buckled down to work, he could do a forty-pound story *every* two days, and in ten days catch up with the deficit, except for what he might have to borrow to live the ten days. He knew, although he refused to admit it to himself, that while a man may write a story in two days, or even in one, the writing is only the final stage of production. It is impossible to maintain such a pace over any considerable period. His optimism, therefore, was a typical example of a writer's gift for economic self-delusion.

The Whilomville stories, about small boys, were an inferior Crane sideline, but he could write them easily, and there was a steady market for them in America. As he fell farther behind, he concentrated on the pieces that were easiest to produce, and as the sickness gained on him he produced them with more difficulty. There was no more time for "Blue Hotels," for which three years intervened between germ and finished tale. The space rate was about the same for quick job or masterpiece. What the editors wanted was his byline. There was a far larger market in 1899 than today for magazine fiction addressed to the general reader, and a less clear dividing line between art writing and slick writing. Crane worked in both specialties, and sometimes forgot which side of the line he was on, or pretended to. Here, as in his money life, self-deception was a necessity. But he was like a man in a sandpit, who with each struggle to get out brings more earth tumbling down upon him.

Cora's business background had not fitted her to run an author. She believed with all her heart, which was as big as an outsize grapefruit, that Crane sold something harder to come by than her merchandise at the Hotel de Dream. Cora was more than a literary buff; she had an eye for good writing and was modest enough to know that good writing was hard. "I am of the opinion that it is criminal for people to write who know nothing about it," she said. Since she so highly esteemed Crane's product, she could not credit its low market value. When she was told that any girl at the Hotel de Dream could outearn the comet of the literary firmament, it made her incredulous as well as indignant. She urged Crane's stories—written, about to be written, and barely foreshadowed in the writer's mind—on poor Pinker. On one of the rare occasions when Crane got a rejection, she wrote:

> I cannot understand what can be the reason for the English publishers refusing such stuff as those children stories and "God Rest Ye." They seem to fancy themselves as judges of literature but to me they seem to be a good set of idiots to refuse really clever and artistic stuff and print the rot they do.

The tempo rises. Cora writes to Pinker that Crane has sixty-seven thousand words on a novel, but

> is going to run very short. He has a wine dealer who threatens to serve papers tomorrow, if his bill for £35 is not paid at once (today). . . . This has

nothing to do with my former request for £20. . . . Of course I don't know how Mr. Crane's account stands with you.

But she could dolefully guess.

Cora's letters to Pinker become more frequent than Crane's; he is too busy trying to write the Cranes out of the hole. The letters show that Pinker was an angel among agents. He let the Cranes get into him for two hundred and thirty pounds, a vast sum in the literary world. Pinker sold a stupendous number of the words Crane wrote, and even of those he contracted to write. (Crane was fluent to the end, writing in his bed when he was too weak to sit up, although the force of the tide diminished as he sank and his need became more acute.) The insuperable difficulty was the gap between the prices, which were scaled to support writers in lodging-houses, and Crane's American inner need to keep up a prosperous front. He complained constantly about the "Comanche braves" who descended uninvited upon Brede in platoons—Americans unknown to him or, at best, acquaintances of acquaintances—but he turned none away. He had a double American fear—that he might be thought to have a swelled head or no money.

THE editors of the "Letters" have provided excellent footnotes identifying Crane's correspondents and references in the text, in addition to a running argument that serves to string the years on the fraying thread of the young man's life. From the arrival at Brede, though, the letters mesh so tightly that they need no exposition. The editors' auxiliary narrative becomes a distraction, like the ice-cream vender's bugle outside the courtroom in "The Stranger." "Mesh" is an appropriate verb, for the story, deadly as a net, is, netlike, intersticed with light. Here are the letters, and the good times they tell about—of H. G. Wells and Henry James and Joseph and Jessie Conrad and some writers, charming people, who would be lost to the world forever if they had not been associated with Crane and these others. Some of the nicest writers are those who don't write very well. Like stable ponies, they serve the purpose of keeping the racers company, and as their rewards in Heaven they receive small bags of sifted footnotes.

The letters indicate that Crane now began to realize the scrape he was in, but there was no quit in him. He may have remembered that when his Open Boat capsized in 1896 and he swam toward land, an offshore current held him until he thought he would die. But he kept on swimming, the current unexpectedly set him free, and he lived to write a great story about his escape. A note he sent to Mark Barr, a fellow-expatriate, in September, 1899, however, shows that by then he had a clear premonition. Crane wrote to congratulate the Barrs on the birth of a son, Philip, for whom, he said, he had ordered "a cheap mug—from me to him":

> Anyhow, it is all the boy now. The boy! May the time-of-his-life rock him gently in ease and may the cradle spill only enough to give him those shocks which inform men, inform men that everything is already well-combined for their destruction and that the simple honest defeated man is often a gentleman.
>
> Rubbish—Salute for me our dear Mabel. Yours ever, my dear boy.
>
> S. Crane

(I saw Philip Barr in a restaurant on Fifth Avenue the day I wrote this. He tells me that someone long ago stole the mug.)

A creature of another culture, an Elizabethan or a Regency gent, would have a hard time understanding why the Cranes did not slip their cables. It would have been wiser even from the point of view of their creditors if they had abandoned Brede. With a few months of complete rest, body and mind lying equally fallow, Crane might have recovered his health and his form, in which case he would have attacked the accumulated debts. His compulsion would have forced him to it. Melville, finding himself in a similar cul-de-sac, had solved *his* problem by abjuring writing. Consequently, he had managed to die solvent, and at the expense to posterity of only nineteen years' production. "Dollars damn me!" old Ishmael had written to Hawthorne in 1851, after a week spent trying to get in the potatoes at Arrowhead while he finished "Moby Dick" and to finish "Moby Dick" while he got in the potatoes. Harper's had refused him an advance; they reminded him that he already owed them $695.65 on the last one. Melville had been forced to borrow, at nine per cent, to keep going. The book about the whale was only passably successful. It is noted in Jay Leyda's "Melville Log" that a year later the author still owed Harper's $145.83. Melville, therefore, after a few more years of feckless struggle, took refuge in a job at the New York Customs House, at four dollars a day. This was more than a fairly distinguished author could count on earning regularly by his pen. He had three children, and Mrs. Melville, his bourgeois wife, was no Cora Taylor.

The fear of bankruptcy haunted the Melvilles all their lives; Herman's father had died bankrupt, of a "brain fever" syncope. Herman's elder brother, trying to revive the family fortunes, had gone bankrupt, too, and his mother's self-pitying letters, preserved by Mr. Leyda, allow us to imagine how deeply she must have impressed the horrors of their situation on her children. A convincing thesis could be written to prove that the fear of bankruptcy is the most potent American trauma, and was the most influential factor in the settlement of the continent. Fleeing their creditors, pioneers exterminated the Indians. Those who stayed solvent remained in place until the next panic. Crane, a cockier type and happier in his choice of a spouse than Melville, continued the enterprise of authorship. He was like Patsy Tulligan, a character in one of his own Bowery tales who had a misunderstanding with a Cuban exile in a Sixth Avenue café and was challenged to a duel with swords. Patsy had never seen a sword, but he acceded. "I'll fight wid anyt'ing," he said. "I'll fight yeh wid a knife an' fork." Crane had written, "Patsy was not as wise as seven owls, but his courage could throw a shadow as long as the steeple of a cathedral."

The Cranes might have given up if their doctors had told them that he must surely die if he did not rest. Instead, the medicos encouraged, or at least tolerated, his notion of writing until he could afford a long journey to a curative climate. Rest and antibiotics are the basis of treatment now, doctors tell me. In the absence of antibiotics, rest was even more essential then. Curative climates are an exploded legend; Crane would have been as well off in Sussex as anywhere. By sending their depleted patients on long, exhausting trips, the lung doctors of the time advanced the dates of their extinction, and if the consumptives survived the voyage itself, the sanatoriums finished them off by exposure to cold. (I know a lung man who says that he rereads "The Magic Mountain" every year to remind himself of what not to do to a patient under any circumstances.)

But the deterrent that I think would have held Crane in place, even if he had had proper advice, was shame. To "put up a front" and then be unable to pay the bill—to be denounced therefore as a four-flusher or dead beat—would have been for him complete ignominy. Insolvency was the hardest sin to confess, and still is in our civilization. Western man can easily joke about most sins, but not debt. "Forgive us our debts as we forgive our debtors" strikes the subliminal keynote; "debt" is the test question even for God. To forgive it is divine, and nobody truly expects that mortals will. Late–Victorian England, dominated by Gladstones and Chamberlains and nice Nellies of every description, had come full circle from the Regency days, when debt and venereal disease were alike considered benign afflictions that supported one's claim to being a gentleman. The worse a man bit his creditors—as John Mytton and Mytton's biographer Nimrod both did, by skipping to Calais—the better the unbitten public liked him. Thackeray's novels display an intermediate stage of feeling. In them, debt is cause for pity. Later it inspired loathing.

Also, Crane's life in England afforded him great satisfaction. He remained outwardly the Golden Boy, or visiting star, in an environment vastly more complex and sophisticated than he had known in America. His friends included Wells and James and Garnett, George Gissing, and, above all, Conrad. In England, too, the upper classes associated more freely with this upper crust of bohemia than in New York. Few peers were as stiff as their American fathers-in-law. The young man who had slept three-in-a-bed with friends over the Art Students League only a few years earlier was sensible to the gracious life, although, as we shall see, he eyed it hard. The writers were of a higher calibre than the Elbert Hubbards, the Hamlin Garlands, and the William Dean Howellses, who were their opposite numbers in New York.

Crane must have found it hard to contemplate leaving all this—especially Conrad, the writer most like him, with whom he delighted to talk about their work. Naturally, he wrote to no one that he was considering a bolt, but at the beginning of 1900, when he was sicker than ever before, he may have thought of it. His friend Robert Barr (no kin to Mark and Philip) reported in a letter to a third party that Crane had said he had booked steamship passage for February 1st. As a rationalization, perhaps, Crane had added that the British press had offended him by loose rumors about his parties at Brede. He announced, according to Barr, that he would take Cora to Texas, buy a ranch, and live in the open air. If he had got there and reached a porch hammock, he might have made it. "But if Crane ever seriously intended leaving England then," Professor Stallman and Miss Gilkes note, "Alfred Plant, the solicitor, must have been the one to nip any such plan. Plant could hardly have failed to point out that Crane would lay himself open to the charge of running out on his creditors if he left the country then." The taboo had its usual effect, and Crane remained at Brede, where, two full months later, on March 31st, he suffered a series of severe hemorrhages that sewed up the game for anxiety and the doctors. In February, he was still mobile. The hemorrhages flattened him. Abed, he continued to try to write.

Cora, distraught, went up to London and appealed to the American Embassy for help—the forlorn hope of an expatriate when all else has failed. The Embassy was moved by the plight of a great American author. It is an oddity of Crane's case that even the Embassy knew he *was* a great author, and so assumed him prosperous. It sought out the leading chest specialist in London and sent him down to Brede, at the Cranes' expense. He was the fellow who got the two hundred and fifty dollars, and he insisted that his consultation be prepaid. Cora gave him an uncovered check, and then dispatched another frantic note to Pinker to deposit the sum at the bank ere it bounce. This un-socialized croaker told Cora that to save Stephen's life she must drag him off to the Black Forest. There were neither airplanes nor automobiles to smooth the journey, so Crane had to be placed on an "air bed" (a pneumatic mattress) and joggled off by carriage to a country railway station, carried by train to London and then to Dover (where he arrived so exhausted that he had to rest a week before continuing), then ferried across the Channel, carried by train half across Europe to Basel, and moved by rail again to Badenweiler, an environment in no way more favorable than Brede. I am informed that the portage thus imposed was enough to shorten his life by at least three months.

Besides being lethal, the consultant's advice was as binding as a priest's injunction on a Mexican Indian mother to carry a child to a miraculous shrine. Cora begged, badgered, borrowed. Conrad, Crane's best friend among writers, wrote to Cora regretfully:

> The daily subsistence is a matter of anxious thought for me . . . I am already in debt to two publishers, in arrears with my work, and know no one who could be of the slightest use. . . . My future, such as it is, is already pawned.

Conrad, fourteen years older than Crane, survived him by twenty-four. He had had no early success to trick him into overconfidence.

Cora's caravan, made possible by the money she had scraped up, consisted of a doctor and two nurses, Crane's niece Helen, Cora, the sick man, and his favorite dog. Mrs. Conrad reported that at Dover Cora often went without meals to save money. They arrived at Badenweiler on May 28th. On June 5th, he died. Cora brought the body back to England and then to the United States, where it was buried in the Crane family plot at Hillside, New Jersey. (Crane was born in Newark, a New Yorker *manqué* by a few miles.) After that, the lovers' paths diverged. Crane has had a long and accidented posthumous career, but public opinion expunged Cora from it until Miss Gilkes restored her.

MRS. MARK BARR, the Mabel of the note about Philip, was the latest-surviving person I knew who had frequented the Cranes in England. She died in 1955, and to the end of her life, she resented aspersions on Cora. "Rubbish," she would say. "Cora Crane was a perfect lady." Since Mrs. Barr herself was a great lady, Cora must have been the goods. Her charm for the British aristocracy survived Stephen. From a letter of a young woman of fashion in London written the year following his death, Miss Gilkes quotes this passage:

> I began to hear a familiar voice at the next table. And, lo, there was Mrs. Crane in a black lace frock with Lady Randolph Churchill and some young men. . . . When she recognized me she ran over to our table and made a lovely American fuss. I had lunch with her several times. . . .

Miss Gilkes adds, "Years later, when Vere [the young woman] knew all the gossip, she wrote: 'I do not know how she lived and do not care. She was "on the level." She was plucky and gay and kind.' "

But this did not help. Cora returned to London to salvage the odds and ends of Crane's literary estate. The principal care was to arrange for the completion of an unfinished novel, and a bad one—"The O'Ruddy." But since there had been no marriage, she had no dower rights, and Crane had left a will so ambiguous that she could get nothing. She went back to the United States broke, although equipped with a letter to Vice-President Theodore Roosevelt, who, when he was Police Commissioner of New York, had been a chum of Stephen's. Roosevelt could find nothing for her in Washington. So she returned to Jacksonville in 1902, put the arm on a number of her old customers for capital, built a new house on the Row, and soon was rolling in a carriage of her own again. Miss Gilkes observes, sentimentally, at the apex of Cora's woes, "Now Cinderella was back in the kitchen, the Prince lay dead under a stone in the cemetery of his people, and Cora found herself, all of a sudden, a woman with neither marital nor social status. And no longer young." (Miss Gilkes researches a lot better than she writes.) But Cinderella knew how to turn pumpkins back into coaches fast.

Her style changed with her milieu. The rest of her life resembled "Sanctuary" more than a novel by Henry James. Prosperous again, she took up with a bartender twenty years her junior, married him (by now Stewart was dead), and then had to throw him out because he was a mean drunk. The bartender heard he had a successor in her favor, a boy of nineteen. He met Cora's carriage on a dusty road in the hot sun. The boy was in it, along with Cora and her housekeeper. The bartender shot him dead. He pleaded self-defense, although the victim was unarmed. Cora could not, even if she had wished to, testify against her husband, but the housekeeper displayed a prudish streak. She told the coroner a story that, if repeated at the trial, might result in conviction. As a reward for *not* testifying, Cora offered to take her employee on a junket to England, so that she would be out of reach of subpoena until the trial was over. And so, in a more secure financial position than she had ever enjoyed as Mrs. Stephen Crane, Cora returned again to the scene of her life with him, visited the Conrads and the Wellses and left a card for James, who had heard about her and ducked. She went motoring in Ireland, a novelty (the car broke down), and arrived back in Jacksonville with the housekeeper a few days after the acquittal. The bartender then divorced her—to marry a woman who shot *him*—and she adopted as house pet an alcoholic real-estate man of good family. It was her last emotional investment. She died in 1910, aged forty-five. She was certainly the least boring author's mate in American literary history, and I can think of only Scarron, in France, who had one in her class.

CRANE'S disembodied fortunes, meanwhile, were at their nadir. Critics, like sportswriters, have a special idiom tangential to ordinary English. "To discover," for example, means "to write about when nobody else has recently." Thus, in 1952, when Crane had been adrift for more than half a century, Professor Stallman himself wrote, in his foreword to "Stephen Crane: An Omnibus," "Crane has been discovered twice since he died, in 1900—more than any other American author except Henry James." (James is in and out as frequently as a drunk caught in a revolving door.) An author not discovered for six months or more is known, in the same odd lingo, as "forgotten." Nineteen-ten, the year of Cora's death, fell midway between Crane's death and his first professionally accredited discovery, by Thomas

Beer, in 1923. (He was being industriously read and personally remembered, but that doesn't count with the professionals. He was also posthumously teaching a number of young men who found him on the shelves of public libraries to write.)

Crane's American contemporaries of note, all of them his seniors, had celebrated his departure with a round of qualified praise, modified by regret that he had not "fulfilled his early promise." By this they could only have meant, if they were objective, that he had failed to show any advance between the ages of twenty-eight and twenty-nine and a half, while he fought the Battle of Brede. But they had in fact resented both his quick rise and his abandonment of them for faster company. The British had been his "discoverers" while he was alive. "The Red Badge" had been received in America with the equivalent of a pat on the head for an exceptional child. The crashing acclaim of the British critics, who constituted a higher court, had promoted him over the heads of his older compatriots, who never forgave him. Accordingly, they gave him a headstone marked "F.I.P.," for "Flash in Pan," and congratulated themselves on their prescience. "After Crane's death at twenty-eight in 1900, his reputation disintegrated rapidly," John Berryman, a fairly late and Freudian Crane discoverer, wrote in 1950, in his critical biography "Stephen Crane."

The run-of-the-mill critic is a Linnaean; he likes to pop his specimens into plainly labelled phials, and Crane, genus Doomed Genius, went into the one labelled "Edgar Allan Poe." Because of the brief span between his late birth, in 1871, and his early death, in 1900, he became the least in focus of American masters, like a man seen through binocular lenses with one set for short distance and the other for long. He was born in the same year as Theodore Dreiser and Samuel Hopkins Adams, his contemporaries on Park Row, who survived him by forty-five and fifty-eight years, respectively. But he has been dead longer than Tolstoy or Ibsen and almost as long as Melville himself, who was born in 1819. Because of Crane's youth, much of the writing about him has a patronizing tone, as if he were eternally junior to discoverers born from ten to twenty years after his death. It has become standard procedure to reproach him for his limitations—although death allowed him little time in which to explore his limits—and to demand why he accomplished so little, although he accomplished a prodigious amount for his age. His legacy of viable masterwork is more considerable than those combined of all the provincial *petits-maîtres* who condemned him when he died. Beer, a slick-fiction writer turned informal (another way of saying careless) biographer, picked up and continued the pair of unfounded suppositions—that Crane was "unfulfilled" and that it didn't matter, because he lacked the capacity to improve. Beer was sympathetic, in the sloppy fashion of the early twenties. He made Crane a romantic figure, like Dick Diver.

Reforgotten, Crane drifted, a sitting duck for the new, Freudian-critical rediscovery. (The reason that a man doesn't write more than he does is that he never wanted to write more than he did. If he dies before he does, it proves that he didn't.) John Berryman said in his biography of Crane that he had an obsessive interest in women older than himself that gravely affected his subliminal retrospective intentions toward his mother, and an interest in horses that showed him pregnant with violence, of which the horse is a symbol. It had not occurred to Berryman that a man whose "idea of happiness" is a saddle might just like horses, or that if a man is much with horses, rides horses, covets horses, and thinks a good deal about horses, a high percentage of the images in his prose and verse are likely to be horse images. Or that most very young men spend a lot of time thinking about women older than they are, because the women younger than they are are still children. This is a circumstance that the years rectify; at forty, had he lived so long, Crane might have preferred women of twenty-five, and, at fifty, women of twenty. When he left America with Cora, in 1897, he was twenty-six and she thirty-two. (She said, incidentally, that she was twenty-nine.) This is scarcely a monstrous discrepancy.

Freudian criticism reaches full frenzy in Berryman's assertion that when Crane, in an unpublished play, called a mythical city in China Yen Hok—it was a humorous play—he was still dominated by the horse cult. "Hock," Berryman reminds the reader, means a "horse's ankle"—violence again. "Now Crane had already written the story of a dying dope fiend named 'Yen-Nock Bill.'... Nothing just like these names have I found; Crane evidently invented them." Here I suspected, when I first read it (and I still suspect, but only faintly, because Berryman is for the rest so serious), that the annotator was having us on. "Yen hok," "yen hock," and "yen nock" are variant phonetic spellings of the Chinese—or at least of the Chinatown—word for "opium pipe," used with self-conscious knowingness by police reporters of Crane's era when they wrote of tong wars. Crane was a reporter and wrote about opium for the *Sun* and *Journal*, as Berryman knew when he detected the symbolism in "Yen-Nock." Can he possibly have missed Crane's attempt at a burlesque dateline ("Opium Pipe, China") or have failed to dig "Opium-Pipe Bill" as a pseudonym for "hophead"? The "hock" in "yen hock" has no more to do with a horse than the "hock" in a Rhine-wine bottle. Again, when Berryman notes, with the air of a discoverer, that another character in the Yen-Nock Bill story is named Swift Doyer, and that a swift is a bird (also an adjective and a brand of bacon), which, it seems, has even direr significance than a horse, it appears that he does not know that Doyers Street is one of the three thoroughfares of New York Chinatown (Mott and Pell are the others), and that because of its indirection it gave rise to the old New York gag description of a dishonest fellow: "As crooked as Doyers Street." Swift Doyer, then, is as obviously a joke name as Yen Hock, or Yen-Nock Bill.

"Sadism grinds strong in Crane's work," Berryman writes, "and its counterpart, masochism, does." He explained that Crane's overt bravery betrayed his inner fear (just as, to the initiate, abject cowardice reveals inner security, because it is not afraid of ridicule). "Death ends the terrible excitement under which he is bound to live—death is a way out, a rescue." *Bref*, Crane scared himself to death.

"Crane wasted his genius," Professor Stallman wrote nine years ago. "What killed Crane was . . . his own will to burn himself out, his Byronic craving to make his body 'a testing ground for all the sensations of life.' " Stallman adds, like a sensible uncle, "He could have retreated from life to calculate it at a distance, as Hawthorne and James did. Instead, he got as close to life as possible." *Bref*, Crane died because he neglected to put on his overshoes—a truly academic mode of suicide. Professor Stallman, incidentally, in his otherwise valuable "Omnibus," descants interminably on the benefits, for an author, of personal inexperience. To describe well, he implies, nothing is so essential as not to have seen. Stallman would have made a great foreign-news editor for Hearst or Luce. "Was there any need for Crane to experience a blizzard in order to write 'Men in the Storm'? Would not an imaginary rather than an actual blizzard have served just as well, the germinal idea of the story being a *symbolic* storm?" or, again, "The locality of 'The Blue Hotel' has symbolic import and could have been painted with no first-hand knowledge of it. . . . The fight that he witnessed and tried to stop during an incident in Lincoln, Nebraska, became the fight depicted in 'The Blue Hotel,' but the germinal idea for the story might just as well have had a literary source." (The heresy of the monks—good wine from a second pressing.) For a clincher, he advances the argument that "Crane reproduced the immediacies of battle in 'The Red Badge of Courage' long before he had seen and suffered actual shellfire." This is to argue that if a man can tie his shoelaces with one hand he couldn't do it better and faster and more easily with two. Also, it ignores a number of special factors. The North swarmed with Grand Army men during Crane's boyhood in small Jersey and upstate towns—roughly from 1880 to 1890—and they were not the graybeards I remember from my small-boyhood, circa 1910, but active citizens, of the age of Second World War veterans now. Most must have been eager to talk, and boys must have been their most willing listeners. Dialogue, personal details, mood are therefore neither imagined nor "from literary sources." The reporter listened. Men talk, moreover, more freely of war, a shared adventure, than of more intimate things; Crane would not have had the same luck if he had asked them about their wives. War, too, is the most fully documented of human activities, and the Civil War is the most redundantly documented of wars. It is a fair bet that the bookcases of the Reverend Mr. Crane and all the families the Cranes knew bulged with sets of bound volumes of *Harper's* and *Leslie's*, and probably of the *Tribune* or the *Times*, and with volumes of war memoirs. These all contained first-hand reporters' reporting; they have since become the sources of the sources of our factual Civil War books.

Most important, Crane did not "reproduce the immediacies of battle;" he made a patterned, a rhetorical, war such as never existed, to test the heart of his hero. The readers who wasted their admiration on his backdrop were the ones who raved over the scenery in David Belasco's productions of Civil War plays—"so natural you would have thought it was real"—and who bought paintings because the Spanish dancers' mantillas made you think that if you touched them they would feel like lace. The luxurious detail was a concession to the only taste, besides his own, that Crane knew then. It is extraneous to the true merit of the book, which is about a boy in a dragon's wood, and timeless. After Crane had seen war, he drew more sparingly, as in "The Upturned Face." He could, I suppose, have later worked up other vicarious subjects as convincingly, except that he never again had ten years to spare.

To bolster his "Red Badge" line, Stallman invokes the testimony of Harold Frederic, who, "discussing this question in his *Times* article on Crane, pointed out *why* it is that the best accounts of battle have been written by novelists who never saw warfare, and the least realistic accounts by trained correspondents who were on the spot." Neither Stallman nor Frederic names his novelists. Stendhal, whose first chapter of "La Chartreuse de Parme" is one "best account," saw war in Germany and Russia under the most illustrious of captains. Tolstoy, when he wrote "War and Peace," had behind him the experience of the Crimean War, which he reported factually in "Sevastopol," and of the Russian campaigns against tribesmen in the Caucasus. The English novelists who wrote so well of the First World War—Siegfried Sassoon, Richard Aldington, and Robert Graves—all had their personal bellies full of it, in the front line. Preëminent among eyewitness-participants' accounts of battle in the Civil War were those of John William De Forest, a novelist *and* a captain in the Twelfth Connecticut Volunteers, first published in *Harper's New Monthly Magazine* from 1864 to 1868—"The First Time Under Fire," "Forced Marches," "Fort Hudson," "Sheridan's Victory of the Opequon," and "The Battle of Cedar Creek." In 1946, all were published again, with other articles by De Forest, as "A Volunteer's Adventures." (I have never ceased to wonder, since reading them in their book form, whether the boy Crane saw them in *Harper's*.) In "The First Time Under Fire," a regiment, rather than one soldier, is the protagonist; the narrator, De Forest, is older and surer of himself than Crane's boy. In "Cedar Creek" the battle is won and lost, as in "The Red Badge."

I can see no merit, then, in the notion that observation is useless, or that Crane, because he had once, laboriously and against his will, dispensed with it, did not gain from experience. His steady and rapid "development" as a man is clear through the curve of the letters. The callow kid who shyly presented himself to Garland and the hardly-better-than-Garland Howells in the first years of the nineties, thinking them the real thing, would have been incapable of the equal-to-equal discussions with Conrad five years later. There was a full lifetime of experience between the youngster, his first victories already behind him, who started West for his first long journey in 1895 and the hardened adventurer who turned up at Brede four years later.

Most of all, perhaps, Cora, his grown-up partner, represented an advance over the Asbury Park summer widows to whom in 1890 he addressed his long, self-explicatory screeds—flashes of young genius mixed with swatches of pure Willie Baxter. Crane at Brede had grown. What he needed, and should not be discounted for not having had, was time to think over what he had learned. Had he escaped the trap at Brede, he would have taken with him material for a new, maturer cycle.

England was his first experience of a civilized society. In America, he had been by turns a college freshman (one semester at Lafayette, another at Syracuse), a hallroom boy, and a newspaper reporter. Because of his fame, he entered the London literary world—at a point where it merged with the nobs'—as an equal at an age when other young men would still have been held at its fringes. He brought to it an eye less reverent than Henry James's and better supplied with material for comparison—the Bowery, Mexico, the Plains, real war, and the relation of society, through the police, to the low classes. When I was a beginning reporter, the city had plenty of newspapermen who had worked with Crane and of senior detectives who hated his memory. He had intervened publicly in favor of some street girls who were being shaken down by plainclothesmen. This marked him indelibly, in the cop mind, as one subversive of public order.

The letters reveal early insights. From one to James Gibbons Huneker, in 1897, for example:

> You Indians have been wasting wind in telling me how "Unintrusive" and "DELICATE" I would find English manners. I don't. It has not yet been the habit of people I meet at Mr. Howells or Mr. Phillips or Mrs. Sonntag's [in New York] to let fall my hand and begin to quickly ask me how much money I make and from which French realist I shall steal my next book.

This was a good beginning, and Crane had other insights ahead of his time; Oscar Wilde, he reported, was "a mildewed chump. He has a disease and they all gas about him as though there was a hell and he came up out of it."

Of James's attitude toward the same milieu, Harold Frederic, the author of "The Damnation of Theron Ware," had written to Crane in 1898, "Henry James is an effeminate old donkey who lives with a herd of other donkeys around him and insists on being treated as if he were the Pope. He has licked dust from the floor of every third-rate hostess in England." Crane, as perceptive, but kinder, wrote:

> I agree with you that Mr. James has ridiculous traits and lately I have seen him make a holy show of himself in a situation that—on my honor—would have been simple to an ordinary man. But it seems impossible to dislike him. He is so kind to everybody.

CRANE might not have survived long in Texas; Robert Barr, in the letter in which he reported Crane's plan, wrote, "He may last two years but I cannot bring myself to hope more than that." This is not conclusive. Lay prognoses were as fallible as those of doctors; the chief difference was that they were free. Crane had been a tough, muscular youth—a varsity baseball player in college, although he weighed but a hundred and twenty pounds. "Small, sallow and inclined to stoop, but sinewy and athletic for all that . . . a capital catcher of curved balls," Garland wrote of Crane when they first met. He was the best player at Syracuse, and although he was there for only one semester he was elected captain of the team. The adventure of "The Open Boat" demonstrated what toughness and what will to survive he had in 1897, only a couple of years earlier. A final argument for his chances was his relative youth.

If he had lived on, even if he had not "developed" beyond the point already reached in his best stories (a point that few others have ever reached), he could hardly have failed to write others as good. We have seen in our time that the best writers as they mature become journalists—Sartre, Camus, Mauriac, Hemingway. Crane might have been the great correspondent that the First World War failed to produce. It fascinates me to speculate on the kind and quality of the work Crane would have done if he had recovered, even partially, and gone through with his escape to Texas. I cannot agree with Professor Stallman's opinion, expressed in 1952, that Crane's "death at twenty-eight resulted in no loss to literature. He had exhausted his genius." Stallman supported this by quoting Garland, an older man who was in the beginning kind to Crane but became resentful when outstripped by him. Garland, a congenital stuffed shirt, couldn't write for free seeds. It is perhaps unfair to tilt against the Stallman of 1952. His researches show such devotion to Crane that he may well have shifted his attitude on the young author's capacity for growth. But he wrote then, "He produced too much, he kept repeating himself, and he never developed."

As a workman, Crane developed sharply between "The Red Badge," written in 1893 and published in 1895, and "The Blue Hotel," which was conceived during his Western trip of 1895 and written in 1898. The only period of his brief life during which he produced too much, kept repeating himself, and so on, was in 1899 and 1900, the time of Brede. Even a baseball player is not ruled through because he has one bad season, and that under dreadful circumstances, and a tenor's high C is not judged by how he performs with one leg in a bear trap. The quality of the work admittedly fell off. As a beginner, Crane had had to cure himself of writing pastiches of Kipling, and at Brede he began to write pastiches of Crane. He had no time to let themes ripen in his mind. Once he began, he always wrote swiftly, but now when he began wrong he could not afford to tear up his work and start on a better line. I think, myself, that Crane might have written long novels of an originality as hard to imagine, in retrospect, as "Maggie" and "The Red Badge" would have been to anticipate. His chief problem would have been to keep free of another syndrome of advances and effort to catch up with them.

Dostoevski said that not one of his novels was two-thirds as good as it would have been if he had not had to hurry it in order to extract another advance. In the years leading up to his exile, in 1849, he wrote to the publisher Kraevski, "I struggle with my small creditors like Laocoön with the serpent!" (or Crane with the wine merchant at Brede), and, again, "To keep my promise and get the work in on time, I forced myself, and wrote things as bad as 'The Lodger;' I was stupefied and humiliated by having written it, and for a long time afterward could not concentrate on more serious work. Each of these botched jobs brings on an attack of my illness"—an "inflammation of the brain," later identified as epilepsy. Relief came from an unexpected quarter—he was exiled to Siberia for eight years, during which he was forbidden to publish. Crane had no such luck.

31
The Soul of Bouillabaisse

Ever since 1918, when I ate my first bouillabaisse—an event that in my mind overshadowed the end of the First World War—I have been hearing from French waiters and cooks that it is impossible to produce the genuine article in this country, because the essential ingredient is missing. In memory, that initiatory bouillabaisse—at Mouquin's, on Sixth Avenue—remains impossible to ameliorate, but Roberto, the Mouquin waiter with the grenadier mustache, informed me that the dish, although sufficiently successful, was but a *succédané,* or substitute. "It lacks *la rascasse,*" he said. "It is like a watch without a mainspring. The *rascasse* does not exist except in the Mediterranean." He offered no details, and though I did not know whether the *rascasse* was a crustacean, a fish, or an aquatic mammal, I did not ask, for fear of revealing my ignorance. In the years since 1925, when Mouquin's closed its doors, a victim of prohibition, I learned that the *rascasse* was a fish, but nothing more, although when I came to eat bouillabaisse in Marseille—good, but not as memorable as Mouquin's—I inferred that some of the fragments in the broth were it. A friend of mine—Dr. Samuel B. McDowell, a zoologist now teaching at Rutgers' branch in Newark—could have identified the fragments for me immediately if he had been there, but he wasn't. Dr. McDowell is a student of comparative anatomy, with stress on its ichthyomorphological aspects, and not long ago I made the mistake of mentioning *rascasse* to him while we were lunching at a seafood restaurant called the Lobster, on West Forty-fifth Street. It is a mistake to mention anything unclear to McDowell, because he will go to entirely extravagant lengths to clarify it. The Lobster is not French, but it is a fine place for broiled fish, lobster, and beer. It no longer attempts bouillabaisse—largely, the proprietors once told me, because when it was put on the menu, customers brought along travelled friends who said that it couldn't possibly be the real thing.

When I passed this information on to McDowell, he asked me why the authenticity of the bouillabaisse should have been denied. I answered that the essential ingredient did not occur on this side of the Atlantic. I felt that my explanation was safe, because a note in the American edition of Larousse Gastronomique says, "Many of the fish used in the bouillabaisse, such as the traditional *rascasse,* are not found except in the Mediterranean; they are virtually unknown in England and America, and no English name for them exists." As for the preëminence of *rascasse* in bouillabaisse, I was leaning heavily on a distinguished and sensible authority, Waverley Root, who, in "The Food of France," has written, "The subject of bouillabaisse is a complicated one. . . . For the ingredients, only one fish is agreed upon by everyone—*rascasse.* No two lists are the same, and *rascasse* is the only name common to all."

McDowell asked me the name of the fish in English, and I said I did not know, here again relying on Root, who wrote, "My French-English dictionary has no idea of what *rascasse* is." If I had looked in Randle Cotgrave's 1611 Dictionarie of the French and English Tongues, the only French-English dictionary I own, I would have found, under "*rascasse,*" "[In Languedoc], the Sea Scorpion," and, further on, under "*scorpion de mer,*" "The Sea Scorpion; a red, great-headed, and wide-mouthed fish, which hath but a few, and those verie small, teeth; but in lieu thereof he is armed with many prickles, both on his backe and about his head." Had I been able to give McDowell the "scorpion" clue, it would have saved him a lot of time. But I had not thought to go beyond Waverley Root. "What is *rascasse?*" Root asks, and answers himself, "It is a coarse fish, armed with spines, which lives in holes in the rocks, and would be allowed to stay there if it were not for bouillabaisse. Alone, it is not particularly good eating, but it is the soul of bouillabaisse. Cooked with other fish, *rascasse* is one of those catalytic foods, like the truffle, whose own contribution to taste seems meagre but which has the gift of intensifying other flavors." Root is more the cook than the taxonomist; his description is not as specific as Cotgrave's, but Cotgrave says nothing at all of the *rascasse's* higher function.

Prosper Montagné, the learned compiler of the original French Larousse Gastronomique (1938), and himself a *toque blanche hors con-*

cours, quotes in support of the indispensable-*rascasse* doctrine Joseph Méry (man of letters, 1798–1865):

> To prepare without flaw this masterpiece Phocian,
> The *rascasse* is the sine qua non of the ocean.
> A fish by himself rather like an old shoe,
> He suffuses with marvels the goo of a stew.

(The translation is a rough one. Massilia, the Greek predecessor of Marseille, was a colony of Phocis. The Phocians are said to have brought into pre-France the olive, without which bouillabaisse, even with *rascasse*, would be impossible, since there would be no olive oil.) M. Montagné (as does Root) recites the neo-Phocian legend that Venus invented bouillabaisse in order to fill her husband, Vulcan, with it and make him fall asleep while she turned a trick with her lover, Mars. Like Root, he pooh-poohs it. "In ancient times, it was held established that fish soup flavored with saffron was soporific, an opinion exploded today," Montagné writes. Root says, "It is based on the superstition that fish chowder made with saffron is a soporific (it is not, but any food taken in on the gargantuan scale that bouillabaisse encourages is likely to make the eater sleepy)." I cite both Montagné and Root on this particular point because of the new light cast upon this old story by McDowell's subsequent investigations, which indeed exonerate saffron but indicate that Venus may have known a thing or two about the *rascasse.*

M. Montagné, then reflecting upon the etymology of "bouillabaisse," strikes out the superficially easy derivation—"slow boil"—as unlikely, since bouillabaisse, despite what its name says, is the product of a quick boil over a high flame, instead of a long boil over a low one. He equally decries the Marseillais tradition that it was the invention of an abbess—the *bouilli à l'abbesse*—to kill the monotony of the Friday diet. My own speculation—that it may have been named for the miraculous taste of a *bouilli* containing an *abbesse*—apparently did not occur to M. Montagné, himself more resourceful at *plats* than at derivations. How the *abbesse* got into the stew is a matter to be settled later—perhaps she was a victim of cannibals. Alternatively, admirers, anticipating her canonization, may have boiled her to separate flesh from bones for the preparation of relics, as was done with the body of Louis IX of France. A dish need not take its name literally, as witness the Scotch woodcock, which is not game but a form of rarebit, which, in its original form—"Welsh rabbit"—was an example of the same thing, since it is not a rabbit.

"Have you any notion of the Latin name of the fish?" McDowell asked, not very hopefully, after I had recited what I remembered of *rascassiana.* When I said I hadn't, he fell briefly silent and then began to tell me of his fears that if we ever learned to desalinate the ocean, the fly-casting lunatics would try to stock it with rainbow trout, a species for which he has great contempt as a parvenu in the zoological scale, since, by fossil evidence, it appeared only in the Miocene epoch, twenty-five million years ago. (His favorite fish, the halosaurs, have been around three times as long as that.) "They'll poison all the more interesting fish with rotenone, in order to make life easier for Sparse Gray Hackle's little playmates," he said. "They've done that in a lot of fresh-water streams already. The game-protection organizations and the tackle-makers have an invincible lobby, and comparative anatomists are politically unorganized." McDowell is a man of many interests, all associated with fish.

ABOUT a fortnight later, McDowell sent me the following letter, the gastronomic as well as ichthyological implications of which should be clear to all:

"I want to thank you for the delicious lunch of red snapper the other day, and to apologize for the peculiar way I squirmed in my chair and bulged my eyes whenever a busboy cleared a nearby table. Because of years of exposure to tobacco smoke and formaldehyde preservative, my taste buds are in no condition to make me a judge of the delicacies of fine cookery, but I am a connoisseur of fine fishbones. The sight of that menu, with its marvellous variety of fishes, immediately suggested to me what delights in fishbones there must be in the kitchen garbage can. I could visualize a huge can of codfish skulls, with striking enlarged intercalary bones; Spanish-mackerel vertebral columns, with articulating processes designed with a fine precision and economy; and the skull of my own red snapper, with a magnificent supraoccipital crest. Through the years, I have learned not to follow the busboy out into the kitchen and rummage through the garbage, but the desire still comes over me, and I am not quite myself when the seductive hints of a fishbone-connoisseur's paradise pass before my eyes on an otherwise emptied platter.

"On the matter of our discussion, if French chefs say they cannot make proper bouillabaisse in America because they cannot get *rascasse,* they either are pulling your leg or haven't been trying very hard. I found a perfectly good *rascasse du nord* by looking under the porgies in a Newark fish market. It seems to me that lifting up a few porgies is little enough to expect of a man who claims a devotion to excellence in cuisine. The *rascasse du nord,* despite its name, occurs in the Mediterranean and goes into the pot there with the other *rascasses.*

"The hardest part of my *rascasse* hunt was finding out what a *rascasse* is. A little book by Hans Hvass and Jean Guibé entitled 'Les Poissons' helped me immeasurably. Since I know Jean Guibé to be topnotch on African frogs and Madagascar snakes, I put my complete confidence in his judgment of fish. Not only does this handy little book, which just misses fitting in my pocket by an eighth of an inch, give an excellent colored picture (page 54) but it has a brief and pungent discussion, on page 100, of the '*Sebaste dactyloptère, ou Rascasse du Nord.*' ('*Dactyloptère*' means 'finger-finned.') Here it is revealed that this fish is known to science as *Helicolenus dactylopterus.* If the chefs had just said that first, I could have helped them sooner. *Helicolenus* is one of the Scorpaenidae, or scorpion fishes [at this point, I reflected that Cotgrave was no mugg]—a family of fishes made famous (as fish families go) by one of its members, *Synanceja horrida.* This is the notorious stonefish. According to the 'Guide and Historical Souvenir of Stage One of the New York Aquarium' (1957), it is considered the most venomous of all fishes. It has thirteen large spines on its back, each with a pair of venom sacs attached, and persons who have stepped on these spines say that the pain is almost unbearable. At first, I was skeptical of this report and thought it might be a cautionary parable, in the 'Slovenly Peter' vein, put out by the Aquarium to discourage children from wading in the fish tanks, but the report is, if anything, an understatement. A more serious understatement is on the next page of 'GAHSOSO,' where it is said of the closely related lionfish (*Pterois volitans*), 'It was once believed to be venomous, but this seems not to be correct.' The New York Aquarium learned the penalty for scoffing at old wives' tales a few months later, when, at 9 A.M. on December 12, 1957, an Aquarium employee, Edward Dols, was stung on the right thumb by a lionfish. Mr. Dols found the pain almost unbearable, and it was probably only speedy medical attention that saved his life. Carleton Ray and Christopher Coates, both of the Aquarium, reported the incident in the journal *Copeia* (1958, page 235), and observed, 'There has been a tendency to underestimate the seriousness of the poisonous nature of this fish. Some ichthyologists and dealers in marine tropical fishes report—irresponsibly, we believe—that the sting is not serious. . . . We believe that this fish is capable of causing death to humans, either directly or through shock.'

"None of the books available to me claims that the *rascasse* is venomous, but my *rascasse du nord* has a groove on the front face of each spine in the dorsal fin, and I refuse to step on it until someone else does. [The newest edition of the common, or Petit, Larousse says of *rascasse:* "Name given to several teleostean fishes of the Mediterranean, comestible but covered with venomous spines."]

"If some of your lazy chefs who don't look under the porgies try to wiggle out by claiming that *Helicolenus dactylopterus* is not the proper *rascasse,* and insist on having a Mediterranean *Scorpaena—scrofa* or *porcus*—don't let them get away with it. We have several species of *Scorpaena* on the American coast, including *Scorpaena agassizi, Scorpaena plumieri, Scorpaena grandicornis,* and *Scorpaena braziliensis.* It is true that these are tropical fishes, but there should be no more difficulty in bringing them to the New York market than in importing from Florida the red snapper we enjoyed together. *Helicolenus dactylopterus* is probably the only instance of the same species of *rascasse* occurring off both Marseille and our Atlantic coast, but *Scorpaena plumieri, S. grandicornis,* and *S. braziliensis* are so similar to the Mediterranean *S. scrofa* and *S. porcus* that gourmets should find them interchangeable. Haggling over the number of scales along the lateral line is for rug traders, not for connoisseurs of fine food.

"We have another member of the Scorpaenidae in our waters that is available in almost any quantity from the market. This is *Sebastes marinus,* variously called 'redfish,' 'rosefish,' 'hemdurgan,' 'Norway haddock,' and (in one of the fish markets I frequent) 'baby red snapper.' This last identification is quite erroneous, as a glance at the third suborbital bone will show, since in scorpaenids this bone covers the cheek and in snappers it does not. Possibly this fish could be used in an emergency when *rascasse* is not available.

"But I doubt whether the emergency is real. I try to take a charitable view, but I am forced to think that some gourmets have been irresponsibly spreading the rumor of our lack of *rascasse* without consulting Goode and Bean's 'Oceanic Ichthyology,' first published in 1896. According to Goode and Bean (page 250), *Helicolenus dactylopterus* 'occurs in the western Atlantic in numerous localities, having been first discovered by the trawler Fish Hawk in 1880, off Narragansett Bay.' Even better, another species, *Helicolenus madurensis* (or, as Goode and Bean spell it, '*maderensis*'), is known from many points in deep water along the Atlantic coast, and Goode and Bean list at least twenty-nine specimens in the United States National Museum. (Museum preservation makes a fish inedible, and in any case these specimens are the property of the federal government and beyond the call of bouillabaisse.)

"My own *rascasse* is also inedible, since I soaked it in formaldehyde for a day and then transferred it to isopropyl alcohol. It now bears my personal collection number F.1766100. My fish collection is not really that big, but it seemed to me that a fish that indirectly inspired Thackeray to an ode deserved a museum number bespeaking an ancient and respected institution. It is still a handsome fish, although the red color has largely faded in the alcohol. I can't help thinking, though, as I ponder my *rascasse* in odd moments, that it is a rather ordinary-looking fish to make such a difference to gourmets. It looks a bit like a sea bass, except that it has spines on its head, like a sea robin, and notably large, inquisitive eyes. If someone told me that a sea horse or an electric eel or an angler fish changed the flavor of a stew, I would believe it without a moment's hesitation, but the *rascasse* proves that there must be more to a fish than meets the eye.

"In many ways, the *rascasse* reminds me of a sculpin. I am not alone in this opinion, because the scorpaenid fishes and the cottoid fishes (sculpins) are regarded as closely related by all right-thinking ichthyologists. We have loads of sculpins around, notably the hacklehead (*Myoxocephalus octodecimspinosus*). As far as I know, fishermen never eat sculpins but use them instead for purposes of augury. The capture of a large and ugly sculpin is widely regarded as an omen, although there seems to be no general agreement as to what it presages. A number of years ago, when my wife and I were vacationing in Maine, a cry came up from the pier of 'Sculpin! Sculpin!,' and half a dozen small boys fanned out in all directions to spread the news. Those of us interested in an advance tip on the weather gathered at the small pier where the sculpin had been landed and was now holding a séance. It was a particularly large and ugly sculpin, nearly two feet long, mud-colored, and with an unpleasant pimply array of spines on its toadlike head. It sat there on the boards, making no motion to escape into the water, and looked at us all very solemnly. We looked back at it expectantly, and for a few moments there was a strange stillness as we stood humbly in the awesome presence. Then the sculpin puffed a ripple along its ample belly and said 'Harrumph.' It repeated this a minute later, and we were transfixed, waiting for the announcement to follow the preliminary throat-clearing. After about twenty minutes of harrumphing, it became apparent that the sculpin had nothing to say. The crowd of watchers thinned out, some predicting a storm and others a cold snap, and when the sculpin finally expired, I was the only one at its side. It made a fine skeleton.

With best wishes,

SAM McDOWELL

"P.S. If I get any more *rascasses,* I shall certainly send them to you. Please save the bones for me, and be particularly careful about the third suborbital. It is a very important bone."

MY first reaction to McDowell's letter was one of stupefaction, as if I had stepped on a stonefish. This is a world of constantly diminishing certainties, and the disappearance of even a negative one is a heavy loss; never again would I be able to say with assurance that there was no *rascasse* in America. My second reaction was one of joy for the Frenchmen I knew who worked in kitchens and would no longer have to deprive themselves of the pleasure of making an authentic bouillabaisse. Root, ever a pragmatist, had said in his book that, *rascasse* or no *rascasse,* the best bouillabaisse that *he* had ever eaten was at the Restaurant du Midi, a small place on Forty-eighth Street, west of Eighth Avenue, "before society discovered it." Root may have eaten his bouillabaisse there long ago, under the regime of the *ancienne patronne,* a woman known only as Ida, but the du Midi still makes a pretty good specimen now and then. (I have seen nobody more social there in the last ten years than an old six-day bike rider named Maurice Letourneur, who now makes wire wheels for racing sulkies.) Jean Pujol, the boss, is from Toulouse, not Marseille, but that still makes him a meridional, so I thought he would be glad to hear of the discovery.

I found him behind his bar, a heavy but active man whose large, inquisitive eyes take pleasure in all that goes on in front of him, which is sometimes considerable.

"M. Pujol," I said after the ritual handshake, too much agog even to ask after the health of his wife, who runs Les Pyrénées, over on the other side of Eighth Avenue, "M. Pujol, can you believe it? The *rascasse* exists in America!"

Monsieur thought an instant, and then said "*Et alors?*" in a tone that made it translatable as "So what?" It was most disappointing.

"The *rascasse,*" I said, to jog his memory. "You know, the fish they say is indispensable for bouillabaisse."

"What they say is not true," M. Pujol said, like a parent who finally admits to a small boy that there is no Santa Claus when he sees that the boy is on the point of finding it out for himself.

A FEW days later, I received a second letter from McDowell. It said:

"I regret I haven't found any more *rascasses* for you. Lately, teaching duties have reduced my visits to the fish markets where I have browsing privileges, but I did step into a Newark market last week, and found a mossbunker, or menhaden (*Brevoortia tyrannus*). This is a fish of some distinction as the World's Least Valuable Food Fish. Its generic name suggests a now departed hotel once noted for its restaurant, but while the zoological affinities of the mossbunker with the shad, the herring, and the sardine are very close, the mossbunker is nearly inedible, and even cats prefer a mackerel smoked over hot road tar. I have saved my mossbunker in case you want it.

"But my news is not all discouraging. Two Mediterranean *rascasses* are living right here in New York, down at the Coney Island Aquarium. My family and I paid them a visit, and Mr. James Atz, the curator, gave us some special attention and put them through their tricks. The *rascasse* does not have many tricks, but it can do two things well: it can sit as still as a stone and look most inconspicuous among the rocks at the bottom of the tank, and it can flit about in a blur of speed when tempted with a bit of fish on the end of a wire coat hanger.

"It would be very unwise to attempt to spirit the *rascasses* out of their tank. The Aquarium has arranged their quarters as a synoptic exhibit of the Scorpaenidae, and the *rascasses* (either *Scorpaena scrofa* or *Scorpaena porcus*) share their home with a lionfish (*Pterois volitans*) and two stonefish (*Synanceja horrida*). Mr. Atz, who wrote the 'Guide and Historical Souvenir' containing the unfortunate underestimate of the lionfish, has done penance by collecting literature on the venom of scorpaenid fishes. He showed me his collection, and the more I read, the less I liked the genus *Synanceja.* The venom of the stonefish is potent and is kept in plentiful supply in glands attached to the spines of the dorsal fin. The toxic component is protein in nature, and when injected into a mammal causes the blood pressure to drop toward zero. (Zero blood pressure is a serious debility.) Natives of New Guinea fear the stonefish, and make very accurate models of it for instructing the young in its avoidance. This is noteworthy for two reasons: the New Guinea natives live among a large and lethal variety of snakes of the cobra family without paying much attention to them, and their art is normally of a highly stylized sort that does not stoop to mere photographic naturalism. Very likely, all members of the *rascasse* group are poisonous.

"As I wrote you before, besides *Helicolenus dactylopterus* we have several species of *Scorpaena* on our Atlantic coast. Jordan, Evermann, and Clark's 'Checklist of Fishes of North and Middle America' names six species from our coast, not counting the Gulf coast and Puerto Rico. *Scorpaena braziliensis* regularly extends north to Charleston, and *Scorpaena grandicornis* and *Scorpaena plumieri* occasionally wander up to Woods Hole, Massachusetts. *Scorpaena plumier* is variously known as *rescacio,* poison grouper, and Plumier's pigfoot. As you well know, commercial fishermen discard from their nets many fish believed to have poor market value. If the gourmets would just tell the fishermen they want poison grouper or Plumier's pigfoot to make soup, I am sure the fishermen would save all they catch. I have found fishermen exceptionally willing to make allowances for exotic tastes and mental aberrations on the part of customers, and my requests for stargazers, toadfish, and lumpsuckers have always been honored without so much as a raised eyebrow. I have no idea how a fish got a name like Plumier's pigfoot, but Jordan, Evermann, and Clark show some tendency to bowdlerize fishermen's names for unrespected fish, and their transcription may not be accurate.

"The more I think about it, the less I can believe it a mere coincidence that the *rascasse* is venomous and also essential to bouillabaisse. Is it the venom—or some metabolic precursor of the venom—that makes the *rascasse* essential?

Yours concernedly,

Sam

"P.S. If it *is* the venom, and there aren't enough Scorpaenidae available to meet the demand for fresh *rascasse*—I imagine that no hostess would now venture to serve bouillabaisse without the essential ingredient—perhaps the venom can be extracted and sold in small bottles, like Worcestershire sauce, while the irrelevant parts of *Helicolenus* and his kin can be ground into cat food. Or perhaps tarantulas can be substituted for *rascasse* in the traditional recipe. Maybe we can make money exporting them to Marseille."

THE note on the effect of stonefish venom on the blood pressure led me to reconsider the legend of the invention of bouillabaisse by Venus to serve to her husband as a soporific. It may be true that saffron is no sleeping potion, but an unduly large proportion of *rascasse* in the quick stew might have the same effect as a weak dose of the related stonefish poison. It could well have put even Vulcan to sleep, let alone an ordinary Provençal husband, and it may have served as a catalyst, or latchkey, in many a meridional love affair. A phenomenon generally reported is not to be brushed aside because of a wrong popular ascription of its cause. Proving saffron blameless does not exculpate bouillabaisse as a form of conjugal knockout drops, if *rascasse* is present. (It would be, incidentally, the kindest form of sedative yet invented, and a tribute to the savoir-faire of Venus, who understood how to keep husband and lover concurrently happy.) However, if I were a Marseillais husband with a pretty wife, I would always be careful to ask her how much *rascasse* there was in the bouillabaisse.

A THIRD letter from McDowell followed shortly, and this one began:

"Since I know that for many years you have admired France and the French, it is difficult for me to tell you of the shocking discovery I have made. At first, I thought it best to forget the matter and pretend that nothing had happened, but as a scientist I am committed to truth, and truth must speak out. It is my very painful duty to report that the French have known all the time that we have *rascasse* in America. Cuvier and Valenciennes, in the fourth volume of their monumental 'Histoire Naturelle des Poissons' (published in Paris in 1829), say this in their account of '*la petite scorpène brune, plus spécialement appelée Rascasse (Scorpaena porcus, Linn.)*': 'M. Milbert sent us a specimen from New York.' I think it improbable that Milbert's specimen was actually the Mediterranean species *Scorpaena porcus*—more likely it was a Plumier's pigfoot on its way north—but any fish enough like *Scorpaena porcus* to fool Cuvier and Valenciennes should do perfectly well in a bouillabaisse. In a previous letter, I promised you my next *rascasse.* I hope you will understand that it is only patriotic duty that forces me to break that promise. I intend to send my next *rascasse* to André Malraux, together with an anonymous note saying, 'Your secret is known.'

"I confirmed that America's lack of *rascasse* is a baseless canard through a telephone call to Dr. Giles Mead. Dr. Mead used to work for the government's Fish and Wildlife Service in Washington, but not long ago became a curator of fishes at Harvard's Museum of Comparative Zoology (a bit of swimming against the current that makes him the equal of the Chinook salmon). Dr. Mead told me that *Helicolenus dactylopterus* is not uncommon off our coast but that fishermen throw them overboard. News of this high potential of a native *rascasse* fishery came at a fortunate time, for I was overhasty in suggesting the tarantula as a substitute. Our supply of tarantulas is severely limited now, and my suggestion was impractical. Once, you could pick up all the tarantulas you wanted down at the docks where the banana boats unload, but today the holds of the banana boats are fumigated, severely restricting our imports of tarantulas, baby boa constrictors, cat-eyed snakes, and Schlegel's palm vipers. We have some native tarantulas, particularly in the Southwest, but they are smaller than the banana-boat kind, and when a man wants a tarantula at all he generally wants the biggest he can get. French tarantulas are even smaller than our tarantulas and, as far as I know, are never used in bouillabaisse. It is probably just as well not to flout tradition, particularly when it would be expensive. Biological supply houses charge a dollar seventy-five apiece for the relatively small American tarantulas. This is a dollar and a half more than I paid for my *rascasse.*

Your obedient servant,

SAM

"P.S. Going back to Goode and Bean's 'Oceanic Ichthyology,' I find that the two species of *Helicolenus* they mention—*H. dactylopterus* and *H. madurensis*—are so similar that only an expert can tell them apart. There are grounds for suspicion that this *expertise* is not possessed by the fish themselves, and that the two species recognized by Goode and Bean are probably only one, *Helicolenus dactylopterus.*

"P.P.S. The above letter, along with my previous letters, summarizes all that I know about the *rascasse.* This is probably as much as anyone should know, for all reputable philosophers are agreed that the world's unhappiness results from the rapid expansion of scientific knowledge, which has outstripped our learning in the social spheres. The world is unhappy enough already without my finding out more about the *rascasse* than our social and religious institutions can cope with."

A. J. LIEBLING (catalyst)

32
To Him She Clung

ABOUT a year or so ago, I was frightened by a story I read in the *Times*. It said that the Metropolitan Life Insurance Company had decided not to tear down its seven-hundred-foot tower on the east side of Madison Square but merely to deface it a bit, in conformity with contemporary taste, and let it stand. I was, of course, glad that the tower, which was the tallest building in New York when it was finished, in 1909, would continue to lend one graceful outline to the otherwise utilitarian *chevaux-de-frise* of hypodermic needles and upended glass caskets. But I was dismayed to learn that the owning company, so actuarially expert, should have begun to consider it obsolete, because the tower is five years junior to me. The company spokesman quoted by the *Times* said that although the building had lost its economic validity, it had been used so long in the company's advertisements as a symbol of invulnerability that to destroy it was out of the question—like the Prudential tearing down the Rock of Gibraltar, I gathered. The tower would therefore be gutted and refitted with smaller offices, from which the insurance-company executives, more numerous than the army that followed William the Conqueror, would whip on the agents, more numerous than Genghis Khan's horde, and keep track of the capital, now estimated at innumerable billions of dollars, fragmentarily detachable only by the death gasps of policyholders.

I must have seen the building when it was new, because it was smack in the middle of my father's noontime life, on which I sometimes impinged at lunch. He was a manufacturing furrier in a loft building he owned on Twenty-sixth Street, between Sixth and Seventh Avenues. The building was on a block that he had made respectable by retaining the Reverend Dr. Parkhurst, a noted crusader against vice, to drive out the brothel-keepers, its former shame. He did this by making a generous gift to the crusade, with no strings attached. The Doctor got the message and cleaned Pop's block first. It was a good touch for the Doctor, and it raised the real-estate value of the three eleven-story loft buildings that Father had just put up on a pretty thin equity. Father lunched regularly at the Café Martin, on the Fifth Avenue side of the Square; he transferred his allegiance to Mouquin's, on Sixth, only after M. Martin retired to France. At Martin's, I was fed nothing more exotic than roast beef and a baked potato, but the vanilla ice cream that followed was yellow, which made it "French" in the usage of the day. It contained bits of broken vanilla bean—an effect probably dictated by showmanship, like the shot that restaurateurs insert in tame pheasant.

Seen from the Café Martin after lunch, Buckingham Palace would have seemed presentable, but the Metropolitan's new pile was impressive even on an empty stomach. A vertically protracted version of the campanile of St. Mark's, in what a company brochure of its youth called "a style combining dignity with refinement" (both qualities now in short architectural supply), it rose, shimmering white, like a frosted cake. The corporate effusion summed it up as "a monumental structure, beautiful in design, gigantic in size, substantial in construction, complete in its appointments," and that's just the way it was. The name, mouth-filling and with operatic associations, further disposed me in its favor. (The Metropolitan Museum of Art was another prestigious homonym.) My parents went to the operatic Metropolitan regularly, and talked about it a great deal in the interim. Caruso, I may have thought, *lived* in the Metropolitan Tower. Madison Square had additional magic for me, because it shared its name with Madison Square Garden. That palace of pleasure, redolent of elephants and horses, stood at the northeast corner of Madison and Twenty-sixth, and I went there twice a year, to see Buffalo Bill's Wild West Show and Barnum & Bailey's Circus. The Buffalo Bill show featured mock battles and galloping horses; it was a series of Westerns in the flesh, and in color and *smell.* The smells were horse sweat and gunpowder—perfumes that hung over the ring from "The Attack on the Stagecoach," in the first act, to "The Battle of the Little Big Horn," in the finale. The combatants fired thousands of rounds of blanks. Buffalo Bill had it all over Barnum & Bailey for me, but at the circus there was always the chance that an aerialist would fall off the high wire, so that interested me, too. Thanks to Buffalo Bill, I saw more Indians before I entered elementary school than the average boy born west of the Rockies gets to look at in a lifetime. They whooped and hollered and rode their ponies around the arena, meanwhile shooting blanks at the troops, who wore blue uniforms out of Bannerman's old army-stores shop on lower Broadway. But although I rooted for the Indians, in whom I saw my prototypes, the soldiers, representing authority, always rounded them up.

It is not the association with Sitting Bull and the smell of elephants, however, that most endears the Metropolitan Tower to me but the fact that it is a historic shrine—or, rather, a *pre*-historic shrine, pre-history in this sense meaning history that is scheduled but hasn't happened yet. If this is hard to follow, I should explain that in 2712 A.D. the forty-eighth floor of the Metropolitan Tower proved to be the cocoon that had preserved the two last survivors of the white race, after the rest of civilized humankind had been wiped out by an unspecified blight. It was here that the pair, Beatrice Kendrick and Allan Stern, opened their eyes again, after eight centuries of coma, to look out upon an uninhabited city—or so they thought for a while, until the cannibals came. The almost unimaginable height above street level had partially protected them from the lethal effect of whatever it was, and they had spent all that time in suspended animation, from which they awoke to their distressing situation. I met Allan and Beatrice—he was an engineer, and she his secretary—on the evening of March 4, 1912, in the columns of the *Evening Mail,* a newspaper bought and burked by Frank Munsey in about 1920, and they have been with me ever since, as the man and the girl in the Metropolitan Tower, although, I confess, I long ago forgot their names and the exact date of our encounter, and had to do a bit of research to refresh my memory.

In the year 1910–11, I had begun school and been taught to read. Miss Flynn was the name of the teacher who taught me, and at first I did not realize what she had done to me. My first year of reading was like the summer, a little later, when I learned to swim and all my care was to stay on top of the water. But the second year of reading was like the second summer of swimming, when the knack came back without thought and nobody could get me out of the ocean. At any rate, my world was no longer limited by my field of vision. It expanded erratically, by the hazard of encounter or recommendation; new lines of investigation opened in every direction. Instead of asking my parents questions, I was keen to find out what they had been concealing from me. Many of these lines led through the *Mail.* My father took the *Times* away with him in the morning, before I went off to school, but he brought the *Mail* home with him at six in the evening. I was not allowed to have the newspaper before the evening meal, which was served at about six-thirty. My father would have looked at it on the way uptown in the subway, and Mother was allowed to have it before we sat down. My chance for a part of it—usually the sports page and Rube Goldberg's cartoon—came afterward, when the maid had cleared the table and my parents had moved on to the sitting room, behind the green plush portières. (The more formal parlor, done in lighter green, was used only when we had company.) I was allowed to read my section of the paper before doing my homework, but the homework often went undone. The burnt-oak dining table, under the hanging dome of green stained glass with its dependent skirt of beads, was a fine place to spread a newspaper. My sister, aged three, was in bed, and so out of the way, like my parents. My current *Fräulein* and the woman who served as cook and maid were in the kitchen, at their own meal or washing dishes, and I was alone with Christy Mathewson, Ad Wolgast, Jim Thorpe, and the other objects of my admiration, who could strike you out, knock you out, or kick you fifty yards for a field goal if you looked at them cross-eyed. Christy—Big Six—was a Giant pitcher invincible in his own league but perennially bedevilled by the crafty Athletics in the World Series. Thorpe had the double glory of being an Indian as well as an All-American; he ran for a touchdown every time he carried the ball against the dudish Harvard palefaces. Wolgast, the lightweight champion, was so unbelievably ferocious that the sportswriters called him the Cadillac Bearcat. I didn't know what a bearcat was, and still don't, but Wolgast was it. Cadillac referred to Cadillac, Michigan, the Bearcat's habitat, and not to the young automobile. Goldberg, whose cartoon appeared on the sports page, was the *Mail's* best bet. He did sets of cartoons with gag titles that became a part of popular speech, like "Foolish Questions," "Mike & Ike, They Look Alike," and "Keeper, Sweep Out Padded Cell No. 414,673." (In the last tagline, the numbers varied but were always high.) His drawing was marvellously divorced from the rule book, and his wonderfully complicated inventions for keeping peas from rolling off a knife blade or stopping grapefruit from squirting in your eye foreshadowed the mobile Calder and the diagrammatic Steinberg.

The story about 2712 A.D. was on what was labelled "The *Evening Mail* Magazine Page," and the illustration that accompanied the first installment has ever since remained in my mind: a man with a long, blond beard and a girl with long, all-enveloping hair looking down through a window of the Metropolitan Tower at the city of New York in ruins. In subsequent installments, as I never forgot, they had Swiss Family Robinson or Robinson Crusoe adventures in recuperating useful articles from the wreck—only theirs was the wreck of a city, and they salvaged their tools from showcases rather than ships. Then, still in the Crusoe tradition, they had to fight bluish-black cannibals who appeared on what the castaways had considered their private island—in this case Manhattan, which was mine, too. The cannibals were of a strain so coarse that they had resisted whatever it was that had killed the higher types. One reason the story so impressed me was that it was supposed to happen in a building I had seen. Another, I imagine, was that I was at a stage of readership when I was not altogether sure, for a couple of installments, whether I was dealing with fact or fiction. It was also, I think, the first intimation I had that my tangible world was destructible.

For whatever reason, the essential framework of the story remained with me for fifty years, although I am not good at remembering plots—names, characters, and phrases are more likely to stick in my mind. Sometimes, after the first thirty years or so, it seemed to me improbable that I should remember anything so odd so clearly and for so long, and I wondered whether I hadn't read the story more recently, although there was internal evidence to the contrary, because no writer would have placed the survival chamber in the Metropolitan after it had ceased to be the highest building. It would have been simple to check, because I was fairly sure that the New York Public Library had a file of the *Evening Mail.* Still, I hesitated, because I had a haunted feeling that the story wouldn't be there at all, and it was not until I saw the news story about the Metropolitan Tower's narrow escape from the knackers that I finally decided to verify what had happened on the forty-eight floor in the twenty-eighth century. A telephone call established that the Newspaper Annex of the New York Public Library had a complete run of the *Mail* for the suspected years, and when I went over to that bleak depository on West Forty-third Street, almost on the river, I had small trouble in finding what I had not been entirely sure I remembered. The *Mail* was there in person, not having been reduced to microfilm, and the crumbling pages in the bound file seemed themselves relics of a ruined city—an effect due to the extremely bad paper used in newspapers since about 1880. When I hit on my quarry in the issue of Monday, March

4th, I found that the illustration was almost exactly as I had visualized it—hairy man and girl looking out the window at what was left. The caption under it read, "No Familiar Hum of the Metropolis Now Rose."

The initial installment of the serial ran across all eight columns of the Magazine Page. Its title was "The Last New Yorkers," and a two-column line at the right of the page described it as "A Weird Story of Love and Adventure Amid the Ruins of a Fallen Metropolis." The author was George Allen England—a mild surprise, because I had somehow formed the illusion during the intervening years that it was Edgar Rice Burroughs, the man who subsequently invented Tarzan, and I had occasionally cited the Metropolitan Tower story (which, naturally, nobody else remembered) as an indication of the versatility of Burroughs' imagination. How Burroughs had got into my authentic recollection of the *Mail* yarn, I do not know. I have never heard of George Allen England since 1912, and the name may well have been somebody's pseudonym.

The serial, I observed before I began to read it, ran through all of that March, skipping Sundays, when the *Mail* did not publish. Chapter I, "The Awakening," began:

> Dimly, like the daybreak glimmer of a sky long wrapped in fogs, a sign of consciousness began to dawn in the face of the tranced girl. Once more the breath of life began to stir in that full bosom, to which again a vital warmth had on this day of days crept slowly back. And as she lay there, prone upon the dusty floor, her beautiful face buried and shielded in the hollow of her arm, a sigh welled from her lips.

Instantly I was transported back across fifty years to the dining-room table under the green-shaded light, and I was full of solicitude and a vague fear.

> Life—life was flowing back again! The miracle of miracles was growing to reality. Faintly now she breathed, vaguely her heart began to throb once more. She stirred. She moaned, still for the moment powerless to cast off wholly the enshrouding incubus of that tremendous, dreamless sleep. Then her hands closed. The finely tapered fingers tangled themselves in the masses of thick, luxuriant hair which lay outspread all over and about her.

Here I, as of 1963, wondered how many of Mr. England's words, met one by one, I would have recognized in 1912. "Enshrouding incubus," indeed! Also, I was astonished to note an element in "The

Last New Yorkers" that had made no impression on me when I was seven—it was hot stuff. George Allen England combined the appeals of Daniel Defoe, Jules Verne, and Elinor Glyn, a lady novelist of his era whose charm I did not begin to sniff until early adolescence. The full bosom, the vital warmth, the beautiful face shielded in the hollow of the arm—the hair! But the full significance of the last detail did not dawn until a later paragraph:

> Even as she took the first few steps, her gown—a mere tattered mockery of raiment—fell away from her. And, confronted by a new problem, she stopped short. About her she peered in vain for something to protect her disarray. There was nothing! All about her, veiling her completely in a mantle of wondrous gloss and beauty, her lustrous hair fell.
>
> Aloud she hailed: "Oh! Help, help, help!" No answer.

For fifty years there had been a number of lacunae in my memory of important points, but a good many of the gaps, I learned on reacquaintance, were in the story itself—for example, how it happened that if the altitude on the forty-eighth floor of the Tower had been sufficient to preserve the fated pair it hadn't saved other tenants on the same floor, or in the observation tower above. There just wasn't any explanation, and I could only conclude that Beatrice Kendrick and her employer had been doing nightwork—an already suspicious circumstance that gained significance from the way she now went looking for him clad only in her hair.

> About her she drew the sheltering masses of her hair, like a Godiva of another age; and to her eyes, womanlike, the hot tears mounted. As she went, she cried, in a voice of horror: "Mr. Stern! Oh—Mr. Stern! Are, are you dead, too? You can't be—it's too frightful!"
>
> He lived!

I abridge—although with regret—considerably. Allan Stern's clothes were in bad shape, too, but they had not quite vanished, which was fortunate, because his beard would have given him only unilateral defilade.

> But almost at once [I have cut a lot here] the engineer got a mastery over himself. She thrilled at sight of him. And though for a long moment no word was spoken, while the man and woman stood looking at each other like two children in some dread and unfamiliar attic, an understanding leaped between them.
>
> (To Be Continued Tomorrow.)

I must have been slow, to miss all that sex content, but missed it I had. I remembered the hair in the picture, but not that it was all the girl had on. What *had* frightened me for fifty years was the notion of awaking and finding all New York gone—the yellow ice cream, my father's loft building, P.S. 9, at West End Avenue and Eighty-second Street, and even the *Evening Mail.* I was glad that the Metropolitan Tower, at least, had survived.

Chapter II began:

> Then, womanlike, instinctively as she breathed, the girl ran to him. Forgetful of every convention and of her disarray, she seized his hand. And in a voice that trembled till it broke she cried: "What is it? What does all this mean? Tell me!"
>
> To him she clung.

It is not until many paragraphs after "To him she clung" that Stern notices that his companion is technically naked. " 'But—you can't go that way, Miss Kendrick,' " he says. " 'It—it won't do, you know.' " But he was a mealy-mouthed hypocrite. "Deep down in his heart," says George Allen England, "he caught some glimmering insight of the future and was glad."

At this point in the reprise, my eyes, fifty years older, began to be tried by the small print. Determined to have the whole serial and read it, as the author intended, in segments and at home, I carted the volume of the *Evening Mail* containing the installments of "The Last New Yorkers" to the photostat desk and ordered the lot. Leaving the Newspaper Annex after my reunion with Beatrice Kendrick and Allan Stern, I had the feeling that I was four feet high, as on March 4, 1912, and out of my neighborhood at that. I feared that some tough kid from Eleventh Avenue might smack me in the eye, and as the shadows lengthened I hurried down Tenth, longing to be home under the green Tiffany-glass lampshade, where safety waited. Not until I reached Forty-second Street did I remember that home, Mother, Father, *Fräulein,* all had vanished, and that Tiffany glass was now only in antique shops and high-toned bars-and-grills. The familiar hum of the Metropolis still rose, but the Metropolitan Tower and I were on the disimprove. I walked east on Forty-second toward a more familiar part of town, and hit Eighth Avenue before I felt full-grown again.

The date on the first installment of "The Last New Yorkers" had placed me so exactly in the past that I had a hard time getting out of it. I was in 2-B at P.S. 9, and my teacher was Miss Costigan, a lean lady not without elements of what I then considered beauty—blue eyes and blond, almost too blond, hair, bound at the brow with a thin black velvet ribbon, and worn in bangs. The building where we lived, at 307 West Seventy-ninth Street, had the resounding private name of Lassano Court. Lassano, like many of the high-sounding names of firms and buildings, was a combination of the initials of a number of partners, but it sounded more plausible than most—it could have been a city in Italy, like Livorno. Father, composing a corporate name for one of his buildings, had had less luck. He had taken the first two letters, Ab, of my first name and hitched on all those of my sister's, Norma. The result, the Abnorma Real Estate Corporation, suggested that we were both psychopaths. We had moved into Lassano Court in the fall of 1907, when it opened its doors, and from our front windows I had looked down on the construction of the Kelmscott and the Hereford, the equally posh newcomers directly across the street. Somebody, someday, should write a poem about New York apartment-house names, and somebody else a book about the social tugs they reflect. Lassano, for example, is a compound of euphony, the exotic, and masked self-aggrandizement; Hereford and Kelmscott are reversions to the old sales appeal of English solidity and dignity. (There is an old apartment building down on Second Avenue named The U.S. Senate.) You entered Lassano Court by a driveway that led right into the building and under a rotunda, and in the middle of this carriage court was a fountain in which stood Atlas, carrying a Tiffany-glass globe of the world with an electric light inside it. We lived, I am almost sure, on the seventh floor. There was an elevator right outside the door of our apartment, and every evening while the serial ran I took up my vigil behind the door at about a quarter to six, waiting to greet Father and try to get away with the paper while he was taking off his overcoat. Sometimes I managed it without trouble, sometimes I didn't.

"Don't you think *I* ever want to see the paper?" Mother might complain, or "You could say 'Good evening' to your father when he comes home after a hard day's work, instead of grabbing the paper and burying your nose in it." Now that I have had another look at Mr. England's prose, I know that Mother would never have read beyond the first paragraph. Arnold Bennett and John Galsworthy were more her style. She had been a high-school valedictorian and had then attended extension courses at Berkeley. She had had timid ambitions—which she had never got up the courage to exploit—to be a writer or an actress, and she attended the lectures, chiefly cultural, of the Women's League for Political Education every Wednesday afternoon, returning with full notebooks and enthusiastic reports on speakers like Rabindranath Tagore and Alfred Noyes and Nicholas Vachel Lindsay. "Go down to Kew in lilac-time," she would spout when she came home from a Noyes lecture, even before she took her hat off, and "In lilac-time, in lilac-time," as she took out the hatpins. She would give me the whole poem, if I didn't dodge off. It is hard to remember how your mother looked at any given period. The memory blurs and blends—she was twenty-eight or twenty-nine when I think I first remember her, and seventy-eight at the last, but her face and hands and ankles were always pretty, and in 1912 she was still fighting to keep her figure like Lillian Russell's. On March 4th of that year, she was exactly thirty-four years and two months old, less eight days. Like Miss Russell and Miss Costigan and the princesses in Grimm's fairy tales, she was blond and had blue eyes—two points that Father and I considered the indispensable attributes of the American Beauty.

I DID not wait for the photostats, which set me back about thirty dollars, as impatiently as I had awaited my daily adventures with Beatrice and Allan in 1912, but when they came I fell under the spell of "The Last New Yorkers" again. With Chapter III, I noticed, the special illustrations ended, and the serial took a stock heading for the rest of its run of twenty-eight installments: a vignette of Madison Square in ruins and gone back to forest, with the invulnerable Metropolitan Tower looming behind and above it. (Daily repetition of the cut was a colossal hidden persuader for the insurance company, and I could not help suspecting a tieup.) There was a box, in blackface, headed "READ THIS FIRST," but now, as before, I spurned this mnemonic crutch. A man in whose mind this story did not burn itself as it went along did not deserve the opportunity to read it. How could anyone forget "WHAT HAS GONE BEFORE"?

In the third chapter, Beatrice and Allan climb to the observation platform, "nearly a thousand feet above the earth," to have a look around. " 'What this all means we don't know yet,' " Allan says when they arrive. " 'All we definitely know is that some very long, undetermined period of time has passed, leaving us still alive. The rest can wait.' " And then "he drew her to him protectingly, while all about them the warm summer wind swept onward to the sea."

This, at first reading, must have tried my patience. It was what I called "slush." When visiting women friends of Mother's kissed me in those days, I ostentatiously rubbed the profaned spot with the back of my hand.

The next paragraph was even worse:

> In the breeze, her heavy masses of hair stirred luringly. He felt its silken caress on his half naked shoulder, and in his ears the blood began to pound with strange insistence. The presence of the girl set his heart throbbing heavily, but he bit his lip and restrained his every untoward thought.

What, I must have wondered, could the poor sap be thinking *about* to make him waste so much time when a city lay at his feet for pillage? The bookstores! The soda fountains! All the bridges over the East River had either fallen down or buckled in the middle, and the forest filled the streets. You couldn't even tell where Central Park ended. At the sight, Beatrice lost her nerve and bawled, but not Allan. I imagine that I felt sorry for him, burdened with such a boob, and thought how glad he would have been to have had me along instead.

I imagine that I began to tire of the adventure until Stern cried, " 'Hark! What's that?' "

> A moment they listened intently. Up to them, from very far, rose a wailing cry, tremulous, long-drawn, formidable.
>
> "Oh, then there are people, after all?" faltered the girl, grasping Stern's arm.
>
> He laughed.
>
> "No, hardly!" answered he. "I see you don't know the wolf-cry. I didn't until I heard it in the Hudson Bay country. Not very pleasant, is it?"
>
> He broke short off. Again, far off, they heard a faint re-echoing roar.
>
> "I guess," said he, "guns will be about the first thing I'll look for after food. There ought to be good hunting down in the jungles of Fifth Avenue and Broadway!"

That was something like! If my attention had come loose during the tiresome slush passages, the wolves and the guns must have refastened it *statim*, Bronco Billy was my movie hero then—he shot his way through two-reelers without benefit of a sound track, but the piano player provided auxiliary percussion. Paul Du Chaillu, pronounced by me "Dooshaloo," was my current hero on the printed page. He was an African explorer of the second half of the nineteenth century, whom I had found bivouacked between covers in the St. Agnes Branch of the New York Public Library, at Eighty-first Street and Amsterdam Avenue. Du Chaillu, like Bronco Billy, lived by the gun—in his case, an elephant rifle, which he usually emptied at a charging brute only yards away. When Dooshaloo, seeing the brute continue to come on, turned for his spare gun, the bearer had invariably fled. But the first unerring bullet, lodged in the brain, achieved its effect just when all seemed lost. It was lucky that Dooshaloo always got his first serve in.

In Chapter V, Beatrice and Allan come down from the office to explore. "Never before had either of them realized just what the meaning of forty-eight stories might be." Beatrice pooped out, as usual, and shrank with nameless fears, but they made it to the ground, and "thus began their search for a few prime necessities of life." Beatrice naturally wanted to look for clothes first, not realizing that *guns* were what they needed—how could they defend themselves if the wolf pack burst upon them while they searched about the ruins of Best's or Altman's for a tailored suit? I knew that it sometimes took Mother weeks to find one she liked. But "everything at all in the nature of cloth either had sunk back into moldering annihilation or had at best grown far too fragile to be of service." They did better in Chapter VI, however. They found a furrier's shop (this must have given me a thrill of recognition) with garments stored in a cedar chest.

> One effort of Stern's powerful arms sufficed to tip the chest quite over. As it fell it burst. Over the girl's shoulders, Stern flung a tiger skin. Magnificent! he judged. For the woman, thus clad, had suddenly assumed a wild, barbaric beauty. Bright gleamed her gray eyes by the light of the flambeau. Half hidden, the woman's perfect body, beautiful as that of a wood nymph or a pagan dryad, roused the engineer. He dared speak no other word for the moment. A polar-bear skin attracted his attention, and this he chose. Then, with it slung across his shoulder, he stood up.

Then came something that made me ashamed of my nasty adult suspicions, and that must have disappointed a lot of readers even in 1912: Having returned to their nest, "Stern, in the outer office, and Beatrice in the other, wrapped themselves within their furs and laid them down to sleep." Indifference would have detracted from the nobility of the engineer's self-denial. But indifferent he was not. "Yet long after Beatrice had lost herself in dreams, Stern lay and thought strange thoughts, yearning and eager thoughts, there in the impenetrable gloom."

In order to reach more swiftly a high point of the plot, I here pick up a couple of installments from the "READ THIS FIRST" summary:

> Later Stern finds a spring where once stood the old Madison Square Fountain. After bathing in the pool, he explores the ruins of a Twenty-third Street hardware store, where he finds guns and ammunition. On his way back to Beatrice, who has been left at the tower, he discovers a flint assagai point. It raises in his mind the fear that a new and strange race of savages inhabit the vicinity.

Stern made his discovery at the fag end of what had been a sunny interlude in the young people's fortunes. Discovered had he a veritable arsenal, and not a moment too soon for his peace of mind. Forearmed stood he forewarned! Intrepid was he, but terror-stricken I! The twenty-four hours that followed must have been hard for me to endure. I was not up to calling the editor of the *Evening Mail* to ask him what came next, but at school Miss Costigan must have found me more abstracted and boorish than usual. It was Tuesday, the most hopeless day of the school week. On Monday, after the blessed weekend, the monotony had not quite taken hold. Wednesday brought the consolation that it was halfway through the week. By Thursday you could see the shore; Friday was almost pleasant, if you had a bit of imagination.

My route to school lay up the Seventy-ninth Street hill as far as West End Avenue—the slope to the river is sharp here, and the wind in March howled through the draw between the solid rows of apartment houses that now lined it. (Kelmscott and Hereford had filled the last gaps.) The wind stung my face and made my eyes water, and sometimes made me clutch at area railings to keep my balance. At West End—the corner was the blowiest place of all—I turned north for three blocks, to P.S. 9, on the northeast corner of Eighty-second Street. Walking to school, I sometimes met fellows in my class, but none was an *Evening Mail* reader, so I had my anxiety to bear alone. (There were seven evening papers in New York then—the *Evening World,* the *Evening Sun,* the *Telegram,* the *Globe,* the *Post,* the *Mail,* and the *Journal.*) The school still stands; it was far from new then, although it was not one of the slab-sided red brick packing boxes that dated back to the Civil War. It is of yellow brick faced with white stone, in the faintly Germanic style popular in New York during the eighteen-nineties. It was an example, Father used to say, of the extravagance of a reform mayor named Seth Low. Washington Irving High School for girls roosted on the upper floors; the elementary-school classes were on the lower. There were boys' classes and girls', but all had women teachers, and nearly all of these were Irish-American. Miss Flynn, Miss Costigan, Miss Collins, and Miss McCabe were the four I had in three years, and the vice-principal in charge of the elementary school was Miss Duffy. What they taught me was to read and write and do simple sums in my head—"mental arithmetic," this was called. Once the reading came easy, the Misses lost control of my mind. I was there, but it was away foraging with Dooshaloo or nagging Roland to blow his horn.

Another thing that one of the Misses did that changed the whole course of my life was to discover that I was nearsighted, because I could not read the blackboard except from the front row. That meant I went into glasses, and, with the glasses to cut down on my active life and the reading to further my vicarious career, my existence assumed that schizoid pattern to which it has held ever since. As a preliterate, I had liked to fight, but now before I started to fight another boy in Riverside Park I would put my glasses on a bench. Then I would forget which bench, and not be able to see them. Losing the glasses caused such *histoires* at home that I fell into sedentary ways. As I turned intellectual, though, I retrogressed socially, and by my third year I stood barely in the middle of my class in fighting. The champion was a Japanese boy who practiced what we thought was jujitsu—he grabbed all his enemies by the necktie and choked them.

On the day after Stern found the assagai point, I must have made a particularly overt attempt to snatch the newspaper, and I hope I got away with it, because otherwise I must have made a sullen supper. I do not think that "assagai" is a word that occurs in Dooshaloo (it is more of a Rider Haggard word, and I hadn't read him yet), but an ensuing paragraph told what it was—a spear. Even Stern was flustered, but then he rallied again.

> "All I can do," he thought, "is just go right ahead as though this hadn't happened at all. If trouble comes, it comes, that's all. I guess I can meet it. What's on the cards has got to be played to a finish, and the best hand wins!" Then back to the Metropolitan he came, donned his bearskin, which he fastened with a wire nail, and started the long climb.

At the top, of course, is Beatrice, and nothing will do but that they must go right back down again. That makes two hundred and forty flights for Stern in two days, and a hundred and forty-four for Beatrice. Realizing that they are living too high, they choose for their new home a suite of offices on the fifth floor. Then Stern has to walk upstairs again to get some leftover chemicals he has found in his office. The round trip brings his flight-count to three hundred and thirty-one. But before he goes, he tests their antique revolvers. The shells are rusty and green with verdigris, but they work. Here I must have felt intense relief; with revolvers, two white people could lick anybody. Roaming the city, Stern shoots a lynx off the remains of the Farragut monument, and finds moose tracks at Nineteenth Street and Broadway. But as he warily hunts, he comes across disconcerting evidence of the nature of the as yet unseen enemy. It is a human thighbone, "broken and splintered, and of no very great age, gnawed with perfectly visible toothmarks."

> Long mused he over this find. But not a single word did he ever say to Beatrice concerning it or the flint spearpoint. Only he kept his eyes and ears well open for other bits of corroborative evidence. And he never ventured a foot from the building unless his rifle and revolver were with him, their magazines full of high-power shells. The girl always went armed, too, and soon grew to be such an expert shot that she could drop a squirrel from the tip of a fir, or wing a heron in full flight.

Romance pursued its course: "The rapproachment between this beautiful woman and himself at such times became very close and fascinatingly intimate. At her he gazed, a strange gleam in his eyes." He might better have been gazing about him for the enemy, I probably thought. During this lull, Stern and the girl built their little domestic world—a pause that has its parallel in every desert-island story, from "Robinson Crusoe" to "The Lord of the Flies"—but I, waiting for the cannibals, must have thought this pretty thin stuff.

I DO not know why Father brought home the *Evening Mail,* unless it was for Goldberg's cartoons. It was a paper without marked character, political or otherwise. It was middle-class, but so were the *Sun,* the *Globe,* the *Post,* and the *Telegram.* Only the *Journal* and the *Evening World,* old rivals in sensationalism, were not receivable in the homes of solid businessmen. (The *Journal* had the most and, in my view, the best comic strips, and I often bought it and smuggled it in, so that I could read about Harry Hershfield's character, Dauntless Durham of the U.S.A., and his foil, the villainous Desperate Desmond.) The *Post,* during all the time that Father was growing up, had had about it the aura of the mugwump highbrow Edwin Godkin, its holier-than-thou editor. The *Suns* (morning and evening) had curled up in their offices in about 1890, like Beatrice and Allan, and had remained in a state of suspended animation ever since. The *Mail* was in the middle of the middle, and the photostat pages on which the installments of "The Last New Yorkers" appear give me an idea of what the rest of the paper must have been like. There was another *feuilleton* running neck and neck on the Magazine Page with the one I remember. It was called "The Woman Who Tried: The Experiences of a Girl Who Came to New York to Earn Her Living," and the writer was identified only as "The Author of 'Her Husband's Letters.' " It was more *terre à terre* than "The Last New Yorkers." Marion, the heroine, lives in a boarding house, where she pays seven dollars a week for room and board. "A girl friend offers to get her a position on the stage," the synopsis says, "but the work is distasteful to her." The rest of the serial is a quest for Mr. Right. There were almost daily feature stories of adventure at sea—the experiences of the commanders of ocean liners. There were bits of travel notes, quite without news pegs, and an anecdotal feature called "Strange Meals I Have Eaten," by an epicure named Bassett Digby. There were also countless humorous sketches that were bad analogues of O. Henry's most maudlin and George Ade's most banal—about office characters named Madge McKimbo, the Most Rapid Stenographer at Ticker & Tape's, or about a poor man's Mr. Dooley named Uncle Gav. There was often a column of gossip about the opera, which in that halcyon day had Hollywood's place, and there was a persistent effort to be refined and yet knowing, even in the Campbell's soup ads, which spoke of saving the maid trouble but never said that tinned soup was a great timesaver for a woman just home from a long day on her feet behind a counter. The *Mail* never had been the top paper, and never would be, but it flaunted self-assurance, like the manager of a branch bank. The *Times,* which Father read in the mornings, was where he got his serious information; it was also a paper on the make, but in a more subtle and, as time has proved, a more effective manner. It presented a front of such dull austerity that to be seen with it in the subway improved a man's credit rating; he was clearly interested in none of the lighter aspects of life. The *Mail,* as I see it now, was an unworthy setting for a jewel like "The Last New Yorkers," but it was like the occasional bad race horse that sires a champion.

The story reached its high point aesthetically, I have decided on rereading it, with the fourteenth installment, which is as nearly midway as you can get. That is where the cannibals make their entrée. It is night, and Beatrice and Allan see, far out on the Hudson, a galaxy of lights approaching from the Jersey shore. The lights, Allan fears, must be torches in war canoes.

> "Hark! What's that?" the girl exclaimed suddenly, holding her breath.
>
> Off to northward, dull, muffled, all but inaudible, they both heard a rhythmic pulsing, strangely barbaric.
>
> "Heavens!" ejaculated Stern. "War drums! Tom-toms, as I live! Two tribes, one with torches, one with drums. And they're coming in here to parley or fight or something. Trouble ahead, whichever side wins!"

At Lassano Court, when I first read the story, I had to wait twenty-four hours, as was proper, to see how each crisis would be resolved. During the return engagement, I tried to hold myself to the same aesthetic discipline, but at times the tension grew too powerful for my feeble capacity for self-restraint, and the tom-toms lured me over the edge of the next installment, which I read at a redwood table under a sour-apple tree in East Hampton, Long Island, putting off useful work, as I had fifty years ago.

> "Two revolvers, one shotgun, and one rifle, all told," said Stern. "All magazine arms. I guess that'll hold them for a while, if it comes down to brass tacks! How's your nerve, Beatrice?"
>
> "Never better!" she whispered, from the dark. He saw the dim white blur that indicated her face, and it was very dear to him, all of a sudden—dearer, far, than he had ever realized.
>
> "Good little girl!" he exclaimed, giving her the rifle.

And well he might, for Beatrice, under her shimmering hair and womanlike exterior, gives houseroom, as she soon proves, to the heart of Calamity Jane, that talented exponent of mass homicide.

The two savage hordes, moving together with the speed of airliners headed for Idlewild seven hundred and fifty years earlier, make contact along the line of Fourteenth Street, now a forest lane. There is "a confused tumult of shrieks, howls, simian chatterings, and dull blows." Are they apes on the way up, or regressing men? The question is soon cleared up. " 'Ugh! A beast war!' shudders the engineer, drawing Beatrice away from the window." And not too soon, for the Jersey Torchbearers, having vanquished the Tom-tommers (from Westchester? the Bronx?), are building a vast fire around the statue of Chester A. Arthur (did they identify that rotund statesman with an Aztec blood god?), on which to cook their prisoners. Stern remains at the window to witness the culinary operations, which revolt him. " 'The swine!' he breathed. 'Wait—wait till I make a pint or two of Pulverite!' " Pulverite is an explosive he knows how to manufacture from his do-it-yourself kit of chemicals preserved in hermetically sealed jars from the twentieth century. It is Stern's analogue of the atomic bomb, not yet invented because the mysterious scourge had aborted both World Wars. Pulverite is clearly just the thing to curb the ferocity of the Lower Races.

But Stern has been almost fatally careless. He has forgotten to renew the water supply in their flat, and he needs water with which to mix his Pulverite. And when he reaches a reconnaissance position where he can see the *Untermenschen* he is up against, the need of water to make his demolition charge is clearer than ever.

> The feature which, above all else, struck him as ghastly and unnatural, was the color of the Things. Through the fog, it struck him as a dull slate-gray, almost a blue. Some of the Things were darker, some a trifle lighter. And the skin, moreover, looked dull and sickly, rather mottled and wholly repulsive, very like that of a Mexican dog.

I did not need to read this passage from the photostat to remember the color of the cannibals. I had never forgotten it, and it has put me off blue, mottled people ever since. Never was there a *priora facie* case for genocide, and I was glad to know, having read the story once, that the Things were going to get it where the chicken got the axe, to revert to a 1912 idiom. We have, in the intervening years, reached a point where we can allow people to be brown, black, or yellow. But *blue!*

Stern "knew at once that these Things were lower than any human race ever recorded, yet they had the use of fire, of the tom-tom, of flint, of spears, and a rude sort of tanning—witness the loin clouts of hide which they all wore." This is a fortunate touch for Beatrice, who otherwise would have had to shoot at them blindfolded. "Far lower than De Quatrofoge's Neanderthal man, to judge from the cephalic index," he estimates. And then, Beatrice joins him at his observation post.

"I found you gone," she whispered. "What is it, Allan? Tell me, have you seen them? Do you know?"

Even excited as the engineer was, he realized that for the first time the girl had called him by his Christian name. Not even the perilous situation could stifle the thrill that ran through him.

He adjures Beatrice not to look at the sub-Neanderthals just yet, until he prepares her for the shock.

"Perhaps all the white and yellow peoples perished utterly in the cataclysm, leaving only a few scattered blacks," [he says]. "You know blacks are immune to several germ infections that destroy other races."

Here Stern goes into a sort of White Citizens' Council talk that I wouldn't have identified in 1912. I may have skipped some of these Mendelian passages, as I did the mush parts, when I first read "The Last New Yorkers," but now came something that I remembered as well as the cannibals' color. "Then a misfortune happened: trivial yet how direly pregnant!" (My theory about how I understood sentences like that is that I got the first part complete and accepted the second as lagniappe—pure fancy sound.) Stern dislodges a bit of stone, and it rolls down among the Things.

On the instant, three of the Things raised their bulbous and exaggerated heads. Plain to see that their senses, at least, excelled those of the human being, even as a dog's might. An instant agitation took place all through the forest.

(To Be Continued Tomorrow.)

At this point, I broke off my reading under the apple tree and went for a walk in my pasture, looking for young puffballs—the only variety of edible fungus I am confident that I can tell from a poisonous mushroom. I am not a brave man, like Allan Stern, who would be eighty years old by now, if suspended animation had not kept him young. (Beatrice would be seventy-four—not much younger than Miss Costigan.) The two of them were lucky to have gone to sleep when they did. In the first fifty years of their snooze, I have survived a couple of cataclysms awake, and have seen too much of the violence that seemed so improbable and alluring when I read about it in the circle of light cast by the Tiffany-glass chandelier. Mother never wanted to believe in the unpleasant, and Father kept it to himself, like Allan Stern with the gnawed thighbone. We lived up there in nine rooms and two baths like Allan and Beatrice in their snug hideout before the coming of the savages. Elinor, the maid, was the only one who had her *private* bath, although it was exiguous. Father knew that everything was precariously balanced, because he had made his money from scratch. Mother preferred not to know, because her father had made *his* money—from scratch—thirty years earlier, and had passed her to Father, like a beanbag, before he lost it. The bourgeoise of that now yearned-after time of security was an Eliza pausing to make a cozy home on each cake of ice. The father, when about to be tackled, tried to lateral-pass his daughter before he went down. And yet the illusion of permanence succeeded. When things go ill, I have a nostalgia for the green chandelier, vicarious violence on the comfortable printed page, and *Fräulein,* contemned but within easy hail, in the kitchen eating *Palatschinken* with Elinor. *Palatschinken* are thin egg pancakes rolled around jam or applesauce. They are a great bracer for a sedentary warrior against cannibals.

I retrieve the feeling of this world whenever I read an installment of "The Last New Yorkers." That day in East Hampton, I did not get back to the serial until the evening, over a bottle of Juliénas, but wine is associated with a more sophisticated period of my youth and did not fit the text. George Allen England wrote *Palatschinken* prose.

"At Stern the girl peered, eagerly," this next began. Since the cannibals already suspected their presence, the last New Yorkers decide to sally out boldly and get the water, shooting their way through if necessary. It seems at first that the savages will let them get away with it—a prospect that must have depressed me in 1912, looking forward as I was to a satisfying slaughter. Stern fires over their heads.

> "Here goes!" he cried. "Let's see how this will strike the hellhounds!" His face white with passion and with loathing hate, he raised the automatic.

He does not seem here to be sincerely seeking a peaceful solution. When he fires, the Things fall grovelling to the ground, like the Mexicans at the arrival of Cortez; they have never seen a white man and are impressed. " 'Look, Beatrice,' cried he. 'Look, we're gods!' " And they run off to fetch the water. This episode combines elements of "The Conquest of Mexico," "The Man Who Would Be King," and "Jack and Jill." If the Things had maintained this sensible attitude, they might have saved their lives, like the Czechs after Munich, and Allan and Beatrice could have put them to work clearing the streets and repairing the Fifth Avenue buses, which would hardly have been affected by so little additional age.

It was not to be. The Obeah, or chief, attacks the apostles of civilization, as natives always do, and they have to shoot their way out. "Stern saw the Thing's red gleaming eye fixed on Beatrice. And as the woman screamed in terror, Stern pulled the trigger with a savage curse." The Obeah has eyes of different colors; earlier on, his other eye has been described as being black and glittering, like a chimpanzee's. But even with his red eye fixed on Beatrice, he can aim a spear at Stern, and it passes through the fleshy part of the engineer's right arm. (He probably aims with his black eye.) Stern's arm falls helpless by his side. With his left hand he grabs the rifle by the muzzle and, "with a formless roar of living rage," brings the butt down on the Old Blue's head so smartly that he breaks the stock. Then Beatrice stumbles, as you might expect, and spills the water. When I read the story first, I must have howled a formless roar of despair at that point, and even this time I pounded my fists on the table.

Like a problem drinker testing his will power, I laid the photostats by, and did not pick them up until next day. ". . . With a ghastly screaming, the Thing was upon him," I read then. "Out struck the engineer with the rifle barrel. All the force of his splendid muscle lay behind that blow. But before he could strike again, a moan from Beatrice"—that hopeless dope again!—"sent him to her aid." Beatrice has been hit with a stone and knocked cuckoo.

> Stern, with a strength he never dreamed was his, caught up the fainting girl in his left arm as easily as though she had been a child. "The gate!" sobbed he, between hard-set teeth, and stumbled forward, ever forward, through the horde. To him, protectingly, he clasped the beautiful body in the tiger skin. He must break through!

Then Stern taps an unsuspected source of strength. He is, it turns out, a Harvard man. From his profession, I would have thought him M.I.T. or Georgia Tech—more probably the latter, considering his views on the color question. Now I understood better his violent reaction to Blue.

> Break through!
>
> Where had he heard those words? Ah! Yes! To him instantly recurred a distant echo of a song, a Harvard football song. He remembered. Now he was back again. Came the crash and boom of the old Harvard band, with

Big Joe Foley banging the drum till it was fit to burst, with Marsh blowing his lungs out on the cornet, and all the other fellows raising Cain. Uproar! Cheering! And again the music! Everybody was singing now, everybody roaring out that brave old fighting chorus.

Which brave old fighting chorus reverberated across those eight centuries, the author does not tell. No matter. "Right and left he dashed them with a giant's strength"—doubtless using Beatrice as a club—until he crossed the goal.

Barricaded inside the Tower, the wounded man sinks into a fevered sleep, and Beatrice takes a kettle and sneaks down to fetch water from the old boilers of the building, a natural cistern. When Stern awakes, Beatrice already has coffee on, and he cannot but congratulate her on her womanly common sense. He does not say "Why the hell didn't you think of that before we got our brains knocked out?," and in 1912 this did not strike me as strange, but on reading it over again, it did, rather. Remained enough water, even after coffee, to use in making the Pulverite, and after that, I knew, even when I was seven years old, that they were in like Flynn.

"But, my Lord!" burst out the man. "D'you mean to say you—went down there—alone?"

Once more the girl laughed.

"Not alone," she answered. "One of the automatics was kind enough to bear me company."

"To work!" Stern cried, and they began preparation for the manufacture of the terrible explosive, Stern's own secret and invention, which, had not the cataclysm intervened, would have made him ten times over a millionaire.

Here, I thought, not for the first time, internal evidence pointed to my friend Colonel John R. Stingo, who was thirty-six years old in 1912, as being the man behind the pseudonym of George Allen England. The style is that of the Colonel in writing prospectuses, or prospecti, as he chooses to call them, and I could imagine him following up the serial in the *Mail* with a flotation of Pulverite stock and discreet reminders of how much money Nobel had made. "More precious now to him that knowledge than all the golden treasures of the dead, forsaken world," I read, and I could have sworn that the same hand had written copy for the Great American Hog Syndicate, one of the Colonel's most successful early-in-the-century promotions.

Stern was still mixing his dope when the curtain rose on the next installment. Because but one utile hand had he, Beatrice to help him had.

> And one by one as she filled the little flasks of chained death, the engineer stoppered them with his left hand. When the last was done, Stern drew a tremendous sigh and dashed the sweat from his forehead with a gesture of victory.
>
> "Take care! Don't tip one over, as you love life," he warned.

If I had been Beatrice and Allan, I must have thought when I came to this point in the operational log, I would have chucked some Pulverite right away and wiped them out. What was the good of holding off when you had something decisive? (It was a thought that was to occur to a lot of men I had not yet heard of before they ordered the bomb dropped on Hiroshima.) For once, Allan acted on my suggestion, projected to him across eight hundred years from the table at Lassano Court.

" 'Give it to 'em!' " shouts the engineer in the next day's paper. "And from the window, aiming at a pine that stood seventy-five feet away—a pine whose branches seemed to hang thick with the enemy—he slung it with all the strength of his uninjured arm." (He is either a southpaw or ambidextrous.) The result is a huge geyser of annihilation, and corpses keep pattering down for a quite a time. Then Stern generously sows seven more bombs from the windows, and that does it. The Things are stilled—as pacified as Arawak Indians. Stern makes a speech along lines that would become familiar to all of us in the late thirties.

> "Gods!" he exclaimed, exultantly, "Gods we are now to them—to such of them as still live. Gods we are—gods we shall be forever! Whatever happens now, they know us. The great white gods of terror! They'll flee before our very look! Unarmed, if we meet a thousand, we'll be safe. Gods!"

After that, they resume their idyll. Allan and Beatrice move to the suburbs. Madison Square, they decide, has too many unpleasant associations. They find a twentieth-century millionaire's summer place and move in.

> "You and I, Beatrice," said he, and took her hand. "Just you and I."
>
> "And love," she whispered.

That is probably as far as I read when I was seven, but there follow several paragraphs of the blurry Jack London-Harry Kemp blend of Socialism and eugenics that was current then, although I didn't begin to catch up with it until I read "The Iron Heel" and "The Valley of the Moon," a few years later. (Racism and that early informal American radicalism often went together; London himself worshipped the Great Blond Beast legend, and it was labor that fell hardest for the Yellow Peril.) " 'And hope and life!' " Stern says. " 'A kinder and a saner world this time. No misery, no war, no poverty, no strife, creeds, oppressions, tears—for we are wiser than those other folk, and there shall be no error.' " His pacifism—after the natives have been wiped out—is in an older American tradition, but his ban on creeds would not go down today, when everybody has again agreed that formal religion is a good thing unless the Russians take it up.

> He paused, his face irradiate. To him recurred the prophecy of the greatest oratory of that other time. "Beatrice, it shall be a world where thrones have crumbled and where kings are dust. The aristocracy of idleness shall reign no more! A world without a slave!" [He had pretty well assured this by his use of Pulverite.] "Man shall at last be free! A race without disease of flesh or brain, shapely and fair, the wedded harmony of form and function. And as I look, life lengthens, joy deepens, and over all in the great dome shines the eternal star of human hope!"

Beatrice, as yet undismayed by the prospect of acting as audience at a permanent mass meeting, responds,

> "And love?" She smiled again, a deep and sacred meaning in her words. Within her stirred the universal motherhood, the hope of everything to be, the call of the unborn, the insistent voice of the race that was here in embryo.

When had it all happened? It was only a few installments back that they began calling each other by their first names, and I thought I had been watching them all the time.

On the same page with one of the last installments of "The Last New Yorkers," the Sunday *American* ran an ad for *its* new serial: "Another of the Adventures of Raffles, the Society Burglar." But I was not to meet Raffles until three summers later, when I found him in a bookcase at Schaefer's Hotel, in Lake Hopatcong, New Jersey.

He displaced Allan Stern, and even Dooshaloo, in my pantheon. But no building will displace the Metropolitan Tower as my favorite skyscraper, and I never walk up Fifth Avenue past the Square without looking at the floor two down from the top and thinking of Beatrice Kendrick and her lustrous hair.

33
Paysage de Crépuscule

FROM the window at which I write, I can look west between two walls of high buildings to the North River. A warehouse stands at the end of the street, and the Palisades, on the other shore, appear suspended above it; the interposed river is invisible. Beyond the Palisades, a taller range, which I take to be the Orange Mountains, forms a horizon. The skyscrapers that make up the two walls date from the twenties, the period of the hollow ziggurat. The signature skyscraper of our own age is the upended glass coffin. When I look at the set-back shoulders of the old ones, I visualize them at the date of the crash, with suiciding holders of mortgage bonds cascading from level to level, like spent fish coming down a salmon ladder. It was a brilliant epoch.

The highest peak on the uptown side of this brief canyon on Forty-third Street is the Paramount Theatre Building; the downtown side is dominated by the Hotel Dixie, a hundred yards to the west. Each blots out the lesser heights behind it. I tell time by the clock on the Paramount, but the Dixie is my moral beacon. Colonel John R. Stingo, my favorite writer, lives there, as snug as a Mexican jumping bug in a bean. I work best at night, when the Dixie is easy to identify by the red electric sign on the roof which reads "DIXIE HOTEL," and by the vertical one:

H
O
T
E
L

D
I
X
I
E

Whenever I look over there, I think of how the Colonel is cheered by the sight of hundreds of lights in office buildings at night. "It reminds me of Ricecakes," he says. "Ricecakes" is his *petit nom* for George Graham Rice, a departed Wolf of Wall Street. " 'Just think,' Ricecakes would say. 'Behind each of those windows, a man is awake, scheming to take somebody else's money.' It gave him a group feeling, and I was never mean enough to advert him that they in most instances signalized the nocturnal labors of honest charwomen. He would have detested the thought."

I, in turn, am cheered when I think of the Colonel up in his room, which faces the Flea Circus, on the Forty-second Street side of the hotel. He is better company, even two blocks away, than a bust of Pallas sitting up above my chamber door, and of more solace than a good conscience, for he indicates that the future is long. When I first knew the Colonel, in 1946, I congratulated him on his *bonne mine.* He was then, by his own count, seventy-two. "I have three rules for keeping in condition," he said. "I will not let guileful women move in on me. I decline all responsibility. And, above all, I avoid all heckling work. Also, I shun exactious luxuries, lest I become their slave."

Along the approaches to the Dixie I can see foothills, one of them a narrow hotel called the Strand, just west of Seventh Avenue. There, once, in the early nineteen-thirties, when I was a reporter for the *World-Telegram,* I interviewed a man with an electric shirt front, a dickey filigreed with the name of a brand of cigars. He wore an electric bulb, worked by a battery that was fastened to his chest behind this display space, and he could turn the light off and on from a switch in his left pants pocket. With his right hand, he would move a cigar in and out of his face. He would stroll along Broadway of nights, an ambulatory rival of the spectaculars on costly rented space. He wore a high silk hat, a white vest, and tails. This self-propelled illumination was of a most impressive appearance—six feet plus, with a cherry-pop complexion and a gray mustache and goatee. He told me that his ambition was to manage a heavyweight champion of the world, and that the excess of his income over his needs during the depression permitted him to subsidize a succession of towering louts. All of them deserted at their first chance to obtain employment. They lacked what Colonel Stingo calls the Divine Inflatus. The electric man, for revenge, beat them up when he could catch them. He was an arrogant man, and bibulous. I remember that on the morning when I talked to him he had a hangover, and the high hat and the rest of the glad rags, strewn about his small room, made it look as if he had been out celebrating New Year's Eve in about 1898. The room was darkened by the shadow of an electric sign just outside. Years later, the wartime dimout extinguished his profession, since the Civilian Defense authorities deemed him an air-raid risk, and I do not know what then became of him.

On my own side of the canyon, the top third of the old Hotel Woodstock intervenes between me and the lower stories of the Paramount. I have no intimate memories of the Woodstock, which is perhaps evidence of its respectability, but I know a fellow who lives there when he is not at sea as a physiotherapist on the America, of the United States Lines. He is an astrologo-nutritionist, yogist, and poet, and is even more distinguished in my book by being the only prizefighter I've ever known who was ruined by orange juice. Jack Willis, to give him his public name, or William Hamby, as he signs ships' articles, changed his name when he was young, so that his father wouldn't find out what he was doing. He came out of Texas in 1924 carrying a bag that contained a spare shirt, a tube of vaseline for his hair, boxing trunks, a pair of ring shoes, and a roll of bicycle tape. Wrapping the tape around his hands before each fight, he left a wake of concussions from Baton Rouge, Louisiana, to Portland, Maine, having successively established himself in each place as a local boy with a job in the lumberyard. He reached his peak in California. But during the second half of the twenties, when he was a prominent middleweight, he began to notice that fellows like Mickey Walker were getting up off the floor after he knocked them down. As he usually broke a hand with the first knockdown, he lost several fights. "It wasn't until I began to study nutrition, years afterward, that I understood what had happened," Willis told me. "I used to drink orange juice by the bucket, under the impression it was good for me, and it leached all the calcium out of my fists, leaving them brittle. I might as well have been hitting those guys with a china cup. Unconsciously, I began to pull, and then they didn't even go down the first time. If I had stuck to whiskey in moderation, I would have been all right. Of course, it might have made some difference that the California Boxing Commission made me quit using the bicycle tape. But the orange juice is what did the business."

Willis became convinced of the power of yoga during a scheduled twenty-round bout with a light heavyweight his manager had erroneously selected for him as a soft touch on July 4, 1930, in Reno,

Nevada. He had a broken rib from the previous soft touch when he went into the ring—his manager was an optimist—and the Reno soft touch, twenty-five pounds heavier than Willis, was killing him when my friend suddenly achieved perfect concentration and flattened the bum with a punch. His hands were already going then, though. It was too late to start a new career on a Vedantic basis. Astrology, yoga, and poetry are the troika of humanities that most interest him now, and he has driven them in harness ever since the failure of an attempt to hitch astrology with horseplaying. The horseplaying fiasco is still a sore subject with Mrs. Willis-Hamby, who is an astrologist, too, but does not think that the science should be milked for safe long shots. The Willis-Hambys say that when they met, at a party in London while the America was turning around, they knew at once that they were predestined mates, and their true selves have never quarrelled since. Each has *two* selves, however, and the short-tempered *Doppelgänger* sometimes tangle over things like betting. Willis is a big, impressive man, a heavyweight now, who walks with his face tilted upward, as if he were looking for a star working three furlongs. (It is a shipboard habit, he says; nights at sea, he can stargaze full time without fear of being run over.)

Willis's verse, in which he shows a frequent preoccupation with the transmigration of souls, is published every now and then in the magazine *American Astrology.* A pretty fairly typical stanza from one poem goes:

I was king, and a god in India,
  You were Sita, my heavenly queen.
I was both Rama and Indra,
  Lord of the storms, supreme.

After a recent retrospective discussion of horseplaying, though, he sent me the original manuscript of a poem that he had just dedicated to his wife:

TO YOU WHO SPOIL THE PRESENT BY ALWAYS TALKING ABOUT THE PAST

When the past is gone forever,
  Lost in an avalanche of time,
Why bring it back to the present
  By your concentration of mind?

Why destroy the present moment
  By dragging back a painful past?
Perhaps it could be forgotten,
  If this attempt could be your last.

All the money in the world
  Can't but your happiness today,
So enjoy these precious moments,
  Don't you know they're slipping away?

I said that it showed he still had a smooth shift, and he said that Mrs. Willis had not referred to gambling since she read the lyric, which showed she got the message.

THE Paramount Theatre Building itself is haunted for me by the memory of a romance in which I didn't get out of the starting gate. It was there, to a dressing room above the backstage, that I went in about 1931 to garner, for my newspaper, the words of Pola Negri, a *femme fatale* I had first glimpsed in the German-made silent film "Passion," which was the "La Dolce Vita" of my adolescence. I had seen it at the Nugget Theatre in Hanover, New Hampshire, while I was a junior at Dartmouth, shortly to be expelled for overcutting chapel. That preliminary ogle had made me Negri's slave forever. I had acquired a carapace of savoir-faire in the intervening eight years, but it melted to the texture of cold jellied turtle soup in her sensed proximity, and when I knocked at her starred door I felt like a pitcher from a prison team starting for the first time in the Yankee Stadium.

Miss Negri was making a personal appearance at the Paramount which was designed to prove she had a voice for the new talkies. Previous to my call, I had caught her act from out front. She floated upon a swing and growled a refrain that went, "And when I *hold* your hand, mm-mm-mm-mm, mm-mm-mm-mm . . ." She was a kind of basso-contralto. When, at the door, I heard "*Komm*," with a couple of added "mm-mm"s that I read in, my legs started to fold under me, but I braced myself on the doorknob and managed to stay upright as I entered. Miss Negri, who used dead-white makeup and had jet-black hair, lay in a white peignoir along a white chaise longue—like a passion-crumpled gardenia petal, as I jotted down on my folded copy paper as soon as I could control my trembling fingers. *Her* fingers trailed limply from her arm, as if dabbling in a stream—"like Cleopatra in the simmering moonlight of a sheening night on the Nile" is how Colonel Stingo once described a lady in a similar pose. The Colonel is a much better writer than I am, and I call him from the bullpen when I cannot get the simile across the plate. By Miss Negri's water-lily-white digits stood a champagne cooler filled with ice. An unopened bottle nestled in its core.

I settled in a straight-backed chair, as if at Camille's bedside. A retainer who looked like the electric-shirt-front man entered and twirled the bottle, but he did not open it.

"*Merci,* Baron," Miss Negri murmured, and he withdrew.

Miss Negri smiled faintly. Her performance had evidently been a great strain upon her. The air was heavy with a scent of tuberoses.

"You have a lovely perfume," I began. "What is it?"

"It is not a pairfume," Miss Negri said, sounding wounded. "It is me. It is my naturahl o-door."

Cursing my clumsiness, I recoiled to think of another overture.

Upon her dressing table stood a photograph of Rudolph Valentino. It was in a silver frame about two feet by eighteen inches and weighing, I estimated, four or five pounds. She had, I remembered from the newspapers, flung herself upon his bier, in what must now seem to her, I imagined, a lifetime of agonies ago.

"Can you bear to speak of him?" I asked, tilting my head in the direction of this Comstock Lode.

"Why not?" Miss Negri asked bravely, like one long accustomed to having thorns stuck in her heart. "He was the only man I evair lawved. But I am fated always to be unhappy in lawv."

The retainer reëntered and twirled the bottle again. This time, I hoped, he would open it, and she would pour out her confidences with the wine. Then I might have the courage to console her. But the henchman left the bottle in the bucket.

"*Merci,* Baron," Miss Negri said, and he withdrew, enveloping her in a glance of unrequited passion.

"He is so loyal, so faithful, the Baron," Miss Negri said. "But he is not for me. Always I am disappointed."

Shocked, I cried, "But surely you, you with all your beauty . . ." I was pleading for another chance for a sex that had failed in its mission.

"No!" she groaned. "No!" And then, apologetic but resigned, she said, "You see, I EXPECT SO MAWCH!"

I fled, and in the corridor I passed the reporter from the *Journal,* who had been waiting his turn. Behind his shoulder, the Baron awaited his cue to twirl the bottle.

I CITE these associations because I do not wish readers to think Manhattan has no soul. Every corner is fraught with memory. In the Dixie, the Colonel is poised midway between the raffish penny arcades of Forty-second Street and the ecclesiastical atmosphere with which the *Times* invests the block on Forty-third. "The *Times* is the modern Herodotus," the Colonel often observes. "It soothes as it informs. What a marvellous institution!"

The Colonel's geriatric rules have worked well, because today, at what I calculate to be eighty-nine, he is, in his own terms, running easy on the last turn. He has even, it seems to me, begun to step up the pace a little, because he avers himself ninety-one, and has thus run his last nineteen years in seventeen flat. He is levelling on the century, and, like a good jockey, taking the short way home. My encounters with the Colonel have become less frequent in these latter years, however, because he makes a practice of not answering the telephone. He says it is almost always somebody who wants to know how he is getting along, and this makes him nervous. The protocolary way to arrange a meeting is to call him up several days in advance and leave a message for him to call you, but this does not always work, for he sometimes lets messages accumulate in his box until he finds it quite hopeless to try to cope with them retroactively, and so throws all of them away.

The Colonel has been fated to turn out most of his own stylistic exercises for publications less sedate than the *Times.* He was the racing editor of the old *Evening Journal* in the early nineteen-hundreds, before the anti-betting law promulgated by Charles Evans Hughes as governor blighted New York State. He wrote then under his civilian name, J. S. A. Macdonald. (The "S.," which he has since dropped, stood for "Stuart," he says, adding as explanation, "The Young Pretender.") To his colleagues, in this period, he was known as Alphabet Macdonald. It was while he was running a small periodical called the *Wasp* in San Francisco during the horse hiatus, he says, that he became smitten with pseudonymity and commissioned himself a colonel. As Colonel John R. Stingo, for thirty years he wrote a column called "Yea Verily" for a Sundays-only paper called the New York *Enquirer* and its successor, the *National Enquirer,* which bills itself as "The World's Liveliest Newspaper," in order, no doubt, to avoid confusion with the Chicago *Tribune,* which is the World's *Greatest* Newspaper. He received no direct emolument for what he wrote, although he is in my opinion the best curve-ball writer since Anatomy Burton and Sir Thomas Browne, making the prose of his contemporaries look shabby and unfurnished. His sentences soar like laminated boomerangs, luring the reader's eye until they swoop in and dart across the mind like bright-eyed hummingbirds, for a clean strike every time. A column was principally useful as leverage, the Colonel said. In his, he treated frequently of people who won large sums of money by following the advice of turf consultants, analysts, and figurators. The touts, by coincidence, advertised in the *Enquirer,* and the Colonel received a fixed percentage of the advertising revenue accruing to the newspaper. The column, however, was no mere congeries of puffs. It was the best reading in the paper—or, for that matter, any other paper—and the profitable allusions were no more conspicuous than birdshot in quail. His income was subject to no editorial whim but was like a permanent Guggenheim or Ford Foundation grant. It left him a free man.

A couple of years ago, I was walking up Sixth Avenue on a sunny October day when I saw a familiar figure, small, erect, and infused with a military jauntiness, well ahead of me. (The Colonel took over, with his rank, the other attributes of a retired officer of the Seaforth or the Coldstream.) I caught up with the Colonel, not without difficulty, and hailed him; then we dropped into a worthy saloon, which has since been displaced by a new claptrap hotel. I proposed a cup of coffee, but the Colonel remonstrated that his physician had enjoined a moderate amount of alcohol for the benefit of his ticker, and that he had not yet had his daily dosage. "May I be so bold as to suggest a Jack Daniel's Sourmash Perfecto?" he said. He had three before our conversation ended. The Colonel told me he had retired—or, as he phrased it, "assumed the emeritus"—owing directly to trouble with his left typewriter hand. He was not the kind of author who dictates, being convinced that style is a visual as well as an aural matter. "As a consequence, I am just learning the benefits of fresh air," he said. "I was on the way to Central Park, where it abounds." The Colonel appeared as cheerful as a cricket, or a wasp, and averred himself to be "holding"—an expression by which he denotes a state of solvency, with no threat of the Plug in the Door, the Damoclean sword that hangs over all habitual hotel guests, preventing their use of their key until they adjust their bill. Racing was experiencing a period of unparalleled prosperity, he explained, and with investors extant in redundancy the turf analysts were prosperous. They advertised, and the management of the *Enquirer* held itself honor-bound to continue payment of the Colonel's commission. "It bears out what I have often told you, Joe," the Colonel said. "Shun commodity. Avoid it like the plague. The tangible is perishable, but a concept bears fruit perpetually. Had I invested in dill pickles or steel rails, I might not be able to sell them, but Si and Smudgie, the Kentucky Colonel, Flying Horse, the Masked Jockey, and my other benefactors will continue their pursuit of the turf investor's dollar, and I will sit snug."

This particular meeting with the Colonel took place during the season when Governor Rockefeller was calling for an air-raid shelter in every back yard and the public press was full of a debate as to whether the antlike *prévoyant* who built his family a proper shelter would, in the event of atomic war, be justified in shotgunning to death his grasshopper-directed neighbor who tried to get into it with him. The paroxysms of anxiety are, like the worst moments of toothaches, hard to remember. I forget why during the early autumn of 1961 the country was so shelter-minded, but it was. (It would seem equally rational or irrational to be so today, but the country isn't.) "Man," the Colonel abruptly began, as if addressing an audience, "can build no structure that will withstand the Blight of Atomic Might." This reminded me of the opening of the speech with which, he used to tell me, he was accustomed, as an associate, to introducing Hatfield the Rainmaker in the drought areas of California in 1912: "Rain—its abundance, its paucity—meant Life and Death to the Ancients, for from the lands and the flocks, the herds, the fish of the sea, the birds of the air, the deer and the mountain goat they found sustenance and energized being. All the elements depended upon the Fall of Rain, ample but not in ruinous overplus, for very existence. Through all human history, the plenitude of Rain or its lack constituted the difference between Life and Death." This time, the Colonel did not fill out his speech to the old orotundity but proceeded summarily—a mere sketch. "Only the Divinity has been able to fabricate the Perfect Answer to the Menace His shortsighted children were to produce," the Colonel intoned. "A Mountain!" And he looked up at me from under his heavy lids and smiled happily. As I did not at once catch his drift, he repeated, chiding me for being so slow, "A Mountain!," and went on, "Joe, if I were only seventy again, I would by now have every mountain in New York State under a ninety-nine-year lease. All I would need to get the thing started is five thousand dollars. I would give that to a smart lawyer who knew all about leases, and then I would go to those boob legislators and lease every mountain in the state parks, without saying why, except to the occasional thief who could penetrate my purpose. Naturally, I would declare such, when inevitable, in. I would then deposit conspicuously several old bulldozers and steam shovels on the slopes of a couple of the mountains and let it be known that I was going to install vaults, living quarters, swimming pools, and air-conditioned handball courts in their recesses. I would put on an advertising campaign, by radio, television, and the good old press, addressing myself to the three hundred and ninety-eight people who enjoyed incomes of a million dollars or more last year, but promising to consider applications from those of lowlier, though amply holding, status. The Survival of the Fittest, I would imply subtly, was a Law of Nature, and who Fitter to Survive than a man with the price of a Mountain? My text would be based, roughly, on a story a racing friend of mine once told me about some trainers who went on a fishing expedition in Louisiana with a horse owner, an oilman of transcendent wealth. A great storm arose, and the trainers, though apprehensive, pretended to make little of it. But the owner, impatient, said, 'Boys, this may be all right for you, but *I've* got a hell of a lot of money.' All I lack now," the Colonel said, in regretful conclusion, "is the energy."

I took the Colonel home to the Dixie in a taxi. The lobby of that hotel is as far from New York as you can get. It is like a tropical-fish tank, insulated from the streets on either side, and windowless. It is accessible from the Forty-second Street side only by a long arcade—like the snout of a steamer clam buried beneath the surface—and from the Forty-third Street side by a staircase. Within the tank, the accents of all regions of the United States except New York are pervasively to be heard, and the transient occupants of the lobby chairs appear to be inhabitants of Little Rock, Arkansas, and Moline, Illinois, who have carried their environment with them in the form of a vast plastic bubble. In the Plantation Bar, which has a décor like that of the lobby of the Capitol Theatre in 1926, a virtuoso at a mammoth console organ plays afternoon and evening, on a podium with a tilted back mirror of glass that exposits his technique to the audience, which crouches back among the luxuriant shadows; I sometimes wonder that the waiters do not carry flashlights, like movie ushers, in order to find their way. It seems a perfect environment for a confidence man, although, as I shall explain, it isn't. I myself, always on the lookout for a hideaway after my contemplated perfect crime, encountered the Dixie through my acquaintance with the Colonel, and adopted it as the address to which I would move with my booty rather than head for Brazil. I was sure that nobody I knew would ever turn up there, and I was sure that it was a haven for minor-league hoods, the womanless men I saw lurking in the corners of the barroom with the lids of their hats pulled down over their eyes. Nothing could be further from the truth, I learned after years of lulling myself with my illusion. It was fortunate that I had not yet committed my crime or taken refuge in that inviting trap. The men in the hats are for the most part G-men, Internal Revenue fellows, and narcotics inspectors, who frequent the Dixie because of the paucity of the government per-diem allowance for federal employees on missions in New York. Mr. Hyman B. Cantor, the proprietor of the Dixie, himself explained this to me one day, in discussing his business policies. "I know those guys haven't got money to throw away, so I let them stay five in a room, for three dollars apiece," he said. "That way, we get fifteen dollars for a key, and they are happy, too; they get a clean bed and a bathroom." If Mr. Cantor, who is a high type, noticed that I blenched, he could not have understood that it was because I recognized the gap that had been yawning at my feet. "It insures a nice class of customers, too," Mr. Cantor said. "Like having a cat in the house. The mice stay away."

In the middle of the lobby stands a glass case containing a scale model of a ninety-thousand-ton, two-hundred-and-sixty-thousand-horsepower ship, Mr. Cantor's pet project. It is one of two ships that, when his plans work out, will ply the Atlantic in four-day shuttles, carrying six thousand passengers at a minimum fare, applicable to one-fifth of the berths, of fifty dollars, not including food, which the passengers will buy, if they feel like it, in the ships' cafeterias. The seasick passenger will have the consolation of saving money. It is a sensible proposition, as Mr. Cantor, a vast, towheaded man in his early sixties, explains it, and it gives the Colonel a sensation he loves—that of living in the midst of a giant promotion. Pictures of the ships, and brochures on the projects of what Mr. Cantor calls the Sea Coach Transatlantic Lines, are handed out regularly throughout the hotel, and you have the feeling while you are there that they actually exist. Compared to the Sea Coach Transatlantic Lines, a scooped-out mountain seems as simple as a baked potato.

High above the lobby and Mr. Cantor, the Colonel lives in a room-with-bath that effectually preserves him from the danger of enslavement by exactious luxuries. He moved into the hotel in 1940, when the Dixie was relatively new and, like other hotels in New York, was making a determined effort to keep full by offering special terms to residents over long periods. When war came, these people attained the rent-protected status of tenants in apartment houses, and the Colonel's economic position, consequently, has been privileged. For a decade or so, the management demanded an almost inhuman punctuality in the rendition of rent. This inspired his haunting fear of the Plug in the Door. Afterward, finding him immovable, the hotel management first acquiesced and then gloried in his tenancy, and he is now the Dixie's senior resident. Age, too, has helped stabilize his finances, by diminishing sudden demands upon them.

"Some Friday nights, I sit up there in my room at the Dixie, working away on my column," he once said to me, in those days that were only the afterglow of his middle age but now seem like the white heat of youth. "I finish, and it is perhaps one o'clock. If I were sagacious, I would put on my hat and go to bed. I always keep an old felt hat by my bedside, because I like to sleep with my windows wide open and bedclothes make no provision for the protection of the thinly veiled cranium. The brain, like Rhenish wine, should be chilled, not iced, to be at its best. Women, however, are best at room temperature. Up there in my retreat, I feel the city calling to me. It winks at me with its myriad eyes, and I go out and get stiff as a board. I seek out companionship, and if I do not find friends, I make them. A wonderful, grand old Babylon."

Times have changed. "Now," the Colonel said to me a while ago, by telephone, "when I hear the city calling, I just turn over on the other ear and go to sleep again. It's ten o'clock to bed every night."

But when I am in my office at night, looking over at the Dixie, it pleases me mightily to know that the Colonel is still there.

34
A. J. Liebling

ABBOTT JOSEPH LIEBLING—Joe—died on Saturday, December 28th, and the preceding article is one of the last pieces of writing he did. That Saturday, in his office at *The New Yorker,* unsorted, unfiled, within reach, scattered and heaped on his desk, tables, chairs, shelves, and air-conditioner, and, in some cases, hanging at odd angles on his walls, were such items as the latest *Annual Report of The New-York Historical Society,* a 1927 biography of Boss Tweed, two lithographs of jockeys, a drawing of Bob Fitzsimmons just after he defeated Jack (Nonpareil) Dempsey for the middleweight championship in 1891, Robert Aron's "Histoire de la Libération de la France," the *American Racing Manual,* a volume on "The Theory and Practice of the Preparation of Malt and the Fabrication of Beer," Harold Nicolson's "The Congress of Vienna," a month of issues of the Las Vegas *Sun,* General Freiherr von Bernhardi's "Cavalry in War and Peace," three volumes of Pierce Egan's "Boxiana," the 1955 edition of the *Guide Bleu Algérie-Tunisie,* a Christmas card from "The Officers and Men of the First Infantry Division," the third volume of Stendhal's "Journal," the November 28th edition of the Miami *Labor Tribune,* and the collected works of Albert Camus. Those items came close to making up a summary of Liebling's passionate interests, among which were New York, Paris, North Africa, England, boxing, military theory, horse racing, newspapers, labor, food, medieval history, Broadway life, Stendhal, Camus, Colonel Stingo, Pierce Egan, Stephen Crane, and Ibn Khaldun. These were some of his subjects, and he knew them all thoroughly; he was the most protean of scholars. An immense variety of people and things gave Liebling delight, and he was impatient to pass along his delight to everybody else, in his writings. He wrote about only what he cared about deeply; there was no searching for material, no writing for writing's sake. Moreover, his memory was so abundant and his mind so supple that he was able to call upon whatever he knew in one field to clarify a situation in another; he drew on Pierce Egan to make a point about European history and he drew on Ibn Khaldun to make a point about horse racing.

Liebling joined the staff of *The New Yorker* as a reporter in 1935, and in the next twenty-eight years he wrote a prodigious number of articles—in the hundreds—for this magazine. As time went on, he wrote with greater and greater elegance, and the journalism he was ostensibly doing somehow turned into the kind of writing that endures. Liebling was physically a big, heavy man, but the writer was lithe and light on his feet; the words were dancing words. His special humor—the Liebling humor—quickened almost everything he ever set down on paper. He wrote with real joy. His comic flights, his sudden aphorisms kept surprising him, and even thrilling him; in the most innocent possible way, he chuckled at his own funny and brilliant and original sentences as they emerged from his typewriter. And he was right. The sentences were just as funny and brilliant and original as he thought they were.

Liebling was born in New York in 1904, and he wrote about it ardently until he died. His love for the city was not something abstract or general; he knew it and loved it in detail. He walked its streets constantly, and made discoveries about it every day. He liked the sound of Broadway speech, and of the city's sporting talk, and of what he called "the side-street New York language," and he preserved it faultlessly in his pieces. He was one of New York's best, most learned, funniest historians. If New York was Liebling's first love, Paris was his second. Each was his true home. Neither ever disappointed him, and he managed to be faithful to both. As a young man, he studied history at the Sorbonne, and through the years he returned to Paris again and again, to be restored and to celebrate the city in his reports for the magazine. While Paris was still occupied during the Second World War and our First Infantry Division was slowly making its way across Normandy, Liebling was with the troops as a correspondent; he was, as he put it, on "the road back to Paris." And on that bright day in August of 1944 when Paris was liberated, he was right there, having arrived with the troops. A week later, he was writing, "For the first time in my life and probably for the last, I have lived for a week in a great city where everybody is happy." Not long afterward, Liebling received the cross of the French Legion of Honor for his writings about France and, in a shy way, he was very proud of it. Years after that, he returned through Normandy to Paris, and wrote a remarkable series of articles in which he moved about on three planes of time at once, mingling the present with a past that was a present to another past. In a final delirium, as he was dying, he spoke only French, and went back once more to Paris.

Liebling's account of D Day, his accounts of the campaigns in North Africa and France, his story of the wartime voyage of the Norwegian tanker Regnbue, his chronicles of the "foamy fields" of Tunisia, his articles on the Jollity Building and the I. & Y. Cigar Store, his marvellously digressive "Memoirs of a Feeder in France," his exuberant pieces on boxing, his valuable commentaries on the press—all these and many others will be read for years to come. He was an inspired reporter, and one of the writers who created *The New Yorker's* reporting tradition; his contribution to the magazine was beyond measure. His colleagues at *The New Yorker* will always cherish what he wrote, and will always remember his sweetness of spirit and his warmth and his gallantry. It would be appropriate to quote from his oldest and closest friend among those colleagues, Joseph Mitchell, who, at Liebling's funeral, said:

"Shortly after I heard that Joe was dead, I went over and looked at his books in a bookcase at home. There were fifteen of them. I looked through 'The Road Back to Paris' and reread 'Westbound Tanker,' which is one of my favorite stories of his, and when I finished it I suddenly recalled, with great pleasure, a conversation I had had some years ago with the proprietor of one of the biggest and oldest stores in the Fourth Avenue second-hand-bookstore district. I had been going to this store for years, and occasionally talked to the proprietor, who is a very widely read man. One day, I mentioned that I worked for *The New Yorker,* and he asked me if I knew A. J. Liebling. I said that I did, and he said that every few days all through the year someone—sometimes a man, sometimes a woman, sometimes a young person, sometimes an old person—came in and asked if he had 'Back Where I Came From' or 'The Telephone Booth Indian' or some other book by A. J. Liebling. At that time, all of Joe's early books were out of print. 'The moment one of his books turns up,' the man said, 'it goes out immediately to someone on my waiting list.' The man went on to say that he and other veteran second-hand-book dealers felt that this was a sure and certain sign that a book would endure. 'Literary critics don't know which books will last,' he said, 'and literary historians don't know. *We* are the ones who know.

We know which books can be read only once, if that, and we know the ones that can be read and reread and reread.' In other words, what I am getting at, Joe is dead, but he really isn't. He is dead, but he will live again. Every time anyone anywhere in all the years to come takes down one of his books and reads or rereads one of his wonderful stories, he will live again.

"Tim Costello once referred to Joe as 'that good, kind, brave, decent man.' In the last two days, I have recalled a multitude of examples of Joe's goodness. I will refer to only one, and to that only because, for some reason that I don't understand, it haunts me. We had been up to the Red Devil Restaurant for lunch. It was one of those times when he was in bad shape physically; his right hand was red and swollen from gout, and his feet were giving him trouble. Also, he was apprehensive about an income-tax matter, and he was having doubts about something he was writing. At lunch, he had been talking about Stephen Crane, and evidently this had put something in his mind. All of a sudden, as we were walking back to the office, he asked me to go with him over to a flower store on Madison Avenue. Joe had an amazing variety of friends, and one of them was an elderly woman who was living in a nursing home in the Bronx. Joe liked her for two reasons. As a young woman, she had been a friend of Stephen Crane. Also, although she was crippled and couldn't get around and had outlived all her old friends and was pretty much alone in the world, she still had a great appetite for life and could find pleasure and delight in things as commonplace as a cup of tea. We went into the flower store and Joe ordered a dozen red roses to be sent to her. We started out of the store. The woman had lived in France for many years long ago and loved France, and Joe must have thought of that. He went back and asked the man to put six blue irises in among the roses. Then we went down to the office, and, walking beside him, I thought of a line in Yeats. I felt that he 'was blessèd and could bless.' "